Also by J. Lee Ready

Forgotten Allies: The Military Contribution of the Colonies, Exiled Governments, and Lesser Powers to the Allied Victory in World War II (McFarland, 1985; two-volume paperback 2012)

The Forgotten Axis

Germany's Partners and Foreign Volunteers in World War II

J. Lee Ready

Volume 1

Part One; Part Two (chapters 9–23)

McFarland & Company, Inc., Publishers
Jefferson, North Carolina, and London

The present work is a reprint of the library bound one volume edition of The Forgotten Axis: Germany's Partners and Foreign Volunteers in World War II, *first published in 1987 by McFarland.*

Volume 1

LIBRARY OF CONGRESS CATALOGUING-IN-PUBLICATION DATA

Ready, J. Lee, 1947–
The forgotten axis : Germany's partners and foreign volunteers in World War II / J. Lee Ready.
p. cm.
Includes bibliographical references and index.

2 volume set—
ISBN 978-0-7864-7169-0
softcover : acid free paper ∞

1. World War, 1939–1945—Germany. 2. Germany—Foreign relations—1933–1945. 3. National socialism. 4. Germany. Heer—Recruiting, enlistment, etc. 5. Military service, Voluntary—Germany—History—20th century. I. Title.
D757.R43 2012
940.54'13'43 87-42519

BRITISH LIBRARY CATALOGUING DATA ARE AVAILABLE

Front cover flag images Wikipedia

Manufactured in the United States of America

McFarland & Company, Inc., Publishers
Box 611, Jefferson, North Carolina 28640
www.mcfarlandpub.com

Table of Contents

• Volume 1 •

Acknowledgments

I must give my thanks to the following, who have aided me in this venture. The idea first came to me years ago when I served alongside Displaced Persons Labor Troops of the U.S. Army (Europe). Once these Poles, Ukrainians, Lithuanians, Estonians, and Latvians realized that I was not just after another "war story," they began to relate their sad tales. Since then I have received invaluable help from veterans of the Allied and Axis armed forces. I especially thank Vart Anivian, once a Romanian flak gunner; Karl Schneider, a Yugoslavian Volksdeutsch veteran of the Prinz Eugen Division; Yuriy Yatskievitch, a Ukrainian eyewitness to the retreat to Vienna; Kazimierz Cywinski, a Home Army veteran of the Warsaw Uprising; Vladas Dargis, a Lithuanian eyewitness to the retreat to Germany; Ivan Rawluk, ex-member of the 1st Division U.V.V.; Jack A. Ready, U.S. veteran of the Ardennes and the Battle of Germany; Charles Weber, ex-U.S. denazification officer; and Jerzy Wysniewski, veteran of the Polish anti-fascist resistance and eyewitness at Auschwitz. I also need to mention the encouragement and assistance of Marvin Lowe, Jerry Kirk, David R. Charnley, Constance T. Horan, and my wife, Kay.

The following organizations have been most helpful: the Lithuanian Association of Great Britain; the Royal Draza Milhailovich Association of Great Britain; the Association of Ukrainian Former Combatants in Great Britain; the Public Record Office, London; and the Imperial War Museum, London; as have the library staffs at the University of Lancaster, University of Manchester, University of London, London School of Economics and Political Science, and the University of Tulsa.

KARELIA
FIN LAND
1
KOMI
RUSSIA
RUSSIA
Leningrad
14
6
15
TATAR
BASHKIR
17
18
Moscow
16
RUSSIA
7
RUSSIA
8
BYELO-
-RUSSIA
KAZAKH
9
Kursk
Don
Stalingrad
11
Kiev
UKRAINE
KALMYK
10
13
12
CAUCASUS
MOL-
-DAVIA
3
13
5
4
Crimea
Black Sea
GEORGIA
2
19
TURKEY
2
1. LOST 1940
2. AZERBAIJAN
3. CHECHEN-
-INGUSH
4. OSSETIA
5. KABARDIN-
-BALKAR
6. MARI
7. LITHUANIA
8. VILNIUS
9. WEST BYELO-
-RUSSIA
10. NORTH BUKOVINA
11. EAST GALICIA
12. BESSARABIA
13. DAGHESTAN
14. UDMURT
15. CHUVASH
16. MORDOVIA
17. ESTONIA
18. LATVIA
19. ARMENIA

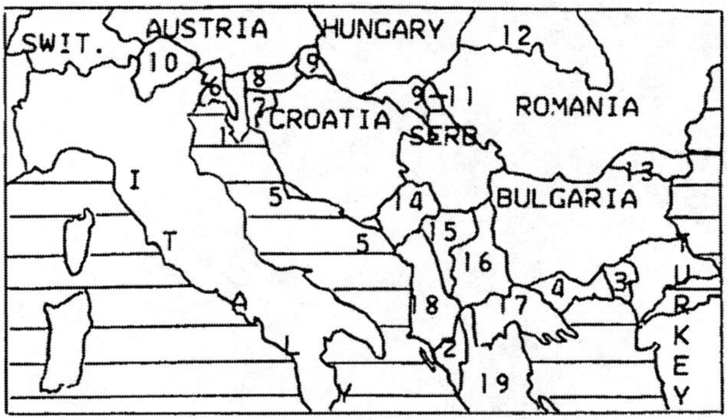

1. TRIESTE-ISTRIA
2. CHAM
3. EAST THRACE
4. WEST THRACE
5. DALMATIA
6. KUESTENLAND
7. ITALIAN SLOVENIA
8. GERMAN SLOVENIA
9. TO HUNGARY 1941
10. SUED TIROL
11. BANAT
12. TRANSYLVANIA
13. SOUTH DOBRUDJA
14. MONTENEGRO
15. KOSOVO
16. BULGARIAN MACEDONIA
17. GREEK MACEDONIA
18. ALBANIA
19. GREECE

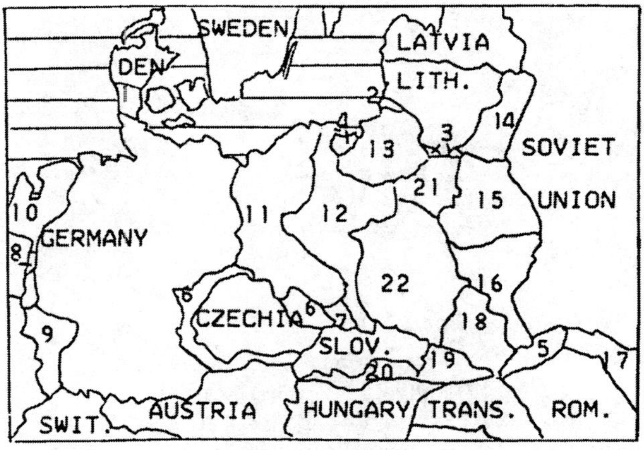

1. NORTH SCHLESWIG
2. MEMEL
3. SUWALKI
4. DANZIG
5. NORTH BUKOVINA
6. SUDETENLAND
7. TESCHEN
8. EUPEN-MALMEDY
9. ALSACE-LORRAINE
10. NETHERLANDS
11. POMERANIA
12. WARTHELAND
13. EAST PRUSSIA
14. VILNIUS
15. WEST BYELORUSSIA
16. EAST GALICIA
17. BESSARABIA
18. WEST GALICIA
19. RUTHENIA
20. TO HUNGARY 1938
21. BIALYSTOK
22. WARSAW GEN. GOVT.

PART ONE: The German New Order and the Unification of Europe

Chapter 1

Conversion by the Sword

The Germans: United by the Sword and the Cross

In the 1930s the population of the German state was about sixty-six million, almost entirely German-speaking with one solid culture, though naturally in such a large country there were regional differences. A small part of Frisia overlapped into northwestern Germany and here about 15,000 Frisian-speakers were accepted by the government as Germans without any respect for their language. Along the border of Denmark there were about 30,000 Danish-speakers, but these people were recognized as such, though this meant in reality that they were looked upon as class II citizens, and every effort was made to forcefully culturally assimilate them. The few thousand Lithuanian-speakers in the northeast were treated in like manner. The language and culture of the few Wends in East Germany were totally ignored.

The largest cultural minority was the Polish-speaking group of East Prussia, Pomerania, and West Silesia. Numbering almost one million, including immigrants, they could not be ignored, but only the German language offered any path for social advancement. Once the nazis had taken power and had begun instituting their confusing racial laws, the Christian Poles were accepted as citizens under the guise of racial Germans who had somehow lost their language and culture. The Jewish Poles were not accepted and they were eventually expelled to Poland. It is ironic therefore that when the German and Polish armies faced each other in the tense summer of 1939, some of the German soldiers were Polish-speaking and some of the Polish soldiers were German-speaking.

Not only did the nazis ignore all languages spoken in the country, other than German, but a conscious effort was made to eradicate those German dialects that proved barely comprehensible to speakers of standard German. The habit of writing in the old Gothic script was discouraged, to the benefit of foreign tourists, and Germans in all walks of life braced themselves for a totally new Germany and a New Order.

Yet Hitler continuously harped back to the past as well, and the New

Order took on a similarity with the Italian Renaissance, which had looked to a scientific future while it longed for the classical past.

There was one major flaw in this idea of a new Germany, and it was not the presence of non-German-speakers in the state, or the presence of half a million Jews who were suddenly excluded from the tribe. It was that one-seventh of the German-speaking people of Europe resided outside the borders of Germany as prescribed by the Versailles Treaty and other subsequent international agreements. Half of these were the Austrians, and the others were the Volksdeutsch, German-speaking minorities controlled by several governments.

With a series of arguments, debates, threats, and above all bluffs, Adolf Hitler intended to reunite the Germans, and the land they occupied. The nazis believed his propaganda and that of racial theorists like Alfred Rosenberg that the German tribe had a collective mentality and that one segment could not function correctly without the other segments. They felt that only when all the Germans and the homeland were united, and only when Germany had enough food-producing areas, could the tribe have living space (*lebensraum*), and only then could the New Order be fully realized.

Adolf Hitler therefore launched his people on a crusade, a march of liberation and purification. In the end he failed, for instead of expelling undesirables he recruited them, instead of rebuilding his cities he destroyed them, and instead of unifying his people he split them asunder. In the last few days of his life, he did not believe himself to be unworthy of the German people, but found them to be unworthy of him, while outside his bunker a European army of non-Germans, owing allegiance to a united Europe rather than a united Germany defended him to their last breath.

However, in 1938 this could never have been foreseen when Hitler united Germany with Austria without foreign interference and seemingly with the blessings of all concerned.

Hitler's propaganda machine, directed by the ingenious Dr. Joseph Goebbels, might not have convinced too many non-Germans of the righteousness of the German cause by the late 1930s, but the German people did not need international propaganda, only domestic propaganda, and Goebbels had already used that to set the mood since Hitler took power in January 1933. The need for the liberation of the Volksdeutsch had never really been questioned, only the method by which it might be accomplished. Once the German forces had been launched against Czechoslovakia, achieving victory without bloodshed, and once the war against Poland seemed to be going very well, it was difficult for the Germans to think rationally in the heady atmosphere of victory. The Germans were quite convinced by October 1939 that all major fighting was over. The fact that Britain and France had declared war, and British planes were bombing German soil, was irrelevant, for it was assumed by most people that the Allies would not be so foolhardy as to launch another campaign such as had been seen on the Western Front twenty years earlier. The German general staff, wishing and hoping for peace talks, dragged its feet, repeatedly putting off Hitler's demands for an offensive in the west, coming up with excuse after excuse, some of them valid, until in early May 1940 they ran out of excuses.

The British acts of aggression against Norway were seen by the Germans as evidence that the British at least were willing to wage a major war, especially if it meant German cities could be bombed, but not British cities, for German aircraft did not have the range to bomb Britain, and that on the new Western Front it would be French soldiers rather than British soldiers who would bear the brunt of the battle.

The German offensive against the West, which was viewed as a pre-emptive strike by Hitler's followers that might cripple the Allies and bring about a swift surrender, was so surprisingly successful that it did indeed seem that Germany's troubles were all but over. The anti-nazi resistance movement in Germany now had to lie low and await the waning of the euphoria before it could even begin to make a move. It must be remembered that although life for German Jews was no picnic, the majority were still "safe," and there was no serious hint that this situation might not continue.

Despite the fact that Germany currently had peaceful relations with the Soviet Union, Goebbels' propaganda ministry began shifting emphasis from the enemy, the land-grabbing British imperialists, towards the potential enemy, the communists. It was done in such a manner that even Stalin, the dictator of the Soviets, was not given any indication that Hitler really planned to attack. When British diplomats warned him, he refused to believe them.

It was Goebbels' propaganda that began to unify Europe, at least to the degree that it was possible to do so after Hitler's wars of conquest. Other groups were intrigued by the prolific information as well. The British fascists were stifled by their government, as were the South African fascists, but the American fascists were going strong, and Hitler hoped they might still be able to prevent that great industrial power from supporting Britain. The people of Europe, and their New World offspring, were susceptible to a crusade and therefore that is precisely what Goebbels provided.

The original crusades of the medieval period of history had been started by a group of French noblemen who believed they had a just claim to the Kingdom of Jerusalem, but they required financial backing for such an undertaking. Church propagandists gave it to them as a crusade was seen to be mutually beneficial. Sadly, the idea of a tiny expedition to a far-off country got out of hand, and religious zealots preached a crusade towards all non-believers, that is, people who were not Roman Catholic.

For centuries thereafter the Europeans responded. The process took the following form: one, preach a politico-religious ideology; two, form a special armed force of crusaders; three, rid one's own land of non-believers; and four, assault and destroy the foreign home of the non-believers. In practical terms this meant: preaching the tenet that God sanctioned the idea of a religious war and gave immunity from punishment for sins committed while on a crusade, no matter how horrendous the crimes may be; forming religious orders of soldiers such as the Templars, the Knights of the Teutonic Order, and the Brethren of the Sword; ridding one's own land of Jews, Moslems, and Pagans; and lastly, assaulting the Middle East Islamic kingdoms and the vast continent of pagan tribes east of Christian Germany.

The English butchered or drove out their Jews and set sail for Jerusalem. The French slaughtered the Cathars, sects of Christians which believed Jesus was man not God, and also fought for the Holy Land of Jerusalem. The Spaniards assaulted the Moor kingdoms in Southern Spain. The Germans advanced eastwards and conquered the pagan Slavs. Adventurers from every European nation flocked to these various theaters of war.

Hitler's new crusade was created to mirror the old. First he needed an ideology—National Socialism, which preached economic equality and social mobility for all believers within the racially acceptable groups. He preached that Divine Providence smiled upon this. Hitler rarely used the actual word God. He also informed his soldiers during the bitterest campaigns that their crimes against unbelievers, especially Jews, would not be punished as normal crimes, thus absolving them from legal prosecution, as priests of the medieval period had absolved warriors of sins before they were committed.

The second step was to provide a special armed forces of crusaders, and indeed he stated that the modern German armed forces were such a thing. However, Heinrich Himmler claimed that his own S.S., partially modeled on the Jesuit Order of Roman Catholic priests, was the true crusading force. The medieval crusading emblem was a black or a red cross on a white background. The nazi emblem was a black cross on a white circle surrounded by red. This swastika, called a crooked cross by the Germans, is a valid Christian religious symbol, as any trip to an ancient cathedral will prove. Other forms of crosses used by the nazis on occasion were the Baltic and the Maltese crosses. Devoutly religious peasants in Eastern Europe were impressed when they first saw the German armies and the cross emblems. The belt buckle of the German soldiers was inscribed with *Gott mit uns*—God is with us.

The S.S. inscription on the uniform was in runic letters, an ancient Germanic/Nordic script, and in parades S.S. men sometimes appeared in medieval armor on horseback with a shield bearing the swastika.

The next phase was to rid the German homeland of non-believers, and the S.S. Security Police and the Concentration Camp Service did their best to achieve this aim. The actual extermination of Jews was not abhorrent to medieval crusaders of any nationality, but its very mention was so to the modern German populace. The anti-Jewish campaign had to proceed with slow caution therefore and the policy of murdering the incurably insane was stopped after a public outcry. Of far more popularity was the arrests of communists, for the atheistic communists had replaced the Medieval Moslems as the enemy. Indeed the Moslems were now part of the crusading force. In Spain Franco's victorious Catholic, nationalist, and fascist armies depended greatly on Moroccan Moslem divisions. In Africa the Catholic and fascist Italian army used tens of thousands of Moslems. Hitler would eventually recruit Moslems into his forces, and the Moslem religious leader, the Grand Mufti of Jerusalem, was in the German camp as early as 1940, and became an S.S. general.

The last step in the crusade was the greatest, the invasion of the enemy homeland, the Soviet Union, the heart of the communist beast. In the Middle Ages the onslaught of the Germanic crusaders was called the *Drang nach Osten* (throng to the east) and Hitler gave this name to his own onslaught. Its military codename was Barbarossa, named after the crusading medieval king of the Holy Roman Reich, who, legend has it, will rise from the dead to lead Germany once more in her hour of need. The Second Reich was the royal period from 1870-1918. The nazis named their period of rule the Third Reich.

Within Europe the memories of crusaders of the past, still looked upon as heroes to this very day, were invoked in the new crusade against the atheistic communists and their cronies. It was difficult to argue the matter if one was a Roman Catholic, because fascist Italian soldiers waged war with the permission of the Church, at times Italian soldiers were blessed by the Pope on their way to battle, Franco's fascist/nationalist government was recognized as the bona fide legal force in Spain by the Vatican two years before the end of the Spanish Civil War actually decided the issue, special legal arrangements were signed between the Vatican and nazi Germany, which could only lend credence to Hitler, and in 1939 the College of Cardinals elected a new pope, Pius XII, who was not only an Italian, but an outspoken friend of Germany.

Hitler was desperate to possess holy relics to legitimize his claim to leadership of the anti-communist crusade, and his S.S. espionage agents scoured the world looking for legendary lost items, the Ark of the Covenant, the Holy Grail, the spear that pierced the side of Christ, and pieces of the True Cross. S.S. archeology teams excavated relevant sites in Europe, Africa, and Asia. One of Hitler's reasons for having troops in North Africa was that he hoped to liberate Jerusalem from British occupation.

There were of course loopholes in Hitler's argument. Within the borders of the Third Reich the Roman Catholic Church was ignored. Only outside Germany were German officers and diplomats ordered to treat the Church with respect. Within Germany the concentration camps were full of Catholic and Protestant clergymen who had dared to challenge the nazis. Hitler crushed Poland, a devoutly Catholic nation and warred with Catholic France. These inconsistencies were overlooked, though, by a segment of the European population who saw the fascist armies as the only bulwark against atheistic communism, and only after the Soviets had been destroyed should they then seek a more palatable form of government than that supplied by the fascists and nazis.

Although the Soviets did not fear attack, they were not slow in the uptake in the propaganda war, and they dug deep into their history books to find out how they had managed to resist the Nordic and Germanic invaders of the past. As early as 1938 Stalin had the famous Russian film director Sergei Eisenstein put together the motion picture *Alexander Nevsky* to remind the Soviet people how that hero had smashed the Nordic invaders on the banks of the Neva River in 1240 and the Germanics on frozen Lake Peipus in 1242. The fact that he had been a nobleman and was later made an Orthodox saint only helped reinforce in the mind of the people that all of them must unite against any future German invasion regardless of their personal beliefs.

The Soviets were perfectly aware that they might have to face this crusade someday and they intended to defeat it with their own counter-crusade, just as the world of Islam had long ago defeated the medieval crusades by a Jihad, a Holy War.

The Austrians: Hitler's Converts

The Austrians are proud of their independent nation, yet they are also aware of the common ethnic bond they share with the Germans. The very name of the country, meaning Eastern Reich, suggests that it is only part of a greater nation, and implies that the Western Reich is Germany. Pan-Germanism was thus at odds and at the same time at one with Austrian nationalism, and therefore the term Germanic became as popular as German and Austrian.

It was only natural that Austria and Germany should ally with each other in the war against Slavic nationalism that was to become World War One, and when that war ended in bitter defeat both empires went down together. Like a wounded animal, Austria fought back at the vultures that now closed in upon her. Despite peace having come in 1918, a year later militant Austrian nationalists were still skirmishing with these invaders. It was bad enough, the Austrians felt, losing the ethnic minorities, but whole chunks of Austria proper with German-speaking people were carved off—three hundred thousand Austrians to Italy, six hundred thousand to Hungary, and over three million to Czechoslovakia. Yet a few thousand Slovenes remained in Austrian-occupied Carinthia.

For years pan-Germans had been trying to unify Austria and Germany, but while Austria was powerful she did not need Germany and while Austria occupied so many different ethnic nations Germany did not want her, but in 1919 shorn of her excess baggage Austria was now in need of protection. For self-defense the Germans and Austrians expressed a wish to unite, but the victorious Allies announced that they would never allow that.

Economically Austria was in a ridiculous position. One person in seven lived in the city of Vienna, where culture and industry fought each other for space. The industrial districts sprouted political and social actionaries, and the cultural and rural areas sprouted political reactionaries. In such a situation street brawls were inevitable. The police, army, and Heimwehr, a right-wing militia, supported the government, which was a coalition of several right-wing parties and the Christian Democrat Party, while the paramilitary Republican Defense Bund supported the opposition, made up of the Social Democrats and the communists. In 1927, when some Heimwehr members were acquitted of murdering two socialists, an angry left-wing mob burned the law courts in Vienna in retaliation. The mob was dispersed by Heimwehr and army troops in a bloody manner—85 died. The leftists replied with a general strike, but the rightists flocked to the city from the countryside and by performing necessary occupations without pay they broke the strike.

In May 1930, Prince Starhemberg, the leader of the Heimwehr, was made Minister of the Interior, but this was not enough for some right-wing fanatics. They attempted a putsch in Styria, but failed miserably. This was not because the government had much support, though. Recently the government had announced intentions of creating a customs union with Germany, but France had reacted by crippling Austria financially, and the government was forced to forget the union, and to beg a loan from the League of Nations. This diplomatic retreat lost the government what few supporters it still had.

Engelbert Dollfuss formed a new government, but the ultranationalists were not impressed. In fact they began to flock to a new party modeled on a German party, the National Socialists, the nazis. The Heimwehr was somewhat placated when Dollfuss put Prince Starhemberg into his new cabinet. In March 1933, two months after the nazis had come to power in Germany, Dollfuss banned them in Austria.

In February 1934, Dollfuss tackled the Republican Defense Bund, but this proved to be far more difficult than simply issuing a ban. The leftists resisted with guns. The army was called out, and within hours a major battle was being fought in the working class districts of Vienna. Only after several days, in which the army shelled the large apartment buildings of the industrial workers with artillery, and 300 people had been killed, was the power of the political left crushed.

Dollfuss now planned to disarm the extreme right, but the illegal nazi party beat him to the punch. On 25 July 1934, they assassinated him. Though Hitler applauded the move, it embarrassed him, for he had only just destroyed his revolutionary cronies in Germany and had yet to consolidate his power base. He was thus unable to intervene in Austrian affairs. The nazis were forced underground by the police directed by the new chancellor, Kurt Schuschnigg. By 1936, the Heimwehr had also been rendered harmless.

By 1938, though, Hitler was in a far stronger position, having remilitarized Germany and won a plebiscite in the Saar, and therefore he chose to intervene now. By intrigue and threats he forced Schuschnigg to appoint Artur Seyss-Inquart, a nazi, as the new Austrian Minister of the Interior, on 12 February.

However, Schuschnigg was not beaten yet. He countered the move by calling for a plebiscite for 12 March to judge the idea of unification with Germany. He hoped that anti-German nationalists, socialists, communists, and the Jews would all vote to keep Austria independent, and he made the minimum voting age 24 to keep out the younger, and more pro-German, nazis.

This move forced immediate action, for Hitler could not depend on the Austrian people, and in a secret telegram dealt through an intermediary, Odilo Globocnik, another Austrian nazi, Hitler ordered Seyss-Inquart to acknowledge ownership of another telegram requesting German armed forces' aid in order to pacify Austria. The puppet did as he was told, and within hours German troops began pouring over the border. The soldiers had been prepared for a battle, but named the march the Battle of Flowers, when they saw Austrian villagers greeting them with garlands. Schuschnigg's plebiscite was still held, but under Gestapo control, and 99.75 percent of the voters chose unification—according to Hitler's count.

Austrians were rewarded with positions of power, and a fighting unit of the S.S. was formed from Austrian volunteers, the S.S. Der Fuehrer Regiment. The 58,000-man regular army was weeded of undesirables and then integrated into the German army, along with the list of army reservists. When possible Austrians were allowed to serve in their own units of the German army, navy, and air force. The Austrian mountain divisions were welcome reinforcements.

Just six months later, these Austrian troops were poised for the invasion of Czechoslovakia, but saw no action. However, eighteen months after the Anschluss, the unification of the two states, Austrian troops fought in Poland. As a department of Germany, now simply known as Ostmark, Austria and her people were subject to all German laws, including military conscription. During World War Two Austrian units distinguished themselves, and many Austrians became known for one reason or another: General Rauss who became commander of the Fourth Panzer Army, General Loehr who became a high-ranking Luftwaffe (air force) officer and commander of the defenses of Yugoslavia, Otto Skorzeny who became an S.S. colonel and a famous commando leader, Seyss-Inquart who ruled the Netherlands, Odilo Globocnik who became an S.S. general, Walter Nowotny who became a great fighter ace, Franz Stangl who commanded an extermination camp, and many others. Of course the most famous Austrian of the Third Reich was Adolf Hitler himself.

Czechoslovakia: Ally and Enemy

Czechoslovakia has gained a sympathetic reputation for tragedy due to its experiences in the twentieth century. Years with the number 8 have been significant for this state. Created at the fall of the Austrian Empire in 1918, it then fell victim to Germany in 1938 and to communists backed by the Red Army in 1948. Its brief passive revolution, crushed by Soviet tanks, was in 1968.

However, there is another side to the story. Though the state was in the inter-war years to the English people "a far away country . . . people of whom we know nothing," to quote from Neville Chamberlain the British prime minister, it was not far away from and was in fact well known to, the people of Russia, Ukrainia, Poland, Hungary, Germany, and Austria. Even before the state existed it was a thorn in the side of communist Russia, for during World War One the Czech Legion had been raised by the Tsarist Russian army from captured Czechs who had been serving in the Austrian army in order to fight against the imperialist Austrians and liberate their homeland, which in practice meant manning a segment of the Russian front line. However, the Bolshevik (communist) Revolution of 1917 in Russia effectively did away with the Russian front line, so the legion commanders accepted an offer from the French. The French government, though, soon saw a better use for the legion than dying in the trenches, and they slowly committed the legion to the anticommunist forces in the Russian Civil War that broke out. After many battles against the (communist) Red Army, the Czech Legion was shipped home from the port of Vladivostok, but this was long after World War One had ended and after the legion had cut a swath clear across Russia and Siberia. The Soviets (communists) would never forget this, and the Czech legionnaires would never forget the brutality of the communists.

Like most underdogs who were suddenly thrust to the top of the heap, the Czechs lusted after power and at once created their own empire. With hindsight it would be wrong to state that the Slovakians were oppressed by the Czechs, but there was a definite distinction between the ruling industrial Czechs and the ruled agricultural Slovakians. Different spoken dialects and literary scripts and a religious division—the Czechs being mostly Protestants and the Slovakians being mostly Roman Catholics, helped to accentuate the distinction. Unfortunately this was not the only problem. In 1918, as Austrian military might collapsed, the Czech politicians who had been lobbying the Anglo-French for the right of self-determination managed to gain from them recognition of the new state of Czechoslovakia as consisting of Czechia (Bohemia and Moravia) and Slovakia, but once peace came and Czech soldiers stood on Czech soil the Czechs demanded other lands too. They demanded the Sudetenland with its three million Austrians, and along the borders there were armed clashes with the Austrians.

In the summer of 1919 the Anglo-French recognized the Czech claims and henceforth the Sudetens would be Czech citizens. The greedy Czechs also swallowed a mouthful of Poland with about a hundred thousand Poles, a morsel of Romania with about 14,000 Romanians, a meal of Hungary with half a million Magyars, and a veritable banquet of Ruthenia, taking all of that Ukrainian province. In addition the new Czech empire ruled over two hundred thousand unassimilated Jews and 33,000 nomadic Gypsies. These were large meals for such a tiny state of 2.6 million Slovakians and 7.1 million Czechs, and ethnic indigestion was to trouble the state throughout its period of independence. However, as long as Austria, Poland, Hungary, Romania, and Ukrainia remained militarily impotent the Czechs knew they would be left alone to digest in peace. To be fair, their rule was not exactly abhorrent. They even experimented with democracy.

In Bratislava, the chief city of Slovakia, a provisional communist government had been established in the last days of 1918, but Czech troops had rooted out the rebels in a 36-hour gun battle. A far greater threat to Czechoslovakia came in June 1919 when the 46th Regiment of the Hungarian army, currently answering to a communist regime, occupied Kosice and Presov, where on the 16th a Slovakian Soviet Republic was established by Slovakian communists led by Antonin Janousek. The Czechs chose diplomacy this time and as a result on 4 July the Hungarian troops withdrew. The communists fled to Hungary and their influence quickly waned. The people of Slovakia did not necessarily want a communist government, but neither did they like the idea of Czechs quashing a Slovakian independence movement. As for the Czechs they now placed the Hungarians and the communists in the same category, as invaders.

Despite the experiences of the Legion in Russia and the brief communist Hungarian invasion the people of the state played politics with no ideological limitations, like children experimenting with new toys. At one time the Communist Party was the third largest. Still ethnicity infiltrated every statewide political question and in 1925 within Slovakia the highly nationalist Slovakian People's Party gained 32% of the vote. In addition to Sudetenland there were villages in Czechia populated by a quarter of a million German-speakers, and in all these Volksdeutsch communities, in Czechia and Sudetenland, there were demonstrations against Czech domination. Altogether thousands of people were arrested and fifty protesters were shot dead. Not surprisingly with Hitler preaching that German-speaking people were as good as anybody, indeed better, many young Volksdeutsch joined the Sudeten Nazi Party.

In 1932, several nazis were arrested by the Czech political police for conspiracy to commit treason, but this only increased party membership. The Czechs themselves had a fascist party, the Vlajka (banner) of General Rudolf Garda, and true to their creed the leaders attempted a revolution in Brno on 23 January 1933. They failed and the prominent figures were arrested.

In October 1933 the nazis were forced underground, and with neighboring Germany now in nazi hands some Volksdeutsch were able to flee there and form the Sudeten Free Corps with dreams of invading Czechoslovakia and liberating their homes. Unofficially the nazis in Czechoslovakia surfaced again in 1934 under the guise of the new German National Front Party led by Konrad Henlein. In the elections of May 1935 this party got 62% of the Volksdeutsch vote, a large percentage when one realizes that the people knew it had no hope of influencing decisions made in Prague.

Suddenly the situation became serious in February 1938 when Adolf Hitler publicly denounced the Czech oppression of the Sudetens and pledged that he would do everything in his power to aid them.

By September 1938, the world was holding its breath as the newly expanded army of the Third Reich faced the smaller but well-trained and -equipped Czechoslovakian army, the latter dug in a concrete bunker line slicing across Sudetenland. Within Sudetenland there were demonstrations and Henlein's people rioted in Eger and Karlsbad. The Czech police called out reinforcements to fight them and even used armored cars.

At the last moment, Prime Minister Chamberlain forced France to renege on her defense pact with Czechoslovakia, and then he offered the Sudetenland to Hitler on a silver platter. The Czechs withdrew from their defenses and not a shot was fired. Hitler could hardly refuse, but he was angered for not only did he not get all of Sudetenland, missing out on 238,000 people, but he failed to liberate the 250,000 Volksdeutsch in Czechia, and most important of all the Czech army remained intact and therefore a threat to Germany. Being ignorant of the excesses of nazi Germany, the Sudetens were jubilant for they had been liberated—by the Germans rather than the Austrians it was true, but if one believed Hitler then there was no longer any difference between the two.

The Hungarians took advantage of Czechoslovakia's dazed condition and with German and Italian mediation annexed a large slice of long-claimed territory. At one swoop the state lost another 800,000 citizens. In addition the Poles stepped in and liberated Teschen and the long-lost people, and took 133,000 Czechs as well.

Throughout the winter, Hitler consoled himself with a pogrom against the Jews in Germany (now including Austria and Sudetenland) while brooding over his lost opportunity to crush the Czechs.

Then the Slovakian nationalists solved the problem for him. With Hungary as an ally Hitler knew he had the Czechs all but surrounded, and with the Slovakians in his camp he had a fifth column. It was time to move.

By quite literally bullying the Czech President Emil Hacha in a face to face meeting in Berlin, Hitler forced him to agree not to oppose the entry of German troops.

The world was aghast. Hitler had actually conquered non-German-speaking people and no one had lifted a finger against him. The great Czech armaments factories and the equipment of the Czech army were his. What is more, Germany now outflanked Poland.

Hitler kept his word and recognized Slovakian independence and Ruthenian independence.

Within Ruthenia members of the Ukrainian National Defense of Stepan Rosokha had set up the Sich, a militia force of 2,000 regulars and 13,000 reservists, which hoped to protect Ukrainian (Ruthenian) rights. Led by Dmitro Klampash, the men raided Czech police posts in the winter of 1938-39 for arms. The German liberation changed everything. On this day, 15 March 1939, the Ukrainian leaders declared independence and named the Sich to be the Ruthenian National Army for this state of half a million people. Unfortunately, within hours Hungarian troops crossed the border. Under Colonel Serhii Yefremov the Sich resisted, but many men, including Colonel M. Kolodzinsky the chief of staff, were killed. Within days only 600 men managed to reach Slovakia and safety.

Within Czechia the German invasion troops, who met no resistance, were accompanied by the S.D., Gestapo, and Kripo, and with Volksdeutsch helpers they made short work of the 2,000 names on their hit list. In Prague the Czech police were ordered to make most of the arrests, and they obeyed at once. The victims were local rabble rousers, communists, trade unionists, Zionists, religious activists, socialists, and German refugees who had fled here from the nazis. Some Czechs aided the Germans and they and the local Volksdeutsch helpers were soon given jobs within the new administrative apparatus. A few became Gestapo agents. Soon the Gestapo, S.D., and Kripo were all controlled by the R.S.H.A., a department of the S.S. headed by Gruppenfuehrer Reinhard Heydrich. Henceforth these departments were usually referred to as S.S. Security Police.

German labor office recruiters also followed the troops, and within three weeks of the takeover 30,000 Czechs, in addition to many Volksdeutsch, signed up for voluntary work in Germany. Within two years 140,000 Czechs would be voluntarily working in Germany. Thousands more worked for the Germans within the Protectorate of Bohemia and Moravia, as Czechia was now officially known. The armaments factories churned out a high percentage of Hitler's war material.

The residents of the protectorate were classified as either Jews, Volksdeutsch, or Czechs. Naturally at first only those citizens who were German-speaking declared themselves and their children to be Volksdeutsch, but as time went on and it became obvious that job opportunities and food rations were far better for Volksdeutsch, many Czechs swallowed their national pride —they had little else to swallow—and signed up as "long lost" Volksdeutsch, Rarely was any genealogical evidence asked for and a knowledge of the German language was not even required. Only those with Jewish connections were turned down. As better food was one reason for this move, the Czechs who remained Czechs christened these people "Margarine Germans."

The German ruler of the new protectorate was the lukewarm nazi Konstantin von Neurath, who was either too strict or not strict enough to rule. His Czech puppets were President Emil Hacha and Premier General Alois Elias. The Czech police force was screened and then let loose again to enforce the laws of the new province as it had done the laws of the old state. As political arrests were soon taken over by the German S.S. Security Police, the Czech policemen saw no reason to risk their necks for the cause of patriotism. Indeed they were glad that with new powers the crime rate soon dropped, except for the black market which sprang up everywhere and involved even high-ranking Germans.

For show purposes the protectorate was allowed to retain 7,000 of its soldiers. The rest of the Czech armed forces were disbanded.

For some Czechs the arrival of the German forces brought bounties, but for many others it meant total dislocation. Hundreds of thousands of Czechs had settled in Sudetenland after 1919 and in October 1938 these were forced out of their homes. After the protectorate was created about one hundred thousand Czechs were forcefully thrown off their land in Czechia to make room for German colonists. This caused great heartache to be sure, but its more serious consequences were the sort of problems that any influx of refugees causes, unemployment, overcrowding, petty theft, disease, and hunger. For the Jews the arrival of the S.S. Security Police meant persecution, and fully 25,000 emigrated before the coming of the war put a stop to that. Beginning in late 1939 some of the remaining 90,000 Jews were shipped out to ghettos in Poland, and in 1942 the deportations increased and this time the destination was the extermination camps. By the end of 1942 the administration of the protectorate was satisfied that it had been rendered Jew-free.

As for the Volksdeutsch, the German S.S. and military recruiters plied their trade and many a young idealist volunteered to serve in the S.S. in order to liberate other unfortunates, that is, the Volksdeutsch of Eastern Europe. Soon conscription became a reality and later in the war parents and wives began to receive telegrams declaring that their loved ones had fallen for the Fatherland. The Volksdeutsch learned that the price of liberation came high.

Within Slovakia the situation was totally different, for though the Slovakians are more racially Slavic than the Czechs the German government recognized them as independent led by a sovereign government of Father Josef Tiso, a Roman Catholic priest. German soldiers stationed in the country were reminded that they were guests whose duty was to protect the fledgling state from outside aggression. However, a mountain of proposals was submitted to Bratislava from Berlin, and the Tiso government found it imprudent to ignore too many of them.

Among the first proposals was a request for anti-Jewish legislation. Already the fascist party militia, now an official body known as the Hlinka Guard, had begun committing scattered acts of violence such as the burning of synagogues.

The government replied by taking a census and stating that there were 90,000 Jews in the state, but that unlike in Germany a racial Jew or half Jew who had been born into, or converted to, a Christian religion would be considered a Gentile and not a Jew.

There was another border of ethnic non-Slovakians in the state and these were the Volksdeutsch. A few thousand were native to small villages, but many more had been officials and colonists of the old Austrian Empire and had simply stayed on after World War One. Now the S.S. was demanding to be allowed to recruit from these people. Under German pressure the government was forced to give way and soon the Slovakians were watching a home-grown S.S. being created in their midst.

Of course the Slovakians needed an armed forces of their own and with the aid of German advisers and Slovakians who had served in the Czechoslovakian army a six-division force was raised. Anti-fascist resistance at this time was so ineffective that the Slovakian police and the guest German S.S. Security Police could easily handle it, and the army was able to concentrate on training for national defense.

Chapter 2

The Poles and the Racial Crusade

After more than 120 years of oppression by foreign military forces it was not surprising when the Poles, who suddenly saw a chance for freedom, seized it with a vengeance. In this cold November of 1918 Poles who had distinguished themselves culturally as well as politically were cheered, praised, almost adored. Indeed some entered politics on the strength of their artistic endeavors. Poles who had lived in the United States brought back newfangled capitalist ideas, and Warsaw and Cracow became centers of dialogue. Poland seemed to be on the verge of a new golden era.

Unfortunately, for the vast majority of Poles there was constant argument stemming from the fact that there were two Polands. One was where the Poles lived, and the other was where the fanatic nationalists thought they ought to live. The territory of the Poles was landlocked, bordered by the Germans on the north and west, the Czechs and Slovakians on the south, and the Ukrainians, Byelorussians, and Lithuanians on the east. In itself this was not cause for alarm now that German military power was destroyed, but the Poles who had gained political power this month were extreme nationalists who felt that Poland should have access to the Baltic Sea, control of the Silesian coalfields, possession of the Teschen industrial area, and ownership of the vast food producing lands to the east, places which had at one time been part of a Polish Empire.

What made the situation worse was that in the 19th century Poles of Russian citizenship had moved to the great cities of Lwow, Minsk, and Vilna, and by 1918 their descendants were eager for Polish sovereignty to include them—a sort of "mountain coming to Mohammed." As far as the Ukrainians, Byelorussians, and Lithuanians were concerned this was a ridiculous excuse for territorial expansion. After all, sons of Poles were living in Chicago, U.S.A. Did the Poles want sovereignty over that city too?

In the past any sign of Polish national spirit had been put down with brutality and that memory was still present in the minds of the Poles. Plus Poland had too many veterans of the armed forces of Germany, Austria, and Russia, many of whom still carried their weapons, who were willing to fight for their beliefs. The result of this was military conflict between the Poles and the Ukrainians.

By the summer of 1919 and the signing of the Versailles Treaty, Poland was recognized by the Allies as having access to the sea through West Prussia, and use of, but not ownership of, the German port of Danzig. The existence of Polish sovereignty roughly corresponded to the land occupied by Polish troops.

However, a great crisis had arisen. The Imperialist Russians had been replaced by the communist Russians, who demanded not just the subservience of the former Russian territories but of the whole world. It was only a matter of time before the expanding Poles and the expanding Red Army clashed in the forests, swamps, and plains of Byelorussia.

By the summer of 1920 the Poles were facing defeat, for a massive Soviet army had pushed the Poles back to the gates of Warsaw. Apart from a few French advisers the Poles stood alone, in their minds not just defending their homes, but defending the world. Yet the miracle of the Vistula turned the over-extended Russian flank and Polish horse cavalry sliced into the Russians. Atheistic communism was repulsed and Christian civilization was saved.

In their desperation the Poles had offered the Ukrainians an autonomous Galicia in return for manpower at the front, but once the Reds were on the run the promise was forgotten. Polish troops reoccupied Galicia and never instituted the ethnic freedoms that the Ukrainians had been enticed with. A large piece of Lithuania, including the capital Vilna, was added to Poland after a Polish-controlled plebiscite, which is generally accepted to have been rigged.

However, plebiscites controlled by international bodies produced startling results. The Masurians, who are Poles, gave a majority in favor of German citizenship and sovereignty, and in Eastern Silesia, which is overwhelmingly Polish, the people opted for Polish citizenship by a majority of only 56%. The actual Poles of Western Silesia were just as split in their vote and this together with the German vote in the area put the district under German control. Teschen was assigned to Czechoslovakia, and this together with the loss of Silesia and Masuria was a bitter pill for the Polish government to swallow. The economic implications were grievously felt.

By the 1930s, Poland consisted of a nation of 24.5 million Poles surrounded by districts under Polish control of 200,000 Lithuanians, 620,000 Volksdeutsch, 1.1 million Byelorussians, and 4.5 million Ukrainians. As well the total area was dotted with villages and suburbs of 1.7 million Yiddish-speaking Jews who were considered by mutual consent to be foreigners. In addition to the obvious problems this caused, the Poles argued, rioted, and fought among themselves. Only a strong authoritarian government could rule this mess, and in 1926 that is what Poland received. The government allowed its citizens to consider themselves to be of Volksdeutsch, Ukrainian, or whatever nationality, even Kashubian—there were 100,000 of them in the northwest—or Gypsy, there were thousands of these deliberately suspicious characters—as long as they agreed to be good Polish citizens, paying taxes, keeping the laws, and reporting for military conscription on the required date.

Understanding Poland's wish for territorial gain and realizing that the government of 1938 was even more nationalist than that of twenty years earlier, it comes as no surprise that Poland took advantage of Czechoslovakia's problem with the Sudetenland in the autumn of 1938 and peacefully occupied the disputed territory along the Polish border. Over 1,000 square kilometers were occupied, 75,000 Polish-speakers liberated, and 20,000 Volksdeutsch and 133,000 Czechs taken over. Some postwar Polish thought is that the move was an attempt by Poland to rescue these people from possible German occupation. But this assumes these people asked to be rescued. At this point in time there was no serious indication that German rule would have been worse than Polish. Civil rights violations and anti-Semitism were rife in both states. Polish Jews kicked out of Germany where they had emigrated were not welcomed with open arms by Polish border guards, but were incarcerated in concentration camps.

Still the move was popular throughout Poland, and the mood of the Poles in the summer of 1939 was perhaps the most arrogant in their recent history. Their government stood behind one of the most powerful armies in the world and defied Hitler over the Danzig question. With their rear protected by the Soviets, who it was believed would never ally with the nazis, the Poles could concentrate their army, heavy in horse cavalry, along the northern, western, and southern borders.

However, Poland was not a very solid fortress. Her army consisted of large ethnic groups that might not fight—desertion among Jews and Volksdeutsch was already high. Her right and left flanks were held by the enemy, her opponents were as heavy in tank battalions as the Poles were in horse battalions, and only Britain had offered to help, but Britain could physically do nothing without Soviet support, which the Poles would not agree to—they had already tasted the bitterness of Soviet brotherhood.

The summer bliss was shattered on 23 August when nazi Germany and Soviet Russia signed a non-aggression pact. Now the Poles knew they would have to keep a large part of their army facing the Soviets for fear of a stab in the back, while the remainder of their forces tried to hold off the Germans. The pact was a death warrant for Poland.

On the morning of 1 September German artillery opened fire on Polish defenses and troop concentrations, Luftwaffe planes riddled the Polish aircraft with bullets while most of them were still on the ground, and German tanks charged across the border aiming at road junctions. Within hours, those Poles who lived near the frontier began to hit the road with suitcases, bundles, and hand carts filled with household belongings. The rich traveled in motor cars, but they could only drive at the speed of the walking refugees who packed the dusty dirt roads. Once in a while, a German plane strafed the columns, smashing the bodies of women and children for the military purpose of clearing the roads for the advancing German tanks.

The Poles fought bravely, but their strategy was wrong from the start. The same nationalist fervor that had caused them to conquer other people's lands in the first place now caused them to try to defend every yard of it rather than withdrawing to the interior and holding a shorter defense line.

Some Volksdeutsch rioted, but more in a celebratory manner than a violent one, and not unnaturally hundreds were arrested by the Polish police and army. Unfortunately in some places these unarmed prisoners were shot by the Poles, and in the Bromberg (Bydgoshcz) area there was an actual massacre. Nazi war correspondents eventually claimed that 7,000 innocent Volksdeutsch civilians were murdered by Polish troops. This was a highly inflated account, but the massacre was tailor-made for Goebbels' propaganda machine. Any Germans who had doubts about the truth of Polish atrocities against the Volksdeutsch minority now accepted them as probably true, and accepted the conclusion that Hitler had been justified in invading Poland to free his German brothers.

Practically unknown to the world, Germany had two military partners in the campaign. A Slovakian motorized division charged through the Dukla Pass and headed for Lwow in Galicia against light uncoordinated resistance, and the Ruthenian Sich, a force of 600 Ukrainian nationalists under Roman Sushko, advanced alongside the Slovakians, intent upon liberating their Ukrainian brothers and establishing a free Ukrainian state. Their military goal was quickly achieved, in that they reached Galicia, but their political goal fell afoul of German plans for the future of the Ukrainian nation.

On 17 September, the thing that the Poles feared the most took place. The Soviets invaded Eastern Poland. Defeat by Germany was staring them in the face, and this simply confirmed the inevitable. Some Polish officers committed suicide, such was the feeling of despair.

Only a few thousand survivors of the once proud Polish army, air force, and navy managed to reach Romania and safety.

The Polish state was divided into three areas: the eastern section comprising 134,000 Volksdeutsch, 200,000 Lithuanians, 1.1 million Byelorussians, 1.1 million unassimilated Jews, 4.5 million Ukrainians, and 5.3 million Poles was annexed by the Soviet Union; the western section consisting of 71,000 Czechs, 100,000 Kashubians, 580,000 unassimilated Jews, 620,000 Volksdeutsch, and 9.2 million Poles was annexed by Germany as the province of Wartheland; and the remainder which was made into a German colony consisting of 60,000 Volksdeutsch, 357,000 Ukrainians, 1.2 million unassimilated Jews, and 9.8 million Poles, was christened the General Government of Warsaw, which despite the name had its capital at Cracow. The name Poland was not to be used again, and this was a hint of what Hitler had in mind for the Poles.

Within the Soviet zone all members of the intelligentsia, that is, people who had proven they could think for themselves, were arrested along with their children and other family members. The prime goal of the Soviets was the ridding of their newly conquered lands of anyone who might be able to form an anti-communist resistance movement. Small guerrilla groups, some made up of Polish soldiers still on the run, were organized to fight the Red Army and the N.K.V.D., the security police, and these took on nationalist flavors almost at once. The Polish groups coalesced into the N.S.Z. (National Armed Forces). As the young men here were now Soviet citizens, they were conscripted into the Red Army. Failure to report meant arrest and deportation to a concentration camp for the draft dodger and all his family, even cousins. Persons who might be useful in Russian industry, for example welders, skilled machinists, engineers, and the like were deported as slave labor, and of course anyone who caused "trouble" was liable to arrest. Within twenty months of the Soviet invasion 1,060,000 people in this zone were taken from their homes by force for one reason or another—one person in twelve.

Within Wartheland the situation was not all that different. Here too Polish intellectuals were arrested and either shot or transported to concentration camps. The Volksdeutsch felt threatened, despite the presence of the German army, and they soon formed a defense militia, the Selbstschutz, controlled by Volksdeutsch officials of the local police. There was already a militia in Danzig, the Heimwehr, which had been formed to defend the people against Polish oppression, but now this was commandeered by the Totenkopf branch of the S.S.

The subjects of Wartheland were divided into categories: the Jews and Gypsies, who were unwanted and had to leave; the Poles, who would eventually be forced to leave; and the Volksdeutsch, who could remain.

To implement these laws the Polish police, containing Poles and Volksdeutsch, were assisted by newly raised units of S.S. called Einsatzkommandos, who rounded up known Jews, searched for unknown ones, rounded up Gypsies, arrested undesirables, and put them all on the roads leading to the General Government. The tragedy of this cannot be expressed by these few printed words. Careers were cut short. People were dragged from their ancestral homes, the elderly and handicapped were abandoned to fate, and in some cases resisters were shot dead in the streets. Many families were torn apart, because Polish-Volksdeutsch-Jewish intermarriage had not been uncommon. Throughout the winter the roads were jammed with pitiful refugees who had nowhere to go.

In one incident an S.S. man murdered fifty Jews. He was at once arrested and tried by his superiors, convicted and sentenced to death, but certain unscrupulous senior officers in the S.S. commuted the sentence to life imprisonment. Then Heinrich Himmler himself stepped in and ordered the sentence quashed. The man walked free.

As for the Poles, there was a problem as to who was a Pole and who was a Volksdeutsch for since the late eighteenth century no one had bothered to ask.

Many Poles soon found that they could put their names on the Volksdeutsch list without having to produce evidence of German race or having to speak German. They only had to prove they did not have more than two Jewish grandparents. It must be realized that a million Polish males were either in German or Soviet prisoner of war camps or elsewhere serving in the Allied-controlled forces, and that as a result there were many families that were without a breadwinner. Knowing that Poles with good jobs were being fired to make room for Volksdeutsch, many a man, faced with supporting a wife and children, and perhaps a mother and a sister and her children too, chose to opt for the Volksdeutsch list rather than lose a job that was the only thing standing between his loved ones and starvation.

To be sure some Poles volunteered for the list out of sheer greed, always wanting to be top dog. Those Poles who knew they had German ancestry had an honest claim to the list, but it is regrettable that once having been placed on the list few of these Poles would ever have the opportunity of being forgiven by the vast majority of the Poles who stuck it out through the cold, hungry winters and did not surrender their birthright.

This was evidence of how silly the racial ideas of the nazis really were. Poles, some of whom had fought the Germans in the September campaign, could be regarded as German citizens, albeit class IV and thus on probation, whereas real Germans who had served their country proudly for years, some in the hideous trench warfare of World War One, were suddenly divested of all rights, including the right to live, simply because more than two of their grandparents had worshipped God in synagogues. Unlike Polish Jews who maintained a closed culture and spoke their own language, German Jews were indistinguishable from other Germans.

More ridiculous still, included on the Volksdeutsch class III list were the Danish-speaking Germans and a few Lithuanian-speaking Germans, and on the Reichsdeutsch class II list were the Austrians, whose loyalty to Germany was ambivalent to say the least, and on the most prestigious Reichsdeutsch class I list were Germans who spoke Frisian and Wend.

The fate of the true Poles of Wartheland would not be determined for another two years, and these Poles never knew whether or not they might suddenly be turned out of house and home.

There was also a movement of refugees from east to west, and these were no less pitiable. By a secret protocol the 134,000 Volksdeutsch of Eastern Poland which had fallen to the Soviets were expelled by the Soviets—they were glad to leave—but they arrived in Wartheland in a state of poverty. They had been allowed only what they could carry. The accoutrements of generations, including precious land, had been confiscated. These refugees, victims of Hitler as well as Stalin, were placed in displaced persons camps run by the VOMI branch of the S.S.

Within the General Government the communities of Volksdeutsch were small, but they gained in size as some Poles opted for the list and some Reichsdeutsch (from Germany) arrived seeking their fortunes in the new frontier. Here too, any good jobs held by Poles were given to Volksdeutsch if someone could be found. Naturally positions in munitions factories, water works, power stations, and so on, were necessary and Poles were allowed to remain in these jobs if their departure was deemed detrimental.

The German S.S. Security Police (Gestapo-Kripo-S.D.) arrived in Warsaw with insufferable arrogance. Other government agencies also sent teams from Berlin. Recruiters of the S.A., known as the brownshirt stormtroopers, came to enlist local Volksdeutsch. Actual German city policemen were also brought in to aid the Polish police and to keep an eye on them.

Under S.S. orders the German 301st Police Battalion, a field force organized on paramilitary lines, arrested hundreds of people for real or imagined crimes and shot many of them in the prisons of Warsaw. The German city and Polish city and rural police arrested throughout the General Government 300 actors, 2,500 university instructors, 17,000 schoolteachers, and innumerable members of the intelligentsia.

Overriding all the problems of the Poles was poverty. Seemingly everything from collaboration, volunteer work, German service, and informing on one's neighbors, to anti-nazi resistance had economic overtones. Within weeks of the German invasion, 110,000 Poles (not Volksdeutsch) had volunteered to work in Germany and by May 1940 the figure had risen to 210,000. Evidently the need to survive was understood and these Poles were not looked upon as traitors by their compatriots. Many more Poles willingly worked for the Germans at home, but then again soon all Poles were working for Germans as all Polish and Jewish business ownership was soon replaced by Volksdeutsch ownership. Not a few Volksdeutsch became wealthy in this manner. The result was that the Volksdeutsch who had been reasonably good Polish citizens for twenty years were now totally alienated from the Poles. Many a family was torn asunder by the German policy.

The influx of refugees from Wartheland added to the problems of the General Government, especially in the case of the Jews. The city of Lodz in Wartheland had kept its Jews, but they had been confined to a section of the city christened the ghetto. Here enough Jewish community leaders were found to form a Judenrat (Jewish Council) to administer the new nazi laws, and soon a leader emerged, Mordecai Chaim Rumkowski. To enforce his orders he organized a Jewish police force, the Ordnungsdienst. Though these Jews were unarmed they were feared for not only could they attack in disciplined groups with clubs, but they could call upon the armed German police if necessary. At first the Jewish police were respected, but as time went on they came to be resented as tools of the nazis.

Within the cities of the General Government the Germans set up Jewish ghettos on the Lodz model as the local Jews and refugee Jews from Wartheland, Germany, and Austria arrived, some of them having walked hundreds of miles. Warsaw had the largest ghetto as its population of Jews was higher. In June 1940, the Germans calculated a rough census for the city. Not counting military formations and field police units, the population was believed to be 895,000 Poles, 393,500 Jews, 5,000 Ukrainians (ex-Polish citizens from Galicia), 2,500 Reichsdeutsch (newly arrived from Germany), 5,500 Volksdeutsch, and 5,000 foreigners.

The Jews were walled up in their section of the city with access to the outside world only in work parties marching to and from the place of employment while under constant guard by Werkschutz (works or factory guards) consisting of Poles and Volksdeutsch. The perimeter of the ghetto was guarded by Polish police and German advisers and in theory the laws were strictly enforced. In practice, though, bribery was commonplace, at least in the first few months when the Jews still had something with which to barter. Even high-ranking S.S. officers could be bribed on occasion.

In the Warsaw ghetto some of the Jewish police were Christian and anti-Semitic. Naturally any dealings with these Jews proved most disagreeable to the Jewish populace at large. The best example of how this had come about was that of Josef Szerynski. Prior to the war he had been a Christian and a colonel in the Polish police. After the German invasion, however, he was declared to be a racial Jew by the nazis—his real name was Scheinkman—and he was made chief of the Jewish police. There were enough Catholic Jews in the ghetto that several churches were filled to capacity on Sundays with mass being said by priests who were racial Jews.

The Germans also set up in the ghetto a body staffed by Jews called the Central Office to Combat Black Marketing and Profiteering in the Jewish Residential District. In reality, this force, run by Abraham Ganzweich, took orders from the Gestapo, and it spent its time battling conspiracies of dissatisfied Jews in order to prevent organized resistance.

Ghettoization was not just inconvenient. It could be fatal. It is estimated that the starvation rations, lack of heating fuel, rampant disease in ridiculously overcrowded conditions, and of course executions for infringements of the rules killed upwards of half a million people, a large part of them the elderly and the children. Continuously the Judenrat had only just managed to find lodgings for the latest influx of Jews, when a train or a marching column arrived with a hundred or a thousand more. There was always more. The numbers of Jews seemed endless, but the senior nazis were debating a solution to the problem, a final solution.

In order to assist the Polish police to combat the anti-nazi terrorists who soon appeared, the German police created several field regiments from volunteer policemen serving in Germany, including police reservists who had been called to full-time duty due to the war emergency. Eventually the following regiments were established in the General Government: Cracow, Warsaw, Lublin, Radom, 4th, 10th, 11th, 12th, 22nd, 23rd, 24th, and 25th. They took orders from German police chiefs not Polish chiefs. Each district had a German KdO in charge of all police and a KdS in charge of all S.S. Security Police, both of whom were responsible to a higher S.S. and police leader. In the General Government the higher S.S. and police leader was in theory responsible to the governor, Hans Frank, but over the years Frank sent complaint after complaint to Berlin stating that the S.S. were a law unto themselves. All Polish police chiefs were responsible to their German counterparts.

In Galicia the differences of the Ukrainian population were noted, and the local Ukrainian police were responsible to German not Polish police chiefs. Twelve police regiments were formed to combat guerrillas, numbered 201 to 212. The 202nd Regiment was made up of Poles, and the rest consisted of Ukrainians. The official name of the non-German regiments and battalions was Schutzmannschaften (guard man squads), hence the nickname schumas.

The Ruthenian Sich had been disbanded, but its members found homes in the schumas and the Werkschutz.

Within Wartheland the Germans extended their civil administration as this area was now just part of Germany, and this meant that 18-year-old male and female Volksdeutsch were subjected to conscription into the Reichs Labor Service—R.A.D., which used these youngsters for a few months to perform government labor, often agricultural work. Officials of the force were older career members. As of March 1940, 19-year-old males were eligible for conscription into the armed forces and in addition all males up to the age of 45 were eligible for call-up as reservists, though some of these class IV citizens did not speak German, and all were really reservists in the defunct Polish army not the German army. All children of the Volksdeutsch were forced to join one of the branches of the Hitler Youth. The Volksdeutsch soon learned what it cost to be a citizen of Germany.

Of course anyone could express discontent with the system, but if the wrong person overheard the conversation it could mean incarceration in a concentration camp for several months.

The Selbstschutz, originally formed to protect the Volksdeutsch of Wartheland, had become overbearing and arrogant. The men treated even Volksdeutsch with poor conduct and were abominable with the Poles. As for Jews and Gypsies, they felt it to be open season on them ever since the murder trial in which Himmler intervened. Everywhere, wearing civilian clothes and an armband, and carrying an assortment of rifles and shotguns, the Selbstschutz aided the police and the Einsatzkommandos to round up undesirables. But by the spring of 1940, even the S.S. officers had had enough of this unit's brutality, and the force was disbanded. The S.S. complained that this undisciplined mob had given the Germans a bad name. Little could they have realized that what Hitler and Himmler had in mind for the future would make the most vicious Selbstschutz members look like naughty children.

While Poland was regearing towards full employment in the service of the Third Reich, a large surplus of manpower was identified. The Germans therefore organized forced labor in which men and women who were judged not to be in useful employment were forcefully dragged off to work in Germany, where off-duty hours were spent restricted to a certain town or in some cases actually imprisoned in a camp near the work site. By early 1941, 800,000 Poles had been placed into this bottomless pit of slavery. Forced labor was also used as a means of punishment for petty infringements of the rules, for example being caught in possession of a ham or a chicken leg, food which was not authorized for "sub-humans." The unluckiest slaves were sent to labor camps owned by the S.S. economics office and guarded by S.S. men. Some slaves were assigned to aid Organization Todt workers in repairing battle fortifications, sometimes under fire. The luckiest slaves were those sent to help German farmers, where they sometimes became friendly with the Germans.

The Soviet occupation of the Baltic States (Lithuania, Estonia, and Latvia), Bessarabia, and Bukovina in 1940 brought the German government more expelled Volksdeutsch. The S.S. VOMI eventually had to place in camps 363,000 of these unfortunates. By the end of 1940 the camps in Wartheland were full to the brim with impoverished and angry Volksdeutsch. Their only way out was to enlist in the S.S. or one of the civilian organizations of the German government or to accept positions as colonists on land stolen from Jews and Poles.

Chapter 3

Nationalist Crusades: The Politics of Desperation

The British Empire

Ever since the first Jew set foot in Britain there has been anti-Semitism there, but it rarely took hold of the people as it did in some other nations. One Jew, Benjamin Disraeli, became one of Britain's most respected prime ministers. At the end of the nineteenth century, though, an influx of Russian and Polish Jews who were fleeing Tsarist persecution created a Jewish district in East London, and this fanned the flames of political anti-Semitism, which soon allied with reactionism to form the fascists.

By 1923 British fascists had begun talking of purifying Britain and in May of that year the British Fascist Party was founded by Miss R.L. Lintorn-Orman, a member of a fine old military family. Later the party president was R.B.D. Blakeney.

There were also purely anti-Semitic organizations that were not necessarily fascist, for example, the Britons of Henry Beamish and Dr. John Henry Clarke, which had been founded in 1918.

By 1926 the leading fascists in the country were Blakeney, Lord Hamilton, Brigadier Sir Ormonde Winter, who had been the rather vicious deputy police chief for Ireland during the Anglo-Irish War, Arthur Hardinge, Nesta Webster, Viscount Down, and Rear Admiral W.E.R. Martin. The rallies and marches of the fascists were by and large peaceful affairs, but there were occasional clashes with anti-fascist groups, especially the communists.

Then the fascists were suddenly in their element as the political left brought the country to a halt with a general strike. The right organized the Organization for the Maintenance of Supplies, which began to perform all the jobs necessary to the survival of the state. This broke the strike.

The Labor Party called this legal fascism, but though all fascists had worked for the Organization, their own leaders had been outmaneuvered by the Conservative Party, which had controlled everything.

The National Fascist Party, which had been trooping around in black shirts, had been thoroughly overshadowed and it never recovered. In 1927 as a means to reestablish itself the British Fascist Party created a blue-uniformed militia. In 1929, some fascist dissidents founded a new party, the Imperial Fascist League led by Arnold Leese and they paraded in black shirts. None of these ultra-right groups were blessed with charismatic leadership. It remained to a volatile British member of parliament to supply that.

Oswald Mosley had been educated at Sandhurst, the British military academy, and had been wounded in the Great War while serving with the Royal Flying Corps. In 1918, he became M.P. for Harrow, the youngest in the Conservative Party, but four years later he declared his independence from the party, and then in April 1924 went over to the opposition by joining the Labor Party.

In 1920, he had married Lady Cynthia, the daughter of the Marquis of Curzon, in a society wedding in which the king and queen were guests. She too was a political figure and for four years, until her premature death in 1933, she was a labor M.P.

Having swung from right to left, Mosley swung back again, retiring from Parliament and his position as chancellor of the Duchy of Lancaster in 1930, to form his own right-wing political party in March 1931. After several discussions at mass meetings and not a few fist fights, the party emerged nineteen months later as the British Union of Fascists.

The manifesto of the party was highly controversial, and the marching members angered many a bystander, but Mosley became more and more accepted by his peers, and he visited several heads of state, including Adolf Hitler. Mosley's strongholds were East London and Preston, Lancashire, and it was one of his Lancashire rallies, at Manchester, that caused a great furor. When the meeting was attacked by communists and anti-fascists the police charged against all concerned. For a placid England this brought memories back of the general strike and was alarming. Mosley blamed the police and soon formed his own black-shirted defense militia. In October 1933, another Manchester rally caused police intervention. In London there were several pitched street battles, though firearms were never used.

The controversial fascists of Mosley continued to gain recruits, and some of the more notable people who joined his ranks were Major General J.F.C. Fuller, the historian; Francis Yeats-Brown, the author; Lord Rothermere, the publisher of the *Daily Mail*, a popular national newspaper; Sir William Morris, owner of Morris Motors; Sir Henry Deterding, chairman of the Dutch Oil Company; Viscount Lymington; Admiral Sir Barry Domville; B. Philby, the explorer; the Earl of Glasgow and Walter Runciman, both brothers-in-law of Sir Thomas Inskip the Minister of Defense, and William Joyce, who became the party's propagandist. Joyce, an American-born son of loyalist Irish parents, bore a facial scar received in a street brawl with communists.

In 1936 Mosley, now a widower, married another society debutant, Diana Mitford, sister of one of Hitler's girlfriends. Despite Mosley's wish to emulate the Fuehrer, this was his only real connection with the man. Hitler knew that, though Mosley had important people on his team, his popular support never numbered more than 40,000.

Several of the younger fascists, like John Amery, son of the Secretary of State for India, joined Franco's army in the Spanish Civil War. Those who returned from that bloody conflict did so with a more complete understanding of what the differences between extreme right and extreme left could lead to.

Despite Britain having fought Germany for four terrible years in the Great War and the fact that the ruling class had sworn to the masses that the Germans were evil, the British and German ruling classes had always maintained high social intercourse. The Royal Family had many German relatives. One of the public manifestations of this was the Anglo-German Fellowship, and though not fascist in outlook the Fellowship did not shrink from maintaining contacts with Germany after Hitler's rise to power. Leading members of the Fellowship were Lord Londonderry, Minister of Air 1931-35; Lord Home, whose son was Prime Minister Chamberlain's private secretary, and Sir Barry Domville, who had been director of British naval intelligence at the time of the signing of the Anglo-German Naval Treaty.

Clivedon, the home of Lord and Lady Astor, was one of the many jovial gathering places for such intellectuals of the ultra-right, and here the German ambassador was always welcomed. For a time this was a Joachim von Ribbentrop, who became Hitler's foreign minister. To be fair to the Astors, though, proponents of contrary political ideologies were also invited.

Sir Neville Henderson, whom Chamberlain appointed British ambassador to Berlin, wrote and stated in the summer of 1938 that he was glad that Czechoslovakia was going to get a turn of the screw from Hitler, and he eagerly requested that Chamberlain allow Hitler his demands. Geoffrey Dawson, editor of the prestigious (London) *Times*, published his agreement with this idea, and the *New Statesman* agreed that the Czechs should let go of their minorities.

Only in late August 1939 when Hitler allied with Stalin did many of these fascists feel betrayed, realizing that Hitler was not a true fascist but an opportunist, and they supported Chamberlain's declaration of war against Germany on 3 September. Few dissented. The leaders of the British Union of Fascists were arrested and imprisoned—Mosley, Domville, Philby, and some lesser members. Joyce and a handful of others managed to escape to Germany. Those fascists who had family connections remained at large. It has long been suspected that a financial supporter of the fascists was none other than King Edward VIII, who abdicated in 1936 and became known as the Duke of Windsor. It is known that he was in contact with German representatives throughout the early part of the war and that Hitler wanted to put him back on the throne. The F.B.I. (American domestic counterespionage) considered the duke and his wife to be security risks every time they visited the United States, and the British government as of the date of this publication has still refused to name all of the financial supporters of the British fascists of the 1930s.

Once war had come there were a few businessmen who were either pro-German or simply unscrupulous who continued to trade with Germany through neutral Spain, putting British money ahead of British lives in priority. In fact it was only when the Americans ceased to trade with Spain in January 1944 that the British government cut off this channel through which Germany had received indirect British aid. Postwar Britain was full of rumors that senior government members had had monetary interests in German companies throughout the war, though so far this has been seen to be without foundation.

Actual recruitment of Britons by the Germans was practically negligible, however. John Amery, who had fled to Germany, was assisting the Germans in the propaganda war when he came up with the idea of forming a force of Britons to fight alongside the Germans against the communists. The force was soon founded, but the result was poor and Amery lost interest in it. The greedy S.S. soon took control of the recruitment, but despite there being tens of thousands of British prisoners of war currently in Germany, only about sixty men were induced, bribed, and coerced into the British Free Corps. The men were kept together for propaganda purposes.

After this poor showing more faith was placed in two ethnic segments controlled by the British—the Irish and the Indians. At first glance it seemed that the Irish could provide a major force. The Eire Free State, though a dominion of the Commonwealth, had not joined in Britain's war as its people were violently opposed to the British government, but the Germans made the mistake of believing that the Irish were also opposed to the British people. Eire had become independent by waging the Anglo-Irish War 1919-1921, and though there had been atrocities on both sides relations between the two peoples survived. Indeed Irish factionalism caused more problems, resulting in civil war 1922-1923. This was the result of the rebel leadership having accepted a compromise peace in which six counties in the north remained British.

The Protestant majority of the six counties of Northern Ireland had sided with the British and were happy with the outcome, but the Catholic minority felt betrayed by their fellow rebels. They fought the Eire government but lost and retreated to a sort of truce condition.

By 1933 General Eoin O'Duffy took control of the Army Comrades Association, made up of veterans of the Government side in the civil war. Wearing blue shirts the members under his direction took on an increasingly fascist appearance and stance. The other fiercely nationalist group was the I.R.A., Irish Republican Army, which had taken the anti-government side in the civil war. Naturally they hated the blueshirts and as well as believing they were more nationalist they also had a left-wing social program.

The Irish people are conservative and Catholic to the core, but at this time they were also poor and social arguments had as much prominence as nationalist arguments. Poverty had caused many young men to join the army, and if there was no room—to join the British army.

The outbreak of the Spanish Civil War in 1936 gave the fascist blueshirts a chance to fulfill their boasts, and to be fair it must be noted that many did do just that, fighting well for Franco. The I.R.A. remained uncommitted to that war, but launched its own war against Britain in 1939. These 2,000 or so men and women, citizens of Eire from the south and of Britain from the north, began a terrorist bombing campaign. Their targets were rail lines, power stations, and such, chosen to embarrass the British rather than kill them, but on 25 August 1939 a time bomb exploded in a Coventry shopping center, killing five and wounding sixty.

The Irish people were as stunned as the British by this act, and the Eire government soon began a serious crackdown on the I.R.A.

In 1940, German intelligence agents landed in Eire to recruit the blueshirts and/or the I.R.A. for the crusade, but they found only a few I.R.A. fanatics willing to enter Northern Ireland and battle the British police and troops. The naivete of the terrorists was matched by the incompetence of the agents. Guerrilla raids did take place in the north, but they were so harmless that the local residents rarely took notice. There were a few gun battles in Eire as the police quickly rounded up the I.R.A. and their German friends.

Of better aid to the Germans were the 140 Irish men and women who worked in propaganda and espionage training departments. When the British Channel Islands had been occupied by the Germans in June 1940 about 800 Irish laborers had been taken over. Asked to either go home or work for the Germans in France, almost all took the offer of employment.

The Irish who worked in the German government departments were favorable towards the creation of an Irish Legion and they assisted the German recruiters when they visited Irishmen in the prisoner of war camps. Though many of these captured Irishmen had originally joined the British army only for the sake of steady employment, it is a credit to them that so few accepted the German offer, despite the offer of free booze and prostitutes—a powerful inducement to any prisoner—if they joined and a beating if they did not, that the legion was never constituted.

The Germans had greater success with the Indians. The many ethnic groups in India had warred against the British from time to time, but none had won their independence. Having served Britain well in World War One, the people's leaders were angry that the British dismissed all petitions for freedom once that war had been won. The independence moves began to split into the pacifists led by Mohandas Gandhi and the militant groups, one of which was led by Subhas Chandra Bose.

The prisoners of war captured in North Africa were depressed that their homes were still under the thumb of the British and because they felt the British officers had abandoned them. The Germans judged them to be ripe for recruitment, especially as the great Moslem leader the Grand Mufti of Jerusalem was in the German camp. When Bose also arrived in Germany to preach a war of liberation, that was enough to sway about 2,000 Moslems and Sikhs. The men were retrained with German equipment as the Indian Legion and then given occupation duty in France. As this unit did not serve in the east it did not witness German-sponsored atrocities, and the men considered themselves to be members of a new Indian army.

The Finns: Crusaders of the North

Finland emerged onto the world scene as if from nowhere, for Finnish nationalism had always been suppressed by her neighbors. In February 1917, Finland was a province of the Tsarist Russian Empire, a land of 3.5 million Finns, 400,000 Swedish-speakers on the southwest coast, and a handful of nomadic Lapps in the Arctic north, but when the tsar abdicated, Finnish- and Swedish-speaking politicians assembled together in Helsinki to proclaim the independence and neutrality of Finland. Finnish deserters began coming home from the Russian army and for a while it looked like the move might succeed in peace. But it was not meant to be.

At the end of the year, a few Finnish communists and some Russians began taking over the country building by building until by January 1918 they controlled the towns.

In the forested areas an anti-communist (White) army began to form led by several nationalists including General Carl Gustav Mannerheim, a Swedish-speaking Finn who had served well in the Tsarist Russian army. The German government also released a unit of Swedish-speaking Finns that had been serving in the German forces. On the political front in March the Communist Russian government signed a peace with Germany and gave up her claim to Finland, thus depriving the Red Guards, as they called themselves, of support. The Finnish White army now began an offensive and together with German troops who landed on the coast they easily drove out the communists, who fled to Russia. The territory inhabited by Finnish Protestants was declared to be Finland, but the area of Karelia which was occupied by Finnish people of the Orthodox faith remained in Russian hands.

In the Finnish mind the Russians were the invaders and the Germans were the liberators. Naturally anti-communism became solidified in Finnish politics and several right-wing organizations sprang up. One of the more well known was the Lapua Movement, which became more and more militant as time went on.

However, when the great World Depression struck Finland in 1930, it brought economic hardship to the lower classes and by 1932 they had created a strong left wing in the country. Though the socialists were still anti-communist and anti-Russian, nonetheless even this was too much for some people and a right-wing revolt was attempted in February 1932. It failed miserably and on 2 March the police arrested the leaders of the Lapua Movement. This move was not without side effects. Two cabinet ministers resigned in protest and much of the bourgeoisie deplored the act.

The right wingers were even more alarmed when French intelligence proved that a Soviet Russian spy network was operating in Finland. Still, in 1936 a left-wing party managed to get elected. Evidently not all Finns were fanatic enough to associate the socialists with the communists.

As is often the case, an outside threat unified the nation. In 1939 the Soviets informed the Finns that they wanted to protect their port of Leningrad by gaining bases in Southern Finland and they wanted the Petsamo area for a series of air and sea bases on the north coast. The Finns made it quite plain that Finnish soil was sovereign and not for sale, lease, or rent. By November, the Anglo-French and the Germans were locked in a major struggle, and the Soviets saw their opportunity.

With a discrepancy in population of four million to the Soviet Union's 180 million, everyone in the world expected a very short conflict—everyone that is but the Finns. They had been alarmed by the constant demands and proposals of the Soviets, and when the Red Army invaded Eastern Poland it shook the Finnish cabinet into action. Violations of Finnish air space by Red Air Force planes only added to the warnings. However, when Finnish troops were posted to the border, the Soviets claimed this to be a warlike move. The Finns were only on the defensive and could hardly be otherwise. By 29 November the Finns were still trying to negotiate their way out of the situation.

The Soviet invasion came only hours later.

The Finns immediately mobilized all available manpower by calling up all able-bodied males up to the age of sixty and taking on female volunteers. This gave them a force of 127,800 soldiers, 100,000 replacements, 100,000 male and 100,000 female Civic Guards. Counting the small navy and air force there were slightly less than half a million Finns in arms.

The main hope of the Finns was the Mannerheim Line, which had recently been refurbished, but it contained only sixty-six machine gun nests to protect eighty-eight miles of line. Even if it could have held back the Soviet Seventh Army, the enemy still had another 900 miles of border from which to choose for an assault. The Soviets placed the Fourteenth Army in the far north targeted on Petsamo, the Ninth Army in the center with bases at Repola, Ukhta, and Kandalaksha, and the Eighth Army of nine divisions and a tank brigade between Lakes Onega and Ladoga. To fend off the Soviet hordes the Finns rushed their reservists to their IVth Corps of two divisions to face the entire Eighth Army, and were employing the Civic Guard to stop the Ninth Army on a 650-mile front. Only one battalion defended Petsamo. The bulk of the Finnish army, the IInd and IIIrd Corps with six divisions, was holding the Mannerheim Line between Lake Ladoga and the Gulf of Finland, and it was soon under pressure from thirteen Soviet divisions and five tank brigades.

After three days of battle, though, the sheer bulk of the Red Army was giving the Soviet generals logistical headaches, as the units were strung out along narrow roads which sliced through the snow blanketed forests. The Finns had already planned a campaign of delaying tactics, and their ski troops were especially useful, imitating the American Indians of the wild west who had harassed wagon trains. Still nothing could prevent the Soviet Seventh Army from cutting through the Mannerheim Line in several places on the 7th, and soon Soviet tanks were advancing towards the city of Viipuri. Elsewhere the Soviets had made good mileage, but Finland is a large country, and so far the only serious loss had been Petsamo.

From the sea the Red Navy bombarded coastal installations, and in the air the Red Air Force inflicted casualties on civilians with scattered bombing, but the morale of the people, the expanse of terrain involved, the time of year, which allowed only four hours of daylight in the south and even less in the frozen north, the bad flying weather, and the one hundred or so Finnish fighter planes that fought like hornets, prevented the Red Air Force from becoming a decisive weapon.

By the 10th the Soviets had halted everywhere. The Finns were relieved and the rest of the world was amazed. Now foreigners realized that there might be time yet for them to give a lick for freedom and they began to leave their peaceful secure homes to sail for Finland—Americans, many of them of Finnish descent; Hungarians, who share a common linguistic stock with the Finns; a few hundred Norwegians; 3,000 Estonians; 800 Danes; and fully 8,000 Swedes, who came to help their Swedish-speaking brothers of southwest Finland. It was interesting that so many Estonians should volunteer, for some of the Soviet warplanes were using bases in Estonia.

Prime Minister Neville Chamberlain of Great Britain went further than any foreign leader and began to form an expeditionary corps of the British army to aid the Finns. Many Britons felt this to be politically unwise, as Britain was at war with Germany not Russia, and the Germans had yet to be brought to battle. On the diplomatic front France showed an interest in Finnish survival and the League of Nations expelled the Soviet Union for this unwarranted aggression.

Further hope came when Colonel General Paavo Talvela ordered a counterattack which sent his troops across the frozen Lake Tolva north of Lake Ladoga on the 12th. Within two days the Tolvajärvi area was in Finnish hands and the panicky troops of the Soviet 139th Division were fleeing through waist-high snow in pitch darkness through a strange forest in temperatures of -40°F, with Finnish ski troops chasing them. The Red 75th Division was sent to the rescue but finished its days joining the retreat. But the price was high. Finnish casualties were 35% of those engaged.

Now the heartened Finns launched battalion-sized counterattacks everywhere to keep the Soviets occupied and therefore unable to continue the offensive. On 6 January the IVth Corps made a major assault against the southern part of the Eighth Army and in a week of bitter fighting chopped up the Russians into pockets. Four Soviet divisions assembled to rescue the besieged troops, but the Finns held them off with one hand while finishing off the pockets with the other. On 18 February the Soviet 18th Division capitulated, and a tank brigade followed suit on the 29th. The Soviet 168th Division still held out on the north shore of Lake Ladoga.

In the Karelian Isthmus the "new" Mannerheim Line, which consisted of just dogged determined men and women, withheld attack after attack as Russian infantry and light tank forces tried to find a path through the defenses so that a new offensive could be undertaken. On the map the armies were not going anywhere, but on the ground the days and nights were never quiet.

In the exact middle of the country the fresh Finnish 9th Division went over to the attack in December and continued to cut away at the Soviet line of communication east of Suomosalmi. On 5 January, a general offensive was called for here and within just two days the remnants of the Soviet 163rd and 44th Divisions were destroyed. The Finnish losses had been high here in relation to forces engaged, 900 dead and 1,770 wounded, but all thought of a Soviet offensive here was cut short.

On 1 February the Finns were subjected to a new offensive in the Karelian Isthmus. From south to north the Finnish 4th Division faced odds of three to one, the 3rd (ex 6th) Division faced two divisions and a tank brigade, the 1st Division faced an enemy division, the 2nd Division between Lake Muola and Vuoksi faced two divisions, the 8th Division faced a Soviet division south of Sakkola, and from there to Lake Ladoga the 7th Division was supposed to stop two divisions. In reserve the Finns had two divisions and the Soviets had three divisions and a tank corps.

Eleven days of shelling, bombing, and massed infantry charges brought the Russians nothing but casualties. Lest it be totally destroyed the 3rd Division was replaced by the 5th Division on the 11th, and these new men now took upon themselves the sickening duty of alternating between cowering in fear under Red artillery barrages and mowing down screaming Russian infantry.

On the 14th the Russians breached the line and all Finnish reserves including half-trained recruits were thrown into the battle, but on the 15th the Finns were already falling back. By March the Russians were at the gates of Viipuri.

By now the Swedish volunteers were ready for action and two battalions were turned into rearguards to make a fighting withdrawal. The Estonians also entered the line as the 200th Regiment, and the Americans and other volunteers were alerted.

One of the more unusual foreign aids went into operation in early March. Boris Bajanov, who had once been Stalin's private secretary, had approached Field Marshal Mannerheim requesting permission to raise a group of emigre Russians and defectors like himself to propagandize the Red Army. Quickly granted permission, Bajanov recruited 450 such people and trained them in rudimentary psychological warfare. In March these "troops" began speaking to the men of the Red Army at night with loudspeakers, and though it was obvious the Finns were now losing and in retreat this unit managed to gain 300 defections in less than two weeks.

Throughout the first two weeks in March the Finns held the enemy advance to a crawl as Mannerheim plugged each new gap with men plucked from his dwindling resources, but on the 13th the Finns were outflanked on the southwest of Viipuri when Soviet troops crossed the partially frozen bay.

The Finnish government already knew that total collapse was inevitable. French and British promises of reinforcements were not enough as it was known that these would have to cross the sea in the face of German and Soviet air and sea power. The ministers accepted Mannerheim's advice, and ceding to the somewhat inflated Soviet demands they surrendered.

The Karelian Isthmus was annexed by the Soviet Union as were the Petsamo area and a slice of terrain in the center. Over 450,000 Finnish civilians fled rather than live under communist rule. Tiny Finland, a country with a smaller population than London or New York, had suffered casualties of 24,923 killed and 43,557 wounded.

Yet the Soviets would think twice about taking on the Finns again, for the four-month war had cost them 900 planes, 1,600 tanks, and according to Stalin 48,000 killed and 158,000 wounded. However, the Finns maintain that Soviet losses were closer to half a million killed and wounded. In the post-Stalin era Nikita Khrushchev admitted that Soviet casualties were one million.

In the summer of 1940 as Germany won victory after victory, a few hundred Finns moved to Germany to join the elite Waffen S.S. The Swedish-speaking were put into S.S. Regiment Germania and the Finnish-speaking into a Finnish Battalion. By May 1941 both were ready for action—except that there was no enemy.

Adolf Hitler would soon remedy that oversight. Secretly meeting with the Finnish government, German delegates informed the Finns that the Soviets would soon have their hands full, so much so that they would not be able to prevent the Finns from reclaiming their lost territory. The Finnish generals were told to plan anew. Only fifteen months after the devastating Winter War the Finns were about to go to war again.

Norway and Denmark: Survival of the Viking Spirit

The politics of the extreme right in Norway was soon tied for better or for worse with Vidkun Quisling. Having served as a military attache to the communists during the Russian Civil War, Quisling then became an official of the League of Nations responsible for aid to refugees in Ukrainia, Russia, and the Balkan states. In this capacity he acquired a Ukrainian wife and an international reputation as a humanitarian. He switched his career to politics in 1930 and served as Minister of Defense for a year until 1932. Then, realizing that many people were not taking the outside threat of Soviet expansion seriously, he set about creating his own political force, the NS, Nasjonal Sammling (National Unity).

The NS was the only real expression of ultra-nationalism in this country of 3.5 million and by its very nature was anti-German, though from 1938 onwards Quisling secretly accepted funds from Germany. There had been a minor flurry of nationalism when a sovereignty problem arose with Denmark over Greenland, but other than that Norwegian nationalism was good-natured and was funneled into cultural pastimes. Norway had remained neutral during World War One and maintained only a small reservist defensive capability, preferring to rely on diplomacy. In 1939 the government refused a non-aggression pact with Germany because it was believed it just was not needed. After all, who would want to conquer Norway?

In early 1940, however, the officer corps suffered from morale problems when British naval forces boarded a German merchant ship while it was anchored in neutral Norwegian waters. Then Winston Churchill publicly pleaded for the small nations to ally against Germany. The ultra-nationalists believed that if left unchecked the British would soon be treating Norway like one of their colonies. In addition, the Soviet invasion of Finland disturbed many. Quisling had denounced this of course, but he urged his followers not to volunteer for the Finnish forces. He could not explain at that time that he needed them for use at home. Caught between Britain on one flank and the Soviets on the other the Norwegians could only turn to Germany for support, believed the conservative right.

In early April the British committed an act of war. The Royal Navy placed sea mines in Norwegian waters. The intended targets were German vessels that carried Swedish ore from Norwegian ports, but naturally a Norwegian ship might just as easily be sunk. At this moment Quisling was in Denmark for a meeting with Frits Clausen and representatives of the German government. The latter wished to know the reaction of these men if German military intervention were necessary. Both pledged their support, but neither were informed of anything concrete.

On 8 April the Norwegians mobilized as a German troop convoy set sail in their direction. The reservists were hardly in place when the next morning German ships bombarded coastal defenses, marines landed on the coast, and paratroopers landed on the airfields. Some units fought like hell, but others obeyed their officers who ordered them to refrain from firing. Colonel Sundlo, an NS supporter, surrendered the strategically important port of Narvik. The government and Royal Family fled northwards and eventually went to Britain.

Quisling barged into a radio station and broadcast to the nation that he was taking control, but just about everyone including the Germans ignored him. The senior members of the NS were as astonished by the move as anyone. Four days after the invasion, by which time the populated districts were under German occupation, the society people of the nation pleaded by radio, leaflets, posters, and newspapers for the troops to cease fire. The Germans were continuously informing the Norwegians that they had come to prevent an invasion by the British, and to be sure there was logic in this statement.

On the 14th, the Germans installed a governing administration of several prominent Norwegians. Quisling was not among them. A week later the Germans installed a Reichskommissar, the German politician Josef Terboven, who held the real power, and General von Falkenhorst changed from invader to military garrison commander. The NS was ignored.

However, Quisling was not one to submit so fast. He traveled to Berlin and spent the next months trying to drum up support for his own personal crusade. He finally found a patron, the racial theorist Alfred Rosenberg.

Denmark

Denmark had been in an unusual position at the end of World War One, in that she had remained neutral, yet shared in the spoils of victory. Up to this date a slice of Denmark had been under German control for half a century, and when the Allies authorized plebiscites for the region a substantial portion of these Danish-speaking Germans voted for the Danish border to come south to include them. Unfortunately not only did the new border not encompass all of them, leaving 30,000 of them in Germany, but it did trap several thousand Germans, making them Danish citizens. Of course the people could have moved, but agricultural people can rarely afford to do this, and then again why should they have left their ancestral homes?

The 1920s saw Germany and Denmark try to get along with each other despite each occupying a slice of the other's land.

It was the economic collapse which arrived with the World Depression that polarized Danish politics. In January 1932 unemployment rose to 136,000, a high figure for a nation of only 3.5 million souls. When the following year the major employers ordered a 20% reduction in pay for their employees, the unions reacted by ordering a general strike for 1 February. The government stepped in now and banned all strikes for twelve months. Those who felt that the capitalists were taking advantage of the situation to return to the old ways in which the poor would get poorer swung to the left. Those who felt that the unions were not willing to sacrifice for the sake of the nation's long-term future swung to the right.

The ultra-right at this time was the Danish Fascist Party, which in April 1933 claimed a membership of 15,000. This was not very many, and political argument never threatened to break out into warfare. In fact by May 1939, when Denmark signed a non-aggression pact with Germany, things were definitely looking brighter. The threat of another Anglo-German war brought foreign industrial orders to Denmark and supplied cargoes for the fine merchant fleet and this led to decreased unemployment.

On 9 April 1940, the Germans invaded the country without any clear warnings. The battle was fought and lost before most people had digested their breakfasts. It came as a swift blow to the man in the street and the Danes were stunned. Total Danish casualties were only twenty-six dead.

Prime Minister Thorvald Stauning announced that the Danes were to look upon the Germans not as invaders but as guests, and he instructed them to forget the little misunderstanding of the morning of the 9th.

The Danish army remained in being, but was reduced in size from 7,000 to 2,000, and the navy remained. The German ambassador to Denmark, Cecil von Renthe-Fink, would remain the German representative. At once German labor officials opened their recruiting offices, offering foreign employment to Denmark's unemployed and job-dissatisfied, and within a few months 25,000 took the offer.

The Dutch: The Other Germanic Empire

Dutch nationalism was revived in the 1930s but it was nothing new. The spirit of nationalism had created the country out of a Spanish colony and had made the Dutch go on to create an empire of their own controlling ten times the number of people that resided in the Netherlands, which had 11 million in 1940.

All of the Dutch were of one ethnicity, and even the Jews were totally assimilated, but for the Frisians, though they were just as Germanic and they retained enough linguistic rights that there was never any serious political conflict between them and the Dutch. The many descendants of French Protestants who had fled to this Protestant country were recognizable only by their surnames. The Netherlands was a peaceful nation that put its nationalist fervor into building and maintaining a large merchant fleet, a fair-sized navy, and a paternalistic style of colonialism in the West Indies and East Indies. Indeed it had been the nationalist spirit that had kept the nation out of World War One, even though the Flemish, the linguistic neighbors to the south, had been overrun by the Germans.

This was pacific nationalism. There was another kind in the country by the 1930s, a militant nationalism that was funneled into the National Socialist Party (N.S.B.). Founded in June 1933, the party, led by Anton Adriaan Mussert, pledged to seek a new way to fend off the World Depression. Moulded in part on the nazis of Germany, the party had its own black-uniformed defense militia, the Weer Afdeling, which was used to protect the party leaders and to control the many mass rallies. Left-wing agitators were always a problem at these meetings. Unofficially, many members of the militia blackmailed, ran protection rackets, bullied, and broke up rival political meetings. By and large, though, the Dutch ultra-nationalists were not as ignorant or as brutal as their German counterparts. They were not even anti-Semitic as a matter of policy and the party actually had Jewish members. Surprisingly, for such a homogeneous nation, the Dutch nazis considered citizenship rather than race or religion to be the basic requirement for membership in the Dutch tribe.

As extreme nationalists these nazis preached against German interference in the affairs of the Dutch nation as much as they did against French, British, or Soviet interference.

After clashes between police and the Weer Afdeling in Amsterdam, the government banned the wearing of political uniforms on 25 July 1933. The nazis replied that the government should spend less time hurting political rivals and more time doing something about the country's 700,000 unemployed. The government was already publicly admitting that there was no economic relief in sight and they did not know what to do for the best.

One thing not to do, according to the nazis, was to allow more unemployed people into the country, but in March 1934 that is exactly what happened. The government opened its borders to German Jews who were fleeing persecution. As mostly the professional classes of Jews were the only ones who could afford to leave, they soon began to take vacancies away from Dutch applicants, and this caused a wave of anti-Semitism, especially as Jewish employers appeared to prefer Jewish refugees who could not speak Dutch to local Christians. When the trade names of Cohen, Goldberg, Moskowitz, and Steinberg and so on began to appear on small shop fronts and on pushcarts, they were looked upon as a blight by the more fanatic Christians, more so if the Christian was without a job. Jewish companies and societies often funded the immigrants in order to buy into failing Christian shops and businesses. In 1935 in the national election the N.S.B. received 294,000 votes, giving the party four seats in each house.

However, by 1939 the Depression was receding as full-scale war in Europe seemed probable. Yet the government seemingly did nothing to prepare military defenses. This angered all Dutchmen who had a love of independence. Even the nazis were not sure that Hitler would respect Dutch neutrality the way the Kaiser had done. Indeed there was evidence that Germany intended to invade the Netherlands. In answer to their complaints that the government was leaving the country defenseless, the N.S.B. leaders were arrested on 19 April 1940. Mussert fled into hiding.

On the morning of 10 May, the rumors were confirmed as German troops marched across the border, paratroopers dropped onto airfields and near bridges, and bombs fell on barracks and ports. In addition, thirty Dutchmen and eighty Germans donned Dutch police uniforms in order to capture a bridge for the advancing German tanks. They failed, but this single incident panicked everyone into thinking that all Dutch police and army patrols were in fact Germans in disguise.

The use of the army reservists seemed to be haphazard, and the first military order was to retreat across the Greebe River into the major population area, which an overconfident military staff christened Fortress Holland.

Yet, after four days the plan was working, and it looked like the Dutch might be able to hold out until they were relieved by an Anglo-French counter-offensive. Then on the 14th came an ultimatum from the Germans, while the Dutch intercepted Luftwaffe orders to bomb the heart of the city of Rotterdam, which was by no stretch of the imagination a military target. Still, the government refused the German demands, hoping that rescue was only hours away. In a confused atmosphere the Germans recalled their bombers for this was a bluff, but the pilots did not receive the message and proceeded to flatten the beautiful city center. By later standards the bombing of Rotterdam was a minor affair, but to a city that had not experienced war in 145 years it was a disaster. Upwards of a thousand people were killed. British propaganda inflated this to twenty thousand.

Those politicians who had not already fled the country were stunned. Believing that the British and French, who had brought about this war, albeit due to good intentions, had left them in the lurch, they agreed to the German demands and called an immediate ceasefire. The navy and merchant service sailed to Britain under German air raids, carrying the Royal Family and a few statesmen.

The Dutch people were in shock as they slowly began to try to salvage their country, but not even the N.S.B. had any definite ideas as to how this could be done.

Chapter 4

Cross of Fire: French Nationalist Elan

In 1918 France emerged victorious from the Great War. Not only was her soil intact, but two German provinces were turned over to her. To the French-speaking people of the border districts of these provinces this was liberation, but to the German-speaking people it was occupation. In addition France gained overseas colonies at the expense of Germany and Turkey, and a reparations agreement promised to France finished German manufactured goods and some raw materials for many years either for free or cheaply.

However, the cost of the war had been disastrous. France, which had been one of the economic mainstays of the world, was devastated. The northeast was gutted. There were thousands of refugees. A quarter of a million civilians had been killed. Of the male youth, 1,357,000 had given their lives, and 4,266,000 had been maimed. These were tremendous losses for a nation of forty millions. Worse, the emotional scars were greater than the physical. Many French men and especially women were convinced that no cause was worth such high casualties, and only the political extremists remained militant—the communists and the fascists. Without the willingness to fight for their ideals the moderates were becoming increasingly impotent.

Yet by a combination of diplomacy and intrigue the moderates managed to cling to power. By 1933, there was common talk of potential civil war in France, and in January 1934 the arguments exploded in the streets. The activities of Sergei Stavisky, an immigrant Jew, who had conned millions out of investors, came to an abrupt end when he died, apparently by suicide. As the case had brought evidence of government connections with Stavisky, many extreme right wingers were convinced that he had been murdered by the government to shut him up. The newspapers *l'Action Francaise* and *l'Echo de Paris* denounced the affair, tying together Jews, capitalists, and the left-wing government.

This belief in government corruption was stretched to include accusations that some government ministers had been bribed by Hitler to turn a blind eye to his rise to power in Germany. To be sure all right wingers thought the government had been weak if not corrupt. There were some groups of the militant right that were prepared to redress this despicable situation by force if necessary—the Camelots du Roi of Charles Maurras, the Jeunesse Patriots of Pierre Taitlinger, Francois Coty's Solidarite Francaise, and the largest political army, the Croix de Feu of Colonel de la Rocque, which had about 100,000 members.

By January 1934, there were nightly marches and parades through the streets of the major cities by all the different political groups. The left wingers were angered that the police permitted this. On the 25th, Premier Camille Chautemps resigned and President Albert Lebrun chose Edouard Daladier to succeed him. When Daladier's call for a national government was refused by both right and left, he set up a Radical cabinet with policies based upon lower-middle class socialism. His immediate dismissals and promotions of various characters angered his opponents, and on 6 February the communists and extreme rightists both began street demonstrations in Paris.

Now at last the police intervened, but this only caused a full-scale riot. Buses were overturned and burned by the mob, and in retaliation policemen mounted on horses charged in and out of the crowds. When a policeman fell with a bullet in him near the Pont de Concorde his colleagues opened fire. Many rioters were shot, six of them fatally. Later in the evening more gunfights broke out.

By the following morning the mobs had been dispersed and the police commanded the field, but one of them had died and 700 had been injured. The rioters had suffered 14 dead and at least 650 injured. During the next few days other riots killed 13 and injured thousands.

However, the mobs were victorious. Daladier resigned, to be replaced by ex-President Gaston "Papa" Doumerge. The fervor died down and the political temperature cooled. France returned to its normal political atmosphere of heated debate and fratricidal denunciation.

New problems arose, though. By 1936 unemployment had risen to 470,000, though this was not at all disastrous compared to other European nations. Still it caused political friction.

The beginning of the Spanish Civil War in the summer of 1936 took the heat off, as extreme leftists and extreme rightists flocked to fight on both sides. Still the antics of successive French governments angered the right, and this was especially so when the next Daladier cabinet was formed in April 1938, for it was Daladier who sold out Czechoslovakia and French honor to the Germans. To add more fuel to the fire, in December Daladier signed a Friendship Pact with Germany. When Daladier did nothing to stop Hitler's armies from taking over all of Czechoslovakia in March 1939, this was too much even for the moderates. When Britain suddenly guaranteed Poland and Romania, Daladier was forced by the Chamber of Deputies to follow suit.

After a summer of war fever Britain declared war on Germany on 3 September, and France seconded the motion. Daladier's followers entered the war with a feeling of relief mixed with anxiety.

Daladier's paper war was not enough for rightists, though, and in early March after he had refused to aid Finland in her struggle against Russia he was ousted by his own supporters. The militants hated him for having held back the French Army and creating the "Phony War," and the pacifists hated him for having declared war in the first place. Unfortunately his successor was Paul Reynaud who had been Daladier's finance minister and who was hated almost as much as Daladier. At least Reynaud did aid Norway in her battle against an invading German army by sending a brigade of mountain troops and a Foreign Legion brigade.

Between them pacifism, communism, fascism, and gangsterism had removed the power of the French nation to wage war, and this was all too evident on 10 May 1940 when the Germans launched a massive invasion of the Netherlands, Belgium, Luxembourg, and France. The French military was not prepared for a war of movement and the lightning war that the Germans unleashed took the generals by surprise so much so that they were stunned into inactivity. The Belgian surrender after just eighteen days of fighting and the British decision to evacuate from the port of Dunkirk shocked them out of their trance, but it was already too late. The French admirals organized a sea lift off Dunkirk to pull out the Seventh Army while the major portion of the French Army began building a defense line on the Aisne River.

The French were aware that the British were telling the world that they had evacuated only after the Belgians had deserted them and after the French Seventh Army had refused to fight, but the French knew that the British had begun to retreat after holding their defenses for only one day, had failed to fight a battle yet, and had begun evacuating their rear-echelon troops three days before the Belgian surrender. In the last two days of the Dunkirk evacuation it had been French troops who had held the rearguards.

The Germans assaulted the Aisne Line on 5 June, and at once found the defenders to be unexpectedly courageous. Only after tough fighting for several days, in which each French division on average inflicted three times the casualties upon the enemy that each British division on average had done, did the German tanks manage to advance.

Naturally German propaganda took advantage of the anti-British feeling by dropping leaflets which described the British evacuations from Dunkirk and other French ports as desertions and stated that the British had vowed to fight on to the last drop of French blood.

On the 14th Paris was declared an open city, and on the 17th Reynaud resigned. President Lebrun appointed Marshal Henri Petain to be the new premier. Petain, who had recently been French ambassador to Fascist Spain and had been bombarded by fascist propaganda there, was a World War One hero. His first acts were to ask the Germans for an armistice and to request that his soldiers cease fire.

Not everyone obeyed. Some units fought on for days, and this was especially true of the Foreign Legion. However, most units obeyed, and in some instances French officers who ordered continued resistance were shot by their own men. Anti-aircraft gunners were prevented from firing at German planes by defeatists who did not want to attract a bomb at this late stage. At Vierson a French officer in charge of defense was shot by villagers who then removed all barricades and allowed the Germans to drive through. French army engineers mined the bridges at Blanc, but the villagers ripped up the fuse wires and surrendered the bridges intact to the Germans. The mayor of Poitiers ignored the presence of a French unit which was forming up for battle and he surrendered his city. In countless cases soldiers were prevented from carrying out their duties.

On the 22nd the Franco-German armistice was signed, and as an act of German revenge the ceremony took place in the same rail car that had witnessed the German surrender to France in 1918.

Petain was hailed as a hero for his surrender in this war as he had been hailed for his defiance in the last Great War. More than half of France was and would remain unoccupied by the Germans, and Hitler agreed that all French colonies would remain, and he allowed the continuing existence of the French armed forces, though on a reduced scale.

The forty-three-day battle in which the French refused to fight, according to British propaganda, had cost the French armed forces 92,000 dead.

Chapter 5

Unfinished Crusades: Greece, Yugoslavia

Greece

It is understandable that a people with such a magnificent heritage as the Greeks do not like being pushed around, but indeed that has often happened to them. They liberated themselves from the Turks in 1830, but after that found they had to toe the Anglo-French line in foreign affairs. Later they had to suffer the humiliation of having a foreign king thrust upon them by the British.

In 1912-13 the Greeks liberated more of their people from the Turks, but in 1914 when Turkey allied with Germany against Britain in World War One, the Greeks were divided as to whether belligerency or neutrality was the best course. They had no love for the Turks, but then again they did not like the British either and their king was the Kaiser's brother-in-law.

The British tired of waiting for the Greeks to make up their mind and forced the issue by invading Greece in 1915 in order to create a front line out of the Greek-Bulgarian border. Bulgaria was by this time an ally of Germany. Fortunately the Greek government did not order resistance to the attack, but this caused near civil war as officers and men deserted the Greek armed forces to join the new Greek nationalist force being organized at Salonika.

The fall of the king's government and the emergence of Prime Minister Venizelos who allied with Britain prevented the outbreak of civil war, and Greece came out of the Great War victorious.

However, the pro-German faction in Greece, which had become incensed by the arrogance of the British, was determined to seize power and place Greece in her rightful position, that of an equal to Britain and not that of an unofficially subjugated state.

Then came the peace treaty, and at once the Greek people realized they had been double-crossed by the British. True, the Greek towns in Turkey were all to return to Greek control after hundreds of years of oppression, but several Greek islands were handed to the Italians, and Cyprus was to remain part of the British Empire. To add insult to injury, there was a revolution in Turkey and the new government refused to acknowledge the treaty.

The Greeks reacted by invading Turkey and within weeks the Greeks were victorious. Having gained his demands Venizelos halted his troops, but the extreme right-wing nationalists were now on the warpath and they could not understand their government. There was still Greek land to be freed, from the Albanians, the Italians, and the British, and the Turks still occupied land that had once been part of Greece centuries before, though no Greeks lived there now. In November 1920 an election was held largely on this issue and the rightists won. The king, who had been in exile since the British "invasion," returned to a triumphant welcome. Within days his ministers ordered a new military offensive in Turkey and before the end of the year the Greeks were once again victorious.

Things began to go wrong in the summer of 1922 when the British and French withdrew their moral support from Greece, and in August the Turks launched a massive offensive. The Greek armies were devastated, and as well as the troops being forced to evacuate Asia Minor about one million Greek-speaking civilians were also forced to flee lest they be massacred by the returning Turks. Several thousand Greek-speakers also had to flee their villages which were just inside Bulgaria. These refugees who arrived in a strange land totally destitute caused critical economic problems for the small state. The people demanded vengeance and a revolutionary committee forced King Constantine to abdicate in favor of his son Georgios. The king had been lucky. His prime minister, four other ministers, and the commander-in-chief were all shot.

The ultra-rightists were by no means destroyed and they attempted a revolution in October 1923. It failed, and soon King Georgios was also driven into exile by the newly elected Venizelos government. This was not the end of left versus right political strife, though, for the disaster in Turkey and the British insults of the Great War had caused too much anger among the Greek people.

It was an angry country that now had one million refugees to care for, and yet could not free the Greek villages in Albania, on Cyprus, or on the Italian-held islands. In addition to its own population the Greek government had to control the Chams (Albanians in Greece), Macedonians, Bulgarians, Arumanians, and Turks whose villages had been conquered by Greek arms. There were also unassimilated Jews. In fact the Greeks drove out 400,000 Turkish-speakers in 1922-23, and 100,000 Bulgarians in 1924. Several thousand Macedonians were also driven into Bulgaria and Yugoslavia, and 60,000 Albanians were forced across the border into Albania. This left a more manageable 191,000 Turkish-speakers, of which 87,000 were Moslem and the rest Christian, in Western Thrace, 81,000 Macedonians in Southern Macedonia, a few thousand Chams near the Albanian border and in an ancient suburb of Athens, a few thousand Bulgarians, and 150,000 Arumanians in their Vlach Mountains homeland.

Following a coup in 1925 General Pangalos ruled as a dictator for a year, being then overthrown by General Kondylis and Lieutenant Colonel Napoleon Zervas. These two republicans immediately held elections and Venizelos proved to be the choice of the majority once again.

The World Depression reached Greece late and affected the state less than it did the more industrialized nations, but its effects were enough to put Panayiotis Tsaldaris into the premier's chair for a month in 1932 and then put Venizelos back in until he was defeated in the next election in March 1933. Another coup failed to stop Tsaldaris' right-wing cabinet from exercising power. The British mentioned possibly bringing King Georgios back to the throne, and when Venizelos heard of this he too plotted against the government. The revolt came in March 1935, but it was highly uncoordinated and after a barracks skirmish his men surrendered. Only three rebels were executed. The rest suffered island exile, a common form of punishment for Greeks.

Tsaldaris took the opportunity to crack down on all left wingers, especially the communists, and as a result he won the next election.

Even this was not enough for the ultra-right, though, and led by General Kondylis they revolted in October 1935 and succeeded in a well-coordinated operation. King Georgios was invited to resume his reign in return for legitimizing the junta. A surprise move came on 4 August 1936, when Prime Minister Joannes Metaxas announced that henceforth he would be the sole ruler of the country.

The Metaxas regime put all previous dictatorships to shame, as the wily general, ably assisted by his security chief, Maniadakis, began a true reign of terror. Opponents were arrested, imprisoned, exiled, and even executed. Some simply disappeared. One of Maniadakis' favorite tricks was to torture a prisoner until he or she publicly renounced the cause and betrayed others. After such an event the prisoner was often let loose upon the people.

A large number of Metaxas' officers were pro-German and anti-British and they looked upon Bulgaria as the next potential enemy. These men were instrumental in getting a defensive line built in the northeast, in case of Bulgarian attack. Of course we now know they were looking the wrong way, for in 1940 Mussolini, the fascist dictator of Italy, began speaking out against the oppression of the Chams in northwest Greece. This angered Metaxas, but not enough to provoke him. So on 15 August, which was a Greek religious holiday, an Italian submarine torpedoed the Greek warship *Helle* in Tinos harbor. Yet even this was not enough to make Metaxas overreact. At the end of October Mussolini threw all pretense aside and invaded Greece.

Within the Greek military the rightists were informed by the Germans that the Italian move had taken them by surprise—it had. However, as Germany and Italy were partners there was little the Germans could do to help Greece.

Britain was already at war with Italy, though, and Churchill offered aid at once. Metaxas refused at first, but later accepted some equipment, a few air squadrons, and rear-echelon units. In return Crete became a British naval base.

The Italians had attacked at the wrong time of year, as any schoolboy could have told them, and a day after they became stuck in the snow-covered mountain passes, the Greeks struck back. Within a week the Italians were driven back across the Albanian border.

Metaxas did not live to see the outcome of the static winter campaign in Albania, dying on 29 January, and the new government of Alexandros Koryzis became apprehensive when Bulgaria allowed a German army to enter that state in March 1941. Spurred by this Koryzis asked Britain for more aid, and at once Churchill supplied more air squadrons and an army corps. Ironically, some of the ground troops were Cypriots of the British Army.

The Commonwealth ground troops arrived just in time to face a new threat. On 6 April the Germans invaded Thrace. Within days the Allied base at Salonika had fallen, a Greek force was trapped against the Metaxas Line, and the Commonwealth troops were forced into a walking retreat up and down the mountains of northern Greece. German and Italian aircraft shattered these columns time and time again, and whenever the Germans almost caught the retreating Allies their long-range artillery destroyed them in bunches.

At the same time the Italians launched a major offensive. Now some Greek officers suggested that they should throw in the towel, but the government politely refused their advice. However, any officer who did not wish to fight Germans was allowed to take indefinite leave. Many availed themselves of this offer.

This sudden military collapse and betrayal was too much for Koryzis. He committed suicide. He was replaced by Emmanuel Tsouderis, who learned almost at once that the Epirus Army, which faced the Italians, had surrendered. Three days later, the Macedonian Army also gave up.* On the 24th, the government and king fled to British-controlled Egypt.

The Commonwealth troops and a few Greeks evacuated as best as possible, but the Italian and German aircraft ran up a high score of Allied vessels sunk and thousands of Allied soldiers were taken prisoner.

One of the first moves of the Axis troops, after by-passed units had been mopped up, was to divide up the spoils. The German Fifth Army occupied Eastern and Western Thrace including the city of Salonika, plus a few Aegean islands and Crete. The Bulgarian Ist Corps sneaked in after the battle and grabbed Central Thrace. The rest of the state went to the Italian Eleventh Army of twelve divisions. Italy actually annexed the Cham districts and the island of Corfu. Then the Axis partners set up a favorable Greek government under General Tsolakoglou, the very man who had surrendered the Epirus Army.

*Macedonian in name only, though some Macedonians were in the army.

The Germans soon withdrew their combat troops, leaving only the XVIIIth Mountain Corps with its 5th Mountain and 6th Mountain Divisions on Crete, 164th Division on the islands, and 125th Regiment in Salonika.

The Bulgarians and Macedonians who had been thrown out of Greece now returned to their villages and tried to resume normal lives again. A difficult move after such a long absence. There was no opposition by guerrillas to the occupation troops, but there was deep animosity between the returning Bulgarians and Macedonians and the Greeks who had usurped their homes. Many of the latter had themselves been refugees from Turkey. Almost at once the Bulgarian forces had to crack down on the rebellious Greeks in their sector. To help defend themselves the Bulgarian settlers formed a militia.

Yugoslavia

A better name than Yugoslavia would have been "the Serbian Empire," and indeed until 1929 the state was named the Kingdom of the Serbs, Croats, and Slovenes. The Serbian monarchists ruled the new state, created as such at the end of the Great War, which contained several ethnic groups which believed they were entitled to sovereign status. In the early years the state had economic and agrarian problems which only served to accentuate the ethnic problem. The communists had been actively engaged in anti-nationalist debates and had even held seats in the assembly, but as early as December 1920 the government deemed the Communist Party to be a greater danger than the nationalists and it was declared illegal. From this date the communists led by Josip Broz waged a non-violent resistance campaign against the government.

The Serbians, who made up 40% of the population, were identified by having their own national consciousness, separate dialect of the Serbo-Croat language written in the cyrillic alphabet, and their own Orthodox Christian religion. The largest minority in the state was the Croats, with 22% of the population, Roman Catholic religion, own territory, culture, history, national consciousness, and own dialect of the Serbo-Croat language written in the Latin alphabet.

At first glance it might not be realized what difference dialect can cause, but it must be realized that even in the United States a difference in dialect can hold a person back in some professions, and the difference between Serb and Croat was written as well as spoken. This difference would cause enough headaches, but Yugoslavia was a state plagued with nationalist headaches. The Slovenes made up 8.2% of the population. These people were Roman Catholics, but had their own language and territory. The Montenegron 2.5% of the population spoke Croat, but prayed in Serbian Orthodox churches. Moreover, as they had been fiercely independent until 1918 they were a hard people to control. Northern Macedonia was under the control of the Yugoslavian government containing 5.6% of the state's population. With their separate language, own territory, and own Orthodox Christian faith, they were sincere nationalists.

The greatest danger to the Yugoslavian state was those ethnic groups whose brothers ruled sovereign nations just over the border. Part of Albania was under Yugoslavian control, with 6.5% of the state's population, speaking their own language, and having either the Albanian Orthodox Christian faith or being Moslems. Part of Hungary was under the state's control, too, with 2.3% of the population being Roman Catholics and speaking Magyar. Part of Bulgaria also lay on this side of the border with .3% of the population having their own language and Orthodox faith. A similar-sized chunk of Romania also lay within the state's borders. These people spoke Romanian and had their own Orthodox faith.

In addition there were pockets of "foreigners," Turks, Czechs, Ukrainians, Slovaks, Italians, and over 700,000 Volksdeutsch.

Lastly there were people who did not want their own state here, but did not want anyone else's either, the Gypsies, true Romany-speaking people who recognized no national boundary, the unassimilated Jews who spoke German or Yiddish, and the Moslems, for many of the latter had adopted the local language but had not adopted local nationalist spirit. These latter three groups were scattered throughout the state in villages and ghettoes.

All of these people were indigenous. That is, they were not considered to be immigrants. The Yugoslavian government spent its time delivering edicts in sixteen different languages, and yet kept the naive belief that it controlled a unified nation. Whoever created such a patchwork state should have been certified insane. It was the Allied leaders at the end of the Great War who share that guilt of insanity.

To make matters worse there was an immigrant problem. The largest group was the Russian emigre refugees who had fled the communists. In 1936 there were 15,000 male Russian immigrants.

Finally coming to the conclusion that no ethnic group was going to cooperate with the Serbians, King Alexander personally took control and formed a new constitution in September 1931. Unfortunately, almost at the same time the World Depression hit the state and within a year the peasants of Croatia were starving. Their frustration was channeled by the Ustaci, a Croatian nationalist political organization, into an anti-Serbian revolt. It failed and this only made things worse. All the ethnic minorities now became convinced that the Serbians were determined to survive the depression at the expense of the minorities. In October 1934, while on a visit to Marseilles, France, King Alexander paid the price for his indifference, being assassinated by a member of a Macedonian nationalist group.

In theory Prince Paul became the regent for the 11-year-old King Peter, but in reality he became dictator, albeit a moderate one. Indeed by February

1939 he agreed that it was time for a more representative form of government, and he appointed Dragisa Cvetkovic as premier and appeased the Croats by appointing one of their leaders, Vladko Macek, as deputy premier.

During the first months of World War Two Prince Paul assumed that there were only two directions in which his country could tread the narrow path of peace—as a friend of France or as a friend of Germany. No consideration was given to siding with the land-hungry Soviet Union. But with the sudden collapse of France in June 1940, only Germany offered a chance for survival. Negotiating with Hitler, Prince Paul got the best deal he could from that uncompromising dictator and then signed the Anti-Comintern Pact, which was aimed at the Soviet Union, on 25 March 1941.

The ink was barely dry when the Serbian people rose in revolt at the news and ousted the regent's government. They did this in anger, but they were naive to think that their government could remain neutral in the conflict that was slowly engulfing all of Europe. The Germans wished to liberate their Volksdeutsch brethren from Serbian control as the other nations surrounding Yugoslavia also wished to liberate their ethnic brothers. It was not a question of would Yugoslavia be invaded, but rather by whom.

The answer was by four neighbors. Hitler had taken the revolt personally, and now he raged over the insult to the point of risking his venture against the Soviet Union. In other words, deep down he thought more about his own pride than he did about the crusade that he had been preaching since 1919.

On 6 April 1941, German forces drove across the northern and eastern borders of Yugoslavia, and Italian troops entered from Italy, Albania, and by Adriatic coast amphibious invasions. Bulgarian soldiers meekly followed the Germans in order to stake their own claims. In an act of pure vengeance Hitler sent as many aircraft as possible against the city of Belgrade, inflicting heavy casualties on the Serbian population, possibly as high as 20,000.

In places the Royal Yugoslavian Army fought back well and in other areas it collapsed. Some units, especially the Croat ones, actually welcomed the Italians as liberators. Ante Pavelic, a Croat leader, had been living in exile in Italy, and his propaganda was responsible for much of this.

Using as a casus belli the fact that Yugoslavian aircraft had retaliated against German rear-echelon units on Hungarian soil, Admiral Horthy ordered Hungarian troops into that portion of Yugoslavia long claimed by Hungary on 11 April. His men encountered only light opposition.

On 17 April, the Yugoslavian government surrendered its armed forces of 344,000 men, while the king fled to British-controlled territory to set up a government-in-exile.

The Italian forces liberated the Italian-speaking zones and conquered Western Slovenia, part of which with 60,000 Slovenes they already had. They also annexed part of Croatia to add to the homes of 60,000 Croats that they already had. Lastly, as the fascist government considered Albania's problems to be Italy's problems, the Italians annexed several Yugoslavian villages with Albanian-speaking populations. Montenegro became a protectorate of Italy.

The remainder of Slovenia became German territory to add to that strip of extreme northern Slovenia, an area of 45,000 people, that the Austrians already had. This district, called Carinthia, had been annexed by Germany when Austria had been taken over.

Serbia came under German protection, and naturally the Germans annexed Banat, a Volksdeutsch area, as Hungary and Bulgaria annexed their respective ethnic areas. For many of the inhabitants this was seen as liberation.

Croatia, or what was left after the Italians had taken a bite out of it, was given its independence, and the Italian-protected Ante Pavelic set up a government. He also controlled much of Bosnia and Herzegovina.

Most of Yugoslavian Macedonia fell to the Bulgarians, though the Italians jumped in and gained some villages to the chagrin of the Bulgarians. Of course no one asked the Macedonians what they thought of the matter. All other areas fell to the Germans.

The short war had been full of surprises for the people of Yugoslavia, some of them good, most of them bad. The greatest surprise was that the Germans, who had borne the brunt of the fighting, had only lost 151 dead.

In the Banat area the large German-speaking population, the Volksdeutsch, was ecstatic at the liberation, not being aware as yet of the methods of the nazi government. At once the Serbian "oppressors" were ousted from positions of power and authority and replaced by Volksdeutsch. Many young men enlisted into the S.S. in order to help keep the peace in the area, and the actual police force was not only Germanicized but weeded of anti-nazis. For emergency duty a militia, the Heimwehr, was also formed. With nazi fanatics and bully-boys taking over the reins it was not long before the ordinary people were placed in a state of submission. The 3,000 Jews in Banat were robbed and beaten, and a few were murdered. Non-German-speaking Yugoslavians who did not leave of their own free will were soon kicked out without being able to take anything with them.

Eventually the S.S. Security Police created some order out of this confused state in Banat, and one of their more important moves was to kick out all the Jews. Most of these refugees went to Belgrade where the local authority tried to accommodate them. However, within the German-occupied part of Yugoslavia all Jewish "troublemakers" were rounded up, numbering about 5,000, and they were housed in prisons and the new concentration camps that began springing up all over the state. Many Jewish males were shot dead for petty infringements.

To the anger of the Italians, Pavelic and his people leaned more towards friendship with Germany, and this was due in part to the knowledge that Germany was more powerful. German and Italian troops were both "guest" forces in Croatia.

Following on the heels of the invasion troops came German labor office recruiters, and by the summer of 1941 109,000 Yugoslavians had volunteered to work in Germany. Most of them were Volksdeutsch and Croatians. The major attraction was that the pay was high and working conditions were good.

The Croatian nation, supposedly sovereign, had created its own police force and armed forces. An army and small air force were recruited using veteran personnel and equipment from the now nonexistent armed forces of Yugoslavia, but the Italians balked at allowing Croatia a navy. As a further sign that Croatia was not yet completely independent, the Italians imposed a member of the Italian Royal Family upon the nation as titular head of state.

The Croatian police force rooted out its politically suspect members before it began cracking down on political opposition. To assist in this cleansing operation the Ustaci created a militia of regulars and part-timers with initially a force of 15 battalions. Unfortunately for the people, the Ustaci contained many members who were so steeped in frenzied nationalist beliefs that they lusted for the blood of their real and imagined enemies. Every Jew in Croatia was fined for his assumed anti-Croat stance, and within a month of the new state's inception young male Jews were conscripted for slave labor. On 26 June the Ustaci began mass arrests of all Jews regardless of age or sex. An extermination camp was established at Danica, where within the next few weeks many Jews were killed. According to Jewish figures the death toll was 6,000. The Ustaci then moved to a better location at Jasenovac.

Despite these antics the Ustaci had considerable peasant support and much of this was due to the Roman Catholic priests who were outspoken defenders of the Ustaci, for example Monsiegneur Vajislav Nastic, the Bishop of Bosnia, and Monsiegneur Aloysius Stepinac, the Archbishop of Zagreb and Roman Catholic Primate of all Yugoslavia.

Another reason for Ustaci support was economical. With the Serbians gone there was more room for Croatian expertise. Bosnia and Herzegovina had two million Serbians, and Croatia had several thousand Serbians who had been employed by the Yugoslavian government or national companies. The Ustaci made it plain that these Serbians were not wanted, and most of them hit the road as pitiful refugees. In some mountainous isolated areas Serbians were murdered by Croats. The goods, buildings, and land, not to mention jobs that were left behind, naturally went to supporters of the fascist regime. Some Serbians took out their anger on innocent Moslems.

Though Serbia was no longer an independent state, a government was set up with the blessing of the Germans. The new leader of Serbia was Milan Acimovich. The Serbian police under the self-explanatory titles City Guard and State Guard with 17,000 personnel was retained, and 5,600 members of the now defunct Yugoslavian Frontier Guard were recruited into the new Serbian Frontier Guard. The duties of these men were to guard the borders of the new state of Serbia, being responsible for apprehending smugglers, foreign agents, terrorists, escaped prisoners of war, and black market operators. The men were "advised" by 600 German border police.

At first one of the major problems of the Serbian police was the controlling of hundreds of thousands of refugees who were fleeing persecution.

To guard Serbian factories against saboteurs and spies, the Germans formed a Werkschutz made up of Serbians and emigre Russians. The cadre of the force was made up of 250 Banat Volksdeutsch.

Within Montenegro the Italian military administration was smart enough to retain the local police and to form a village milita. In addition, several auxiliary police field battalions were formed from local volunteers. However, the Italians were not smart enough to rule with compassion. Fascist arrogance continued to remind every Montenegrin that the Italians were here as conquerors.

The Italian-speaking Yugoslavians who were liberated were subjected to all Italian laws including military conscription, but many of the new soldiers were allowed to be stationed near their homes.

There were good sides to the Italians. They allowed religious freedom. They brought a slight economic prosperity. They administrated better than the old regime. They did not refuse Serbian refugees, and they refused to hand over any Jew to the Germans or Croatians if the Jew was less than full-blooded Jewish or had a non-Jewish spouse.

The Bulgarian liberators took the form of the Fifth Army of the 1st Cavalry Brigade and the 14th, 15th, and 6th Divisions. The Macedonians were generally-speaking anti-Bulgarian and any expression of their true feelings was brutally repressed. Bulgarian soldiers and police behaved arrogantly and there were some murders. The young Bulgarian and Macedonian males were liable to military conscription just like the Italian- and Magyar-speaking Yugoslavian citizens. However, the Germans were not conscripting their Volksdeutsch youth.

Within the newly occupied districts of Slovenia members of that ethnic community were advised by Slovenes who had been living under Italian occupation since 1919 to acquiesce to the new masters. The Italians retained the Slovene police and created a militia, the Village Guards. Within the German-occupied district of Slovenia the Slovenes were advised by Slovenes from Carinthia that so far the nazis had not been too bad and that they would be all right if they obeyed the Germans. Naturally it was to the advantage of the occupation troops if the people remained docile.

Within the German-occupied district of Slovenia there were a few scattered villages of Volksdeutsch and there were also some Slovenes who were racially Germanic, whether they knew it or not. These "German" communities were cajoled into supplying men to establish a defense militia, the Wehrmannschaften, which was trained to handle infantry weapons and light artillery by the S.A., and upon completion of training the militiamen automatically became members of the S.A.

In the newly liberated Albanian districts of Yugoslavia, the Albanians ganged up on non-Albanian residents. Serbians who had been living here to enforce the economic and governmental oppression by the Serbian kingdom were now beaten and humiliated in revenge for real or imagined crimes. There were also a few villages of Serbians, Montenegrins, and Croats who had been here for hundreds of years, but these too were forced out of house and home. The Italians turned a blind eye to this as their goal was to maintain a friendly, albeit pro-Italian, relationship with all Albanians.

Hitler believed by June that the people of Yugoslavia were no longer a threat to him. Within the large German-occupied area he left only a small ill-equipped garrison, the LVth Corps of the 704th, 714th, 717th, and 718th Divisions. These were security divisions, possessing only two line regiments, little artillery, no mechanization, and being manned by men between 36 and 45 years of age, too old and poorly trained to climb the steep Yugoslavian mountains. Their only real purpose was to prevent sabotage of the rail lines by British agents and to show the flag. The 718th Division was in fact based at Banja Luka in Croatia as a "guest" force.

The Italians were more realistic having sixteen divisions in their sectors, but the equipment of the units was little better than that supplied to German security divisions. The Italian Second Army occupied West Slovenia and defended Dalmatia with eight divisions, and the Ninth Army occupied Montenegro with eight divisions and all of Albania with four divisions.

Chapter 6

Collaboration or Cooperation: Germany's Friends in Europe

Slovakia

In August 1939 the Slovakian 1st Motorized Division, an infantry force with trucks, a few armored cars, and seventy-nine Skoda LT vz35 light tanks, was mobilized for possible duty in Poland if war broke out. When that war did come as Germany invaded Poland on 1 September 1939, the Slovakians loaned the division to the Germans. Charging through the Dukla Pass the division headed for Lwow knocking aside light disorganized resistance. The campaign only lasted a few days for this unit as Eastern Poland had been assigned to the Red Army, but nonetheless the Slovakians now felt that they had a right to be treated as an equal partner by Germany.

Shortly after this the Slovakian government stabilized. The President was Josef Tiso, who was also a Roman Catholic priest. The Prime Minister was Voytech Tuka, with Ferdinand Durcansky as Foreign Minister, and Sano Mach, who was head of the feared Hlinka Guard, was made Minister of the Interior.

By 1940 the locally recruited S.S. had made a reputation for itself as hunters of enemies of the state. Though these men were Slovakian citizens they were Volksdeutsch, and as their bosses were German S.S. officers, and no one could hide that fact, this created a certain animosity between the Slovakians and the Germans.

Norway

After Vidkun Quisling had been lobbying in Berlin for four months he managed to gain some recognition. On 25 September 1940 a new provisional government was created which had some autonomy. All the senior posts went to NS members. Quisling got the best job as Leader of the Council, and the next most powerful post went to Jonas Lie, who was made Minister of Police.

In addition there were Hustad for labor, Skancke for education, Hagelin for interior, and Riisnaes for justice. After this date NS members began taking over the provincial councils.

The members of the Hird, the uniformed but still unarmed militia of the NS, were now in wonderland. They continuously pranced up and down the streets looking for trouble. Fist fights became common as Hird men ganged up on anyone who looked suspicious. The police made no arrests in these scuffles, but at least they hardly ever supported the Hird men, even when the Hird appeared to be outnumbered. Behind the scenes the more intelligent Hird men extorted large sums of money from the Jews.

The S.S. found the youth of Norway to be ideal racial stock, indeed they suited the stringent requirements more than most Germans. S.S. recruiters therefore began asking for volunteers for the Crusade, which at this stage meant protecting installations from British saboteurs and hunting for all those in political opposition. The Soviet Union was not mentioned, at least publicly, for Germany was still friendly with the Soviets and trading heavily. Hitler wanted his tanks full of Russian fuel before they drove across the Soviet border.

Soon enough young Norwegian idealists were gathered together to form two battalions of the Waffen S.S. A few other Norwegians, usually older than the fighting recruits, joined the S.S. Security Police, and there were plenty of informers who would willingly spy on their neighbors for pay.

The Norwegian State Police had already begun harassing the small population of Jews, who were culturally assimilated, and arresting those citizens who were noisy in their opposition to the new system. Hird members on occasion arrested anti-fascists and took them to the police, for the Hird had no actual police powers, but often the poor victim was immediately released. Most Hird members preferred beating opponents until they were half dead.

The German labor office recruiters opened their recruiting offices in April 1940, almost two months before the Norwegian Army surrendered, and within a year over 100,000 Norwegians were voluntarily working for the Germans in Germany or in Norway. Their treatment and pay were judged to be good.

Denmark

The soft treading of the Danish government pleased the Germans and it pleased most Danes, but it did not please the Danish national socialists. Their leader, Frits Clausen, a Danish medical doctor and World War One veteran whose home town had been inside Germany until the end of that great conflict, had expected that he would have been placed in power by the Germans. The German-speaking Danish citizens also felt betrayed by the political deal. Their leader, Moeller, who had been elected to the Danish parliament in 1939, was practically ignored by the German military authorities.

In order to provoke the German Army into intervening Clausen and Moeller organized street incidents and Clausen's party militia, the brownshirted Storm Afdelingr, deliberately brawled with the Danish police. Their plan backfired. Not only did the German Army not intervene in what they saw as an internal Danish affair, but the Danish police force was expanded to meet the threat.

The German S.S. did intervene in one way, though. They recruited Danes for that elitist organization. By the end of 1940 only 250 had been accepted, but many more Danish citizens were allowed to sponsor the Danish Branch of the German S.S.

Netherlands

The Germans replaced the sovereign Netherlands government, the leaders of which had fled the state, with their own civil administration. Its head was Reichskommissar Artur Seyss-Inquart, and this Austrian brought his friends from Vienna with him—Brigadefuehrer F. Wimmir in charge of Administration and Justice, Gruppenfuehrer H. Fischboeck as head of Finances and Economic Affairs, Gruppenfuehrer Hans Albin Rauter as Higher S.S. and Police Leader, and Obersturmbannfuehrer Fritz Schmidt, who was placed in charge of special affairs including the Jewish problem.

At first the regime appeared to act fairly. Most of the Dutch civil servants continued on as before, and most of the 300,000 Dutch soldiers captured in the short war were soon released.

The Dutch political leaders called upon all citizens to refrain from helping the Germans, but this was found to be difficult in practice. Even Mussert joined in this call, but his party members were already conversing with the Germans. When the Germans were seen to be mostly lonely men who felt embarrassed by the entire affair it was hard to look upon them as the enemy. The only danger now came from British aircraft which continued the war on Dutch soil by striking at barracks, military installations, and factories that supplied the Germans.

A few prominent Dutch preached cooperation with the Germans. Professor J.E. de Quay, a Catholic politician, J. Linthorst, the Queen's Commissioner for Groningen, and Dr. L. Einthoven, the Rotterdam Police Chief, founded the pro-German National Union Party. Another outspoken friend of the Germans was Rost van Tonningen, and he led a section of the N.S.B. membership which soon gained the choicest jobs open to Dutchmen.

Mussert was a Dutch nationalist, but he was also a pragmatic individual, and he soon saw which side his bread was buttered on. He joined the Germans.

The N.S.B. began organizing anti-Jewish demonstrations, and almost at once these took the form of brownshirted members hitting passing Jews with their fists. Later some Jews were seriously beaten, and later still tradesmen's hand carts were overturned and shop fronts were smashed in. The German soldiers, who spent much of their time roaming the streets of the cities as tourists, complained of the brutality of the Dutch nazis. However, the Dutch police, and the few German police who had followed the invading army, were warned by Rauter not to meddle.

Apart from occasional British air raids and the odd quiet arrest of an overtly anti-German, the state was at peace. Therefore it was more for political reasons than defensive ones that Mussert launched a campaign to increase the strength of his defense militia, the Weer Afdeling. These men were once again allowed to prance up and down the streets with their handsome black uniforms. There was some justification for this. On 7 September 1940, Peter Ton, a Weer Afdeling militiaman, had been shot dead in a Hague street. As yet the Germans were not allowing Dutch nazis to carry firearms.

In November, as a show of his new strength Mussert paraded 5,000 Weer Afdeling through Amsterdam to the cheers of thousands of spectators. Flowers were tossed at the marching columns. Most of the cheers came from relatives of the militiamen.

Almost as soon as the German invasion had achieved its aim, German labor office recruiters set up shop. Within a year 93,000 men and women had volunteered for work in Germany, and thousands more were employed by the Germans in the Netherlands. Many of the latter were construction workers, who spent their time building German barracks, bunkers, air raid shelters, gun emplacements, and airfields, and repairing the slight bomb damage that had been caused by the short war and the extant British air raids.

There was another way in which a Dutchman could serve Germany, and that was as a soldier. Heinrich Himmler, who was forever on the lookout for foreign volunteers for his S.S. as the German government would not allow him enough volunteers from the military conscription age groups, cast his gaze upon the racially Germanic Netherlands. His recruiters began their trade in September 1940, offering a flashy uniform, a good old-fashioned military style of life, reasonably good pay, good food, access to S.S. brothels, and a chance to join a winning team. Above all they offered each acceptable recruit an opportunity to do his own part in ridding his country of international communism and Jewish conspirators. A few thousand young men took the offer, most of them becoming part-time members of the Allgemeine S.S. A few, though, chose to be members of the fighting force, the Waffen S.S.

The fighters formed a battalion-sized unit with the name S.S. Regiment Westland.

These Dutch members of the German S.S. must not be confused with the Dutch S.S. That organization was founded on 11 September by J. Hendrik Feldmeyer, Mussert's bodyguard. Wearing black uniforms and their own insignia the force imitated their German counterpart. As their duty was to guard installations and senior members of the N.S.B., they were allowed to carry weapons by the German civil government.

By the end of 1940 a mild form of forced labor was introduced in order to place the unemployed and underemployed into necessary jobs. At this time this was no more stringent than the forced labor laws which the British government was currently enforcing on its own people.

By February 1941 the N.S.B. had a quarter of a million dues-paying members and the National Union Party had 800,000 members. Approximately one adult in seven was overtly pro-German. Among the younger age groups the fraction was higher. British air raids increased, rationing became stricter, and almost everyone learned of someone who had been forced out of a good job because he or she had been judged politically unreliable. But by and large the Dutch people were not badly treated.

For the Jews it was a different story. Beginning in 1941 Weer Afdeling raids on the Jewish Quarter of Amsterdam increased, and there were several fistfights as militant Jews resisted. In one clash a militiaman was mortally wounded.

In response, on 12 February, the Dutch police sealed off the district and created a ghetto out of it. Only non-Jews were allowed to leave. Enough Jews were found to create a Judenrat, a Jewish council, which would implement the nazi laws within the ghetto.

Ten days later, Dutch police and German S.S. Security Police entered the ghetto and began arresting men off the street. These innocent men and their friends resisted and a riot broke out, but the police won the day and managed to arrest 450 innocent men, 60 of whom were not Jews.

In answer to this, various workers organizations in Amsterdam, Hilversum, and Zaandam called a general strike four days later. Their representatives demanded the release of the arrested men. The S.S. Security Police ignored the demand, transported the men to a concentration camp, and announced that the men would be shot if the workers did not immediately go back to their jobs. The workers backed down. Within Amsterdam there was now considerable ill-feeling towards the police.

Terrorist outrages now increased, and on 3 March the Germans executed a man for treason. Hitherto, political prisoners had only been imprisoned. Though he was not a Dutchman, but a German Jew, the shot was heard throughout the Netherlands. It was time to choose sides.

Belgium

After the fall of France Gustav de Clerq and Leon Degrelle returned to Belgium and both preached to their respective ethnic groups that they should cooperate with the Germans. At this time it was believed that the wars were over, and only the Germans offered a chance of survival. The people listened and obeyed. Within a year and a half of the German invasion 321,000 Belgian citizens had volunteered to work in Germany and 82,000 were voluntarily working for the Germans in Belgium, though it must be remembered that unemployment was a major cause of this.

The Belgian Secretary of the Interior, Gerard Ramsee, and Victor Leemans, the Secretary of Economic Affairs, both retained their jobs after the German invasion by doing what was required of them by the new German Military Government of General von Falkenhorst.

Degrelle had 50,000 members in his Walloon Christus Rex and his party militia was allowed to parade in uniform. There was little anti-German terrorism and the Walloon Rex and Flemish nationalists were allowed their exhibitionism. As was the case everywhere else, these extreme nationalists soon got the best jobs, at the expense of Jews and citizens who were politically suspect.

In imitation of the German S.S., a Flemish S.S. was formed by Ward Hermans and Rene Lagrou. The force had a small full-time unit, which assisted the police as much as possible in hunts for terrorists and also guarded installations, but the members were rarely armed. The majority of the force were part-time sentries. Men over 35 years of age were placed in a separate section called the Vlaanderen Korps. The V.N.V. did not support the Flemish S.S., and most of the members came from the Devlag party.

The German S.S. also recruited in the country, but only the Flemish were deemed racially Germanic and therefore eligible for recruitment. Many of the recruits went to the part-time Allgemeine unit in the nation, but most asked to enter full-time fighting formations. The result was that a battalion was formed and sent to S.S. Regiment Westland. Himmler was so pleased by the training performance of the Dutch and Flemish S.S. sections that he authorized another regiment to be recruited in April 1941, S.S. Regiment Nordwest.

France

In June 1940 Marshal Petain set up his new government at Vichy, a famous health resort. So many sycophants and political rabble-rousers flocked to the town to see him in order to beg for a job that the many hotels were soon filled. Would-be cabinet ministers were to be found sleeping in corridors. Many fascists were among the jobseekers, hoping that after the Jews, communists, and socialists had been kicked out there would be a vacancy for them. The major fascist parties currently competing for power were the Parti Populaire Francaise of Jacques Doriot, the Rassemblement National Populaire of Marcel Deat, Le Franciste of Marcel Bucard, the Parti Francais of Pierre Clementi, SAR of Eugene Deloncle, Front Franc of Jean Boissel, Ligue Francaise of Pierre Constantini, and Parti Social Francais of Colonel de la Rocque.

Petain's cabinet did not include fascists—Pierre Laval as Vice-Premier, Admiral Jean Darlan as Commander-in-Chief of the Navy, Raphael Alibert as Minister of Justice, and General Maxime Weygand as Minister of Defense. One of Petain's first domestic acts was to coerce the Chamber of Deputies into surrendering their power to him, and one of his first acts as a friend of Germany was to hand over the gold reserves of Belgium.

Anti-British feeling in France was already high, but the British themselves sent it soaring over the top with one of the most despicable acts of the war. The bulk of the French fleet lay in ports out of reach of the Germans, Dakar in French West Africa, Alexandria in neutral Egypt, Mers el Kebir in French Algeria, and Toulon on the south coast of France, but the British were afraid that the ships might be formally handed to the Germans. These fears got the better of their moral judgment and on 3 July 1940 a British fleet sailed to Mers el Kebir and the commander at sea demanded that the French warships either surrender to the British or scuttle. The French captains conferred with each other and with Darlan by radio, but without a sense of urgency. Many of the French officers knew the British officers on a first-name basis, and after all they had been allies just eleven days earlier, so they did not take the ultimatum seriously. They should have, though, for the British have a habit of sinking neutral fleets.

Suddenly the British warships opened fire, and their carrier planes bombed the French. The mighty naval shells bored deep into the bowels of the French ships and blew them apart while they were still tied to the wharves and unable to fire back. Only a few vessels managed to slip anchor and maneuver away from the docks using the smoke of blazing warships as cover. Later these ships opened fire with their stern guns as they ran for the open sea, but British aircraft dogged them for days.

For the loss of two planes and two men wounded, the British had sunk two battleships, a cruiser, and a tug, damaged a battleship and a destroyer, forced a battleship to scuttle, and shattered to pieces the bodies of 1,297 French sailors. Another 351 survived to show their scars to the French people. The same day in British ports and at Alexandria British troops boarded and confiscated all French vessels, naval and mercantile. French planes retaliated with a light raid on the great British naval base at Gibraltar.

In effect, from this day on Britain and France were at war.

On 2 August, the French government sentenced General Charles de Gaulle to death, in absentia, as he had ignored the order to surrender and was forming a renegade army in Britain. This had been a painful move for Petain, for de Gaulle had been his protege for many years.

Other government decrees granted to Germany 400 million francs per day as reparations for having started the war, and ceded Alsace and Lorraine to Germany. Soldiers who were from these predominantly German-speaking provinces and who were currently languishing in German prisoner of war camps could declare loyalty to Germany and be released. Another decree authorized French arms and munitions companies to seek orders from Germany.

One of the most immediate of Petain's problems was that in his unoccupied sector he had seven million refugees, unemployment was high, and 1.9 million French soldiers were in German prison camps. As the bulk of these men had been reservists they were missed by their civilian employers as well as by their families which relied upon them for putting bread on the table.

The German labor office recruiters entered the occupied zone and within weeks gained 59,000 volunteers to work in Germany.

As a move to alleviate his economic problems, Petain did not release his youngest recruits to civilian life where they would compete in the job market, but placed them in labor camps called Workshops of French Youth. There they would perform any work that the government required.

The regular soldiers could remain as Hitler had allowed Petain to keep an armed forces. The navy was left untouched, but the air force was strictly limited. The army retained 100,000 men in unoccupied France, known as Vichy France, 55,000 men in Morocco, 50,000 in Algeria, about 40,000 in Syria-Lebanon, a division in Tunisia, and several thousands in the colonies.

Within the occupied zone the German intelligence organization, the Abwehr, formed a French detachment under Henri Lafont, a gangster whose real name was Chamberlin, but at first relied predominantly on its own personnel and upon the local police, though the latter in theory still obeyed Petain.

Within Vichy France Petain used his police to good effect in order to reinforce his power. He had the urban police forces and to control the countryside the Gendarmerie of the Ministry of Defense. His enemies were rounded up and housed at the first French concentration camps, Gurs and Rivesaltes. Due to rail sabotage a Rail Police was created. But the well-armed Gardes Mobiles was disbanded.

With a little prompting from the Germans Petain also investigated the Jewish situation. All French Jews were assimilated and it took a thorough police investigation just to keep track of all Jews. It was learned by September 1940 that of 300,000 Jews in France, 144,000 lived in Paris, and a third of all Jews were immigrants.

On the 3rd day of October came the first of the anti-Semitic laws, nicknamed the Alibert laws. All persons with more than two Jewish grandparents were deemed to be Jews, regardless of religion. Some Roman Catholic priests suddenly found themselves regarded as legal Jews. Now the dismissals began—49 prefects, 58 under-prefects, and 2,282 civil servants, all kicked out because they were legally of the Jewish race. Jewish members of the armed forces were also dismissed, and major companies were encouraged to "purify" their work force.

The German government took this opportunity to expel all Alsace and Lorraine Jews to Vichy France and even sent along 7,500 German Jews who had literally been kidnapped off the streets. Petain protested loudly but to no avail. Therefore his police arrested these Jews for being illegal immigrants, and they were placed in concentration camps.

In November, 100,000 residents of Alsace and Lorraine, mostly French-speakers but including some anti-nazi German-speakers, refused to declare loyalty to Germany. In disgust the German authorities arrested them. The luckiest were simply expelled into Vichy France, but some became slaves at labor camps. German-speakers who had left their homes in 1919 rather than live under French rule were now returning and they needed homes and jobs, so the disloyal residents would not be missed.

Meanwhile the war against Britain was going badly. British aircraft had damaged the battleship *Richelieu* in a raid on Dakar on 8 July and later a team of saboteurs had damaged her. At sea several French merchant ships had been captured by Allied warships. Worse, some colonies had fallen to British-sponsored revolutions.

Still, Petain was able to make a secret agreement with the British that neither would occupy the other's territory. The British had no intention of keeping the agreement.

On 24 September 1940, the British and de Gaullists tried to invade Dakar, but in a two-day fight the garrison repelled them. The British suffered damage to a battleship, a cruiser, and two destroyers, and lost six aircraft. A Vichy French submarine was sunk and some shore batteries were damaged. In a separate action at the same time a French destroyer was damaged and forced to beach after an encounter with an Allied cruiser.

Due to the colonial revolutions in Africa, the colony of Gabon was cut off from home, that is Metropolitan France. On 12 October, British and de Gaullist troops invaded the lightly defended primitive colony, but the French put up a good mobile defense. One month later, the colony's administrative capital finally fell. The French governor-general saw that all was lost and hanged himself. His deputy surrendered the colony. While attempting to break out, a sloop and a submarine were sunk by Allied ships.

By the end of 1940 many French people were finding the acts of the British to be repugnant, especially whenever they heard the air raid sirens. Almost nightly the western ports were struck by British bombs. The targets were German installations and troop concentrations, but at this stage of air development night bombing was notoriously inaccurate, and many French civilians paid for this fault with their lives. Even the momentary revulsion at the German execution of a young Frenchman for fistfighting with a German soldier did not last.

By Christmas Lafont was happy to report to his new masters that his team had so far arrested 600 active anti-Germans.

Petain found that running even half of France was taxing his strength. On 13 December, the aging general was forced to dismiss Laval, following rumors of a planned revolt. To assist him he chose Pierre Flandin, and soon that man would be running the day to day affairs, taking a load off the old man's shoulders.

On 18 January 1941 all males aged twenty within Vichy France were conscripted for the Workshops of French Youth for eight months' duty. This was not a popular move, but at least it guaranteed some employment and discipline for those young men of this age who were still unemployed or underemployed.

Flandin was ousted in February, and Admiral Darlan took over the day to day running of the government under Petain's watchful eye.

Throughout France there was talk about the budding resistance activity in occupied France, but within that zone there was peace, except for a few coastal air raids by the British and they were falling off. Only the members of the ineffective resistance underground and the Jews had anything to fear. However, even in Vichy France the Jews were now in danger, for Petain had set up in March the General Commission for Jewish Questions. This was a government agency with its own investigators which searched for signs of Jewish conspiracies. The men and women of this organization soon began arresting Jews on flimsy evidence and housing them in concentration camps.

In May Henri Lafont received a better offer from the Gestapo, and he transferred his detachment from the Abwehr to that hateful body. He was soon inducted into the Gestapo and later given the rank of S.S. Hauptsturmfuehrer. His employees were also made members of this secret police organization. He and his men were indeed honored, for under normal circumstances Heinrich Himmler did not allow non-Germanics to enter the ranks of his elite S.S. Within months everyone in occupied France dreaded the approach of men in plainclothes who would suddenly produce an identity card and announce themselves with the terrifying words, "Police Allemand."

Joining Lafont at this time came Pierre Bonny, an ex-police official who had been kicked off the force for accepting bribes. Besides performing a valuable service for the Third Reich, the French Gestapo also became rich into the bargain, as these investigators extorted large sums of money from the rich. A refusal to pay up risked being arrested for a "political" offense.

On 14 May the Paris police rounded up 3,600 Jewish immigrants and accommodated them at a new concentration camp at Beaune La Rolande. All Jews were fearful of arrest now except for those with friends in high places. Within the occupied zone all Jews were now forced to wear a yellow Star of David on their clothes, except for friends of the nazis, including thirteen Jews who were employees of the Gestapo. This mass arrest and lesser-scale arrests in the occupied zone and Vichy territory of immigrant Jews caused indignation within the Roman Catholic Church. Religious dignitaries demanded that all racial Jews who were Catholics should be released.

Throughout France no immigrant Jew was safe, except for the ones in the Italian-occupied zone.

The spring of 1941 was a momentous time for the people of France, for it was time to take up positions in the war. The people had been given a breather after the surrender, and the British attacks on Mers-el-Kebir, Dakar, and Gabon, plus the colonial revolutions in favor of de Gaulle had somehow seemed far away. The people had been too busy adapting to the new conditions. But in May the problems appeared again. They would not go away for the British would not let them go away. They demanded that the French people choose sides now.

The first sign of Petain's choice came in May when he allowed German fighters to set up a base in Syria so that they could raid British forces in Iraq. Though this was the first overt act of aggression by the Vichy French since the beginning of the Anglo-French War ten and a half months earlier, it nonetheless upset the British very much. They retaliated with air raids on French airfields in Syria.

At the end of the month the campaign in Iraq was over and the French ordered the Germans to leave Syria. The last of them were gone by 6 June, and the next day there were no British raids. The French breathed a sigh of relief, believing they had weathered another storm. Their defensive fighter pilots and anti-aircraft gunners had perfomed adequately.

The very next day, however, 8 June, the French were thoroughly aroused. A British army crossed the Syrian-Palestine border.

To defend the large expanse of Syria and Lebanon General Henri Dentz had an armed force of: eight Syrian, three Lebanese, five Senegalese, six Algerian, three Tunisian, one Moroccan, and three white and black African battalions of infantry; plus twelve Circassian, a Tunisian, a Moroccan, and an Algerian horse cavalry squadrons; four battalions of the 6th Foreign Legion Regiment; 6,700 French artillerymen; 90 tanks; a few armored cars; an air force of three fighter, one reconnaissance, four bomber, two transport, and six army-cooperation groups, and one bomber and four naval air squadrons. Offshore there was a naval flotilla. Counting reinforcements and rear-echelon personnel the garrison had 80,000 effectives.

The attacking enemy consisted of a comparable air force, an excellent and larger naval force, and an army of the British 1st Cavalry Division (horsed and mechanized), Australian 7th Division, Indian 5th Brigade, and sadly a light division of de Gaullist Frenchmen, French colonial natives, and foreign legionnaires.

Within twenty-four hours of the invasion Dentz managed to mobilize his defenders. On the Litani River the Australians were stopped, and at the north end of the river mouth a battalion of British commandos was devastated. Only after a full day and night of action were the Allies able to advance over the river. Quneitra fell to the de Gaullists, but on the 11th the defenders of Kissoue stopped them cold. In this tragic action French soldiers battled against French soldiers. If the French Civil War was only a rumor in France, it was a full-blown reality here. The following morning, the de Gaullists, reinforced by the Indian 5th brigade, attacked again. A Vichy French horse cavalry charge failed to restore the situation for the native horsemen were just scythed down by machine gun fire. Kissoue was abandoned, and the French retreated northwards.

The defenders of Merjuym did not retreat, though, and on the 15th they inflicted a defeat on the Australians.

Sidon on the coast and Mezze inland fell, but on the 19th the French counterattacked and encircled the Indian 5th Brigade. By the next morning the two Indian and one British battalions and the British artillery section had had enough and they surrendered.

Now of course would have been an ideal time to launch a full-scale counteroffensive against the Allies, but Dentz and his staff had made the mistake of concentrating on the Indian brigade and had missed identifying an advance by the de Gaullists upon the capital of the colony, Damascus.

On 21 June de Gaullists and Australians battled their way into the city among Arab houses, ancient winding streets, and historic landmarks. The bitterest fighting was between legionnaires who had been friends only one year earlier. By nightfall the defending legionnaires were holding on, but the following morning more Australians arrived to add weight to the assault, and they and the de Gaullists succeeded in their advance. Now the French garrison received the order to withdraw.

Dentz learned of this defeat at the same time that he learned that British units had entered Syria from Iraq. Four days later, the British assaulted the small town of Palmyra. It fell as only a couple of companies of legionnaires were holding it, but they fought like demons and the battle lasted nine days.

On 3 July, the Indian 8th and 10th Divisions drove into Syria just south of and parallel to the Turkish border. This sealed off the French rear. By this date at sea the Allies had defeated the French naval flotilla, and this cut off Dentz's forces from their homeland. Damur was captured on the 9th, and during the fight the city was severely damaged by British naval gunfire.

Dentz studied his dispositions. The weather was hot and most of his troops were in an exhausted state, retreating to nowhere across sandy wastes and over high rocky mountains. Rather than watch more of his men die to no honorable end, Dentz contacted the British on the 10th to request surrender terms.

The campaign cost Dentz 6,000 casualties. As part of the terms all Allied prisoners of war were to be returned, even those who had been transported by sea to German and Italian control. Dentz's men would be allowed to choose either to go to a Vichy-controlled garrison in France or North Africa or be discharged in Syria. None of them were taken prisoners of war, but Dentz and thirty-five senior officers were held hostage until all the Allied prisoners were returned. The Germans and Italians honored the agreement.

Before the French troops were shipped out, de Gaullist officers roamed the camps attempting to recruit the men for their armed forces. Not surprisingly most men spat at the name of de Gaulle.

The Anti-Bolshevik Crusade

June was a momentous month in the life of Europe for this month the struggle between right and left in politics that had always existed since the century began, and which had already erupted into warfare, notably in the Spanish and Russian civil wars, turned into a war of extermination as Germany finally and irrevocably launched the crusade that the fascists had been preaching for years.

Throughout Europe the rabble-rousers preached that the time of decision was at hand. If you were not for the war against the atheistic communists then you were the enemy.

In Norway those who had volunteered for the Waffen S.S. suddenly realized that they were in the vanguard of the crusade. Others who had struggled with the idea of joining were swayed when the war became a reality. Many of these people looked upon the war between Germany and Britain as an entirely different struggle and not their concern. The security forces were placed on full alert as it was expected that the few communists in the country would soon get orders from Moscow to revolt. As an additional front line force the Germans and the NS began recruiting a legion of young men who would not have to take the unpopular step of enlisting in the S.S., but who would nonetheless be fighting for Christian European civilization. By October 1941, the legion contained 1,200 recruits. Many of the men were ex-policemen. Titular head of the legion was Jonas Lie, who was inducted into the Waffen S.S. and sent to Yugoslavia for on the job training. Before the legion had finished basic training Lie returned armed with the Iron Cross 1st Class and plenty of war stories.

It must be remembered that as Norway bordered on the Soviet Union, the Norwegians had an added stake in seeing victory over the communists.

The Danes were in a slightly different situation in that they still had a sovereign government with its own armed forces. However, the result was the same, for the more conservative Danes recognized their chance to help crush the communist menace and at the same time appease the Germans. The government therefore organized its own legion to fight on the Eastern Front. The Danish Frikorps included a large proportion of Danish soldiers and thus was easily trained by the Waffen S.S. into a formidable fighting battalion. In addition, more Danes joined the Waffen S.S. to fight as German servicemen rather than as Danish servicemen.

The Danish government also ordered its police to be on the alert for communist sabotage. In November, the Danish government formally signed the Anti-Comintern Pact, effectively placing Denmark in a state of war with the Soviet Union.

In the Netherlands the 69-year-old ex-Chief of the Netherlands General Staff preached that service in an anti-bolshevik army was a patriotic duty for all Dutchmen. He helped organize the Volunteer Regiment Northwest, but soon General H.A. Seyffardt's force was renamed the Netherlands Legion, to be uniform with the other legions. Volunteers had to be between 18 and 40 years of age and fit.

The Dutch serving in the Waffen S.S. were also earmarked for front line duty and more Dutchmen signed up for that organization now that there was a real enemy to fight. A large number of Feldmeyer's 6,000 members of the Dutch S.S. also joined the German S.S. for the duration of the conflict. Feldmeyer himself joined and rose to the rank of hauptsturmfuehrer.

Many Flemish volunteers had been accepted into Seyffardt's Volunteer Regiment Northwest, but with the Germans taking over control of training the legions the Flemish were placed in their own Flanders Legion. At first glance this might seem to have been a good move for the 900 Flemings, but they lacked officer material, and the Germans made the mistake of putting German Waffen S.S. officers in charge of them, who became very resentful of being put into a non-German unit, became exasperated by the language difference, and of course looked upon all men outside the S.S. as some sort of lesser breed of human. It was a disastrous move and morale problems plagued the Flanders Legion continually.

There were no Walloon Belgians in the S.S. as racially they did not suit Himmler, but Leon Degrelle soon saw that by forming an anti-bolshevik legion his Christus Rex Party might gain equality with the Flemish, and therefore Germanic, Belgian political parties.

However, in an unusual move for a right-wing party leader, Degrelle insisted that he enter the legion as a private, because he had no previous military experience. This humility earned him more than if he had demanded a high rank the way some fascists had done.

The Germans gratefully accepted the Walloon Legion as the 373rd Battalion (Independent) of the German Army.

The Flemish had their own S.S. too, but like the Dutch version it all but disappeared when many of its members joined the German S.S. for the coming struggle. Rene Lagrou joined the Waffen S.S. and Ward Hermans became a radio propagandist for the Germans.

The area of Malmedy-Eupen with its predominantly German-speaking population was now German territory and all its residents, even French-speakers, were being conscripted into the German forces.

As for the French, they were already at war with Britain, in effect, and indeed as the Germans crossed the Soviet border the French were glued to their radios and were searching their newspapers for news from the battlefront in Syria. Within the occupied zone, though, the fascist parties saw a chance to become legitimate by forming anti-bolshevik legions. Soon it was realized that it would be far better to link arms in defense of Europe than to argue over political differences.

When the invasion of the Soviet Union became a reality the police were ordered to be extremely vigilant in case of communist sabotage. This was a real threat, for the communists had gained a greater hold in France than in any other Western European nation.

Under Paul Chack a Committee for Anti-Bolshevik Action was formed, and under this authority an armed force was recruited. On 8 July took place the first registrations for the Anti-Bolshevik Legion. Its commander was to be the 60-year-old historian Roger Labonne. However, the force was rejected by Hitler. This came as a bitter blow, and Germans friendly to the French conveyed their misgivings to the Fuehrer. Swayed by their argument Hitler agreed to the creation of a legion, but its non-officers had to submit to S.S.-type induction qualifications, and the manpower ceiling for the unit was fixed at 15,000. As Frenchmen the troops were to be denied S.S. status, not that they wanted it anyway.

Indeed once the induction restrictions were adhered to it was realized that the ceiling could never be reached. There were several proponents of the legion, the most vocal being Eugene Deloncle, who was appointed President of the Volunteer Legion Association. Another verbal advocate was Cardinal Baudrillat, the Archbishop of Paris. Other clerics also lent religious support to the antibolshevik crusade in defense of European Christian civilization.

The first all-party rally of fascists in France was held in Paris in order to drum up support for the crusade. In case of disruption by a communist mob, or worse an actual terrorist attack, the police kept an eye on the proceedings and the rally itself was protected by 500 blueshirted guards of Marcel Deat's militia.

Still by the end of July only one thousand of the volunteers had been accepted, and six hundred of these had been ordered to join by their party bosses. Jacques Doriot and Pierre Clementi set a good example by enlisting. Eugene Deloncle also offered his services, but only as a political commissar and only if he received the rank of full colonel. The Germans politely declined his offer.

By the end of August the legion contained 3,000 men, but no less than 6,000 had been rejected, mostly for being too old.

27 August was the day. The unit was formally paraded and instructed to swear an oath of loyalty to Adolf Hitler. The parade had been prepared for, but the oathtaking ceremony came as a surprise, a very unpleasant surprise, for these men looked upon themselves as soldiers in a French Army not as soldiers in a German Army. Fortunately, the leading French fascists were present as was a delegation from the Vichy government, and they managed to calm the men and get them to fulfill the requirements of the ceremony.

This was not the end of the affair, for as the leading politicians and officers were passing, one of the legion soldiers, Paul Collet, a 21-year-old ex-sailor, suddenly lifted a .25 caliber pistol and fired it repeatedly. The policemen who were providing security jumped him, but not before he had shot Pierre Laval in the lung and shoulder, and wounded Deat, a colonel, and two legion soldiers.

Collet was quickly tried and sentenced to death, but in an act of clemency Laval himself commuted the sentence to imprisonment for this member of the resistance who had enlisted into the legion specifically with the intention of getting close to a fascist leader.

By October the legion was down to 2,452 personnel, after training by the Waffen S.S. had weeded out the physical weaklings and political indoctrination had thrown out the "morally weak." Those members who were found to be lacking in fervor for the nazi cause were still allowed the opportunity to fight, but as members of German army penal battalions, units that were practically suicide squads.

Chapter 7

The Eastern Axis: Hungary and Romania

Hungary

Hungarian nationalism had been a major enemy of the Austrian Empire and it had not been stifled when Hungarian rebels were militarily defeated in the mid-nineteenth century. Hungarians did indeed achieve progress, gaining autonomy for their nation which in turn allowed them to lord it over other less fortunate ethnic groups. In 1914 Hungary's ties to the Austrians brought her into war with the Allies, and in 1918 when Austria collapsed, the Hungarians looked upon the decision not as a defeat but as a liberation. Hungary was recognized as a sovereign state.

Recognition was not enough for the extreme nationalists, though, for the Allies had by the same token freed those ethnic groups that had recently been subservient to Hungarian authority.

Nationalism to one degree or another permeated every political ideology in the country, even communism.

Bela Kun, a Hungarian Jew, returned to his native land a few days after the Austrian surrender to work towards the goal of a communist but nationalist regime for his country. Incredibly it was only four months later, on 21 March 1919, he succeeded in heading a coalition regime, which began instituting socialist policies on the domestic front while exerting extreme nationalism on the foreign front. He refused the Allied orders that Transylvania be turned over to Romania, that Novi Sad go to the Serbians, and that the northern districts become Czech territory.

With one regiment of infantry he put a communist government into a village in Slovakia, but withdrew his military support within days.

He angered the communists by pulling the props out from under this provisional government of Slovakia. He angered the socialists by not instituting his domestic reforms fast enough. He angered the capitalists by instituting some socialist reforms. He angered the aristocracy by nationalizing the large estates.

Lastly he angered the army and the nationalists by not resisting the Romanian Army when it occupied Transylvania, or fighting for Novi Sad or the northern districts. Not surprisingly, on 1 August his government collapsed.

Within two years Kun was forgotten and communism in the country was so low in membership and esteem that the Soviets withdrew their financial support of the Hungarian Communist Party.

The Hungarians identified communism and Jewry with a failure to govern and a failure to defend the nation.

The nationalists seemed to be satisfied when Admiral Miklos Horthy took control. An ex-admiral of the Austrian Navy, he now ruled the country, which had no ports and therefore no navy, as regent for the country's king, which it did not have either.

Despite three-and-a-half-million Hungarians having been given to other states by the victorious Allies, the rump of Hungary that the Allies graciously allowed to exist was not homogeneous. Only 7.1 million people, 90% of the population, spoke Magyar, while 600,000, that is, 7%, spoke German. These Volksdeutsch were people who had been officials of the Austrian Empire or had colonized the area, or were descendants of colonists. Few of them returned to Austria as they considered their Hungarian surroundings to be home. They remained to become loyal Hungarian citizens. Many of the aristocratic Volksdeutsch were officers in the Hungarian Army.

140,000 citizens of the new state were Slovakians, having been missed by the boundary makers for the new state of Czechoslovakia. There were also 24,000 Romanians, 1,500 Ruthenians, 37,000 Croatians, and 17,000 Serbians living in scattered villages along the badly drawn border. Even among the Magyar-speaking people there was a minority, the Szeklers, who are racially different than the racial Magyars.

All of these citizens were Christians of many different faiths, but there were also 473,000 Jews. About three-quarters of them were assimilated into the Magyar or German cultures, but the rest were Yiddish-speaking and alien to the surrounding cultures.

Anti-Semitism was extant even with such a large assimilated Jewish minority, for more than half the merchants in the state were Jews. It is understandable that some people became anti-Semitic because of an uneven business deal, whether it was really the merchant's fault or not, whether it was a major economic transaction or the buying of a pair of shoelaces. Recompense was often hard to come by, especially as half the country's lawyers were also Jews.

There was also a population of nomadic Gypsies who far from being romantic curiosities were feared by the Hungarians as thieves and evil curse makers.

Horthy found his cabinets to be satisfactory until the World Depression reached the country. In September 1932 he put the ultra-right Gyula Goemboes into the driver's seat to bring the country back to an even keel, but as all statesmen were finding out there was no quick remedy to cure the ills of the depression. Upon the death of this Volksdeutsch army officer, in October 1936 Kalman Duranyi became premier. A much more moderate man, he recognized that the fascist Party of National Will led by Major Count Ferenc Szalassi and the Hungarian National Socialists of Laszlo Endre were very real dangers to basic Hungarian freedoms.

Duranyi's successor was more nationalist than fascist. Bela Imredy recognized the danger of uncontrolled fascism, and he tried desperately to control the domestic scene, which was becoming riotous. On the foreign scene he willingly allied with Nazi Germany to recover Hungarian villages from Czechoslovakian rule in October 1938. Czech troops resisted the move and there was some light combat, but almost at once Germany and Italy intervened on the diplomatic front and forced the Czechoslovakian government to sign the Vienna Award. This placed 12,000 square kilometers under Hungarian control, a territory which not only included the homes of half a million Magyar speakers, that is Hungarians, but also 272,000 Slovakians and 38,000 Ruthenians, the latter Ukrainian-speaking.

This was an extremely popular move within Hungary, but by February 1939 a new premier was on the scene, Paul Teleki. Teleki most seriously did not want an alliance with Germany for he did not trust Hitler, but with the large number of nationalists involved in Hungarian political life he could hardly refuse any offers which might create a greater Hungary. Therefore he conferred with the German representatives about the future of Czechoslovakia. One day after the Ruthenian declaration of independence, which had been achieved with German connivance, the Hungarian army invaded that newborn state and crushed the poorly armed defenders, also with German connivance. With Hitler's help not only was Ruthenia born, but it was born dead.

Teleki's greatest fear was that as Germany had inherited the Austrian state, she might also have inherited Austrian ambitions, one of which was to rule Hungary again. The extreme nationalists were too elated over their victories and too grateful to Hitler to clearly understand what Teleki feared. Of course Teleki was willing to admit that there was really nowhere else to turn to but to Germany.

Teleki had massive support, but a large number of his followers were pro-German. In the 1939 elections the government won easily as had been expected. Teleki's new Hungarian Life Party won 180 seats. The closest opposition won only 49 seats, but that opposition was a coalition of fascist parties led by Szalassi's Arrow Cross. The periodic imprisonment of the fascist leaders had only seemed to make heroes out of them.

Teleki gained even more glory and the nationalists became even more ecstatic when Hitler agreed to restrain Romania while the Hungarians annexed Transylvania. By August 1940 the reunification of Greater Hungary was complete except for a strip of land still occupied by the Yugoslavs. In gratitude Hungary signed the Tripartite Pact with Germany on 20 November.

The next offer from Hitler alarmed Teleki. He would allow Hungary to liberate the Magyar-speaking Yugoslavs, but only after German troops had been allowed to cross Hungarian soil. Germany bordered on Yugoslavia, but Hitler wanted to outflank the Yugoslavian troops in the north of the country. Teleki protested vigorously, for he believed that once the border was opened to the Germans it would culminate in a German occupation of Hungary. Admiral Horthy overruled him.

Teleki protested in the most effective manner of which he could think. He committed suicide. This was the only shot fired when German troops marched into Hungary.

After the Germans invaded Yugoslavia, Yugoslavian aircraft retaliated by hitting the German lines of communications, some of which stretched across Hungarian soil. The Hungarian government used this as an excuse for attacking across the border. Within days the lightly defended areas of Magyar-speakers were liberated.

The local Magyar-speakers now turned against their Serbian bosses. Serbian factory managers, business owners, and government officials were attacked in the streets and beaten. Many were murdered. The more fanatic nationalists, who were in a state of euphoria, also attacked Jews. The Arrow Cross men among the Hungarian Army joined in this butchery. It is believed that on the first day of the liberation of Subotica about 250 people were murdered. Within a few days of the liberation of Novi Sad about 500 people had been murdered there.

Romania

The Romanian victory in World War One was a hollow one. Her casualties had been extremely heavy, her countryside had been laid waste by battle and enemy occupation, and her armies were racked with communist mutinies. Much soul-searching followed the conflict. The relief at just having survived as a nation comforted many, and the very fact that the country had emerged victorious helped hide the many mistakes that had been made. In the first few months following the war Romanian troops enforced the decisions of the peace treaty that awarded Hungarian, Ukrainian, and Bulgarian land to Romania.

Pre-war problems still beset the state, too. In a peasants' revolt in 1907 the death toll had reached 10,000, and the split between the landless peasants and the landed nobility was as deep as ever. The nobility was pro-German, and they blamed Romania's entry into the war as an Allied nation on the liberal politicians. The acts of communists only widened the gap between the aristocrats and the liberals. The petit bourgeois soon allied with the agrarian reformers.

There were nationalists among all walks of life, and the more fanatic and therefore less pensive among them believed that everything had gone well after all, despite the interference of communists and socialists, and they boasted of their liberation of Romanian villages from the oppression of the neighboring states. Unfortunately the Romanian government had become the oppressor, and had ignored the advice of the United States president, Woodrow Wilson, who believed in national self-determination. By the end of 1919, the Romanian government lorded it over 1.4 million Hungarians, 750,000 Volksdeutsch, 780,000 Ukrainians, 366,000 Bulgarians, and 100,000 Gagaus. All of these people lived in areas either sliced off from neighbors or in pockets large enough for sovereignty. In addition, scattered throughout the state were 177,000 Turks, 260,000 Gypsies and 728,000 Jews. About half of the Jews were assimilated into German culture, but the other half lived outside the Volksdeutsch areas and were unassimilated, being Yiddish-speaking. Half the population of the city of Jassy was Jewish. Of the sixteen million Romanian citizens, over a quarter did not speak Romanian as their native language.

When King Ferdinand died and was succeeded by Carol, the conservatives set about trying to reform their new king, who had a reputation as a philanderer and as a rake. His wife, the half-Jewess Magda Lupescu, was ostracized. Their efforts were not too successful, and by mutual consent, it seemed, Carol's six-year-old son Mihail was placed on the throne instead.

By October 1930, however, Carol's volatile interests had turned to politics and with the support of certain politicians he once again assumed the throne. Romanian political life was in the process of swinging to the right, but though the general mood in the country was nationalist and anti-Semitic, the extremists were in disarray. The major fascist groups, the Iron Guard of the League of Archangel Michael, led by Corneliu Codreanu, the League of Christian National Defense of A.C. Cuza, and the National Agrarian Party of Octavian Goga, together held nine seats.

The National Liberal Party ruled the conservatives in the country and had the government. It also had considerable French and British diplomatic support. The fascists were not always satisfied with the political status quo, though. On 19 December 1933, some Iron Guards assassinated Prime Minister I.G. Duca.

In May 1936, the National Peasants Party, which had the moderate middle class as its power base, staged a very impressive rally in Bucharest. The party then proceeded to win the city's municipal election.

In anger at this new rival, fascist bully boys began roaming the streets looking for known political enemies. Fistfights and deliberate destruction of property became widespread. The Blueshirt Militia was especially active in the mob violence. This force was an unarmed militant faction of the new National Christian Party, which had been formed by a merger of Goga's and Cuza's organizations. As a sideline any Jews who got in the way were also beaten and robbed.

Secretly the government had been supporting the National Christian Party as it was deemed to be the lesser of many fascist evils. Therefore the police usually did not interfere in the political violence. In November 1936, the National Christian Party held its own rally in Bucharest, at which 100,000 members pledged support. The Iron Guards, seeing this rival party steal their thunder, also began a campaign of intimidation, beatings, and destruction of property.

In January 1937, two Iron Guards, who had been killed in action fighting for the fascists in the Spanish Civil War, were given a political funeral in Bucharest. The Iron Guards assembled in uniform, and though political uniforms were now illegal the police kept their distance. One of the more noteworthy dignitaries who attended the ceremony was the Patriarch of the Romanian Orthodox Church.

As the political violence increased during the year and especially just before the December elections, the government began to fear the fascists. The election was a chance for the nation to bare its soul. The ruling National Liberal Party drew 36% of the vote. The remainder of the votes were divided among some small unimportant groups, and the moderate National Peasants Party, 20.4%, the Iron Guard, 15.6%, the National Christian Party, with 9.2%, the fascist Neo-Liberal Party, 3.9%, the ethnically nationalist Hungarian Party, 4.4%, and the left-wing Radical Peasants Party, with 2.3%. This meant that 69% of the voters were right wing, and 28.7% of them extreme right wing and anti-Semitic.

Yet King Carol astonished everyone by appointing Octavian Goga to be the new prime minister. Of course this pleased only 9.2% of the voters, and the move was described by all concerned as dictatorial. The Blueshirts were elated, though, and to celebrate they wandered through the streets looking for trouble. As always there were some Jews in their path who bore the brunt of their hatred. Although the Iron Guards had nothing to celebrate, they too roamed the streets, taking the opportunity to show their brainless muscle. For the most part these crimes went unpunished.

However, by 10 February, Goga had proven unsatisfactory to the king, and Carol now dismissed the government and took power himself with a nonpartisan cabinet. This move pleased 0% of the voters.

As his puppet prime minister, the king chose none other than Miron Cristea, the Patriarch of the Romanian Orthodox Church. As a further dictatorial move the king dissolved all political parties. It is now known that Carol had British and French support and advice in this move.

The Iron Guard was not about to take this lying down, and after all other methods appeared to have failed, they attempted a revolt. However, the police and army chose to respect the throne, regardless of who sat upon it, and they defended the government. The poorly armed Iron Guard was dispersed and most of the leaders were arrested. On 30 November 1938, fourteen of the leaders, including Codreanu, were shot "while trying to escape." The fascists were stunned.

When Cristea died in March, the king chose Armand Calinescu to fulfill the role. But Calinescu had been the executioner of Codreanu, and the fascists had sworn to avenge their leader. On 21 September 1939, the Iron Guards murdered him.

The police cracked down even harder now, and the leading Iron Guards, including their new chief, Horia Sima, fled to Germany. Under a new prime minister, Argesianu, the country attempted to get back to normal.

By the summer of 1940 international politics were overshadowing Romania's domestic problems. With the fall of France there were only two power-blocs left, Germany and the Soviet Union. Carol was forced to lean towards Germany for trade and economic survival. To appease the fascists enough to prevent further disturbances, the king not only removed his ban on the Iron Guards but actually invited some of them into his government. This was one price to pay for the alliance with Germany, which was soon formally signed, but the next bill was far too high for the people of Romania to pay. Hitler forced Carol to pull back his border garrisons and then cede territory to Bulgaria, Hungary, and the Soviet Union.

Refugees began to arrive in Romania proper from Dobrudja, Transylvania, and Bessarabia and Northern Bukovina. From the first two came government officials, policemen, and national company employees who were not indigenous to the area, but from the latter two came not just Romanians, but even some Ukrainians and Gagaus. They had fled for their lives, for their new masters were the Red Army and the N.K.V.D. The Soviets had arrived like a savage plague. Anyone who was suspected of possibly contemplating the idea that he might think about possibly speaking out against the communists was arrested. The deportees would soon number in the thousands as the suspects' wives, children, parents, brothers and sisters, and their families were also arrested.

Naturally after such a shameful surrender not even the police were willing to defend the king. On 6 September General Ion Antonescu and Horia Sima siezed power. Carol was compelled to abdicate.

The Iron Guards celebrated in their usual manner. They harassed, frightened, beat, and murdered political opponents. It goes without saying that for a few days the Jews could not walk the streets safely either. For protection Romania now signed the Tripartite Pact.

Antonescu was aware that he was running the risk of turning over the streets to the Iron Guard, and in December 1940 he made his move. The army was mobilized into the streets and the police began to arrest Iron Guardsmen. The German government had graciously provided some extra military equipment for the Romanian Army for this operation. By the end of January the fascists were crushed. Casualties on both sides numbered several hundred dead, but Romania was brought back to an orderly state. Though Hitler had been a party to their downfall, the Iron Guard leaders fled to Germany. There was nowhere else to go. Hitler's price for his aid was that the Romanian government maintain the flow of oil from the large Romanian oilfields to Germany's tanks, planes, and ships. By welcoming the fascist refugees into his country, however, Hitler was keeping an ace in the hole. He might have use for the Iron Guards yet.

Chapter 8

The First Crusaders: Fascist Italy

Starting with the Italian invasion of Libya in 1911 and then the entry of Italy as an ally in the Great War in 1915, Italian patriotism became feverish. Even the communists were proud of the nation's achievements. Such a staunch socialist as the newspaper editor Benito Mussolini ran off to join the colors.

Italy won the war, but disappointment was felt due to the very high casualties, over one-and-a-half-million killed and wounded, which crippled the nation of only forty million. However, the peace was as disappointing as the war. The Italian northeast was liberated from Austria it was true, but Savoia and Corsica were kept by France and the Italians of Dalmatia were not liberated, but rather handed to the Serbians by the British and French who were calling the shots. As some sort of compensation, the homes of 300,000 Austrians in the Sued Tirol were given to Italy, as were the homelands of 60,000 Slovenes and 60,000 Croatians. Remaining under Italian control were the Friulis, the Catalans and Sardinians of Sardinia, and a few Greek villages on the southeast coast of the Italian peninsula. In addition some Greek Islands were annexed by Italy. The people felt betrayed by any politician who accepted this ridiculous offer.

Mussolini and others who believed in recreating the Roman Empire, and who used the fasces as their symbol, hence the term fascists, were determined to liberate all Italians everywhere, but they were not willing to trade the foreign ethnic groups they already had: not the Europeans and not the people of Libya, Eritrea, or Somaliland.

A body of ultra-nationalists took control of the city of Fiume, but they were dispersed by the armed forces. The government seemed to the fascists to be anti-Italian.

In 1922 Mussolini led his own revolt, but it took the form of a march from Northern Italy to Rome. Incredibly, the government collapsed and the King acquiesced to Mussolini taking over the reigns of a fascist government. Before he could comprehend what had taken place, Benito Mussolini was prime minister. It was an astonishing move for the young editor who had been a private in the army only five years earlier.

When Italian delegates to Greece were murdered, the new leader of Italy showed that Italy could not be pushed around any more. He sent warships to bombard the island of Corfu, and forced Greece to pay an indemnity. The Italians cheered. Here at last was a politician whom they could look up to.

Fascism pleased foreign visitors too. Italy was suddenly emerging into the twentieth century. Favorable reports were written by foreign journalists of all political persuasions, except communists and extreme left-wing socialists. Some Italians who had emigrated to the United States actually began to return. The ongoing guerrilla war in Libya only concerned the few regular soldiers unlucky enough to be sent there. Usually, the colonists, who were turning the coastal cities into a clone of Italy, were not affected by the war in the desert to the south.

When Mussolini managed to bring the nation through the World Depression without too much hardship, he seemed to have assured his position forever.

The Italian invasion of Ethiopia was seen by the people as a good move, very patriotic, and long overdue. Italy owed the Ethiopians one since the defeat at Adowa forty years earlier, and as the majority of the Ethiopian people alternated between starvation and slavery, the war was seen as a humanitarian crusade. The devoutly Roman Catholic Italians were impressed when the Pope publicly blessed Italian soldiers who were on their way to the front.

The Church had to keep its side of the bargain. In return for its support, Mussolini had let go of a few acres in central Rome and had formally recognized the land as sovereign territory belonging to the Roman Catholic Church. As it contained the Vatican Palace the land was named the Vatican State.

The world denounced the invasion, and the British and French actually took some half-hearted moves to punish Italy. The Italians felt that the British and French behaved very hypocritically. After all, were not they currently oppressing half the world?

The victory in Ethiopia in March 1936 and the dispatch of Italian troops to fight for the Catholic-Nationalist-Fascist rebels in Spain four months later were cause for jubilation throughout Italy. In Spain the Italians were up against the arch-enemy, the atheistic communists.

Italian communists had been dodging the police for years and enough of them reached Spain to form a very courageous Republican brigade. The communists and socialists in Italy cheered the Republican side in the Spanish Civil War and made a nuisance of themselves in Italy. At times their agents caused illegal strikes. The fascists won the war in Spain by March 1939, but there was not so much jubilation now. Things were beginning to go wrong. In Spain the Blackshirts of the Militia of National Security, who had been allowed to form armed units, had behaved arrogantly towards the ordinary Italian soldiers. All

Italians had been ashamed when their poor quality equipment had been compared with the material of the German expeditionary force. When the war had been won the people began expressing that they had had enough of warfare, but the fascists were searching for further conquests. To placate them, Mussolini turned towards Albania.

By 1918 the one-and-a-half million Albanians deserved independence after such a long period of Turkish rule, but not only did their new state not encompass all of their people, but it was a fragile state upset by internal conflicts. Islam was the religion of 68% of the people, and 21% were Orthodox Catholic, and 11% were Roman Catholic. In addition the state possessed villages along the border of Greeks and Macedonians, each making up about 6% of the state's population. There were also about 30,000 nomadic Gypsies.

Aside from all this lay social problems, such as dialect discrimination, and economic problems, such as are common to all states. To stabilize the nation, Ahmed Zog took power in 1924 and with Italian aid he managed to hang on to it. In 1928 he crowned himself king.

The regime was reasonably stable until 1932, when on top of the problems caused by the World Depression evidence of widespread government corruption reached the people. The king took some measures, but the people lost much faith in Zog. Mussolini also lost faith, for he had an economic stake in the country. In April 1933 Zog insulted the religious leaders by shutting down all denominational schools.

On Good Friday, 7 April 1939, the Italians tired of their economic interests being risked by Zog, and they invaded. The Albanian Army and some armed civilians resisted stubbornly throughout the Easter weekend, but then melted away in front of an avalanche of Italian infantry.

Within days it was realized that the economic considerations were only a minor reason for the annexation. Mussolini's fascists had simply wanted to sate their appetite for military conquest.

A small group of Albanian nationalists led by Abas Kopi took to the mountains and began to wage a low-key guerrilla war against the invaders, but within a few months the landscape was placid. The Italians kept the Albanian police, and enough Albanians were cajoled into joining the Italian Army that two battalions, about 1,500 men, were formed. The four occupation divisions were rarely called upon. The small communist groups in the country merged into one party on 8 November 1939 under Milan Popovic and Dustan Mugosa and also took to the mountains.

Most of the people of Italy were looking forward to a time of peace in the summer of 1939. There had been peace in Libya for a few years, the war in Spain was over, a reasonably humane rule in Ethiopia under the Duke d'Aosta was winning friends there, and the Czechoslovakian crisis was over with.

In September when Britain, France, Germany, and Poland slid into the abyss of war, Mussolini managed to keep Italy from nearing the precipice. Mussolini had to listen to his fascists, but he was not so rash as to tackle the mighty French Army or the mighty British Royal Navy. The fascists had to make do with what Mussolini gave them, the invasion of Albania.

After nine months of world war, the Italians were still basking on their sunny beaches. Socialist cries that Mussolini was a warmonger were scoffed at.

However, Mussolini's greed got the better of him. In June 1940 he made the most disastrous decision of his life.

Seeing that France was already tottering on the brink of defeat, he declared war on 10 June. He mobilized his army on the beautiful Franco-Italian border. In the Alps he put the Fourth Army of General Alfredo Guzzoni, which had twelve divisions facing two French divisions, and along the coast he placed the First Army of General Pietro Pintor, which had thirteen divisions with which to crush just one French division. However, the French defenses were permanent and the fields of fire were well placed. The narrow passes meant that only a few Italians could advance at a time. Counting garrison troops and artillery positions the French had 185,000 men.

Just before the offensive the Italian government ordered all Slovene and Croatian troops dismissed from the army. This order was in fact never implemented, but the very idea caused serious ill feeling among those troops. The Julia Division was particularly affected.

Mussolini urged his generals to win a victory before the French surrendered to the Germans and spoiled everything. On the 20th, three days after Marshal Petain asked his soldiers to lay down their arms in front of the Germans, the Prince of Piedmont, the commander in the field, launched the invasion of France. The front line infantry of the Assietta, Livorno, Cosseria, and Modena Divisions failed to make any headway in a charge reminiscent of World War One. In a freezing rain the infantry stumbled over one another as the machine guns and well-sited artillery of the French minced them. The generals exhibited a complete lack of tactical knowledge, but the soldiers exhibited suicidal courage. Amid the cries of the wounded men, horses and mules, the battle raged for four days and nights. The French were livid that their nation had been defeated by the Germans and they vented their frustration on the targets that Mussolini had offered them. The French government formally surrendered to Germany on the 22nd, and then was forced to suffer the humiliation of surrendering to Italy on the 24th.

When the firing stopped the French saw that the Italians had gained only a few hundred yards. Thirty-seven Frenchmen had been killed, forty-two wounded evacuated, and one hundred and fifty had been captured.

The Italians suffered almost 10,000 casualties—1,247 dead, 2,631 wounded, 3,878 taken prisoner, of which many were wounded, and 2,151 maimed with frostbite!

Italy was rewarded with a few square miles of French soil, and the Italian Army settled down to a peaceful occupation. It was quickly decided that blatant resistance would be dealt with, but most anti-Italian activity could be handled by the French police. Italian occupation in France was not overly oppressive. One of the greatest problems was the influx of refugees, especially Jews who were fleeing the policies of the French and German governments.

Mussolini's greatest error was not the Alpine campaign, fiasco that it was, but the fact that he had challenged the British as well. The Royal Navy was still very much alive and kicking and showing no signs of wishing to throw in the towel.

On the Libyan-Egyptian border British troops had advanced to meet the Italians, and in the Sudan, British Somaliland, and Kenya a British force was massing so that it could surround Italian-held Ethiopia, Eritrea, and Somaliland. In order for Italian merchant shipping to leave the Mediterranean Sea they would have to sail through the Suez Canal or the narrow straits of Gibraltar, both of which were protected by British guns. In other words without firing a shot the British had cut off Italian East Africa and trapped Italy on the seaward side.

The war that the Italian people had dreaded had finally come, and they would have to fight it at great disadvantages. For one thing, too many of her valiant officers and noncommissioned officers were already lying dead in Libya, Ethiopia, Spain, and on the Alpine border. The replacements were either full of cocky overconfidence or disillusioned by fear, depending on their upbringing. The war was not a youngsters' war, though, for reservists up to the age of 54 were called up. Those reservists who had already survived the terrible battles of World War One had no inclination to finish their lives by being shattered by shrapnel, especially as they now had families and careers to go back to.

In Libya the ultra-fascist Marshal Rodolfo Graziani assembled an army, including 30,000 Libyans, and in August he invaded Egypt without meeting opposition. The Egyptian Army refused to fight and the British retreated. After covering about fifty miles of rocky desert the Italians sat down and began to build outposts. Once the construction was done they sat down again and waited, and waited, and waited.

Fortunately for Mussolini his commander in Ethiopia, the Duke d'Aosta, though young, was a very good leader and many of his troops were brave and eager. Of his 288,000 men, 200,000 of them were trustworthy Eritreans, not so trustworthy Somalis, and downright untrustworthy Ethiopians.

The Duke ordered an advance into Sudan and Kenya at once and by this move he put the British off guard, though the invaders found the Sudan Defense Force and the King's African Rifles to be formidable opponents. In terms of Italian lives the occupation of a few mud huts was costly.

These moves were feints, for after they had taken place d'Aosta struck at his real target, British Somaliland. Using 23 battalions of Eritreans and Somalis, two battalions of Blackshirts,* and one battalion of Sardinian Grenadiers, plus artillery, tanks, and horse cavalry, Major-General de Simone invaded on 3 August. The large force advanced across the desert, plagued by flies, sandstorms, and heat, and harassed by snipers of the Somaliland Camel Corps.

On the 12th, the infantry of the Harar Division, and of the 13th, 14th, and 15th Brigades, bravely charged through Tug Argan Pass, which was defended by only two black African and two Indian battalions. After fearful losses a hill was taken, but after another three days the impotent Italian generals had come up with no better idea than massed infantry charges against machine guns. Nowhere did the native soldiers and the Italian sergeants and officers show that they did not deserve better commanders.

The Allied defenders were forced to retreat and evacuate the colony by sea from Berbera, but as well as victory de Simone had brought d'Aosta a butcher's bill of 465 killed and 1,530 wounded.

In Sudan the 2nd Colonial Division fought off raids by Sudanese and Indian armored cars and snipers for five months, but elsewhere there were far more alerts than there were skirmishes. Enemy air raids were light and rare, though they caused panic among the native troops. Italian sergeants often threw up their hands in despair when their native soldiers panicked at the sight of an aircraft without bothering to find out if it was Allied or Italian.

D'Aosta could do no more, for he was not equipped to launch a major offensive. He therefore concentrated on the defense as he knew it was only a matter of time before the British decided to crush him. If he could tie down an Allied army for several months, his defeat would not be in vain.

He divided his command into four sectors. Major-General de Simone would hold Somaliland with ten colonial brigades. General Guglielmo Nasi would protect the western area of Ethiopia with four colonial brigades. General Frusci had three colonial divisions and three colonial brigades with which to defend Eritrea and three colonial brigades and five Blackshirt battalions with which to hold Gondar. The fourth sector was central Ethiopia, which the Duke would hold himself with his best forces, the Africa Colonial Division and the all-Italian Savoia Grenadiers Division.

In December 1940 the poor quality 27th Colonial Battalion, which stuck out into enemy territory like a sore thumb, at Gallabat, Sudan, was attacked by the Indian 10th Brigade. Within hours the town fell. The Allied commander, Indian Army Brigadier William Slim, became confident. When his brigade was reinforced by British troops he assaulted Metemma, just over the border in Ethiopia. However, the garrison of Lieut.-Colonel Castagnola was waiting. It consisted of two colonial battalions of infantry, some Italian artillery, and

---

*By this date Blackshirt troops were members of the army.

machine guns manned by two companies of Blackshirts, and it had aircraft on call.

When the attack took place the defenders fought well, and as they counterattacked Italian aircraft struck the Allied infantry. The British fled and the Indians followed. The attackers had suffered 167 casualties. Victory though this was, it was of such minor importance that d'Aosta was not impressed.

To those Italians at home who had no knowledge of strategy and tactics it seemed that Italian arms were victorious. The truth was far different. Mussolini had added to his blunder of waging war against the British Empire by going to war against Greece. What is more he did it at the wrong time, in the wrong place, and in the wrong manner. The wrong time was to attack just before winter. The wrong place was the very mountainous Albanian-Greek border. The wrong manner was to shove divisions down the narrow mountain passes without bothering to clear the peaks.

The military offensive began on 28 October 1940. After a week General Count Sebastiani Visconti-Prasca had flung into Greece the Centauro Armored, Bari, Julia, Arezzo, Venezia, Piemonte, Parma, Ferrara, and Siena Divisions deep into the Kalamatas and Pindus mountains. The infantry consisted of fifty-one Italian and six Albanian battalions. So far the only problems had occurred when the Ferrara had been caught in an artillery ambush on the 31st.

Then on the 4th the Siena had to battle hard against a tough rearguard, during which a regimental commander was killed. Already the Julia had been fighting against horse cavalry and mountain artillery since the 2nd, but by the 4th the five columns of the large division were each cut off by Greeks who had calmly allowed the Italians in the valleys to bypass them. The mule columns of this alpine unit were especially hit hard. The mountain roads were rough on vehicles and therefore mules were useful, but each Italian division only possessed twenty-four trucks anyway.

The Centauro Armored Division was immediately ordered to send its infantry, who were Bersaglieri, to break through to the trapped division. On the 6th the Julia was ordered to fall back until it could link up with the relief column. This was duly done, but several companies had been cut off in small valleys, and casualties were severe.

Other than this minor setback the offensive was gaining ground. Then suddenly the Greeks struck back on the 14th. Their operation against the Julia seemed to have been an experiment. It had worked and so the Greeks now counterattacked every Italian force in the same manner. At once, the Parma, Bari, Venezia, and Piemonte Divisions were instructed to fall back, and on the 18th the order was extended to the other Italian formations. The Julia prevented the enemy from following too closely by launching a short but fierce counter thrust. All of the divisions were given enough time to set up a defensive line in Albania only by the sacrifice of battalion-sized rearguards. By the 22nd the Italians were back where they had started.

From this date on the Italians and Greeks spent their time in positional warfare. They slaughtered each other in the freezing snow with a tedium of sniping, artillery barrages, and air raids, broken only by periodic night patrols and company-sized and battalion-sized attacks from both sides.

As a direct result of the defeat, the Commander in Chief, Marshal Pietro Badoglio, resigned, to be replaced by General Ugo Cavalero, who could do little for the rot had already set in. In mid-December a Greek coastal offensive captured some small ports from the Siena Division.

The fact that such a strategy had been doomed from the start was not appreciated by the British public which like all publics knew nothing of strategy and tactics. All they knew was that the Italians had been defeated, and this was proof enough to the Englishman safe in the warmth of his local pub that all Italians were cowards.

The British public's disgust of Italians had been one of the successes of British propaganda in World War One. In 1917 with the Russians ravaged by political insurrection, the French in a mutinous mood, and Ireland entering a state of revolt against the British, the British government looked around for a way in which to instill a fighting spirit into the British Tommie, who was close to being at the end of his tether. The Italian defeat at Caporetto was tailor-made. The government bombarded the British troops and people with the suggestion that the Italians had collapsed because they were cowards and could not take it anymore. The Italians had been at war for nine months less, too. The slogan that stiffened the spine of the Britons was "Our boys can take it." Not wishing to let the home front down, the British fought on.

The subsequent victories of the Italians at Piave River and Vittorio Veneto, which knocked Austria out of the war, were placed by the British people at the foot of the handful of British troops who were serving in Italy. The Italian victory did not destroy the British belief that Italian men might make great opera singers, but definitely made poor fighters.

The Italians took half a year to crush primitive Ethiopian warriors in 1935-36 and in Spain the Italians suffered setbacks on occasion. All this helped confirm the British opinion. The debacle in Greece in 1940 only reaffirmed it.

Then came the British campaign in North Africa. The British defeats at Metemma and Tug Argan Pass were quickly explained away, but the fact that the British had retreated without a fight in Egypt went against the grain. It was high time that this situation changed, the British felt.

General Wavell, the British Commander in Chief Middle East, had been very reluctant to tackle the Italians in Egypt, for he did not believe for one minute the hogwash about Italian faintheartedness. By the end of November he only had two divisions and a brigade with about 275 tanks to face twelve Italian divisions and two armored brigades. There were British advantages, though: his tanks were better, thirty-five Matildas—17-ton tanks with a 2-pounder (a .40

mm) solid shot gun—and 240 Mark Is; his aircraft were sufficient to keep the Italian Reggia Aeronautica at bay, and he was in the process of re-equipping his fighter squadrons with Hurricanes; he controlled the Italian left flank, which was the Mediterranean; and most important of all, the Italians were strung along a series of desert camps for miles, and therefore the British could strike at the enemy's weakest links.

With these advantages in mind he agreed to a large raid. At dawn on 9 December, General Malletti's armored brigade was awoken to a cold morning by the blasts of British artillery shells. As the tank crews and artillery gunners ran for their duty stations artillery shrapnel sliced into them. Few of the soldiers had experienced artillery fire before. The Italian artillerymen proved themselves to be brave, like most Italian artillerymen, but unfortunately their guns did not have the range to hit back at the British long-range artillery. They fired nonetheless. Later they were offered an infantry target on the eastern perimeter.

Two hours later, as all eyes were on the massing British infantry, a battalion of British tanks rammed into the west side, which was open, followed by almost two thousand bayonet-wielding British and Indian infantrymen. The Libyan rear-echelon personnel had no choice but to throw up their hands at once, while the tanks turned to do battle one to one. The British possession of superior quality equipment was responsible for blowing the Italian vehicles all to hell. Once a British tank was freed it turned to machine gunning the Italian and Libyan footsoldiers. General Malletti was killed, and the artillerymen, who had no personal weapons, were charged from behind. Yet, they fought back with ramrods, crowbars, knives, and their bare hands. After a bloody six-hour fight the Italians and Libyans finally began to give up.

The British counted over 2,000 prisoners, and had lost only 56 killed and wounded.

Knowing a good thing when he saw it, the British commander in the field, Lieut.-General O'Connor, ordered another assault that very afternoon. Tumar West proved to be defended by 2,000 Libyans with Italian cadre of the 2nd Libyan Division. When the defenders were attacked by a similar number of enemy infantry and a battalion of tanks they fought for two-and-a-half hours, longer than their Italian officers had expected, when one considers the impotence of a rifle in the face of a charging tank. Once the camp was overrun, the British sent their prisoners to makeshift barbed wire camps.

Tumar East was not immune from attack, either. The British tanks charged it, along with a British-Indian brigade, while a heavy artillery barrage was laid on them. This camp, containing the remainder of the 2nd Libyan Division, surrendered quickly. The Libyans could think of no reason why they should die for Mussolini. Thus another 4,000 prisoners entered the British lines. The few hundred Italian cadre and rear-echelon personnel fought on longer, but they knew it was futile. At dusk, they counterattacked and almost broke through at one stage. During the night a few did indeed manage to sneak away in the dark.

These survivors reached the main camp at Sidi Barani, which was defended by the all-Italian 4th Blackshirt Division, but at dawn this camp came under British tank attack. O'Connor had surmised that the Blackshirts would fight well, but like a gambler on a roll, he hated to quit now.

Later in the morning the Blackshirts were attacked by a British brigade and an Indian battalion on one flank and by the British 4th Armored Brigade on the other. Not surprisingly, trench after trench was overrun as the tanks sat aside the ditches and machine-gunned anyone in them who moved. Still the fight went on all day throughout the large flat desert encampment, and into the night. The Allies suffered over 500 casualties here, but the next morning the Italian command surrendered. Over 15,000 Italians and Libyans were taken.

On the 9th the 5,000 Libyans and 150 Italians of the 1st Libyan Division at their camp at Meiktila had begun to panic when they were subjected to several air raids and a bombardment by heavy naval guns firing from out at sea, for they could only sit and take it. The following day, the division received the command to retreat and this panicked the Arabs even more. Throughout the day the long foot column was strafed and bombed by aircraft.

By the morning of the 11th a fresh British tank battalion was nipping at the heels of the column, machine-gunning a few and taking many prisoner. A large part of the division fled from the coast road inland into the desert, but this only meant that they soon ran out of water and had to return to the road to surrender. By late afternoon, though, a strong rearguard managed to stop the tanks.

The following day, the commander ordered the remaining troops of the division to surrender. Some of the Italians thought this disgraceful and they fled towards Sidi Barani, not knowing that that camp was now in British hands and that there was nowhere to run to. If any Italians took off across the desert in small groups they would either die of thirst or be murdered by nomadic Arabs just for their boots.

This meant that the Allies had destroyed the expeditionary force of the Italian Tenth Army and had taken almost 30,000 prisoners, for the loss of only 624 casualties.

General Mario Berti, the army commander who had been on sick leave, was flabbergasted when he returned to his command. The good use of well-trained tank crews had been astonishingly successful, and he only had one armored group left, and Major-General Babini's tanks were little better than those which the British had been destroying with impunity. Marshal Graziani, the overall commander in North Africa, could only hope that Berti's box defense would soon wear down the British. He ordered all the remaining troops in Egypt to concentrate at Bardia on the Libyan coast.

A rearguard of the 1st Blackshirt Division was emplaced to hold up the enemy at Sidi Omar, but the one thousand or so infantrymen were simply swamped by an entire armored brigade on 16 December, showing that the move had been suicidal. Another 900 or so Italians fell into the degradation that was the lot of prisoners of war and another hundred or so Italian corpses fed the lonely desert.

However, Bardia was indeed a major position. Like all Libyan coastal cities it had a large Italian colony, which had built a European district to resemble the best in Italian life. Agricultural plantations offered work to the town Arabs. The military commander of Bardia was a man well respected by his troops, General Annibale Bergonzolli. He had at his disposal some light warships in the harbor, some aircraft, and a ground force of the 62nd Marmarica and 63rd Cirene Divisions, both recruited from the colonists, men who had never seen Italy. In addition there were stragglers from the 1st and 2nd Blackshirt Divisions, and lesser groups from the 4th Blackshirt, 1st Libyan, and 2nd Libyan Divisions. Elements of the Catanzaro Division were held in reserve. There were a few tanks and a few anti-tank guns, none of them of any quality. Most of the soldiers were green, though a few of the officers had served in one or more of Mussolini's campaigns.

The defenders gained confidence when a British tank battalion was repulsed at the perimeter and no further British advance took place. Libya had been Italian for twenty-nine years and it looked like it would remain so for some time to come.

Though individual British soldiers had witnessed Italian bravery, the commanders and supporters in Britain were bragging how well the British had done. The press took up the cheer, claiming in thinly veiled terms that the Italians were still cowards. Few reports mentioned that half of the prisoners were Libyans. Later in the war the British used Libyan soldiers, but they never trusted them to battle.

Once the press had told how easy it was to defeat the Italians the British could hardly refrain from attacking. Therefore O'Connor reconnoitered Bardia and then launched an assault. He brought up the best troops available, elements of the British 7th Armored Division and the fresh Australian 6th Division.

The Italian defenders were subjected to a bombardment by long-range artillery, continuous air raids, and a naval barrage from three battleships, seven destroyers, and a monitor. Then they were attacked by the Australians and a battalion of tanks on 3 January 1941. Despite the Allied firepower the Australians found that they could not advance without tank support, and the turmoil went on for forty-eight hours. The Italians fought back fiercely in some areas, but wavered in others. At no point, though, could the Allies break through in strength. It was cold and the overcoated Australians were often pinned down, but whenever the tanks appeared the Italians were massacred. When five or ten were shot down, the other thirty or forty of the platoon surrendered, but only yards away across the flat sand lay another platoon which was still fighting. Even after being overrun one or two Italians would continue to resist until finished off.

By the morning of the 4th, the Italian line was pierced, and Italian generalship proved once again to be bankrupt. Bergonzolli refused to accept the inevitable, though, and he fought on. That night he gathered his staff around him and picking up stragglers along the way he broke out of the trap. On the morning of the 5th, the defenses collapsed completely. Thousands began throwing up their hands. Countless numbers had run out of ammunition. In the late afternoon the battle headquarters surrendered and by nightfall the shooting was over.

The Australians had suffered 456 casualties, but their booty was immense: 462 guns, over one hundred armored fighting vehicles, naval small craft, and 45,000 prisoners.

Bergonzolli's mob dodged British armored car sweeps, air strafing, and murderous nomadic Arabs, and still with a substantial strength reached the great city of Tobruk. At once, Bergonzolli conferred with General Manella who commanded the XXIInd Corps, and then both inspected the defenses. The long perimeter was defended by only one division of colonists, the 61st Sirte, but there were thousands of unarmed army, air force, and navy rear-echelon personnel. The exhausted survivors of the battles that had been fought so far were therefore put into the line. The largest group of them were from the 2nd Blackshirt Division.

Almost at once the perimeter was alive with Australian patrols, and for two weeks the Italians were unnerved by air raids, long-range artillery fire, and naval bombardments. At last on the 21st the defending infantry were provided with targets. The Australians attacked, along with a British infantry brigade and the ever present tanks.

For the whole day the Allies were held up as the Italians fought feverishly. The Italians knew, however, that six camps had already been overrun, and this naturally led to some defeatism. Towards the end of the day the Italians launched a counterattack that actually had the Australian commanders worried for awhile. At dusk, though, Bergonzolli, nicknamed "Electric Whiskers," due to his facial decoration, recognizing the signs of defeat, gathered his loyal entourage around him and anyone else who wanted to come along and planned a break out. In the darkness he led several thousand men into a counterattack that infiltrated through the tired Allied troops and ran across the desert to the west.

The following morning the British tanks began sweeping across the Tobruk defenses with little opposition. The garrison surrendered stockpiles of supplies, vehicles, guns, smallcraft, and 25,000 personnel. The cruiser *San Giorgio* scuttled. The twenty-four-hour battle had cost the Australians 355 casualties.

Meanwhile the British tanks were racing across the desert to the west overcoming hundreds of stragglers from Bergonzolli's mob. Before noon, British tanks were outside Derna. Here the defending 60th Sabratha Division, minus a brigade, had been reinforced with the remnants of the Catanzaro Division, and when the British 7th Armored Division attacked on the afternoon of the 22nd, the Italians won the day. O'Connor knew that Derna would therefore be a tough nut to crack. Therefore, his armor picked out the sole brigade of the Sabratha at Mechili and charged it on the 24th. However, the defenses proved to be solid here too. While the defense was being bravely directed, the Babini Armored Group counterattacked the 7th Hussars, a British tank battalion. Though the British tanks were far better than the Italian tanks, as had been proven, the British withdrew after a short fight. The British tanks had been damaged by the 47mm guns of the Italians and the Italians had suffered many tanks damaged and two destroyed. The Italians were afraid, but did not let that fear get the better of them when the 2nd Royal Tanks attacked them with Cruiser tanks. After seven of his tanks were destroyed Babini ordered his non-armored units to withdraw, and at dusk he withdrew his tanks. The British did not follow.

The next day, the defenders of Mechili repelled the British 7th Armored Division, but they knew they were pushing their luck. That night the entire garrison withdrew to the west.

Babini had withdrawn his tanks to Derna because that garrison had been under pressure from the Australian 19th Brigade while he had been fighting his first tank battle. He was in time to help the defenders repulse the Australians for four more days. Finally, on the 29th the garrison commander felt that his men had done enough. The entire Derna garrison withdrew to the west.

The retreating Italians had to walk along one road which was devoid of any cover whatsoever. Allied planes made countless bombing and strafing runs, and ships at sea blasted gaps in the column of exhausted, sick, wounded, and cold refugee-soldiers.

Meanwhile the bulk of the British armor charged across the desert, taking a short cut to Benghazi, with the hope of capturing that city before the Italians could form a defense line. In Benghazi the army was trying to organize a defense, but the Arab population was showing signs of rebellion. Within the cities Italian fascist arrogance had angered the Arabs and in the open desert Italian soldiers had sometimes raped Arab village women without being punished by their officers.

At the end of January the retreating Italians learned that the British had not only reached Benghazi, but had captured it almost without a fight. General Tellera was now put in charge to try to bring the Italian Tenth Army out of Cyrenaica, Libya and to take it to Tripolitania, Libya. The retreating soldiers lost many stragglers as the wounded were abandoned to the British, and many sick and dispirited simply waited to be taken prisoner.

On the morning of 5 February, the survivors, who had braved the enemy, the cold, sandstorms, hunger, and sickness, suddenly fell into complete despair —the British were ahead of them and digging a defense line. In order to reach the next Italian garrison these stragglers would have to fight their way through an armored division and an infantry brigade. Still the officers drew on their last ounces of fortitude and organized an assault. Though they had already walked 500 miles, the Bersaglieri charged the British positions. All day the Italians entered the battlefield, and as had been expected since the invention of gunpowder, mere flesh was not enough to stop piercing bullets and slicing shrapnel. The following day, the remaining 110 tanks under the command of General Babini went into the fray, joined by thousands of infantrymen, but at the end of the day the British had not been moved. It had been a slaughter for the infantry, and Babini had lost 80 tanks. Yet darkness did not bring an end to the battle, as thousands of Italian infantry frantically struggled with the British. Indeed the British later admitted that they had some anxious moments this night. During the conflict General Tellera was mortally wounded.

The following morning, Babini saw that it was over, but never one to be called a quitter, he sent his remaining tanks into a death ride against the British guns. Only then could the British advance and begin to round up the filthy, sick, starving, wounded, and shocked Italians. After they had done so they counted 25,000 in the immediate vicinity. One of them was General Bergonzolli. Thousands of other Italians had not yet reached this spot, but they could be rounded up at leisure, the British knew.

By mid-February the British were claiming that total Allied casualties in North Africa since 9 December were 2,000 killed and wounded. Marshal Graziani did not know this for sure, but he did know that he had suffered casualties of 20,000 killed and wounded and that 130,000 of his men were missing.* He had failed utterly and now he asked to be relieved. He was replaced by General Italo Gariboldi.

Only the Pavia Division and a mob of stragglers stood between the British and the expulsion of the Italians from North Africa, but the British did not advance. They too were exhausted. Their tanks were crippled by mechanical breakdowns due to combat and the rough terrain. What is more the British supply line was long. Wavell believed that it would be a couple of months before the British would be able to advance. In the light of hindsight we know this to have been a foolish decision, but at the time it seemed a sensible thing to do.

In Italian East Africa by early January the Italians knew of the defeat in Egypt. Government propaganda could not hide that. They also knew of the defeat in Greece. Now, they wondered, would it be their turn? They were cut off from all resupply and reinforcement, unlike the other Italian armies, so if anything their prospects looked even dimmer than they did in Greece or North Africa.

---

*30,000 of the casualties were Libyans.

In Sudan the British formed a corps of two Indian divisions, the 4th, which had fought at Nibeiwa and Tumar, and the 5th. Indian divisions at this time contained two-thirds Indian and Gurkha and one-third British infantry, with most of the artillery manned by Britons, and the technical jobs performed usually by Britons. The officers of the Indian units were usually racial Britons of the Indian Army.

On 18 January the British learned that the Italian garrison of Kassala, Sudan had fallen back towards Eritrea. Immediately the Indian corps began to follow.

D'Aosta's troops were falling back to Keru, which they hoped to hold for awhile. The duke knew that the British target was Massawa, the large Italian naval base from which Italian ships and submarines were harassing Allied shipping. D'Aosta conferred with Frusci and they both agreed that the Allies could only be stopped along the way, which lay over two routes, Agordat-Keren-Massawa and Barentu-Keren-Asmara-Massawa. The entire route crossed high inhospitable rocky mountains and the major junction at the pass at Keren was the key. This was not tank country and d'Aosta hoped that his men would not have to face armored vehicles, for they were not equipped to fight them.

The first serious action was at Keru. The 41st Colonial Brigade was surrounded by an Indian division and a battalion of tanks. It came as a bitter disappointment to the Italians that they would be up against the tanks of the same army that had defeated them in Egypt. However, the Italian commanders were not defeatist. They ordered a break out, and obeying this command most of the Italian and Eritrean troops managed to escape. They made a run for Agordat. About 900 wounded and sick had been left to the Allies. At least the Italians knew their abandoned wounded would be cared for, for the Italians had fought alongside the Britons in earlier wars and had noted their humanity. During the retreat, sixty native horsemen and a couple of Italian officers swerved off from the dusty column and charged the chasing Indians. Of course this was a futile move as the Indians possessed many machine guns. In seconds most of the horses were shot dead and twenty-five cavalrymen were dead and sixteen were wounded.

At Agordat the column found the 4th Colonial Division, a battalion of Blackshirts, armored cars, horse cavalry, artillery, and rear-echelon units. There were also about 150 German merchant seamen who had been trapped in East Africa. All told, the camp now held 12,000 troops.

On the 28th the British opened fire with artillery and raided the base with aircraft. The civilians remained indoors, fearful for their young men, Eritreans, who were outside in the open, helpless against the Allied firepower.

The perimeter was soon surrounded by tanks and armored cars. Then the infantry appeared. The Eritreans fought well as did the actual Italians, but here and there Italian sergeants were forced to plug gaps caused by native desertions. For three days the battle raged. Only after this did the garrison commander decide to break out. His order was successfully completed when the Eritreans and Blackshirts counterattacked and charged right through the Allied lines, but much heavy equipment had to be abandoned as were those sick and wounded who were unable to walk.

At this same time, the 6,000-man garrison of Barentu, the 2nd Colonial Division, was under attack from the 5th Indian Division. The defenders held out until they heard that Agordat had fallen. Then they also chose to escape the trap. They successfully counterattacked and fled.

Both Italian columns were heading for Keren, where General Frusci was already assembling a defensive garrison. The retreating 2nd and 4th Colonial Divisions found their compatriots to be waiting for them, the 11th Grenadier Regiment of the Savoia Division, which d'Aosta had released from his reserve, three battalions of Bersaglieri, two colonial horse cavalry squadrons, and artillery and rear-echelon personnel. Counting his new arrivals General Nicholangelo Carmineo was eventually able to put 8,500 infantry into the line, slightly more than half of which were actual Italians.

The garrison was given no time for regrouping, though, for the Allies attacked on 3 February. The Indian and British infantry of the 4th Indian Division and a company of Palestinian commandos charged across the slippery, sharp mountain ridges, right into the positions of the Italians and Eritreans. For three days the frenzied men struggled against each other, often in hand to hand combat, but no one gave an inch. Finally, to the relief of all concerned, the Allies broke and ran back to the relative safety of their own temporary lines.

After a day to recompose their senses, the Italians holding the flanks were assaulted by the enemy, but they held their ground. The defenders were then given two days of rest, which they gratefully accepted. The fighting so far had been terrible, but regardless of this the Allies charged again, and again, and again against all the defending zones for two days. The Italians and Eritreans did not waver. Their casualties had been high and it was soon realized that their primitive medical establishment could not cope. Minor wounds were quickly becoming infected. As well the food and water deliveries were irregular. Part of this was due to incompetence, and part was due to the fact that the porters were open to sniper and artillery fire.

From now on the Allies were content to only test a position now and then with a company-sized attack, and to keep the defenders' heads down with artillery barrages and air raids. The Reggia Aeronautica seemed to have disappeared, and the Italian artillery was just not sufficient to counteract the enemy artillery. This constant bombardment was especially unnerving for the native soldiery, coming as it did immediately after the bloody infantry struggles. Some simply took off their uniform and deserted. It was after all their country and they knew where to go.

Within Italian Somaliland the native troops stationed at Afmadu were equally unnerved by an Allied air raid on 11 February. Their officers were unable to convince them to stay and wait for the Allied ground attack which was expected, and finished up retreating along with the natives, trying to retain some control. The following day the British 12th (Black) African Division occupied the abandoned town.

General de Simone organized a defensive line along the Jaba River, but it was thinly manned by the unreliable Somali troops. A bridgehead was soon gained by the 24th Gold Coast Brigade, though it was not exactly handed to them. De Simone ordered counterattacks, and they took place, but they were half-hearted and stood no chance of shoving the Gold Coasters back across the river. A few miles away at Gobaen the South African (White) 1st Division gained the river, but the defenders repelled all attempts to cross. Meanwhile the city of Kismayu was abandoned.

For another five days the Italians held the river and kept the Gold Coasters immobile, though the Allies were now trying seriously to break out into the interior of the colony. De Simone was under no illusions as to the quality of his native troops, though. On the 21st the South Africans captured a few yards of the east bank and for twenty-four hours Italian counterattacks failed to dislodge them. For fear of being outflanked if the South Africans broke out, de Simone ordered a full-scale retreat.

During the march, many of the native troops disappeared, often right after an Allied air attack. The Italians agreed to hold together and to take with them as much equipment as possible, but it was difficult due to the primitive terrain, lack of real roads, air strikes and barrages by long-range artillery. Near the coast the retreating columns were subjected to bombardments by Allied warships. The Italians cursed their navy and their air force. The natives cursed all Italians.

Mogadishu was abandoned on the 25th, and the Italians now conceded Somaliland and hoped to form a defense line at Jijiga in Ethiopia.

D'Aosta ordered a provisional defense line to be built at Marda Pass just west of Jijiga, and by mid-March it was ready. The retreating Somali units had disintegrated and few of the natives had remained loyal. The line here was therefore manned by Ethiopians and Italians. On 18 March Nigerian infantry supported by British artillery and Allied aircraft assaulted the pass, but by the following day the Italians were still holding. However, d'Aosta ordered another retreat, this time to Babile Pass. He knew that his army was disappearing quickly. Not only were his native soldiers scattering to their homes, but now his Italians were running too. Many of his Italian cadres for the native units were colonists from Eritrea and Somaliland who had never seen Italy. Their home towns were the cities that had been swiftly abandoned. Their womenfolk were now at the mercy of rampaging native army stragglers, and one sure way to anger an Italian is to threaten his womenfolk. These soldiers were therefore running not to save their own skins, but rather because they placed their families ahead of Mussolini's dreams of empire, quite understandable under the circumstances.

Within Ethiopia the colonists had only been here five years at most, but Mussolini had encouraged tens of thousands of Italians to settle in Ethiopia and thus even here there were numerous colonist/soldiers who were now very worried about their families. Only some of the smaller all-Italian units and the Savoia Division were made up of Italians whose families were safe in Italy.

On the 24th the Italians successfully repelled an Allied attack at Babile Pass, but that very night d'Aosta ordered another withdrawal to the Bisidimo River. On the 26th, a small rearguard failed to stop the Nigerians from crossing the river.

In order to protect the thousands of colonists at Harar, d'Aosta proclaimed the city to be open, and his retreating army picked up more units and began the long march to Dire Dawa. When South African troops entered Harar they were forced to fight mobs of riotous Ethiopians for two days before they could inform the Italian civilians that it was safe to walk the streets again.

The Allies now took stock of the situation. The 11th (Black) African Division had taken 10,350 Italian and 11,732 native prisoners, and estimated that 30,000 native troops were on the loose. The division had suffered less than 100 dead.

On 5 April d'Aosta declared the capital city of Ethiopia, Addis Ababa, to be open, and chose a new destination for his army, Dessye. His men who struggled with him were sick, hungry, hot, and in some cases lightly wounded. Apart from air raids, his men had to undergo sniping attacks by natives on occasion. Some of the men had walked no less than 1,500 miles over some of the roughest, and definitely the hottest, terrain on earth. Behind them lay a route marked by broken down and burned out vehicles, dead horses and mules, satchels, helmets, rifles, coats, tins, and corpses. They were not beaten yet.

Far to the north the defenders of Keren had not retreated, but had sat it out day after bloody day. The enemy had been reinforced up to two beefed up divisions and had launched several major assaults, but the Italians and Eritreans had held everywhere. They too had been reinforced with sixteen unreliable colonial battalions and three Blackshirt and one Alpini battalions. During the fierce fighting General Lorenzini had been killed, and many high-ranking officers had been wounded.

On 27 March the British tried a new tactic. They shoved a battalion of tanks right down the main road. The defenders had nothing with which to stop these vehicles and soon they found their rear being chewed up. With their line burst open the Italians began to withdraw of their own accord either towards the coast or southwards towards the Duke's army. At Keren the Italians had held up the Allies for fifty-seven days and had inflicted 3,835 casualties.

The bulk of the defenders fled towards Massawa and Asmara, though not all of them could outrun the Allied tanks and armored cars. There was no time to regroup, gather and reassign the stragglers, and build defensive positions, for they were being chased by two depleted Indian divisions and a fresh Free

French brigade. The remnants of the Savoia Grenadiers Division, two Blackshirt and two marine battalions, and the stragglers, joined by the customs police, defended the forts that protected the cities, but it was only a matter of time. Against fierce Indian tribesmen and French Foreign Legion troops the defenders did not stand a hope. Asmara fell on 1 April and Massawa fell on 8 April.

The Italian East African Fleet tried to escape, but after four destroyers were sunk by Allied aircraft, Admiral Bonetti felt he had no choice but to surrender.

In defense of Eritrea the Italian armed forces lost 5,000 dead and 8,000 wounded, of which 3,000 dead and 4,500 wounded were actual Italians.

By 18 April d'Aosta had formed a new position at Kombolchia with his Africa Division, a reliable Eritrean formation. The defenders repelled the first Allied attack, delivered by a South African brigade, but when the Italians and Eritreans counterattacked they were slaughtered by massed accurate rifle fire and machine gun nests traversing their bullets across the fields of fire. The South Africans then occupied some flanking peaks, and reckless Italian charges failed to dislodge them. This had been a very eventful day.

On the 19th the South Africans, now allied with thousands of Ethiopians, who were loosely guided by British officers, swarmed over the first line of defense. For three days lone Italian outposts held out, but then the Ethiopians, who showed no regard for casualties, began to overrun the positions that were running out of ammunition. This sort of maniacal attack was too much. D'Aosta ordered his army to abandon the position and flee northwards.

More than 500 defenders had been killed at Kombolchia and 5,258 Italian and 2,766 native wounded and sick were abandoned to the Allies. Undoubtedly this number also included some soldiers who simply gave up.

The force that d'Aosta took with him was a mere trickle of men compared to the great army he had once commanded. Within a week he assembled his stragglers at Amba Alagi, counting 7,000 men and forty artillery pieces. The excessive heat gave way to excessive rain, as the rainy season began.

The force came under attack on 29 April from Britons, Indians, and Ethiopians who outnumbered them five to one, yet the heavy assaults in the rain were beaten back every day for two solid weeks. On 13 May a massive swarm of Ethiopians swamped an Italian outpost and then noisily tortured to death those Italians they had found alive. Naturally when the Italians defending the position known as the Triangle were attacked by the Ethiopians they fought with a fury and massacred the natives in droves. The following day, using a little bit of thought, South African troops captured the Triangle, and then held off Italian counterattacks for twenty-four hours.

D'Aosta was now at his wit's end. On the 19th he surrendered his immediate command. The prisoners numbered 400 natives and 4,400 Italians including d'Aosta, General Frusci, and four other generals.

This was by no means the end of the East African campaign, though, for d'Aosta had wisely not surrendered the Italians who were holding out elsewhere.

Along the Kenyan-Ethiopian border the 11th (Black) African Division had advanced in April into Ethiopia, crushing each Italian rearguard and capturing Shashamannu. All Italian forces in the area were now ordered to assemble at Soddu. Gathering there were the 21st, 25th, and 101st Colonial Divisions, consisting of unreliable Somalis. Already the British 12th (Black) African Division was closing upon the town.

Generals Baccari and Liberati managed to hold off the enemy for three days of battle before surrendering.

Elsewhere in the south the Colito garrison of 489 Italians and 300 natives was captured by a British African brigade, a force which then went on to capture Siolo. The small garrison at Abalti fell to a Nigerian brigade. In each place, though, the Allies reported a short but tough fight.

In the south the only major Italian force left was the garrison at Jimmu of the 24th Colonial Division, which had been flooded by refugees and stragglers. The town was not attacked immediately and by July the commander was able to work out a deal with the British. If the British undertook to protect the Italian civilians from the natives, he would surrender. The agreement was made and 15,000 members of the Italian Army walked into captivity. Near here, as late as August, some Italians were still holding out in the mountains.

In the southwest a mobile column of Italians and natives moved away from the chasing Allies, fighting rearguard actions at Demli and Gimbi, but in early July General Gazzera learned that a Belgian Congolese unit was ahead of him. With the British close on his heels with East African and Nigerian brigades, he chose to surrender his 5,000 Italians and 2,000 Ethiopians on 3 July rather than fight a suicidal battle.

Only in western Ethiopia were major Italian units still in existence.

In early March the garrisons of Debra Markos, Bahdar, Giorgis, and Bunji, each of two brigades, came under pressure from Ethiopian guerrillas, and soon the Bunji force was ordered to withdraw to Debra Markos as the supply lines could not be kept open. One column of 7,000 Italian and Ethiopian soldiers suffered the indignation of 2,000 native desertions in a few days. General Nasi replaced the commander of this unit, Colonel Natale, with Colonel Maraventano with the expectation that the unit would in future behave better.

In late March Nasi ordered all brigades to make a sweep of the mountains, but after a week it was realized this only gave the Ethiopian troops a better chance to desert. Faced with a growing enemy made up of trained ex-Italian Army soldiers, Nasi came to the conclusion that he had to withdraw to a secure position. On 4 April the withdrawal began. During this maneuver an entire battalion was cut off and forced to surrender, the Italian officers and sergeants reluctantly being forced to follow their native soldiers. The columns were able to make Gondar, except Maraventano's unit. Finding his way blocked, he diverted the column into the area of the Upper Blue Nile.

At Addis Dera, Maraventano fought off the surrounding Ethiopians for several weeks, but even courage cannot overcome hunger, and when his men ran low on food the colonel, remembering his orders from General Nasi, chose to try to break out rather than surrender. However, by this date he was surrounded by tens of thousands of Ethiopians armed with captured Italian weapons, ancient rifles, and spears and swords. The retreating column was assaulted by these fanatics for three days. The struggle was psychologically crippling as hundreds were gunned down to be replaced by thousands. Individual Italians who were overrun were chopped to pieces in front of their comrades' eyes. Though some native troops were fighting well, every Italian was afraid that the men under his command might suddenly turn on him with their bayonets.

Once more Maraventano tried to get his men moving, but heavy, though inaccurate, rifle fire, and some machine gun fire, pinned his men down. Suddenly a British officer stepped forward under a flag of truce. This was Major Orde Wingate, who commanded 8,000 Ethiopians who were reasonably well trained by Sudanese sergeants. Wingate offered to accept Maraventano's surrender and vouch for the safety of the prisoners. Otherwise the Italians would be sliced to ribbons, literally, once they had run out of ammunition. The Italians accepted his offer.

This was the fate of one of Nasi's columns, but he still commanded 40,000 troops—2,500 at Kulkaber, 2,500 at Chilga, 5,000 at Debra Tabor, 5,000 at Wolchefit Pass, and the rest at Gondar. His men were the last organized Italian units in East Africa.

All of these garrisons were surrounded by Ethiopians and a battalion of Sudanese troops. The British later brought up artillery and other combat support units and had aircraft on call. The Italian outposts were not mutually defensive—Debra Tabor is seventy-five rugged miles from Gondar.

The British command could have starved out the garrisons, but too many Allied soldiers were being tied down here and manpower was short in other theaters of war. Besides, the Ethiopians, who rarely obeyed the British, wanted to win now. The British felt therefore they might as well ally and do the job now.

The Italians of Nasi had been up against guerrillas so far, but now each outpost came under reasonably thoughtful attacks, aided by British artillery barrages and air attacks. All arms were used in the defense and many a rear-echelon soldier found himself fighting for his life. Nasi knew he had no hope of relief and it would have been honorable if he had surrendered. Instead he chose to fight on as long as was humanly possible in order to hold down Allied troops and equipment.

In June Debra Tabor surrendered as the garrison had run out of food. Wolchefit Pass' defenders were placed on starvation rations and held out until 27 September. Only then did the emaciated troops give up. They had performed well, repelling attacks by thousands of guerrillas, and battalions of Britons, Indians, and British East Africans.

In mid-November Colonel Ugolino's men at Kulkaber fought like the devil, though hungry and sick, repelling the latest round of assaults. By the time he was forced to surrender, on the 21st, Ugolino and his 2,500 men had inflicted thousands of casualties on the Ethiopians and about 1,000 casualties on troops of the British and South African Armies. In the last attack the British had been forced to throw in Sudanese pioneers, that is, labor troops.

On 27 November General Guglielmo Nasi ordered the complete surrender of all Italian personnel in Ethiopia. He had held on to the last possible minute without allowing his men to starve to death. During the seven-and-a-half months his men had been holding out they had been up against possibly 100,000 Ethiopians and an ad hoc British division.

General Duke d'Aosta had known the probable outcome of the war for his own command ever since war had been declared, but like the true soldier that he was he fought on, holding down a force of comparable size for seventeen months, counting Nasi's stand. If the Allies had been spared the time-consuming East African campaign, and had been able to use the six divisions elsewhere, they probably would not have suffered the defeats in Greece, Crete, and North Africa. D'Aosta's stand should have gone down in history as a great epic. Instead it has been all but ignored. The British prejudice against Italians was largely responsible for this, as well as the Axis governments' reluctance to describe events in a campaign that was doomed to failure. It is tragic that the Duke did not survive his captivity.

In Albania the Italians had reinforced their army to a massive size. They had failed in Egypt and lost half of Libya and in East Africa the garrison was written off, but by spring 1941 they stood a chance in Greece.

The Italian garrison of Albania now stood at two armies, the Ninth of General Pirzio Biroli and the Eleventh of General Geloso. The divisions were the Cuneense, Siena, Ferrara, Julia, Parma, Piemonte, Venezia, Taro, Modena, Bari, Pusteria, Cuneo, Tridentina, Brennero, Pinerolo, Lupe di Toscano, Acqui, Cagliari, Forli, Legnano, Pugli, Sforesca, Feltre, Centauro Armored, and Casale. There were also smaller formations.

After a quick conference with German delegates, Mussolini put four other divisions into Albania facing the Yugoslavian border. At last he would be able to fulfill one of his nationalist goals. He was going to liberate the Dalmatian Italians.

On 6 April, as German forces invaded Yugoslavia from Austria and Hungary and Bulgaria, the four Italian divisions rushed northwards into Southern Yugoslavia. Other Italians landed by amphibious moves onto the Dalmatian shore and General Ambrosio's Second Army of fourteen divisions charged into

Northwest Yugoslavia from Italy. Within days the Italians achieved their goals.

This was Italy's first real victory in the current war and the Italians were ready for it. Mussolini was elated for he knew that more was to come. As part of the same agreement German troops had invaded Northeast Greece on 6 April as well, and within a couple of days the Greeks and a British expeditionary force were on the run. By 12 April the Italians felt strong enough to launch an offensive of their own.

As soon as the Italians charged, the fourteen divisions of the Greek Epirus Army fell back, though it was not a rout. In places the Greek rearguards gave the Italians quite a few nasty surprises. However, on the 20th the Greeks began giving up and the next day it was all over but for some mopping up.

Italy had been victorious, twice, but even the fanatic fascists were aware that they had required German help. Italian losses against the Yugoslavs were negligible, but the cost of the war against Greece had been exceedingly high. The Italians had inflicted 60,000 casualties upon the Greeks, but in turn had suffered 13,755 dead, 50,000 wounded, 12,368 maimed by frostbite, and 20,000 prisoners, most of whom were in British custody and therefore would not be returned.

The losses were dismissed by Italian propaganda. The news from the Balkans was good and the news from Africa had improved. By the end of April 1941 it certainly looked like the Italians might yet emerge from this war victorious.

After the loss of Cyrenaica, Libya in February 1941, the Italians had reinforced the defenses of the western half of the colony, Tripolitania. One of the reinforcements was a division of German lorried infantry, armored cars and light tanks commanded by Lieut.-General Erwin Rommel. German aircraft were also sent to this desert conflict. Against Italian orders Rommel launched a little reconnaissance in force and soon proved that the British victory over the Italians in Egypt and Libya had been a matter of tactics, not a matter of British heroism and Italian cowardice. Within days a small German force defeated an entire fresh British armored division and a motorized infantry brigade, flung the British all the way back to Tobruk, and took thousands of prisoners. The world was amazed. The Italians now rushed to join Rommel who was hundreds of miles to the east of their front line.

The Italian people had been as worried about the sea campaign as they had about the land operations, for they are a sea people and they knew that all of the land victories were meaningless if the Italians could not control the Mediterranean, which the fascists liked to call Mare Nostrum (Our Sea).

When Mussolini took his people into war against France and Britain in June 1940 his sailors were pleased for they had had little to do in Italy's wars so far, but the admirals were not so happy. It is true that the Italian Navy was powerful by the standards of the day, but the British Navy had a reputation for invincibility.

The navy of Admiral Cavignari consisted of four old and three almost brand new battleships, seven cruisers, twelve light cruisers, fifty-seven destroyers, sixty-seven destroyer escorts, 115 submarines, and plenty of small craft. The Royal Navy was currently engaged in warfare against the Germans, but had managed to spare for the Mediterranean three battleships, five light cruisers, and twenty destroyers. Most important of all, the British possessed aircraft carriers. The Italians had some naval aircraft, but they relied on land bases. Cavignari knew that the British might be able to concentrate a far superior force for just long enough to destroy the Italian battle fleet before the war against the Germans diverted the warships to other duties.

The British secret was not that they had produced more and better ships, but that they had produced better admirals. In addition a good deal of luck was on their side. Germany had no warships in the Mediterranean nor any method of getting them there, so Italy protected the Axis southern flank. The British wasted no time in testing the strength of that flank.

Off Calabria, Italy, the opposing battle fleets emerged to do battle on 9 July 1940, having been drawn together while protecting convoys. Admiral Campione had the battleships *Conti di Cavour* and *Giulio Cesare*, the cruisers *Trento, Fiume, Zara,* and *Pola*, eight light cruisers, and sixteen destroyers. At first the British only committed three British and one Australian light cruisers, but then when they realized their opportunity rushed up the battleships *Warspite, Malaya,* and *Royal Sovereign*, five light cruisers, fourteen destroyers, and most important of all an aircraft carrier.

The Italian gunners proved their accuracy once the enemy was within range, but this was hampered by the sudden swerving moves that the Italian warships had to make to dodge attacks by British torpedo bombers.

Campione ordered Admiral Paladini to bring his cruisers in closer so they too could participate, but just as they were moving up the *Giulio Cesare* was struck in the boilers by a 15-inch shell fired from *HMS Warspite* at the range of thirteen miles. As the crippled vessel withdrew so did the *Conti di Cavour*. The cruisers then held the line as the Allied warships came closer and the aircraft continued to attack, and later the destroyers alone held the defenses until the larger Italian ships were safely away. The Italian battle fleet should not have withdrawn, but it did, and by doing so Admiral Campione surrendered the initiative to the British.

On the 19th two Italian light cruisers happily chased five British destroyers, until they espied the Australian light cruiser *Sydney* off Cape Spada. The Italians immediately withdrew, but the Australian gunners accurately struck the *Bartolomeo Colleone* and the *Giovanni della Bande Nere*, sinking the former.

The most spectacular affair came on the night of 11 November 1940, showing the Italian people exactly what it meant to have a hostile fleet offshore. British torpedo bombers took off from the carrier *Illustrious* and attacked the fleet in Taranto harbor by flare light. The battleships *Conti di Cavour, Caio Duilio*, and the new *Littorio* were sunk for the British loss of only two planes. The Italian fleet was forced to withdraw further north to Naples.

The Italian admirals could not really have been blamed for this, for no one, not even the men who launched the strike, could have predicted such a success. Over a year later, the Americans proved they had not learned from the Italian defeat when they suffered an even more humiliating attack at Pearl Harbor.

On 25 November 1940 Admiral Caviglia, who naturally was looking for a quick victory to erase the shame of Taranto, learned that Force H, a British fleet, had just left Gibraltar. Hoping to catch the British ships piecemeal he ordered Admiral Campione to intercept with the battleships *Vittorio Veneto* and *Giulio Cesare* and seven destroyers, aided by Admiral Angelo Iachino with the *Pola, Fiume*, and *Gorizia* and four destroyers and Admiral Sansonetti's force of the *Trieste, Bolzano, Trento*, and three destroyers.

On the 27th the enemies met off Cape Spartivento, but at first only the cruisers were close enough to do battle. Admiral Campione ordered his cruisers to withdraw, but Admiral Matteuci did not like that idea and he challenged the British by opening fire from the *Fiume*. At once, the other cruisers joined the battle. The British cruisers returned the fire, and carrier planes got into the act by diving low among the Italian warships. The sea captains had to spend more time ordering maneuvers that would dodge aerial torpedoes and the other fastmoving ships than they did ordering standard firing positions. With the 6-inch shells of five light cruisers landing among the Italian warships the situation became confused. Then 15-inch shells began hitting the water near the ships. The British battleships had arrived. An Italian destroyer was crippled and the Italians managed to damage the British *Berwick*, but all the other shots were near-misses, more fatal to crewmembers than to ships. The *Vittorio Veneto* opened fire at the incredible range of twenty-five miles, but the *Giulio Cesare* had to plough through the waves for several minutes before she reached her firing range of fifteen miles. Then the mighty warships both traded shots with the British *Renoun* and *Ramillies*. Later high-altitude bombers of the Reggia Aeronautica arrived to lend their weight of bombs, but neither they nor the British aircraft actually hit anything. When the Italian fleet withdrew the British did not follow.

For his result Admiral Campione was relieved of command and succeeded by Admiral Arturo Ricciardi, while Admiral Iachino was made commander-in-chief afloat.

Ricciardi chose a showdown when he learned, falsely it turned out, that German aircraft had crippled two British battleships on 16 March 1941. Admiral Iachino was put to sea with the battleship *Vittorio Veneto*, cruisers *Zara, Pola, Fiume, Trieste, Trento*, and *Bolzano*, light cruisers *Duca degli Abruzzi* and *Giuseppe Garibaldi*, and ten destroyers to threaten a convoy and hopefully draw forth the British light cruisers. Instead he brought forth a hornet's nest of trouble.

On the 28th off Cape Matapan Sansonetti's cruisers engaged a force of British light cruisers, but British aircraft sighted and attacked and struck the *Vittorio Veneto*. With his sole battleship limping, Iachino chose to call it a day. A retaliatory strike by Italian aircraft failed to do any damage. Iachino's decision was confirmed when a second wave of British torpedo bombers attacked his fleet and again hit the battleship. Iachino survived the explosion and called for a withdrawal at once.

Just before dusk a third wave of torpedo bombers attacked and though they missed the battleship one of the torpedoes pierced the *Pola* and stopped her dead. The fleet sailed on.

After dark Admiral Cattaneo decided to risk going back for the *Pola* either to escort her or tow her home. It proved to be a fatal move. The *Fiume, Zara*, and five destroyers while searching for the *Pola* were suddenly lit by searchlights from a whole host of British warships including the battleships *Barham, Warspite*, and *Valiant*. The British gunners had a perfect target, while the Italian gunners were blinded. Only three destroyers managed to outrun the British and escape. Admiral Cattaneo and 3,000 of his fellow sailors went down with their ships.

The Italian Navy had proven itself to be as tactically bankrupt as the Reggia Aeronautica and the Army. Often British aircraft on solo patrols were sighting Italian warships before scores of Italian aircraft were sighting the British ships. In these pre-radar days visual sighting was imperative. Everywhere the British were always one step ahead.

Only a sea chariot raid by Italian frogmen salvaged some Italian pride. In December 1941 these suicidal underwater warriors sank the British battleships *Valiant* and *Queen Elizabeth* and a tanker in the shallow waters of Alexandria harbor.

Mussolini had crushed Albania more because he was jealous of Hitler and because he needed to appease his fascists than because of any economic reason. He had taken over Greece for the same reason. Although he had vociferously staked claims to Egypt, Sudan, Kenya, and British Somaliland, he had really been on the defensive in Africa. The swift French border action and the invasion of Yugoslavia had been opportunities that he had grasped. The performance of his forces should have taught him something. His armed forces required urgent re-equipping and most of all he needed to replace his commanders with men who had sound strategic and tactical sense, even though they might not have been as politically loyal as he would have liked. The promotion of officers for their fascist ardor rather than their ability and the attachment of two Blackshirt battalions to every infantry division had been detrimental to the war effort.

By June 1941 Mussolini had controlled Italy's destiny for nineteen years, and for fifteen of those years he had led the country in war. Within the last year his dreams of recreating the Roman Empire had brought him casualties of half a million. His army had either frozen in the French Alps and the Albanian mountains or died of thirst in Africa. His navy was crippled. His merchant shipping was in danger of extinction, and his air force was too obsolete to survive. In Northern Italy the citizens of his industrial centers were being blasted to bits by British bombs.

Instead of learning from these disasters, Mussolini put his pride ahead of his country and searched around for a further conquest. His gaze soon fell on Russia.

PART TWO: The Battle of the Kingdom of the Mind

Chapter 9

The Crusaders of the Crooked Cross The Invaders of the Soviet Union

Germany equipped three-and-a-half million men for the invasion of the Soviet Union. The Luftwaffe drained the rest of Europe of most of the squadrons, thus ending the Blitz on Britain and denuding Germany of adequate air defenses. In order to continue the occupation of the conquered lands the less physically able soldiers were put into their own occupation units. Usually men over thirty-five years of age up to forty-five were earmarked for occupation duty, excepting officers and senior noncommissioned officers. Hitler wanted Germany's finest young men to be the ones who would do battle against the communists. The officers of this army were veterans and at this stage of the war their men had complete confidence in them.

The German Navy was only given secondary peripheral duties, but that was just as well for it was still bogged down in a naval war with Britain.

The S.S., it seemed to those who looked back upon its short history, had been bred just for this event. All the previous operations could be labeled rehearsals. These were the crusaders par excellence and at last the crusade was about to begin in earnest. The fighting force of the S.S., the Waffen S.S., which had the status of a branch of the armed forces, was still small, numbering only five divisions and some smaller units, but they had been indoctrinated to believe that their untis were the reincarnation of the Teutonic Knights, the Knights of the Brethren of the Sword, and other such religious orders that had christianized the Northern and Western Slavs at the point of a sword. Indeed all Germans had been infused with the crusading spirit, and without mentioning God as such the nazis had nonetheless convinced many people that the destruction of communism and the colonization of the eastern lands was a divine mission.

The Finns were quite literally invited not to take part in a war but to enter into a crusade. As the Soviets had militarily defeated Finland only fifteen months before, bombing civilians, and annexing a part of the Finnish homeland, the Finns naturally were eager to right past wrongs. Her tiny navy had only thirty minesweepers and gunboats and five submarines, and her air force possessed a mixed-bag of three hundred airplanes, but the army was experienced in fighting the modern Red Army and was very familiar with the terrain over which the battle would be fought. Field Marshal Mannerheim was old, but not too old to learn new tricks, and he tried to make sure that the army learned from its mistakes. With a front of over 950 miles he had to hand over the northern Arctic section to a German-Austrian mountain corps and concentrate his own army on certain strategic points. His 400,000 troops were divided into the IInd, IIIrd, IVth, VIth, and VIIth Corps controlling thirteen divisions, while three divisions were independent. There were also some independent brigades. However, only the 1st, 3rd, 6th, 14th, 15th, 17th, and 19th Divisions were up to strength. The 2nd, 7th, 11th, and 18th Divisions were at about half to three-quarter strength, and the 4th, 5th, 8th, 10th, and 12th Divisions contained less than 4,000 men each, about a third of the strength of a Red Army division. In addition the army only possessed one tank battalion armed with purchased and captured vehicles: BA-20s; BA-10s; T-37s; T-38s; T-26s; T-28s; OT-130s; Komsomolets; and Vickers. Every one was inferior to the Soviet T-34.

About ten percent of the Finnish troops were Swedish-speading, and there was one actual battalion of Swedes from Sweden, serving as volunteers. These men faced the Soviet naval base at Hangö. The Swedish government did not like the idea of Swedes serving in the Finnish armed forces, but her neutrality was somewhat anti-Allied at this stage. Regular shipments of Swedish iron ore kept the German armaments industry at full capacity, and there were other lesser industrial deals being made. The Swedish government even allowed the German Army 163rd Division to travel across Sweden on its way from Norway to Finland, knowing full well that the division would probably be used against the Soviet Union.

The 200th Regiment of the Finnish Army contained Estonians, who had joined to fight for Finnish freedom, but were now being prepared to fight for their own freedom as while they had been serving the Soviets had annexed their homeland.

With memories of their glorious past and more recent memories of the ridiculous Bela Kun regime, the Hungarians prepared for their own crusade. Hungarian knights had battled the Slav invader and the infidel for centuries. It was time for the Hungarians to do the invading, and the nationalists were extremely gratified to have this opportunity. The state possessed a massive army of 700,000, but its equipment was poor and its only combat experience had been during World War One. The actions in Slovakia, Ruthenia, and Yugoslavia had been too short for any knowledge to have been gained from them.

The internal divisions that split the country also divided the armed forces. Percentages of the soldiers were Ukrainians, Volksdeutsch, Serbians, Romanians, and Slovakians. Jews also served, but in unarmed labor battalions. The

Szeckler units were Hungarian forces made up of Magyar-speakers of the Szeckler rather than Magyar race.

The units were divided into: the Ist Corps of 1st and 2nd Divisions; IInd Corps of 4th, 5th, and 6th Divisions; IIIrd Corps of 7th, 8th, and 9th Divisions; IVth Corps of 10th, 11th, and 12th Divisions; Vth Corps of 13th, 14th, and 15th Divisions; VIth Corps of 16th, 17th, and 18th Divisions; VIIth Corps of 19th, 20th, and 21st Divisions; VIIIth Corps of 22nd, 23rd, and 24th Divisions; IXth Corps of 25th, 26th, and 27th Divisions; and Mobile Corps of the 1st and 2nd Motorized Brigades and 1st and 2nd Cavalry Brigades. These divisions were smaller than the German ones, being binary, that is, having two regiments of infantry, each with three battalions. The Hungarians possessed a small armored force, using eighty-one Swedish-designed Hungarian-built Toldis, forty-eight Csaba armored cars, and sixty Italian-made CV35s.

The Romanians were anxious to liberate the provinces of Northern Bukovina and Bessarabia, and they needed no propagandizing about a crusade. Though the Iron Guard had been rendered impotent, the government and its supporters were right wingers who had been fighting this crusade for years within their own borders. The Romanian Army was very large, 1.8 million, but suffered from a lack of good equipment and a limited objective. The nationalist feeling wanted to liberate but not to occupy. Unfortunately, the Soviets might not see it that way, they knew. How far, therefore, should they advance?

Only a fraction of the army was to be used for the invasion, and horse cavalry would provide the spearhead. The First Army was to liberate Bessarabia with the 5th, 6th, 13th, and Guards Divisions, and a frontier and an armored brigades. The Third Army was to liberate Northern Bukovina with the Mountain Corps, of the 1st, 2nd, and 4th Mountain Brigades, and the Cavalry Corps, of the 5th, 6th, and 8th Cavalry Brigades. The armored brigade had two tank regiments and the horse cavalry brigades had some tank support, giving the Romanians a total of about 120 armored fighting vehicles—French-built Renault R-35s, Czech-built R-1s and R-2s, and some obsolete FT-17s.

The air force was small and the navy of four destroyers, two submarines, and some small craft would hug the coast. The sailors had no desire to tangle with the Red Navy Black Sea Fleet of a battleship, six cruisers, thirty-seven destroyers, and fifty submarines.

Slovakia had already fought briefly as an ally of Germany and wanted to secure its position with Germany. The Roman Catholic government of Father Tiso could hardly keep out of the war even if it wanted to, for Hitler would have enforced their participation. Besides, a war to destroy atheistic communism could not be bad, and the Catholic politicians felt that they would be betraying their beliefs if they tried to remain neutral in this the ultimate struggle between good and evil.

The government therefore spent much effort informing the people that it was their Christian duty to destroy the communists. An expeditionary force of the 1st and 2nd Divisions and a mobile brigade was readied, in theory to fight shoulder to shoulder with the Germans, but in reality it was agreed that the poorly equipped Slovakians would not be given dangerous tasks, probably protection of lines of communication. The mobile brigade was equipped with thirty VCKD tankettes and one hundred and thirty armored cars. However, in May and June 1941, the Germans gave the Slovakians thirty-two 38ts and twenty-one vz40s.

Italy had borne the brunt of the Axis war effort since 22 June 1940 and could not really participate as fully as Mussolini wished. In comparison to the other Axis partners, Italy's expeditionary corps was only a token force, consisting of Pasubio and Torino (binary) Divisions and the 3rd Celere (mobile) Division. The latter contained a regiment of horse cavalry and a regiment of armor, with L6/40s and Semoventi 47/32s.

The brand-new state of Croatia was not to be left out either, and indeed the Croatians like the Slovaks believed that they could earn respect from Germany by fighting shoulder to shoulder with the Germans. A regiment of Croatians was therefore assigned to the German Army. In addition, two battalions were put into a Croatian Legion to aid the Italians in Russia.

All of these nations were formal Axis partners and considered themselves to be equal in status to Germany, regardless of what Hitler thought. However, there were many other Europeans who wished to take part in the struggle against the communist terrorists and agents provocateurs and, once the invasion had taken place, against the Red Army.

The Waffen S.S. had been recruiting in the nations of Western Europe for fighters for the cause and had created battalions of them for service in the continuing struggle against the communists. When the units were put on the march for the Soviet border, though, it was plain to everyone that a conflict with the Red Army might ensue. The soldiers believed that they had been maneuvered into an anti-Soviet stance, but far from feeling tricked, they behaved as if this was an honorable gift. They were proud that they might soon be taking part in the greatest military struggle in the history of mankind.

The non-German Waffen S.S. were placed into the new Wiking Division. The Westland Regiment of the division consisted of Dutch and Flemish volunteers, who had been given quick courses in the German language as in theory at least all orders were to be given in German. The Nordland Regiment of the division contained a small battalion of about 250 Danes and two battalions of Norwegians. The Germania Regiment had originally been an all-German unit, but it had become international with an influx of Swedish-speaking Finns, Swedes, about a thousand Swiss, some Luxembourgers, Estonian Volksdeutsch, and a small party of Liechtensteiners. Most of the officers were German or Austrian, but there were a few Volksdeutsch. One of the regimental commanders was Artur Phleps, a Romanian Volksdeutsch who had recently been a general in the Romanian Army. The rear-echelon troops were German. All of the personnel of the division were members of the Waffen S.S. The division also received eventually about 400 Finns who were sprinkled throughout the unit.

In reserve, the Waffen S.S. had a battalion of Finns that was still training, provisionally named S.S. Regiment Northeast. A Dutch and Flemish unit called provisionally S.S. Regiment Nordwest would soon supply its manpower to S.S. Regiment Westland. As soon as the first shots were fired in this new war the nations of Europe would provide more volunteers, it was hoped.

There was an ulterior motive for recruiting foreigners into the S.S. Heinrich Himmler saw himself as an army leader, but the German Army had constantly put restrictions in his path. With Hitler's help he had managed to get the Waffen S.S. accepted as a branch of the armed forces, but he was not allowed to conscript and indeed only those volunteers not wanted by the army, navy, and air force could enter the Waffen S.S. A further problem in recruitment was that the S.S. had set itself high physical standards and racial standards, and thus even willing volunteers were often turned down for trivial reasons. Himmler's ambition to build an army was not compatible with his recruiting standards and as his ambition grew the standards of recruitment lessened. He had been forced to mobilize a large number of S.S. reservists through the job of concentration camp guard, which was a reserved occupation, that is, it took priority over army conscription, and into the Waffen S.S. as Totenkopf units. Often later described as brigades of ex-camp guards, they were to gain a fearful reputation, but ironically, few of their number had seen the inside of a concentration camp. To manage a fourth division Himmler cajoled thousands of policemen into volunteering. Police duty, including reservist police, was also a reserve occupation. His fifth division was the Wiking Division, and in order to create that he used men who could not be conscripted by the German Army, namely foreigners. Those Volksdeutsch who had not been liberated yet were also foreign citizens and could therefore not be conscripted. Himmler's recruiting officers were therefore sent to all nations where a Volksdeutsch community existed under foreign control. In the future Himmler's recruiters, often acting illegally almost in a spy-like atmosphere, would bring him new blood from all over Europe. Himmler's greed for an army of his own soon outstripped his desire to create an elite. This is understandable, for after all if his own standards had been applied to himself or Hitler, neither would have been allowed to enter the S.S. The need for quantity quickly overcame the desire for quality.

As for the other departments of the S.S., they were constantly at loggerheads with the army recruiters. As the conscription age was 18 to 45, most S.S. men should have been inducted into the army, navy or air force, but Himmler always pleaded that the person in question had a reserved occupation. If the army won, which was rare, the conscript immediately volunteered for the Waffen S.S. and once the quotas allowed him to transfer to the Waffen S.S. he did so, and once inside that branch of the armed forces Himmler immediately put him back into his old job. In such a way men who were theoretically members of the Waffen S.S. performed non-Waffen S.S. jobs, economics office, camp guards, Gestapo and so on. In addition, members of the Waffen S.S. who were invalided out through wounds or injuries received were given jobs in other departments of the S.S.

This meant that the vast majority of foreigners who joined the S.S. and who felt they were being allowed to participate by a grateful Himmler, were in fact simply enlisted to give the little ex-chicken farmer megalomaniac his own private army so that he could play general.

The man who scraped up Waffen S.S. recruits from the oddest of places was Gruppenfuehrer Gottlob Berger, a man who had to be a soldier and diplomat. His son-in-law, Andreas Schmidt, assisted him as the head of the Romanian Volksdeutsch community.

Chapter 10

The Soviet Union: A Prison for Nations

When the Axis armies lined up along the Soviet border they were still hundreds of miles from Russia. In order to reach Russia they would have to battle their way across Soviet-occupied Lithuania, Byelorussia, or Ukrainia. The nazi leadership looked upon these three nations as enemies, because the populations were Slavic, but the ordinary soldiers of the Axis armies looked upon them as an unknown force. They were prepared for hostility, even from harmless-looking villagers, but the reception they received came as a complete shock. The inhabitants welcomed them with open arms, flowers, food and drink. The local communists were pointed out, and in some areas the inhabitants killed the communists themselves. The Germans, Hungarians, Croatians, Slovakians, and others were glad that they had the indigenous population on their side, but wondered why this was so.

Of course the Romanians already knew. The Ukrainians, Jews, Gagaus, and Romanians of Northern Bukovina and Bessarabia had been Romanian citizens only months before, and through the stories of refugees and smuggled reports the Romanian people had learned of the true spirit of communist brotherhood. Close on the heels of the invading Red Army had come the terrifying security police, the N.K.V.D. Those uniformed terror-troopers had immediately arrested the intelligentsia, that is, all persons involved in politics, and all foremen, managers, trade union officials, civil servants, police officials, landowners, property owners, poets, writers, artists, teachers, scholars, organization leaders, religious leaders, lawyers, doctors, advisers, administrators, army officers, people who were retired from such occupations, and indeed anyone who had shown the ability to think for himself. As well as these "criminals," the N.K.V.D. arrested their wives, mothers, fathers, children, brothers and sisters and their families, and close friends. Those arrested went into the concentration camp system where few emerged alive.

As a high percentage of the intelligentsia were Jews, the Jewish community lost more people than the other ethnic groups. Jewish historians, who only count Jewish losses, estimate that 50,000 Jews were arrested by the Soviets in these two provinces in just the few short months of occupation. A total arrest list of 100,000 persons is probably not an exaggeration.

Naturally when the Romanian troops invaded these areas in late June 1941, there was jubilation among the survivors, even among the Gagaus, Ukrainians, and Jews, who had never been particularly fond of Romanians.

When Finland had lost a province to the Soviets in March 1940, ninety percent of the population had fled into unoccupied Finland. Those who remained behind did so because they had communist or Russian connections or because they naively assumed they could work within the Soviet system. It was the Finns of Eastern Karelia who paid the price for the excellent resistance put up by the Finnish forces, and these Finns had been Soviet citizens during the conflict, not Finnish citizens. In 1918 they had opted to remain under a Russian administration primarily because of religion. Although the Russian government had been communist, there were revolutionary Russian governments around at that time and the victory of the communist government was by no means certain. These Finns were of the Orthodox Catholic faith, unlike the Finns of Finland who were Lutherans.

When the bulk of the population of the newly annexed territory eluded the Soviet oppressors, the N.K.V.D. took out their vengeance upon the Eastern Karelian Finns, their own citizens. Thousands of innocent Karelians suffered for imaginary crimes. Even local communists were arrested. The Finns, whom the Finnish army encountered, welcomed the invaders as liberators.

The Lithuanians cheered as German aircraft shot up barracks, military installations, Red Army trucks, and Red Navy ships. Their experience of the Soviets went back to 1918.

A provisional Lithuanian government had been established on 16 February 1918, declaring the nation of 2.5 million to be no longer part of the Tsarist Russian Empire, but a sovereign state. However, only weeks later, the area had been overrun by a German army. The Germans discussed Lithuanian autonomy during their short stay, but these talks were overtaken as on 11 November Germany surrendered to the Allies. The Lithuanians proclaimed their independence again a few days later.

Meanwhile in Vilnius, the traditional capital of Lithuania, a group of Lithuanian and Byelorussian communists proclaimed a new communist provisional government for the two nations led by Vincas Mickevicius-Kapsukas. The non-communist government gained overwhelming support from the Lithuanian people, although the minorities, ethnic Russians, descendants of mid-nineteenth-century colonists, and Volksdeutsch, descendants of colonists going back eight-and-a-half centuries, and the unassimilated Jews, descendants of colonists going back several centuries, did not favor a Lithuanian nationalist or a communist regime.

The communist government had few supporters and in order to survive asked for Russian communist assistance. The entrance of the Red Army sparked off war as the Lithuanians, armed by the still present, but impotent German Army, resisted the invasion. Some of the German soldiers were demobilized with their uniforms and equipment so that they could fight against the communists in a Freikorps.

On 21 April 1919, a Polish army captured Vilnius and kicked the communists back to Daugavpils (Dunaburg). After a Red Army offensive almost captured Warsaw, the Poles counterattacked in the summer of 1920 and retook Vilnius.

The Lithuanians had managed to fight off the Reds further to the north and by the end of 1920 they longed for only two things, to be left alone in peace and to have their capital city returned. However, despite feverish diplomacy on the part of the Lithuanian government and after some light border incidents that took the lives of Poles and Lithuanians, the Poles refused to return the city and its Lithuanian population, claiming that as it had a Polish minority it was part of Poland.

From this time on Lithuanian schoolchildren would grow up chanting in school every day that they would not rest until Vilnius was returned.

The Russians and the Poles had proven to be the enemies of the Lithuanian people, and the Germans had proven to be friends. The individual acts of Lithuanian Volksdeutsch and the crimes of drunken Freikorps were overlooked. In 1923 the Lithuanians invaded the area of Memel, a German city which was under international control, and even this did not damage German-Lithuanian relations.

However, after this the Lithuanian government opened negotiations with the Soviets and introduced some socialism. This was too much for the nationalists, who had become paranoid due to Soviet excesses. In December 1926, a military dictatorship under Augustinus Waldemaras took control. He made certain that the Soviet Union realized that Lithuania would remain independent.

Trade with Germany was stepped up and good relations were established with Latvia and Estonia. After fighting off an attempted coup in September 1927, the regime handed power to Juozas Tubelis in September 1929. Tubelis guided the nation through the bad times of the World Depression, not letting left-wing agitation rock the boat.

Though Memel was autonomous, the Volksdeutsch were not happy with the Lithuanian government, and in February 1934 the two leading Volksdeutsch political parties were banned. The disabled Volksdeutsch plotted with disaffected Lithuanians and on 7 June they launched a coup. It failed and one of those arrested was Waldemaras.

To the people of the Western Democracies Lithuania appeared to be an unstable nation, but they did not realize that it is starvation, disease, invasion, terror, and unemployment that affect the common man, not palace squabbling. The Lithuanians considered themselves to be relatively free and well off.

Tubelis' days were numbered as soon as he agreed to negotiate with Poland over the Vilnius question, as his supporters knew it was at Poland's insistence, and in any case they felt the issue was not negotiable. Then following nazi stormtrooper demonstrations and noisy rallies in Memel the German Navy invaded on 23 March 1939. Hitler himself witnessed the peaceful takeover. Tubelis had offered no resistance, and Memel once again became German.

Tubelis was ousted by his one-time supporters and the government was placed in the hands of General Jonas Cernius. He was soon faced with a serious problem. When Germany and the Soviet Union invaded Poland in September 1939, tens of thousands of Polish refugees fled over the border into Lithuania. The problem was that this might cause the old Polish-Lithuanian antagonism to explode into rioting. Cernius made certain that the refugees were welcomed and given at least some aid. Many Poles later spoke of the good treatment they received at the hands of the ordinary Lithuanian people.

But the Soviets were now on the warpath again. On 8 October the Soviet government demanded permission to set up military bases inside Lithuania. As the manpower of the Red Army outnumbered Lithuania's citizens, Cernius knew he could not refuse. Two days later, 50,000 Soviet personnel drove across the border to find a peaceful, though sullen welcome.

The Lithuanians were surprised to see how poorly equipped the Soviet troops were. The wives of the Soviet officers, who soon followed the "guest" army, dressed more like refugees than conquerors. For their part, the Russians were astonished at the high standard of living of Lithuanian factory workers.

Finland's heroic resistance during the winter of 1939-40 caused great joy in Lithuania, but when the Finns were forced to acknowledge defeat there were those Lithuanians who said that the Finns would have been better to have given in to the Soviets as they had done, for at least the Lithuanians had preserved the lives of their young men. This was seen to be false, for in June 1940 they too were given a Finnish choice. As the French were surrendering Paris without a fight and the British were drying out their uniforms following defeat at Dunkirk, Stalin mobilized his garrison in Lithuania and sent an ultimatum to the government of President M. Smetona and Prime Minister Merkys demanding he be given the right to choose a new government for Lithuania.

The Lithuanian cabinet studied intensely, but they knew they had no choice as the Soviet troops were already in the country and there would be no help from outside. Germany was busy and in any case was currently professing friendship with the Soviet Union. Smetona was less trusting than his colleagues and he at once fled to Germany.

On 16 June Lithuania began to die as thousands more Soviet troops entered the nation and were this time followed by the N.K.V.D. The towns, factories, streets, and homes of the proud Lithuanians were invaded. Within days the Soviets had one soldier in the country for every nine Lithuanian citizens. The new boss was Commissar Vladimir Dekanozov, a crony of Stalin's from Georgia, and at once he unleashed his security police. Their targets were the intelligentsia. The lists contained the names of those who could think without prompting, and many people were arrested who never knew why. If a member of a family did not come home at the end of the day on time the other members worried. Had he or she been picked up on a trumped-up charge?

A few Lithuanian communists had survived Stalin's purges and together with a host of Russian officials they now came home. Within a few days they organized a spontaneous demonstration in favor of Russian intervention. Only foreign journalists who were half-communist were fooled.

Then on the night of 11 July the N.K.V.D. went to work making mass arrests. Sometimes whole neighborhoods were arrested. Three days later the Soviets held elections, but nationalists who had gone underground urged the people not to vote, for they would certainly be deliberately miscounted as pro-Soviet. In fact so few people turned up at the polling stations that the authorities held them open for another day, and then forcefully rounded up thousands of voters. Accordingly about 16 to 18% of the people voted, according to Lithuanian nationalists, but Dekanozov stated that 99.19% of the people had voted in favor of integration into the Soviet Union. In truth he had been hard put to find the seventy-nine communist party candidates, let alone anyone to vote for them.

Once formal entrance into the Soviet Union came on 5 August, the economic life of the nation became harsh. All the consumer goods had long since disappeared into the homes of the communist elite, and only shoddy Russian goods replaced them. Foreign trade continued, but the people no longer saw the benefit of this. Food lines appeared quickly and many families suffered from too little food. The winter was more terrible this year, but only because the people were less equipped to protect themselves against it, and the warmth of the next spring brought no smiles or hopes.

Stalin knew something that the man in the street did not. He suspected that Germany was mobilizing against him. He had been warned often enough. So, just in case this was true, he launched a new wave of terror. The N.K.V.D. began their inhuman work on 14 June, but could not finish the job as eight days later German bombs began to fall.

The tiny nation had been held in abject terror of their lives and the lives of their children, and they were quite convinced that tens of thousands of their compatriots had disappeared into the bottomless pit of the Soviet concentration camp system. The nationalists claim that no less than 34,260 men, women, and children disappeared in the last ten days of the Soviet occupation, making a total of arrested persons of approximately 60,000. Many of the kidnapped were skilled factory workers whom the Soviets decided they would need in Russia. When the Germans invaded, it seemed to the people that liberation was finally at hand. The nightmare was over, and they had awoken to a beautiful, sunny spring morning.

The Ukrainians had never been as totally oppressed by the nobility as had the Russians, so there were plenty of nationalist organizations in the nation at the time of the collapse of Tsarist power. In March 1917, the state of Ukraine was founded by the establishment of an autonomous provisional government, despite the western half of the nation being under enemy, that is, German and Austrian occupation.

On 25 December 1917, following the creation of a Russian communist government, Ukrainian communists established a provisional government in Kiev, but the two Ukrainian governments bickered with each other and there was even some street fighting. All of this came to an end in March when the Germans invaded and occupied the entire nation. The communists fled to Russia and the nationalists at first went underground. However, the German military soon began negotiations about establishing an autonomous Ukraine government.

The Germans had come here for the harvest, for due to the British naval blockade the German people were nearing starvation. Ukraine is flat and tepid enough that a very prolific grain is grown here. The Ukraine has been described as Europe's breadbasket. Every conqueror who had come here had done so for the harvest. The nation's vast mineral resources were a prize too, but most of that potential had yet to be realized in 1918. The coastal areas were warm enough for ports and holiday resorts.

On 11 November 1918, Germany surrendered to the Allies, and the Ukrainian nationalists now began organizing another provisional government. The people paraded in the streets of the cities to express their political ideas. As the people are devout Orthodox Catholic they did not intend to invite the communists back. They declared a sovereign state. Within the Austrian province of Galicia the Ukrainians are Eastern Catholic, but they too acknowledged the new national government. Ukrainians who had served in the Austrian and Tsarist Russian armies now came home to join the Ukraine National Army, bringing their weapons and equipment with them.

Under the leadership of Simon Petliura, an extreme nationalist and anti-Semite, the more fanatic nationalists celebrated their freedom by butchering the Jews. This notorious pogrom claimed thousands of lives. The fact that many of the communists were Jews did not endear the Jewish community to the hearts of the nationalists.

The communists who survived set up their own provisional government in Kursk and at once invited the Red Army in to protect them. When the invaders crossed the border the Ukrainians resisted and the result was the War of Ukrainian Independence. It lasted for two years, brought much bloodshed and mass starvation. Ravaged by war, Europe's breadbasket could no longer feed the thirty million Ukrainians. In Galicia the Ukrainians had to fight off a Polish invasion and in Ruthenia (Trans-Carpathian Ukraine) the Ukrainians were defeated by a Czechoslovakian army.

By April 1920, as most of his country was now under communist occupation, Simon Petliura made one last gamble to try to save something. He made peace with the Poles and allied with them against a Red Army that was invading Poland. If victorious, the Poles promised that Galicia would become an autonomous province of the Polish Empire.

Not only did the Poles and Ukrainians defeat the Red Army, but they drove it back across the border and thus saved Europe from a great peril. The only aid they had received had been some advisers from France.*

Now came the great betrayal. Galicia became a Polish province, but the Ukrainians were never granted the freedoms they had expected. After an international conference the Curzon Line was established, which gave Central and Eastern Ukraine to the new Russian communist state, the Soviet Union, Galicia to Poland, Ruthenia to Czechoslovakia, and Northern Bukovina and Bessarabia to Romania. What is more the borders were badly drawn.

At least the Western Ukrainians did not have to live under communist rule. In the Soviet-occupied zone life was terrible. The nationalists were naturally still active, and the Union for the Liberation of the Ukraine of Professor Serhiy Yefremov and the Ukrainian Youth Organization of Mykola Pavlushkov were both legal organizations that controlled illegal underground movements. Using the legal organizations as bait, the Soviet security police arrested many suspected revolutionaries. The midnight knock on the door was a constant fear for all of the Ukrainian intellectuals. Only in 1930 did the N.K.V.D. tire of the game and arrest the members of the legal organizations too.

Another source of resistance was the Orthodox Church, but even the pious bearded monks and priests were not immune from the Soviet terror. It is claimed, and may be quite true, that 20,000 clergymen were arrested and sent to the concentration camps. It is known that one of them was the leader of the faith, Vasyl Lypkivsky, the Metropolitan of all Ukraine.

The worst terror was launched against the kulaks. These were farmers who by one method or another had managed to gain ownership of a small plot of land to be used for family subsistence. In times of good seasons the farmers could sell their excess at the local village markets. This free enterprise system was judged by the communists to be a deadly enemy, and in 1928 with the introduction of Stalin's first Five Year Economic Plan these private farms were taken over by force and the homes of the kulaks were bulldozed. The land was incorporated into state collective farms. From this moment on the kulaks were forced to seek employment at these farms, but there were never enough jobs. If relatives and friends could not be found to take in a kulak's family they

*One of them was Charles de Gaulle.

began to die from starvation. In order that the ordinary people would not feel sorry for these peasants, the communists constantly referred to them as kulaks, which in fact was a derogatory term normally used to describe a shyster.

To the communists any peasant who owned land was a kulak, and anyone who complained about the destruction of his home, the ending of his livelihood, and the malnutrition of his children was a counterrevolutionary who had to be incarcerated in a concentration camp to protect the state. By 1932 over half a million so-called kulaks had been arrested. By this time though only a small percentage of peasant plots had been collectivized, and Stalin needed the grain production of the Ukraine to sell to foreign countries in return for industrial equipment. What the Ukrainians would eat if their grain was taken from them was of no concern to him. Indeed their starvation would benefit the communists, for there was no room for anyone who had benefited from a free enterprise system.

As the job was immense, the N.K.V.D. was expanded and the Red Army was brought in, and the enforced collectivization of all agricultural land really began in earnest. All opposition was ruthlessly crushed.

Within weeks thousands of peasants, men, women, children, roamed the country lanes, foodless, homeless, and hopeless. Armed guards were placed on the unharvested fields and on the grain warehouses so that any children who sneaked in to grab a handful of heads of wheat to stuff into their starving mouths could be shot dead on the spot and their bodies displayed as a lesson to others. Anyone who spoke out against this genocide, for that is exactly what it was, was immediately arrested.

Foreign journalists were denied access to the Ukraine, but a few managed to infiltrate through the checkpoints. One was a respected reporter, the Briton Malcolm Muggeridge. Once he reported the truth he was deported. Foreign communists and fellow travelers denied that there was a famine, and when food parcels were sent to the Soviet Union by caring foreigners the Soviets sent them back stating that they were not needed. If the Stalin administration had admitted the existence of the famine then soon the cause of it would be known. The cause was Stalin.

The winter was very bad this year for no one had the health to resist the intense cold, not even those in employment. It had been the habit of the collective farms to pay their employees partly in food, but when Stalin demanded all the food for his industrial schemes this was discontinued. Money was no good if there was no food to buy. Yet in some areas due to poor transportation or bad administration mounds of food rotted before it could be sent to the ports and exported. Armed sentries guarded these heaps while within view women and children lay on the ground writhing in agony. Wherever soldiers and communist officials were barracksed guards had to be placed on the garbage cans outside the adequately supplied food canteens to prevent dying peasants from scraping the inside of the can for a mouthful of food.

There was an active resistance, but those angry enough to fight back were too weak and those who had not yet starved dared not risk the lives of their families. Few peasants could find arms in any case. The most successful type of resistance was sabotage of the transportation system that was taking the food to the ports and sabotage of the farm machinery used on the state farms.

By the summer of 1933, the Russians were learning of the truth and when the N.K.V.D. reported that the Russians were trying to smuggle food into the Ukraine, Stalin panicked. The truth was out and he needed a scapegoat.

He blamed the famine on the mismanagement of the Ukrainian communists and ordered the N.K.V.D. to purge the whole party apparatus. Thousands of loyal communist officials who had massacred their own people on Stalin's orders were now arrested and imprisoned alongside their kulak victims.

Forced enclosure of land in Britain had caused migrations, malnutrition, and disease, but it had been implemented over a period of half a century in the eighteenth century, a time not known for its humanitarianism. Modern man professes that he has learned a few things in the two hundred years since then, but the communists enforced collectivization over a period of two years, while at the same time preaching to the world "land for the peasant" and "bread for the worker."

Conservative historians believe that collectivization caused the death of three million Ukrainians, and the radical Ukrainian nationalists claim that the figure was nearer eight-and-a-half million. The number of people sent to concentration camps was 650,000, of which 27,000 were communist officials.

Years later, Stalin informed Churchill that enforced collectivization had caused the deaths of ten million. Most of these were Ukrainians, but some Russians were also starved out.

After 1933, no decent Ukrainian could look upon the communists with anything but revulsion. The Ukrainian emigres outside the Soviet Union tried to make the world aware of what was happening, but no one took the time to listen. In Rotterdam the leader of the emigres, E. Konowalets, was murdered by N.K.V.D. agents to remind the emigres that no one was safe from Stalinist vengeance.

In September 1939, the Ukrainians of Eastern Galicia were treated to communist brotherly love when the Red Army invaded. By this move Stalin gained control over the destinies of 4.5 million Ukrainians. In addition, about 30,000 Ukrainians fled from Western Galicia into Soviet-controlled territory to escape the nazis. Just in case one of them might have been a German agent, the N.K.V.D. arrested them all. Indeed, the treatment of anti-nazi refugees by the Soviets was so bad that thousands of Jews actually returned to nazi-occupied Poland rather than live under the Soviet system!

It goes without saying that the Galician intelligentsia was erased from the face of the earth. Of the 1.5 million Polish citizens arrested by the N.K.V.D. or forcibly conscripted into the Red Army, about a quarter of a million were dead within two years.

Is it any wonder, then, that in June 1941, only twenty years since the destruction of their state, only eight years after the genocidal famine, only sixteen months after the slaughter of Ukrainian troops of the Red Army in the frozen forests of Finland, and only days since the N.K.V.D. had been arresting people on only hints of suspicion, the Ukrainians began to cheer as the Axis armies began to liberate them?

The nations that the Germans would have to cross in order to reach Mother Russia were potential recruiting grounds, if they could have only realized it, but the leaders of the Axis states wore ethnic blinkers and not until the race was almost over would they realize that they had been running in the wrong direction.

The Soviet Union contained more than just the above nationalities. Lenin had bragged when he created the Soviet Union that his empire was a prison for nations, and this was no exaggeration. Some ethnic groups were tribal and though entitled to freedom and prosperity like anyone else they were not yet ready for sovereign status, but others were deserving of immediate sovereignty to be respected as equals by any European or American state.

Two were Estonia and Latvia, whose history was similar to that of Lithuania. During the twilight of Russian history between the fall of the Tsar and the rise of communism, reasonably fair elections were held in certain areas. In Estonia the communists gained 35% of the vote. This reflected the romantic period when communism seemed to be humane, and also the fact that Narva, a border city, which had the largest communist vote was in the hands of Red Guards and had an ethnic Russian suburb. When the news of the Bolshevik (communist) revolt in the Russian capital reached their ears, the Estonian communists proclaimed a provisional government. Their power base was a mob of sailors and soldiers of the Russian Army and Navy, some of whom were Estonians. The German invasion put an end to this in March 1918.

After Germany's surrender the Estonian nationalists proclaimed a provisional non-communist government, taking advantage that the Red Guards were no longer in the nation. However, on 29 November the Red Army returned. Narva was quickly captured and another communist provisional government was proclaimed. Six weeks later, the Reds were in retreat, chased by the Estonian National Army, German Freikorps, Russian anti-communists (Whites), and Finnish soldiers. The fighting was often more noisy than deadly.

The war continued, but the Reds were unable to reinvade. The British Navy prevented the communists from making an amphibious outflanking move. The Estonians refused to invade Russia, maintaining that they had no claims on Russian territory, but in October 1919 when a Russian White army with British air and sea support advanced against Petrograd (Leningrad) the Estonians joined in. Only the last-minute intervention of 11,000 sailors of the Red Navy fighting as infantry saved the city for communism. Defeated and riddled with typhus the Estonians went home. By the end of the year a peace was worked out.

After so long without a political voice, it was only natural that every Estonian was impatient for reforms. A series of governments, twenty by 1934, pleased only one faction at a time, bringing instability to what was otherwise a normal European nation. Minor unsuccessful revolts created additional difficulties.

In October 1933 the government adopted a rightist constitution, which brought forth cheers from the League of Soldiers of the War of Independence, a right-wing anti-communist organization, but denunciation from the socialists. Tensions rose and in March 1934 Konstantin Päts and General Laidoner seized power. The leadership of the league was crushed, over five hundred people being arrested. Within days, Päts signed a nonaggression pact with the Soviet Union.

Prosperity settled over the land for five years until the Soviets brought it to a close, showing that their treaties were useless bits of paper. On 24 September 1939 the Soviets demanded the right to station their troops in Estonia. With a population of only 1.13 million compared to the Soviet Union's 190 million, Päts knew he could hardly expect his people to resist. By November, 25,000 Soviet personnel were stationed in the nation.

This trespass angered the entire population, and when the Soviets used Estonian airfields from which to bomb Finland the Estonian people became extremely angry. Finland had aided the Estonians to repel the Red Army in 1918 and this was not forgotten. Three thousand young Estonian males crept out of the country by boat to join the Finnish Army. The winter brought false hopes as each day the Finns miraculously held out, but with the Finnish defeat in March the time of hope was over. The people felt that if the Germans would not aid the Finns when they were fighting they would not aid the Estonians who were not fighting.

The Soviet ultimatum which came on 16 June 1940 had been expected. The previous day, the Red Air Force had shot down an Estonian passenger liner. Of course the small nation could not fight back unaided. On the 17th the Soviets occupied the country, and within hours the N.K.V.D. were setting up their offices. Within days their pick-up squads were arresting the intelligentsia, one of the first men on their list being Päts. It is believed by reliable sources that he survived for sixteen terrifying years in a concentration camp before succumbing to the beatings, disgusting food, lack of adequate shelter, and excessively hard labor. He was not alone. Thousands of Estonians, 99.9% totally innocent, including newborn babies, were thrown into the Soviet penal system or murdered outright. Andrei Zhdanov, an N.K.V.D. specialist, ruled the nation as his own personal fiefdom more cruelly than any medieval tyrant.

After a "spontaneous" uprising of the "people," the "workers" invited the Soviets to take control on the 21st. That this happened four days after the Soviets had already taken control, did not seem to faze Stalin and his propagandists. Once a puppet administration had been set up, the N.K.V.D. cracked down even harder. The following twelve months were more terrible than anything written in the history books. One adult in ten was kidnapped off the street or dragged out of bed by the hated security police. Relatives lucky enough not to have been picked up as well usually received no information from the N.K.V.D. office when they inquired of their loved ones' whereabouts.

On 14 June 1941, due to Stalin's fear that the Estonians might aid the Germans if it came to war, the N.K.V.D. arrested hundreds more, and continued their hunt for counterrevolutionaries for the next week, eventually netting about 10,000 innocents.

Suddenly on 22 June hope arrived in the form of German bombers which struck at the Soviet military installations in the country. Unfortunately it was already too late for 62,000 Estonians.

Latvia was a nation of not quite two million people, with a Volksdeutsch minority. Most of the latter were tradesmen and farmers, but some were wealthy nobles. The aristocratic Germans pined for the days of feudal lords and manorial fiefs. Unlike Memel which was really part of Prussia, the Volksdeutsch areas of Latvia were cut off from Germany, and thus any dream of liberation by German troops would of necessity mean an occupation of thousands of Latvians as well. For this reason the Latvians were against the idea.

All of this was just talk while both Latvian and Volksdeutsch (Baltdeutsch) lived under Tsarist Russian rule, but when the empire collapsed in February 1917 both saw their chance. The Latvians negotiated for independence and the Volksdeutsch contacted the German Army.

The Germans invaded in March 1918 and for a few brief months the aristocrats among the Germans lorded it over their compatriots and the Latvians. Then Germany's surrender brought a drastic change in the life of the small nation.

Ignoring the German Army, the Latvians declared independence and neutrality. The Volksdeutsch petitioned the German garrison commander, but his hands were tied by the new revolutionary regime in Berlin. The Volksdeutsch really began to panic when in dead of winter the Red Army invaded. The Latvians also began to argue among themselves. Fearing that civil war would riddle the anti-communist defense full of holes, the British used warships to shell one political faction in the city of Riga. Even then the other Latvians and the Volksdeutsch failed to defend the city and the Reds were victorious.

Fortunately in late January 1919, the Red Army had to retreat as it was threatened by an advance by Estonians on its right flank and by Poles on its left flank. On 9 February, the British shelled the communists in Ventspils (Windau). When a French Navy flotilla entered Liepaja harbor (Libau) the Red Army withdrew completely.

Now the British, who had been inspiring their soldiers for four years with stories of German brutality, ordered the German Army to intervene and trounce the communists once and for all. Eagerly the German officers obeyed.

General von der Goltz ordered a full offensive on 5 March. Together with the Latvians they inflicted heavy casualties.

However, in early April von der Goltz began to play politics, allowing some of his men to be demobilized with their weapons so that they could join the Freikorps, which was not under Allied command. He also equipped the Volksdeutsch. On 16 April the Volksdeutsch and the Freikorps tried to take the nation. President Ullmanis had to hide in the British mission. However, Andreus Niedras, the Volksdeutsch leader, and his Landeswehr (Land Defense) allied with General J. Balodis' Latvian troops and attacked the Red Army, which was trying to regain the nation again. The German Army did not take part in this battle. By June the Red Army had fled the nation, forever.

By September the citizens of Latvia felt safe enough to begin fighting among themselves again. When orders came from Berlin for the German Army to go home, the Volksdeutsch knew there was no time to lose. On 8 October the Landeswehr and the Freikorps attacked the Latvian garrison of Riga, and after three days was forced to withdraw due to tough opposition. On the 15th the British and French warships in the harbor decided the issue by shelling the Landeswehr and Freikorps until they retreated. A British cruiser was damaged by shore batteries.

The Latvians then counterattacked with more British aid, and then struck Russia in November but gained nothing. Partially harassed by the Lithuanians, the Freikorps and many Landeswehr managed to reach Memel and safety.

By January 1920 the Landeswehr had been purged of its more fanatic Volksdeutsch nationalists and under the command of a British officer, Harold Alexander, fought alongside the Latvians in another small offensive against the Red Army on the Russian border. Latvia had proven to be more trouble than she was worth and the communists soon agreed to a peace.

As was the case with Estonia, men unaccustomed to ruling themselves wasted political energy in social experimentation. In March 1932, the Latvian government refused to recognize the German language for the Volksdeutsch areas and in February 1934 smashed the two right-wing Volksdeutsch political parties. The Latvian right wing then got the impression that they would be next, so Prime Minister Karlis Ulmanis and General J. Balodis, drawing support from a rightist paramilitary force called the Latvian Home Guard, dissolved the Assembly, which had been the cause of friction, and banned all political parties.

Of course, this was not democracy, but it did bring stability to the nation at little cost. The militant left and the militant right were both rendered harmless.

Having brow-beaten the Estonians, the Soviets also forced the Latvian government to accept Soviet bases on 5 October 1939. The Latvian surprise at the lack of material goods possessed by the Red Army officers did not lessen their fear any, and that fear was shown to be justified in June 1940. On the 16th, as the Soviets were sending an ultimatum to the Estonian government and as they were already invading Lithuania, Soviet troops attacked a Latvian border settlement, killing two men, two women, and a child, and kidnapping others. The following day Stalin issued his ultimatum, demanding the right to restructure the Latvian government. Twenty-four hours later the Red Army left its bases and occupied the important buildings and set up machine guns on the street corners. Commissar Andrei Vyshinsky organized a demonstration of local communists and several hundred communists imported for the occasion, and then set about dismantling the apparatus of the nation. His N.K.V.D. had a field day. According to figures learned by Tolstoy, within the few months of the occupation 34,250 people disappeared off the streets, of which the security police actually tortured to death 1,217 adult males, 109 adult females, and 29 children of which 4 were under six years of age. The latter were probably tortured in order to force their parents to confess real or imagined crimes.

The winter was terrible for those poor souls who were arrested and transported by freight trains across the frozen wastes of Russia and Siberia to the concentration and slave labor camps. In some cases trains arrived after weeks of travel to divulge nothing but corpses from the locked cattle cars. Whole families were found frozen to death; on occasion the guards were also.

Beginning on 14 June, Stalin's fear brought a major terror to all the three Baltic states. Tolstoy gives figures of 5,371 adult males, 6,257 adult females, and 3,065 children being arrested in Latvia by the N.K.V.D. in the last two weeks of their occupation. This very probably brought the total of arrested persons, native Latvians, Jews, and Volksdeutsch, to 60,000.

It is possible that Lithuania, Estonia, and Latvia might have been able to survive if they had all resisted together in September 1939, but this opinion comes with the hindsight of how terrible the Soviet occupation was going to be. As well, it must be realized that the Soviets tackled only one nation at a time, though within the space of a few days, only moving on to further aggression when a previous effort seemed to have paid off. The Soviets underestimated not only the fortitude of the Finnish people, but their military prowess, but two reasons for the excellence of the Finnish defense were that she could trade space for time and her landscape was primitive and inhospitable in winter. The capital cities of all three Baltic States were less than 140 miles from the Soviet Border and their road system was good, in comparison to Central and Northern Finland. In addition, the Finns had a unified control. The Baltic States had three governments and three general staffs.

The little-remembered nation of Byelorussia contained 7 million people in the early 20th century, and had its own identity, language, and traditions, centered around the cultural areas of Minsk, Mogilev, Vitebsk, and Gomel. The nation, which is the size of England, had been treated like a floormat by the Lithuanians, Poles, and Russians for centuries and the period of World War One and the Russian Civil War was no exception.

The Byelorussians have never expressed their nationalism as fiercely as many others and did not put up too much opposition to the settlement that eventually put a quarter of the nation under Polish control, where they had some freedom and partial autonomy, and the rest under the thumb of the Soviets, where they suffered like everyone else living in that oppressive state.

The Soviet system was also the Russian system, and the culture of the Byelorussians was deliberately submerged. Russians look upon Byelorussians as not deserving of any privileged status and certainly not as an ethnic nation in their own right. Then in September 1939, the Polish-controlled part was invaded, and the Byelorussian culture that had thrived here was also submerged. Thousands of people were arrested as in other areas occupied by the Red Army and the N.K.V.D. The cities were soon crowded by forced labor brought from the countryside to work in the factories and the young men were conscripted into the Red Army. Those who had been captured while members of the Polish Army were allowed to join the Red Army, but many preferred captivity.

The extent of Soviet denationalism is evident if one asks the man in the street in the western world to identify the locality of Georgia. He will invariably locate it in the Southern U.S.A. There is another Georgia, though, a proud nation with its own culture, language, and tradition, which has been submerged in the Soviet pot.

With an approximate area of 25,000 square miles, depending on who draws the border, it is the size of Belgium and the Netherlands together, and in 1939 it had a population of 2.1 million, slightly less than that of Norway. It is an ancient nation, and during the twelfth century it created an empire under Queen Tamara.

In November 1917, various Bolsheviks (communists) and Mensheviks (socialists) created a Trans-Caucasus Commissariat in order to govern several nations, but the proud Georgians would have none of this. Negotiating with the local Mensheviks, the Nationalists created an independent, sovereign, socialist state within Georgia, with its capital at the city of Tblisi. If the Georgians had accepted a communist government they would still have been conquered by the Red Army steamroller, and in fact they were a prime target because the communists hated the socialists as much as anybody. Still the country survived for three years, while the Red Army was busy crushing Russian anti-communist opposition.

On 16 February 1921, a tiny band of Georgian communists slipped over the border into Georgia and at the village of Shulaveni proclaimed a new communist government for Georgia. They then asked the Red Army for aid to repel counterrevolutionary elements. As the Red Army Eleventh and Thirteenth Armies just happened to be nearby, they invaded at once. The Georgian Army resisted, but was quickly defeated and forced to abandon the capital. The Georgians, troops and civilians, fled to the port of Batum, begging for foreign aid, but the Western Allies had had their fill of the effects of the Bolshevik

Revolution and no one answered. On 18 March the Red Army captured Batum, and after a few more skirmishes the Georgians surrendered on 21 May 1921. A year later, the nation was formally annexed by the Soviet Union.

Forcible collectivization of peasant land caused malnutrition and murder, similar to that seen in Ukraine, but Georgia is partly mountainous and suited to guerrilla warfare, therefore the Georgians were able to resist to some extent. As starvation ravaged the population, the people saw it as a double indignity, for Stalin himself was a Georgian. Georgian emigres in the West tried to enlighten the governments as to what was going on, but the West had its own problems.

To the south of Georgia is Armenia, an ancient land with a great historic past. In the second century B.C., the Armenians were a powerful ally of Rome. Like most nations that are situated at a crossroads, Armenia has been devoured many times, most recently by Russia, Turkey, and Iran. With an area as big as Denmark it had the size and population to become an independent state in 1917. Neither a long oppression nor the genocidal policy of the Turks had daunted the Armenians. In February 1915, Sultan Abdul Hamid of Turkey took the opportunity of the world war currently raging to get rid of his 1.8 million Armenians, not just the Armenian Catholics, but the Roman Catholic and Protestant Armenians too. Disarming all Armenians in his army he then ordered that the people be rounded up and marched into the deserts and the mountains. Along the way Turkish villagers and Kurds and Circassians robbed, murdered, and raped the helpless refugees. The purpose of the marches was officially relocation, but in reality it was a cover-up for the extermination of the Armenians. Only women could survive, and then only if they adopted the Moslem faith and took a Moslem husband. By 1917 only one million of the Armenians were left and they had survived only by escaping into the Russian Empire to stay with their compatriots over the border. When the Tsarist government collapsed it seemed to the Armenians that suddenly they stood a chance of establishing their independence again. The possibility looked even more hopeful when the Turks were defeated by the Allies in October 1918.

The nation was free and the state created. In August 1920, by the Treaty of Sevres, Armenia was internationally recognized as an independent nation.

However, this peace and prosperity was not to last. By the end of the year the southern borders were being raided by warlike Iranians and on the western border a Turkish army had invaded. Then in November the Red Army appeared on the northern border. Traveling with the Reds were a few political commissars who had orders to establish a communist government for Armenia. The Armenians were devoutly Christian and hated the idea of being controlled by an atheistic regime, but as the alternative seemed to be genocide at the hands of the Turks there seemed to be little alternative. The Dashnaks, government supporters, negotiated with the commissars and within days a coalition government of Dashnaks and communists was formed. The Red Army occupied a territory containing 1.3 million Armenians and the Turks were offered a smaller area, where the Armenians were oppressed but not murdered. Ironically as time went on Turkish atrocities waned and communist atrocities waxed. Within a year the Dashnaks were forced to hand over complete control to the communists and the nation soon entered the Soviet Union. The Dashnaks and their families were arrested and taken away, never to be seen again. Armenia was lost to history.

Azerbaijan is a wondrous nation with flat deserts, high rocky mountains, and a beautiful coastline. With the area of Portugal and 2.5 million people it links Europe with the Middle East. When the Russian Empire collapsed, the Azerbaijanis saw no reason for tears. They had never really accepted Russian rule, and their compatriots to the south had never accepted Iranian rule. Within Iran an Iranian socialist army under Mirza Kuchik Khan had been battling the Iranian Army for a year and the Azerbaijanis had been aiding him, hoping to win some autonomy out of the contest. By 1918 British troops were aiding the Iranian Army.

In April 1920 within the new sovereign state of Azerbaijan, on land once claimed by the Tsar, all was quite peaceful until a mob of communists seized several buildings in the capital, Baku. It just so happened that a Red Army was on the border and it at once invaded the country. The small Azerbaijan Army was quickly overcome. A month later, the Red Army made an amphibious landing at Rasht to steal Southern Azerbaijan from Iran. When Khan allied with the communists the Azerbaijanis here too were overrun.

Most Azerbaijanis looked upon the return of the Russians as a return of Tsarist rule, but they soon found out that this new type of Russian was a world apart from the Christian Tsarists.

The Russians made a treaty with the Iranians in February 1921, and then in June ignored the treaty and invaded Iran. Assisted by Khan the Red Army marched on Tehran. However, the spearhead of the column was defeated by Iranian Cossacks and by September the Reds had retreated north of Ardabil. A new treaty left some Azerbaijanis under Iranian rule.

Many other nations were freed from Tsarist Russian rule only to be reoccupied by communist Russians. If half a dozen communists or criminal sycophants could be found of a particular nationality, then this was enough to establish a provisional government which would then invite the Red Army into the country to "keep order."

Khiva had been a kingdom for centuries and had become immensely wealthy during the Middle Ages as it sat astride the great caravan trade routes. When the Tsar was overthrown the Khan of Khiva was no longer under restraints. Once again he was the complete lord of several ethnic nations, the Karakalpaks, Tadzhiks, Uzbeks, and Turkmen. However, the Russian communists were bent on conquering the world and so it was only a matter of time before the Red Army reached the border. After a small raiding party captured the palace the Red Army moved in and swiftly defeated the Khanate troops. However, it took five months before all opposition was crushed. The communists created a federalized state, with each of the ethnic groups having autonomy, but as all political leaders were communists, most of them Russian, and as they all took orders from Moscow, this was seen for the sham that it was. The communists were embarrassed when Turkey and Afghanistan recognized the state, now called Khorezm, as sovereign, but eventually in October 1924 the state was formally entered into the Union of Socialist Republics, without a whimper from the outside world.

When Tsarist power collapsed the Emir of Bukhara continued to rule over his Uzbek people, but now as a sovereign lord. When the news came of the Bolshevik revolution in November 1917, the communists among the Russian immigrants in the land declared themselves to be the Young Bukhara Party. The Emir's spies watched these potential revolutionaries, but not closely enough. In March 1919 the communists allied with the bourgeoisie party of Faizulla Khodzhaev and revolted, asking for the Red Army to assist. However, this time the Red Army was defeated by the Emir's forces, and the 200 communists in the country were forced to flee with the retreating Reds.

Only after Khiva was overrun did the communists feel strong enough to try again. This time, August 1920, the Red Army was successful and the Emir fled to Afghanistan. Naturally the new government gave in to Moscow on all matters and in 1924 the state was formally made part of the Soviet Union.

Tannu Tuva had never been incorporated into the Russian Empire but in 1914 it had accepted the Russians as protectors. In March 1918, while the new Russian communist government was being forced to surrender all rights to its neighbors to the west, Russian communist workers in Tannu Tuva were proclaiming a communist government for that nation. The natives ignored the eccentric Europeans. Yet on this flimsy basis the Red Army felt it to be its duty to liberate the people of Tannu Tuva from the counterrevolutionary elements. Little resistance was offered to the powerful Red forces that overran the nation.

South of Tannu Tuva lay Mongolia, a nation which had spawned some of the greatest military conquerors known to history, but by 1919 there was no Mongolian horde to dictate terms to a prostrate Moscow. The shoe was now on the other foot. Moscow controlled an army of millions armed with tanks, artillery, and planes, and Mongolia had been reduced to a collection of shabby huts loosely organized into tribal groups engaged full time in the raising of goats and sheep. Ulan Bator was a market place that served as the capital for the nation that was the size of Western Europe. Chinese troops roamed the area at will.

This year a group of Russian communists proclaimed a revolutionary government in Ulan Bator and invited in the Red Army. In a three-month campaign the Red Army defeated the local horse cavalry and a Chinese warlord's army and placed the local leader of the Lamaist faith on the throne. Bogd served as a puppet ruler and the state remained in theory an independent nation. This situation was allowed to remain as the Soviet government decided that it needed a buffer state here.

Other nations that were submerged in the sea of communism were the homelands of the Khazan Tatars, Crimean Tatars, Chuvash, Mordovians, Bashkirs, Votyaks (Udmurts), Chechens (Shishuns), Mari (Chermiss), Ossetians, Komis, Avars, Lezghins, Kabardins, Dargins, Kumyks, Laks, Kalmyks, Khirgis, Pamirs, Khazakhs, and Siberians. Each of the above nations have their own definable borders, languages, customs, and history, and by the early 1920s each had more people than the sovereign European state of Luxembourg. Khazakh territory is the size of the United States east of the Mississippi River.

The people of these nations thought that they too were entitled to sovereignty in which they could live in peace as they chose, with cultural and religious freedom.

In addition, the Red Army had conquered by 1922 another one hundred nations, which though smaller still had as many or more people than the sovereign European states of Liechtenstein or Monaco. There were also pockets of people in the Soviet Union who were not Russian, the countless unassimilated Jews, the Gypsies, a few Lapps in the frozen north, 300,000 Volksdeutsch along the Volga River and in Ukraine 340,000 Volksdeutsch, 205,000 Bulgarians mostly around Odessa, and 125,000 Greeks in Black Sea coastal villages.

All of these non-Russian people were quickly alienated by the atheistic communists as they were denied complete religious freedom. Whether Buddhist Kalmyks, Moslem Azerbaijanis, Protestant Volksdeutsch, Roman Catholic Poles, or Jews, their religious leaders were under constant threat of imprisonment. In some communities the churches were closed down. In addition, the security police behaved abominably to all the people, and when Stalin's literally murderous economic policies took hold many of the nations saw only warfare to be the last hope of survival.

The Yakuts revolted in 1928 and paid dearly for their failure. A year later, the Buryat Mongols lost their bid for freedom and paid with a tremendous amount of blood and slavery. It is estimated that 35,000 of them were massacred. In 1931 the Khazakh revolt was bloodily suppressed. In the early 1930s, 40,000 Crimean Tatars were marched off to their deaths. In 1935 the nations of the North Caucasus decided that they could take no more. The Chechens, Ossetians, Kabardins, Kalmyks, Avars, Dargins, Laks, and Lezghins rose in revolt against the policies that had brought starvation to their children. The Red Army and Red Air Force were brought in to destroy all opposition with ferocity.

The Soviet Union may indeed have been a prison for nations, but by June 1941 it was also a house of cards.

Chapter 11

In Defense of Mother Russia

When the more free-thinking of the Axis officers studied who might aid them in their struggle against the communists, two groups of people immediately came to mind, the Cossacks and the Russians themselves.

The Cossacks are descended from Ukrainians, Russians, and others, who chose to live outside the sedentary society, and this meant becoming semi-nomadic and fiercely independent. Their reliance on the horse can only be equaled by the Mongol hordes and their descendants and by the North American Plains Indians. By the seventeenth century if an army commander could recruit a large body of Cossack horsemen he was almost assured victory. As the Cossacks remained a useful recruiting ground, the Tsars left them alone. With the coming of the Russian Civil War the Red Army recruited many Cossacks, making them all sorts of promises. However, the Cossacks were religious Orthodox Catholics and the atheism of the communists was a constant source of friction.

The anti-communist Russian armies, called Whites, were ecstatic whenever they managed to recruit Cossacks. For this reason the British sent a military mission to recruit many Cossacks into the White armies to fight in the crusade against Bolshevism. General A.M. Kaledin set up a political body, the Cossack Union of the Don in December 1917, hoping to attract all Cossacks by the promise of a state of their own, one with enough room for them to live in comfort. In Eastern Siberia a force of Cossacks under Gregori Semenov began to raid Red Army installations and attack the trains on the Trans-Siberian Railroad. By 1918 he was being aided by the Japanese.

In February 1918 the Cossacks of the Kuban joined the Whites, but were forced to withdraw south of their homeland when the White armies were defeated by a Red counteroffensive in April.

In June 1918 in Iran, a force of Russian Cossacks under General Bicherakov deserted to the Reds when they realized that their Allies, the British, were just seeking imperialist gain. Bicherakov remained loyal to the White cause, nonetheless.

By September, the Whites, Don Cossacks, and Kuban Cossacks had recaptured their homes and were invading Russia from the south. At the end of the year due to this victory and due to British pressure Pyotr Krasnov, who led a large group of Don Cossacks, threw in his lot with the Whites. He soon proved to be one of the most respected of the Cossack leaders. By May 1919, the Whites had the Reds on the run and the Cossacks were swarming around the city of Tsaritsyn (later renamed Stalingrad then Volgagrad). On 14 June alone over 800 Reds were killed in a Cossack cavalry charge. The Cossacks could not have felt better for it looked like the dream of a Cossack homeland was becoming a reality.

By October the dreams were shattered as hundreds of thousands of Reds poured down from the north, sweeping all before them. On their left flank the Whites were running for the Black Sea ports, and on the right they were heading for the deserts of the Caucasus. In Siberia a White army had also been defeated, and the Cossacks of Semenov were retreating to the coast and Japanese protection.

The last major efforts took place in the Crimea and the Kuban in June 1920, but the White offensives were all repulsed. By early 1921 the Whites were either surrendering or sailing away from the Black Sea ports to an unknown future. The escaping men and women wondered what had happened. They were stateless persons in foreign lands, and they felt betrayed by their supposed allies. They had fought alongside soldiers of the American, British, Finnish, Latvian, Estonian, Lithuanian, Polish, Czechoslovakian, Romanian, Greek, Japanese, French, and Italian armies, and yet they had lost the war. Those who reached the United States found the American people to be ignorant of the Russian Civil War. Most Americans believed that the communists were just farmers and factory workers and that all Whites were simply dukes and princes who had been angered when their vast estates had been taken from them. Nothing could be further from the truth, although there were princes among the refugees, of course. Men who had been colonels were reduced to working as waiters. Countesses had to scrub floors. Of the Cossacks the more fortunate found jobs working with horses, such as in circuses, but most of these fierce warriors found themselves digging ditches.

Periodically the Soviet government announced an amnesty to any Whites who wished to return. Those who were naive enough to do so were never heard from again. The League of Nations counted hundreds of thousands of refugees, from the heir apparent to pig farmers. The League issued many with Nansen certificates in lieu of passports and managed to see them settled, though it took years. Canada accepted 40,000, the U.S.A. 20,000, Manchuria 100,000, Germany several thousand, France no less than half a million, and the rest by the far corners of the world.

Gregori Semenov was one of the luckier ones. With 10,000 men he set up a headquarters in Manchuria and lived like a king under the protection of a Chinese warlord. The rest of the Whites in Manchuria also lived under the protection of one of the many warlords, but life was not always happy or safe. In the cities such as Harbin the crime rate was exceedingly high among the Manchus, Mongols, and Chinese who lived here. One emigre faction formed an armed detachment of 4,000 men under General Konstantin Nechaev and in 1922 earned its keep by fighting for Chang Tsun-Ch'ang against Wu P'ei-fu and Feng Yu-hsiang.

Politics of all kinds rocked the emigre world in Manchuria and naturally one of the parties was fascist, the R.S.O. The greatest fascist leader was Konstantin Rodzaevsky who had fled the Soviet Union at the age of 18 in 1925. Choosing the Italian model, he organized the Russian Fascist Party in 1931. Months later, Manchuria was invaded and occupied by the Japanese. Actually this brought a good deal of stability, and the Japanese created a puppet, but nonetheless effective for all that, government under Henry P'u-Yi, who was renamed Emperor Kang-Te. The power of the secret societies, criminal gangs, and warlords was crushed by the Japanese, and the Whites found more employment on the Japanese schemes, such as railroad building. The Japanese also remembered their friend Semenov and he was left to live in the style to which he had become accustomed.

General Vladimir Kislitsyn was appointed the leader of the emigre population. This man was a member of the Brotherhood of Russian Truth which had been founded by Pyotr Krasnov, and he was still a general for he and his men now and then continued to launch forays into the Soviet Union. Soon, however, the Japanese liked the look of the Fascist Party and they also began to support Rodzaevsky, tolerating the antics of his stromtroopers. They did not like the actions of the Osoby Otdel, though. Led by Alexander Bolotov this group of fascists murdered the political rivals of the fascists. Bolotov had been trained well for this. He was an ex-N.K.V.D. man.

A compromise was eventually worked out and the Japanese took over the Osoby Otdel, using the men as scouts along the Soviet border. In November 1936 the detachment actually made a large-scale raid into the Soviet Union, but the operation was a fiasco and it suffered fifty percent casualties. Hedging their bets the Japanese also set up a monarchist Russian force, owing its allegiance to the heir to the Tsar's throne, Cyril I, whose wife was a German nazi. Later they took over the Manchurian branch of the Brotherhood and also began giving Semenov orders. At times these sponsored soldiers were used to fight against the bandits, who still plagued the countryside, and the communists of Mao Tse-Tung.

In 1938 the Japanese created the Asano Brigade made up of emigres, and appointed Gurgen Nagolen, an Armenian and ex-policeman of the Imperial Japanese Railroad, as its commander. Officially these 700 men were members of the Army of Manchukuo, the name of the puppet state, but Nagolen took orders from a Japanese general. In its early days the unit sent reconnaissance parties across the border, but in the summer of 1938 was involved in an actual

Soviet-Japanese battle. Hopes were raised among the emigres that the Japanese might wrest a significant portion of territory from the Soviets. Then an action in the summer of 1939 showed this to be only a dream. The Japanese entered Soviet territory again and were this time soundly defeated, losing 11,124 men out of a force of 15,140. The Asano Brigade fought in the ten-day battle and suffered 70% casualties.

This was immediately followed by the Nazi-Soviet Non-Aggression Pact of August 1939, which shocked the emigres and Japanese alike. The dream of a free Russia looked further away than ever.

In the Western World the pact shocked many emigres into action. They decided that if the Germans had allied with the Soviets, and the division of Poland by these two powers seemed to bear out this assumption, then Germany was their enemy too. Tens of thousands of emigres joined the French, British, and Canadian Armed Forces.

The emigres in the United States were divided into political groups as anywhere else, but there was no real fascist party, with one minor exception. Anastase Vonsiatsky, a Polish-speaking Volksdeutsch who had married a wealthy American, spent his time trying to create a recognized fascist party for the emigres. His efforts mostly went into attempting to gain recognition by the German-American Bund and the Silver Shirts. He also traveled Europe meeting the fascist leaders there and met Rodzaevsky in Tokyo. His organization was based on the German model, but it was not anti-Semitic. The tailor who designed the party's stormtrooper uniforms was a Jew.

Vonsiatsky was never quite taken seriously, except by the F.B.I. In 1942 he was arrested and sentenced to five years' imprisonment for espionage.

The headquarters of the largest emigre organization, the National Workers Association (N.T.S.), was in Paris, and it had a very large active membership. Unfortunately, the Soviets had infiltrated the association quite early in its history, and any agents who were sent to the Soviet Union were immediately arrested.

It was in Germany where the best chance for the emigres lay, though no one could have known that for sure until 22 June 1941. In the 1920s a great friend of the emigres was Alfred Rosenberg, the chief racial theorist of the German nazis. Rosenberg was an Estonian Volksdeutsch, who had studied in Moscow, and who had not come to Germany until he was twenty-five years old. In effect he too was an emigre. The more fanatic of the emigres joined the stormtroopers, Sturm Abteilungen (S.A.), and formed their own section called the Russian Auxiliary. Unlike the Germans, who wore brown shirts, the Russian members wore white shirts.

By the time the nazis gained power in Germany in January 1933, there were 50,000 emigres in Germany, and many thought that their organization might someday encompass all emigres. Within a few days, A.P. Svetozarov and Pavel Bermondt-Avalov founded the Russian National Socialist Workers Party, an auxiliary of the German Nazi Party.

However, the pact of 1939 destroyed the emigres' hopes. As part of the deal the emigre organizations in Germany were disbanded, and a few emigres were even handed over to the N.K.V.D. by the Gestapo.

Some emigres kept their positions of prestige, but only by becoming good German citizens. For example, Grigori Bostunich had changed his name to Schwarz and joined the S.S. He kept his job and eventually rose to the rank of Standartenfuehrer (colonel). As well, at the same time that the emigres were losing their position their younger members were joining the German Armed Forces to prove that they deserved equal treatment.

When the Germans attacked the Soviet Union the situation was turned around again. The emigres began lobbying the government to be allowed to set up a Russian anti-communist liberating army. None of these men and women realized that their future hopes would bear fruit among Red Army officers, men who had been their enemy for so long.

This was to come about because the communists in Russia were also greatly dissatisfied. Since 1917, the communists had been busy denouncing each other as counterrevolutionaries. The first twenty years of the communist government in Russia, that is the Soviet Union, was fraught with the pitfalls of intrigue, backstabbing, throat-cutting, and kangaroo courts. The infighting was brought to a new high by Stalin himself, a paranoid-schizophrenic who could shake a man's hand one minute and order his execution the next. Already he had shown ruthlessness in his rise to power. He had exiled Leon Trotsky, one of the original leaders of the revolution, but had reserved a more final fate for most of his colleagues. There is even a possibility that he murdered Lenin. His betrayal of the Ukrainian communists during the Great Man-Made Famine showed the rest of the Soviet communists what they could expect. Yet, as each one gambled that he or she could tumble to the top of the heap no one did anything to stop the maniac.

On 10 July 1934 the O.G.P.U. was renamed the N.K.V.D. and taken over by H. Yagoda who like the founder of the communist security police, F. Dzerzhinsky, was a Pole. One must not think of these men as Poles in the nationalist sense, though, for each was an opportunist who would have equally been at home running the Gestapo.

Still Yagoda did not satisfy Stalin, and in September 1936 a new head of the N.K.V.D. was named, N.Y. Yezhov, a Russian. At once he began to purge the leadership of the force, even arresting founder members. He did not want a clique of the veterans to conspire against him. This was Stalin's kind of man. Beginning in 1937 Yezhov began hunting communists as if he were Adolf Hitler in disguise, always under Stalin's orders of course. Reinhard Heydrich, the chief of the German S.S. Security Police, later bragged that he and the emigres had planted false information with the Soviet Union naming loyal communists as anti-communist spies. How successful they were is unknown, but they claimed many successes. One of their claims was that they framed Marshal

Mikhail Tukachevsky, the great hero of the Russian Civil War. He was arrested for treason and executed on 11 June 1937. If he was not safe then no officer was safe, the communists realized.

Following this show trial, the N.K.V.D. arrested three-quarters of the Supreme Military Soviet, thirteen out of nineteen army commanders, and 110 out of 135 divisional commanders. Most of these were executed. The Germans were ecstatic, for Stalin seemed to be doing their job for them.

The N.K.V.D. now stretched its tentacles to include industry, the civil service, the police, the Comintern, and foreign communists. Not only were men arrested, but often their families too, and in some cases the women and children were officially ostracized, that is, if anybody had contact with them they were liable to arrest. The result was that they died on the streets of starvation and cold. To offer food or shelter to such an ostracized person risked death in a concentration camp. With foresight Stalin had passed a law on 7 April 1935 naming all persons over 11 years of age as eligible for adult punishment, including the death penalty. If a younger person was arrested they were held in protective custody until they became old enough to be sentenced to prison. Of 179 members and candidates for the Central Committee, a sham parliament, at the 17th Party Congress of 1934, no less than 98 had been arrested by 1938. Of 1,966 voting and advisory delegates at that congress, 1,108 had been arrested by 1938. Most of these men and women were executed or assigned fatal labor duties in the concentration camps.

Foreign communists suffered too. If they failed to answer the summons to come to Moscow they were branded as traitors. If they did come they were arrested, often at the border. The Polish, Austrian, Czechoslovakian, German, and Yugoslavian Communist Parties were especially devastated. Bela Kun was executed. In Spain communists who were currently fighting against Franco's forces in the civil war there were murdered by N.K.V.D. agents. These agents assassinated "traitors" all over Europe and in the U.S.A. Trotsky was assassinated in Mexico.

The provincial leaders within the Soviet Union were also purged. This destroyed the education system which was teaching the more primitive tribes to read and write and create a literary culture of their own. The tribesmen were not sorry to see the communists arrested, but they were sorry to see their schools closed down for lack of teachers. They felt that once again they had been deserted by Stalin. In Georgia the purge was particularly terrible, where a Georgian and friend of Stalin, Lavrenti Beria, massacred the party leadership. Stalin rewarded this butcher by putting him in charge of the N.K.V.D., while Yezhov was taken to a mental institution for a "rest." There he soon died mysteriously.

However, this was December 1938, and the 39-year-old Beria found that there were not enough people left to arrest. So many faces were new. He did curtail the excesses and by the end of the year it was recognized that the purge had ended.

Most of those punished had simply had their party membership taken away from them, which crippled their careers and often their lives, but they knew they were the lucky ones. By the end of 1938 the Communist Party of the Soviet Union could claim only two million members, less than 2% of the adult population.

By 1941, though, the atmosphere within the Soviet Union was still one of complete terror, for periodic arrests continued to come in waves. The post-Stalin Soviet government has admitted, with embarrassment, the truth of the figures noted above. It is estimated that between 1929 and 1 September 1939, Stalin murdered twenty million people. Note that this was before his forces began their invasions of Eastern Europe.

Chapter 12

Throng to the East

In the early hours of Sunday morning, 22 June 1941, German Army Group North opened fire on Soviet positions in Soviet Lithuania. At the same moment German Army Group Center attacked Soviet Poland and Soviet Byelorussia, and German Army Group South invaded Soviet Ukraine. Within twenty-four hours the thousands of guns and thousands of planes had blasted paths through the defenses, and the Germans, riding in tanks, armored fighting vehicles, self-propelled guns, half-tracks, and trucks, but mostly walking alongside horse-drawn wagons, stepped into the hidden land that was the Soviet Union. This was the moment of decision. The time to live or the time to die, for there could be no diplomatic retreat from this move.

Northern Sector

When the Lithuanians awoke on the morning of the 22nd, expecting to have to face another day of terror at the hands of the communists, and instead saw the smoke and heard the bomb blasts and later heard the rumors in the street that the Germans had invaded, they felt a sense of relief mixed with anxiety. Relief because the Soviets might soon be kicked out and anxiety as they wondered how the Germans would treat them. They knew that if the previous German occupation was anything to go by they would all have civil rights, but not political rights. If so, it was better than going to and from work not knowing if you were going to be picked up by the security police on a trumped-up charge and deported to a concentration camp. The general opinion was that with the Soviets gone life would at least be livable again.

Some Lithuanians decided to aid the Germans. A rudimentary resistance force had been created in answer to the Red terror and now its members came out into the open with what few weapons they had. Individual Red Army soldiers, N.K.V.D. men, and those ethnic Russians who had collaborated with the Soviets were prime targets. Sabotage was also taking place, though on a small scale.

Already on the 23rd the Soviets could be seen fleeing, the N.K.V.D. quickest of all. The sound of artillery fire reached the cities of Kovno and Vilnius, and here the populace was jubilant for their homes would not be damaged by fighting and the communists were leaving. The German invasion seemed to point to the complete disintegration of the Soviet Empire. Naturally the Soviets tried to crush all overt opposition, but generally speaking they were too busy fleeing to fight back. By the end of the second day of the war the cities were abandoned by the Soviets and the German mechanized forces began creeping into the suburbs. The people welcomed the invaders with open arms, cheers, and smiling faces. The soldiers were extremely glad that they were on friendly soil. The German vehicles were festooned with nazi heraldry, for the Germans were so confident of a swift victory that they did not bother to hide their unit identification. The peasants saw that the insignia of the Germans was the cross of Christ in its various forms and this was a welcome change from the God-hating communists. The vehicles were covered in white crosses, the crooked cross (swastika), Maltese cross, and different Balkan crosses, a white border around an invisible cross, a black cross with a white border, a white cross with a black border, a white cross with a black cross superimposed on it, a white cross with a black border and a thin, medium, or fat black cross superimposed on it, invisible crosses with partial black borders, and other combinations. Several German units used cross variations as their own insignia and others used double-headed eagles, which the peasants mistook for Russian Tsarist insignia. To anyone over thirty years of age these insignia were a sight for sore eyes.

The members of the Lithuanian anti-communist resistance and gangs of men and women who had stolen weapons from Soviet soldiers began to loot the installations that their oppressors had been using. Some of these mobs were criminal in intent. When the prisons were reached the mobs were struck dumb. Near Kovno the N.K.V.D. had shot 500 prisoners as they did not have the transportation to take them to Russia. Within hours of the liberation loved ones began searching among the bodies for relatives and friends. In a wood just outside Telsiai 73 corpses were found. They had been tortured to death by the N.K.V.D. Later, N.K.V.D. documents were found, which were authenticated, revealing plans for more arrests of politically suspect people and various technicians and specialists who were to be put into slavery to help the Russian economy, but the German invasion prevented this. Approximately half the population of Lithuania would have been arrested, eventually.

The Jews of Lithuania had suffered as much as anyone, but the N.K.V.D. had deliberately looked for criminals who were Jewish to aid them in their hideous terror operations as sentries, interrogators, translators, and guides and informers. Many Lithuanians hated Jews and the realization of what Jews had been doing inflamed the more rabid anti-Semites. They began roaming the streets searching for male Jews. Any that were unlucky enough to be caught were hanged from trees or lampposts, or stabbed or beaten.

Once the German soldiers came to the conclusion that the Soviets had gone, they declared martial law in the towns and put a stop to the mob violence. Some of the murderers of the Jews were arrested. The Germans had been disgusted by the pogrom, and the sight of hanging civilians was too much even for combat veterans. The majority of the Lithuanians were also disgusted by the fanatics, but the cultivation of anti-Semitism, the repressed frustration of the Soviet terror, the discovery of the N.K.V.D. murder sites and torture chambers, and the sudden release of these feelings at the moment of liberation were too much for some minds. Mob rule has a mind of its own and for a couple of days in Lithuania the mob ruled the streets. It is believed, according to German and Lithuanian sources, that in Kovno alone 3,800 Jews were murdered.

Ironically, the Jews who had aided the Soviets had either fled with the Red Army or had been murdered at the last moment by the N.K.V.D. As usual, whenever mob violence occurs, it was the innocent who suffered.

By the 26th the Germans were pouring into Latvia. Here similar scenes were repeated. In Riga a serious fight broke out between the Soviets and the resistance. The latter often consisted of just men and women with knives. Soviet warships were raising anchor and Red Air Force planes were taking off one after another. Truck convoys of Soviet soldiers raced through the streets. A poorly coordinated Red Army counterattack was hardly noticed, and the Soviets continued night and day to escape as fast as their ships, planes, trucks, trains, and feet could carry them.

When the cities were turned over to anarchy for a few hours anti-Semitism was less rife than in Lithuania. When the Germans entered Daugavpils on the 26th and Riga on the 27th, they found relative calm.

In Estonia the anti-communist uprising was more coordinated. The Germans had parachuted into the nation a force of eighty Estonian saboteurs, under the code-name Operation Erna. These men worked with placid devotion, ignoring the chaos about them. The actual resistance itself, which had received some German arms and money, rose up as one and began to make life dangerous for the Soviets, who at first tried to organize a defense and then tried to escape. Knives were used to kill Soviet soldiers and their captured rifles and machine guns were used to capture more weapons. Within a couple of days the Soviets found themselves under attack from a guerrilla army. The Soviets believed many of the rebels were Germans who had been parachuted in to harass supply lines, so fierce was the determination of the ordinary Estonian civilian to be free.

Riding in a vehicle convoy on his way to Talinn docks, Admiral Panteleyev was ambushed and barely escaped with his life.

Within days of the German attack Estonia was liberated, and the Germans found the Estonians to be most grateful, especially after the N.K.V.D. prisons were opened, and the truth about communist brotherhood was laid bare for all to see. A mass grave was found where 450 men and women had been beaten to death. Medieval-style torture chambers were discovered with the recipients of Soviet displeasure still lying in them. Prison cells, the inmates of which had simply been forgotten by the N.K.V.D., greeted the liberators with the disgusting stench of decomposed bodies.

The Germans disarmed all the anti-communist rebels as soon as possible to prevent mob rule and the extortion of money by criminals. There had been little anti-Semitic violence. The Erna Estonians were kept, however, as these men were soldiers belonging to German army intelligence.

The people of Latvia, Estonia, and Lithuania were more ready to serve in an anti-communist crusade now than at any other time. The opportunity for the Germans to gain allies was staring them in the face.

The Finns waited a week before launching their war, which they would call the Continuation War, as if it was simply round two of the Finno-Russian conflict. The VIth Corps of two divisions and a brigade, commanded by Major-General Talvela, and the VIIth Corps of two divisions, under Major-General Hägglund, advanced towards the Svir River, while the IVth Corps of four divisions and the IInd Corps of three divisions tackled the enemy on the main front in Karelia. One division, which included the Swedish battalion, was left behind to besiege the Soviet garrison at Hangö. In the far north the IIIrd Corps of two divisions and the German XXXVIth Corps walked rather than charged across vast forests towards the thinly held Soviet frontier. Still further north inside the Arctic Circle a German mountain corps that included some fine Austrian veterans of the Norway campaign attacked the Soviet naval bases which were the only worthwhile targets for hundreds of miles.

As Finland was now embarked upon a crusade the government adopted a new insignia, doing away with the white-blue-white stripes. The new symbol was the hakaristi, a black swastika trimmed in white.

Within days the 6th Division was making good progress towards Salla, but the flanking German S.S. Nord Brigade was easily held up. The unit contained German S.S. reservists who had never volunteered for front-line combat duty. Further south the VIth Corps directed its attack towards Lake Onega and the flanking VIIth Corps was approaching Lake Ladoga. The Finns hoped to cut off large numbers of Soviets before the winter froze the lakes and offered the enemy a means of escape. The IInd Corps was well on its way towards the southwest shore of Lake Ladoga and the IVth Corps and a German division were making good progress towards Viipuri. Field Marshal Mannerheim controlled Army Karelia and Army Southeast. The northern sector of the Finnish front was commanded by the German General Falkenhorst of German Army Group Norway.

By 16 July VIIth Corps had momentarily cut off a large number of Soviets around Sortavala, but then they evacuated by ship across the lake, hounded by Finnish and German aircraft. A greater maneuver was in the making in the Isthmus as the IVth Corps began trying to break through at Vuolsalmi on the

31st. The Red Army generals took their time deducing Mannerheim's intention, but once they discovered it they evacuated Viipuri on 16 August before the IVth Corps could break through and surround them. Western Karelia had now been liberated and even if the Soviets had not been trapped this was still cause enough for celebrations throughout Finland.

Central Sector

Byelorussia is a land of large swamps, forests, and plains, and in June 1941 there were few hard-surfaced roads, and only one major one, which led to Moscow. Recent rains had turned the dirt roads into useless scars upon the earth. By the time of the German advance there were few rainshowers, and the temperature was hot and would get hotter, so they did not need to worry about weather as they advanced across this immense land. They did not worry about the local inhabitants either as the villagers greeted them with feelings varying from neutrality to gratitude. Only pockets of Soviet soldiers offered resistance, and if the troops on the ground could not quickly overcome them they could always call upon the Luftwaffe. The Red Air Force did not put in an appearance. Every day some Germans were killed, but a larger number than that of Soviet deserters offered to take their place. Unfortunately the Germans were under orders to pass all prisoners back to the rear.

In a massive battle fought between Bialystok and Minsk over 300,000 Soviet troops were ordered to surrender after only eighteen days of war, and these were added to the thousands who had already given themselves up. On 9 July Vitebsk was liberated and four days later the Germans began to enter Russia itself. This was truly enemy territory, yet here too the villagers were often friendly. The Soviet Union had indeed been a house of cards and one swift kick from a German jackboot seemed to have toppled it.

The German soldiers realized why the local people welcomed them when they heard the narratives of communist brutality. If anything, the nazi propaganda that the Germans had been subjected to had underplayed the horror of communism. Now the Germans could see evidence of the Red terror for themselves. At Chervene in Byelorussia, a mass grave was found to contain the corpses of thousands of victims of the N.K.V.D.

The Poles too, who had been occupied by the Soviets in September 1939, and who had never had anything good to say about the Germans, looked upon the German invasion as a sort of liberation. At this date few realized that nazi horror could be as terrifying as communist horror.

Whenever the Germans discovered evidence of communist butchery they exhibited it to the nearby inhabitants, not that the indigenous population needed much anti-communist propaganda by this date.

By 5 August the Germans who were advancing into Russia proper had captured another 300,000 Soviets between Hoth's and Guderian's panzergroups, and by this time they were three-quarters of the way on the road to Moscow. But now, due to grand strategic considerations, Hitler ordered the two panzergroups to halt on the Desna River.

Southern Sector

The first part of Ukraine to be liberated by the Germans had only been under Soviet occupation for twenty-one months and the peasants and city-dwellers alike welcomed the Germans. When the N.K.V.D. fled Lwow they left a prison full of 3,500 corpses. In other areas too they had murdered their political prisoners rather than evacuate them. Still, most of the prisoners had been found transportation and had been carried into the Soviet hinterland. N.K.V.D. trains had priority over all others, including hospital trains loaded with Red Army wounded.

Once the protection of the Red Army was lifted, the Ukrainian communists were fair game for mobs of Ukrainians. Hundreds were murdered in the streets. In every district where the Germans were near the populace revolted, and in the more remote areas whole villages resisted truck convoys of Red Army troops. A large number of Ukrainians who had been conscripted by the Soviets turned their weapons on the Red Army.

Stepan Bandera had been serving time in a Polish prison for his part in a political murder when he had been liberated by the Germans in September 1939. By 1941, he had connived with the 1st Brandenburg Regiment—a special warfare unit of the German Army—to create a legion of Ukrainian nationalists, recruited from ex-soldiers of the Polish Army who had been captured by the Germans. The Germans armed these men and trained them to operate as guides, interpreters, and scouts. Once Lwow was liberated Bandera's men began recruiting more soldiers, while at the same time hunting down known communists. As a large proportion of the communists were Jews, this operation often took the appearance of a pogrom especially when undisciplined mobs took the law into their own hands.

The Germans were advancing at a rate that astonished their own tank specialists. Everywhere whole Red Army units were surrendering, fleeing, or being overrun. With only 600 tanks divided among his five panzer and thirty-three infantry divisions, the commander of Army Group South had defeated thirty-three Soviet divisions armed with 3,000 tanks. In Ukraine, Zhitomir was liberated by 9 July.

The Romanians faced a Soviet force of six tank and motorized, three cavalry, and thirteen infantry divisions. To oppose them the Romanians only had the Third Army with six brigades and the First Army of four divisions. The First Army, on the southern flank, actually came under the tactical control of German Eleventh Army with its troops on the southernmost flank, but all Axis troops in this area ultimately came under the command of Marshal Ion Antonescu. However, for strategic purposes he in turn was under the command of German Army Group South commanded by General Gerd von Runstedt.

At sea the Romanian Navy cautiously hugged the coast, aided by some German boats that had been brought in parts by truck and an Italian MASboat flotilla. There were also six Italian and six German midget submarines.

This unified command structure was to cause problems for the two nations had different goals. The Germans wanted to advance as far as possible, but the Romanians only wanted to liberate their own soil.

Although the people welcomed the Romanians, there were some tough fights at Kichinev and Tiraspol.

Bandera's men had not been forgotten, and after some discussion he was allowed to keep his legions, Roland and Nachtigall, each approximately of battalion size.* Nachtigall, led by Roman Shukhevych, advanced eastwards towards Vinnytsa, while Roland joined a force of Romanians, Germans, and the 369th Croatian Regiment to take Kichinev on 16 July and then move on towards Tiraspol. With Bukovina soon freed the Romanians threw all their weight into the Bessarabian battle, adding to the First Army the 5th and 13th Divisions, and placing General Dumitrescu's Third Army into Northern Bessarabia, and reinforcing it with the 1st and 7th Cavalry Brigades.

The Romanians achieved their goals by mid-August, but by this time the Germans had talked Antonescu into occupying Southwestern Ukraine, which the Romanians called Transniestra. This extension of their original goals would bode ill for many a Romanian soldier.

The Hungarians had actually been facing northeast at the outset of the war. To face twenty-five Soviet divisions, the Hungarians had only put together a light corps of one cavalry and two motorized brigades. As expected, when the Hungarians advanced the Soviets withdrew on 27 June rather than be cut off by a pincer movement of Germans from the northeast and Romanians from the southeast.

Here, too, the Christian peasants of Ukraine were glad to see a liberation by Christian warriors. The insignia on the Hungarian vehicles was a Maltese cross in white with a green border and a red ring in the center, or sometimes the Hungarian coat of arms which contained an Orthodox Catholic cross. Later on, Hungarian vehicles sported a fat white Balkan cross on a black field, or a fat green Balkan cross with a white border. Many of the non-German Axis vehicles also carried a swastika flag which they could display when German aircraft were in the vicinity, so that the German pilots would not mistake them for Soviet vehicles.

According to the German reports the Hungarians faced no opposition in

*Roland was formed from emigres living in Austria by Colonel Iarii.

their advance, and in relative terms this was true. Nonetheless there was some combat and by 3 August the Hungarians had suffered 977 casualties. General Ferenc Szombathelyi proved to be a reasonably able commander, but he was always under the strategic control of the German Seventeenth Army.

The Slovakian corps of two divisions and a mobile brigade, commanded by General Ferdinand Catlos, had advanced against light opposition, taking casualties of 106 dead, 188 wounded, and 30 missing by the end of the first week in August. Then the two divisions were placed on rear security duty, to protect the lines of communications from Soviet stragglers. The mobile brigade was beefed up to the strength of a division and assigned to the German 1st Panzer Group. The Slovakian vehicles were decorated with the double-armed white cross to symbolize their connection with the Roman Catholic Church.

On 6 August a trapped Soviet pocket counterattacked the German flank around Molodovka, and the nearest Axis unit that could aid the Germans was only a Hungarian force of horse cavalry. Still the Hungarians responded brilliantly, charging into the enemy and giving the Germans the chance to eventually crush all resistance from this Uman Pocket. The Soviet commander surrendered 103,000 men. There were several other occasions in which the Hungarian horse cavalry proved their worth. In October the horse troops were recalled home for the winter.

Part of General von Kleist's 1st Panzer Group was the S.S. Wiking Division. As it was partly mechanized it had to await a breakthrough and then follow the panzer divisions. It was only called upon to fight whenever a pocket had been bypassed by the tanks, but whenever it looked like a major fight might develop the division moved on and left the enemy to the infantry who were walking as fast as possible into enemy territory. These tactics had been tried and proven in Poland and France and the Wiking's personnel performed them well, despite its personnel coming from ten different nations and speaking six different languages.

While von Kleist's panzers thrust eastwards continuously, Hitler overrode his advisers to send Guderian's panzer group southwards into Ukraine around Kiev to pin the enemy against von Kleist. The result was a battle as tough as it was large, and all available panzer and mechanized formations were rushed into it, including Wiking, the Slovakian Mobile Division, and the two Hungarian motorized brigades. By the end of a wet September, 600,000 Red Army troops had laid down their arms. The non-German Axis troops were proud that they had fought in the largest single short battle in history. Hitler's advisers had argued against this battle as in order to fight it they had to halt their drive on Moscow. Evidently they had forgotten that their objective should have been the destruction of the enemy, not the occupation of a city.

During the battle of Kiev the Croatian 369th Regiment had aided German forces to capture Krementshug on the Dniepr River, 12-18 September.

One of Mussolini's reasons for sending an expeditionary corps of 55,000 under General Zingales to aid the Germans in Russia was to convince the Italian people that henceforth the Germans and Italians would always fight side by side, and therefore the Germans in North Africa were there not to do the Italians' fighting for them but as part of this general agreement. Whether or not anyone believed this particular line is debatable. Still, after preaching the evils of communism for twenty years and sending an army to fight them in Spain, Mussolini could hardly keep out of the invasion of the Soviet Union the lair of the communist wolf.

At first the dispatch of the Pasubio, Torino, and 3rd Celere Divisions was done with typical Italian publicity, pomp, and fanfare. It was known that the Soviets were already reeling back from the onslaught of the rest of Europe, and the Italian soldiers felt their presence would probably be just a token gesture.

Once in Russia the troops began to advance against weak bypassed mobs of Soviet troops throughout July and August, reaching the Dniepr River late in the month, where they were placed in a defensive role. There were patrol actions, but their first real battle did not take place until the end of September. The entire corps attacked across the river, using Bersaglieri as the spearhead, and quickly had the Reds on the run. Moving towards the city of Stalino, the Italian corps became the advanced unit for the Germans in this area. It was not the rearguards that hindered the advance, bloody as they were, but the autumn rains, which turned the roads into a sea of mud. The wheeled vehicles had to be hand pushed for miles day after day. By the 17th day of October the horse cavalry Savoia Regiment had reached the Sukyie Yalli River and had forced a crossing. Then the horsed Novara Lancers took up the chase to capture Uspenovka. On 29 and 30 October the 3rd Celere Division took Stalino in a hard-fought battle.

The Germans noted that their losses were becoming extraordinarily high, despite the string of victories that came one after another. It would soon be time for the Romanians to join their German comrades-in-arms beneath the cold, wet soil of Ukraine. Odessa is a major city and port, and in the summer of 1941 it was a military and naval fortress, guarding the southern approaches to Transniestra. In order to safely occupy this district the Romanians had to have Odessa.

The first assaults by the Romanian Fourth Army against the entrenched enemy were bloodily repulsed, and many officers thought that at this stage it might be prudent to besiege the fortress and starve out the garrison. Unfortunately, once a poor general gets his teeth into an object only death releases it, and the only dying done here was by the flower of Romanian manhood which was thrown away in fruitless charges. The 5th, 6th, 7th, 8th, 13th, and 14th Divisions were soon joined by the Guards, Frontier, 3rd, 10th, 11th, 15th, 21st, and 35th Divisions, all of them to be thrown into the slaughter at Odessa. Meanwhile the Third Army with the cavalry and mountain brigades moved eastwards.

The German liaison officers with the Romanian units noted that the Romanian soldiers were brave, but suffered not from the mental strains of overeducation and high intellect, and were simply used by the leaders as cannon fodder. In October the 1st and 2nd Divisions came to add their blood to the battle.

On 16 October the surviving Soviets evacuated Odessa and fought their way across the Black Sea against Romanian and German air attacks. The Romanians had taken the mighty fortress and had therefore been victorious, but they had sacrificed an army for the laurels. Casualties were an incredible 70,000 dead and 100,000 wounded! Even then the killing did not stop, for the Soviets had left behind booby traps and delayed action bombs, one of which exploded on the 22nd and killed General Glugosianu and fifty of his staff.

The Third Army had been far luckier. On 12 September General Ritter von Schobert, the commander of the German Eleventh Army, had been killed, and though the Romanians could not have known it at the time this was the beginning of good fortune for them, for as a replacement came General Erich von Manstein. This general was one of Germany's greatest commanders. Although half Polish—his real name was Lewinski—he had been one of Hitler's favorites since he had planned the defeat of France. As part of his duties Manstein was given control of the Romanian Third Army.

General Dumitrescu had held his army back while awaiting the decision to invade Transniestra. When that decision had come from Antonescu, the Germans had already left the Third Army behind. By the time the Romanians caught up with the German Eleventh Army, the Germans were planning to rush Perekop, a five-mile stretch of hard ground between swamps that led into the Crimean Peninsula, which was practically an island. Dumitrescu was given a German division to add to his Romanian brigades and made responsible for the coastal front east of Perekop, on 20 November.

On 26 September the Soviets riposted against the Romanians, flattening the Romanian 4th Mountain Brigade with their momentum. Through the ten-mile gap the Soviet armor poured, licking at the flanks of the other Romanian mountain brigades. Despite being outnumbered and outgunned, the Romanians held on for three days until Manstein conjured up a German mountain corps and the S.S. Leibstandarte Division, which closed the gap and inflicted crippling losses on the Soviets. Within hours, though, the Romanian cavalry brigades just northwest of Melitopol were yelling for help as the Soviets attacked them in strength. Leibstandarte rose to the occasion and plugged the gap. The next day, the Romanians held off all Soviet attacks.

The following day, it was the turn of the Soviets to be surprised. While the Romanians went over to the offensive, von Kleist's German panzers slammed into the northern flank and within days broke through to the Sea of Azov. This trapped the Soviet Ninth and Eighteenth Armies against the shore. Since the

Soviet counteroffensive had begun on the 26th, 42,000 Reds had surrendered. Now with the surrender of two armies another 65,000 Soviets passed into captivity. The Romanians were left behind now as von Kleist's tanks charged ahead towards Rostov followed by his mechanized units including Wiking.

The Romanian Third Army was reinforced so that it now contained the 1st, 2nd, 10th, and 18th Divisions, and 1st, 2nd, and 4th Mountain Brigades, and 5th, 6th, and 8th Cavalry Brigades, but it was given a passive mission, guarding the coast of the Sea of Azov in case of a Soviet amphibious invasion. However, von Manstein appreciated the courage of the Romanians if not the quality of their equipment and he soon brought the headquarters of the mountain corps, together with one mountain and one cavalry brigades, to the Crimea. He needed every man he could get, for he had only six German divisions to fight twelve Soviet divisions, and the enemy still had air superiority in the Crimea.

Beginning on 18 October the Germans launched frontal assaults on the narrow entrance to the peninsula, the only tactic open to von Manstein as he had no amphibious equipment, and after ten days of bitter fighting they broke through. Now as the Germans charged forward the two Romanian brigades were brought into play. They were ordered to reach the south coast over one hundred miles away as fast as possible, ignoring their flanks. The Romanians obeyed to the letter and after a swift advance, which included cavalry charges, they caught sight of the Black Sea on 5 November. By the 16th the Soviets only held onto Sevastopol at the Western tip of the peninsula and Kerch at the eastern tip, having surrendered 160 tanks, 700 guns, and 100,000 men.

The Romanian 4th Mountain and 8th Cavalry Brigades were placed on coastal guard duty, and fortunately for them the winter, which brings forth freezing snow on the mainland, only brought a freezing rain to the coast. The men hoped that they could pass the winter in serenity.

For a time the Romanians had under their command the Walloon Legion (373rd Battalion), but while it was still new to combat it was transferred to the German 100th Jaeger Division for anti-partisan duties.

Northern Sector

The Finns were pleased with themselves. They captured Olonets on 6 September, Lodeynoye Pole on the 8th, and Petrozavodsk on 1 October. In the isthmus they had already ceased to advance, for Mannerheim had been ordered by his government to liberate occupied Finland and to seek strategically defensible positions, but not to occupy large tracts of Russian soil. The Finns wanted the world to know that Finland had no territorial ambitions beyond protecting her own sovereignty.

Yet the killing would go on. As winter approached, in late October several

Soviet units found themselves trapped against lake shores. As the forests were on fire the terrified men and screaming horses plunged into the freezing water. On one occasion the Finns reached a burned out shoreline to see the heads of hundreds of horses sticking out of the ice. The lake had frozen solid while the horses were still swimming.

The Finns hoped that the major battles were over, though. It was decided that all military personnel born before 1908 could be released, but of course officers and noncommissioned officers were retained as were select necessary personnel, and even then the release process was deliberately slow so that some units could keep their cohesion.

There was still a front line and the Finns launched an attack in December to take Medvezhegorsk, but soon the line came to resemble the Western Front of World War One. The Soviets could not advance and the Finns would not advance. The Soviet base at Hangö finally fell on the 16th. It was now that the Finns announced that due to a request by the Swedish government the Swedish Battalion was being disbanded, its mission being over, and the men were being sent home to Sweden.

To the south of the Finnish lines lay the great city and naval base of Leningrad, which the Germans had reached at the end of August. By the middle of September the Germans had outflanked the city to the east, reaching the southern shore of Lake Ladoga, and cutting it off by land from the rest of the Soviet Union. Hitler hoped he could starve the garrison into surrender, and to this end his Luftwaffe made sailing on the lake an unhealthy prospect. German pleas for Finnish support at Leningrad always fell on deaf ears.

The Germans became impatient, though, and made attacks to get closer so that their artillery could shell the city into surrender. In early October, the German XXXVIIIth Corps of the Eighteenth Army was informed that reinforcements were at last on their way, but the corps staff were surprised to learn that they were Spaniards, for Spain was supposed to be neutral.

Generalissimo Francisco Franco's Spain was indeed neutral, but the Falangists, that is the fascists among Franco's supporters, felt this to be a disgrace. They had won their civil war only twenty-seven months earlier, defeating the republicans, communists, and the few Soviet troops who had come to aid their Spanish fellow travelers. Now that much of Europe was attempting to finish off that political blight once and for all, the Falangists believed they should be in on the kill. To be fair, it must be realized that these fellows had miraculously survived a great catastrophe and they could have been forgiven the urge to lie on the soft, warm sand of a Spanish beach and forget about the war in Russia, but instead tens of thousands of young and not so young men were willing to risk their lives once again for the cause.

The wily generalissimo had to placate Hitler, too, who wanted a formal alliance with Spain in return for the large amount of aid that Germany had sent to Franco during the civil war. As a compromise, Franco agreed to form one division with air support to fight on the Eastern Front, but refused to acknowledge the troops as members of the Spanish Army. Once Foreign Minister Ramon Serrano Suñer had announced the agreement, the numbers of volunteers far exceeded the size of one division, and therefore only the cream of the crop was taken, civil war heroes and current serving members of the Regular Army. General Augustin Munoz Grandes was chosen to lead the force. A 45-year-old war hero, he was much respected by the Falangists. The division would have four regiments commanded by Colonels Rodrigo, Esparza, Pimentel, and Vierna and an artillery regiment under Colonel Badrillo.

Following a parade in their blue Falangist uniforms, hence the nickname Blue Division, the men were entrained for Grafenwöhr training ground in Germany. After the men set up camp on 25 July 1941, the Division was restructured on German lines with Esparza's, Pimentel's, and Vierna's regiments becoming the 269th, 262nd, and 263rd Regiments. There was no fourth regiment. Badrillo's artillerymen were renamed the 250th Artillery Regiment. Colonel Rodrigo was given the position of second in command to the division which received the number 250th. All the men were supplied with German equipment and German uniforms, though some of the men continued to wear their blue shirts underneath.

As the unit was in effect a Spanish division, the German trainers were satisfied with the unit after only four weeks. The 641 officers, 2,272 noncommissioned officers, and 15,780 men then boarded trains for the east. Disembarking at Suwalki, Poland, the men and horses then began to walk to their next destination, 600 miles away. This incredible distance, for Spaniards, was a shock, and the rough forty-day march in heat that killed many of the horses and put many a man in hospital was judged to be completely unnecessary. The Spaniards wondered what they had let themselves in for. Yet, at the end of the epic march lay another train ride, before the division finally reached the front line. They had left Germany in a hot August. It was now a cold, wet 11 October.

The next shock was that Munoz Grandes was given a front of thirty miles to defend, a frontage normally assigned to a corps. It ran from the west bank of the Volkhov River to Kurisko on Lake Ilmen.

The Spaniards were eager for the fight they had come 2,000 miles for, and on the night of the 12th the 2nd Battalion of the 269th Regiment attacked, surprised a Soviet battalion, and forced it to withdraw. After a few patrols the battalion attacked and captured part of the river front, and then repelled counterattacks for three days, until the 22nd. Commandante Roman was commended for his leadership. On the 28th the divisional reserve battalion took most of Dubrovka, but failed to capture a Soviet barracks in the town and suffered badly. The same day the 3/263rd Regiment advanced slightly.

A full-scale Soviet counteroffensive put a stop to all movement, and the Spaniards did well to hold the line until 7 November. It was decided then that the enemy would be susceptible to an attack. The decision proved to be a good one, and leading with the 1/269th the division covered twelve kilometers by 12 November and then stopped a Soviet counter-thrust.

In this last Soviet move the village of Passad was surrounded, trapping 380 Spaniards. By the night of the 15th the tiny garrison was devastated, but the survivors succeeded in sending back 200 wounded on snow sleighs and held out another twenty-four hours until they were replaced by a company of the 2/262nd, a company of the 1/263rd, and a company of engineers. Commandante Rebull remained in the village to command its new garrison, and though the enemy attacks were fierce the Spaniards held on.

By November the Netherlands Legion was at the front, having been attached to the 2nd S.S. Brigade. The first task for the initial draft of 875 men was to become acclimatized and familiar with the peculiarities of war on the Eastern Front. A small cadre of German S.S. was assigned to the legion. Before the year was out the legion would have on or near the front line 2,500 Dutchmen ready to defend European civilization as they saw it.

The Flemish had been placed into their own unit, but being short of officer material they had to take orders from a command structure of German S.S. men. Unfortunately for Belgian-German relations these officers looked upon the Flemings as a defeated people, and this caused constant argument and friction. Still by November the 875 Flemings were accepted as being combat trained, and on the 16th they entered a relatively quiet sector of the Leningrad front. For the next two months the men would concentrate on trying to survive nightly patrols, enemy infiltrations, sniping, artillery barrages, air raids, freezing temperatures, and the nazi ardor of their officers. This introduction to modern warfare was a great awakener for these young idealists.

On 4 December the Spanish 250th Blue Division was subjected to a heavy artillery bombardment and then assaulted by four Soviet infantry regiments under an umbrella of Soviet aircraft. Within minutes the Reds broke through the thinly held line. Commandante Roman held together a surrounded force of two companies of engineers, two artillery batteries, and some anti-tank guns, who dug in the bitterly cold snow. By the 6th the excellent quality of the Spaniards had forced the enemy to withdraw with heavy losses. The outpost village of Passad had just been reinforced by the 1/269th in temperatures around -40°C, but then the garrison was ordered to withdraw on the night of the 7th. To date the 269th Regiment had suffered 120 killed, 440 wounded, and 20 missing. For the next two weeks the front was quiet.

Central Sector

By November the German 7th Bavarian Division had been severely reduced in size by five months of terrible combat, and while holding the line near Golokova it was reinforced by the French Volunteer Legion (638th Regiment). Colonel Roger Labonne at sixty was really too old to be trudging through knee-deep snow under shellfire, but he was here and proving that he was faithful to his creed, and that meant a lot to his 2,642 personnel, who were either entering the line or waiting to do so as replacements. After a few patrols the legion advanced at the end of November and at Djukovo, only forty miles west of Moscow, the Frenchmen captured a position and then held off heavy enemy assaults until well into December. The two front line battalions had suffered badly, though, and they soon had to call upon replacements from the 1,400-man replacement depot just to the rear. About 200 of the French soldiers were Moslem Algerians.

At the end of the first week in December the Soviets began to counterattack along the central sector and by mid-December the whole Soviet line was on the move. Often the attacks were led by Soviet soldiers from Siberia who were used to the intense cold and who had not witnessed the great demoralizing Soviet retreats. The Axis soldiers were barely able to hold their weapons let alone fire them as by this time the young men whom Hitler had thrown into the great battle had become pathetic figures, frozen stiff, and huddling together for warmth in their summer uniforms. Within days the German armies were retreating over ground that it had taken weeks to conquer. Within days some units had been forced back a hundred miles, before the Soviet steamroller ran out of steam. On the day the first Soviet counterattacks had taken place, one German unit had been battling for a factory in a suburb of Moscow. The Axis forces would never come that close again.

Southern Sector

After the battle of the coast of the Sea of Azov the German tanks had rushed onwards to reach Rostov, the gateway to the Caucasus and the Soviet oilfields, closely followed by the S.S. Wiking and Slovakian Mobile Divisions, but, although the Axis troops attacked fiercely, the fortress city withstood the assault. In the first week of December the Axis troops were forced back here too and only managed to stop the Soviets on a line between Izyum and Taganrog. Further attempts by the Soviets to advance were repelled by the bravery of Italian, Slovakian, and German units. For merit and bravery during the fighting at Magdalinovka, the Slovakian Colonel Malar was awarded the Knight's Cross. He was to continue to show courage. Now here too the Eastern Front froze solid.

The Hungarians announced that they were recalling three light divisions, an armored brigade, and three frontier brigades from duty in the east. This left them with no front-line troops on the Eastern Front and only four infantry brigades and a bicycle battalion behind the lines to guard installations against partisans. The Hungarians believed they had done enough and they had no ambition to freeze to death in the long Russian winter. To date in their assault on the Soviet Union they had suffered, in six months of action, 26,000 casualties.

Chapter 13

The Purification of the Occupied Territories

As the German horde swept into the east the civilian administration followed it. The Germans planned to rule the conquered land with an Ostministerium under Alfred Rosenberg, who after all should have known something about the mentality of the Soviet people. His fiefdom was divided into three sections, north, center, and south or Ukraine. Each section was in turn ruled by a Reichskommissar who had at his right hand an S.S. general as a Higher S.S. and Police Leader, who was responsible for security. The area within thirty miles of the front was administered by the German Army.

The Germans brought Ordnungspolizei (ordinary police) with them, but wherever possible they encouraged the indigenous police to remain, where they could continue on as before, except that they would have German overseers and would no longer be involved in political investigations. All native police were known as Ordnungsdienst (order service). For political investigations the Gestapo took over, for espionage and counterespionage operations the S.D. ruled the roost, and in case of major criminal activity, such as black marketing, the Kripo was responsible. All of these were elements of the S.S. Security Police, and one KdS was responsible for all of them in his own small area. He reported to the BdS, who in turn was answerable to the Higher S.S. and Police Leader.

In addition to the German Army, Waffen S.S., Navy, Luftwaffe, Ordnungspolizei, and S.S. Security Police, there were other organizations that set up offices in every town. The Allgemeine S.S. had many departments, often seemingly conflicting in their missions, and also the S.D. sometimes gained control of operations that they were not trained for. As the territory was only just occupied and stragglers and terrorists were still around, the Allgemeine S.S. usually carried weapons. Within time all of the civilian organizations would be issued arms for self defense, the major ones being: fire-fighting units of the German fire service; Feurpolizei, who protected the firemen and investigated possible cases of arson; air raid wardens; Organization Todt, which built and maintained military installations and fortifications, often in the front line; R.A.D. Reichs Labor Service, which supplied seventeen- and eighteen-year-olds for government labor duties, usually construction; N.S.K.K. National Socialist Transportation Corps, which provided drivers, mechanics, and traffic directors for various other organizations including rear echelon military units; Bahnschutzpolizei, which guarded trains and train stations; TeNo, which supplied emergency technical repairmen for rebuilding battle-damaged and air raid-damaged installations; S.A. the stormtroopers, who guarded nazi party offices, government buildings, and the lives of nazi officials; and lastly the various departments of the German government and the Ostministerium. The Soviet rail system was taken over by the Germans and many rail employees were brought in from Germany to help run the trains and maintain them.

Every one of these organizations and all the branches of the armed forces took on Soviet citizens as hilfeswillige (volunteer help), nicknamed hiwis, both men and women to perform various jobs, cleaning, laundry, cooking, driving, manual labor, repairs, interpreting, guiding, scouting, and advising. As the months went by, Soviet partisans began to make nuisance raids on the less-protected installations and vehicle convoys. It was later estimated that only 9,000 partisans operated throughout Estonia, Latvia, and Lithuania, most of them being ethnically Russian, but as it only took one partisan sniper or saboteur to cause pandemonium the occupation forces had to be constantly on their guard. As a result many hiwis were employed as unarmed sentries, so that the Germans and other hiwis could get on with their mission in peace. By the end of 1941 many units and agencies were employing armed hiwis as sentries. The number of hiwis who turned upon their masters was so few that the Germans did not worry about it.

Other German officers wanted to use the citizens of the Soviet Union in a more active role, and at Olevskie, Ukraine a mob of willing Ukrainian males was recruited as an anti-partisan force called the Ukrainian Nationalist Revolutionary Army. The Abwehr, the German armed forces espionage service, also recruited many men and women to operate as informers, interpreters, and agents, not just to infiltrate behind enemy lines, but to infiltrate into partisan bands. These people were known as V-men, and were divided into three sections: Walli I, spies; Walli II, saboteurs; Walli III, partisan infiltrators and "turned" Soviet spies. Naturally the chief of Foreign Armies East, German Army Intelligence, also took on hiwis, and he eventually employed about eighty to a hundred at his headquarters in Germany as advisers.

In each of the Baltic States a militia was formed of full-time barracksed personnel who were to root out communists and Red Army stragglers—in Estonia the Eesti Kaitseliit, in Latvia the Aiszargi, and in Lithuania the Siauliai. All of the militiamen were indigenous.

The partisan menace appeared at once. The fighters were either Red Army stragglers or communists who had been left behind. Few of these groups were in contact with the Soviet government and it would be months before the Soviet government realized the potential of a guerrilla force behind the Axis lines. As early as July the German 8th Panzer Division had to be taken out of front-line combat in order to protect lines of communication in Northern Russia, as the partisans were threatening the resupply of Army Group North. Each German army group already had three security divisions, made up of German Army reservists 36-45 years of age, but these were obviously not enough for such an immense area. By the end of the year almost every one of the German armed forces, government, and civilian organizations had had at least one district section commandeered by army officers, armed hastily, and sent into action against a partisan band. All of these German citizens were eligible for military medals while on such military duties, but the hiwis were as yet not officially recognized. Usually the hiwis wore their own clothing, civilian or ex-Red Army, but those who were employed by a branch of the armed forces wore an armband stating that they were "in the service of the German Armed Forces." All German branches of the armed forces and other organizations used females, but females were never armed or placed into danger areas, though of course some came under attack now and then.

Of all the German formations that crossed the Soviet border the most hideous were the Einsatzgruppen (action groups). These were created in the spring of 1941 and divided into Einsatzkommandos, and must not be confused with the Einsatzkommandos that served in Poland prior to this date. These new formations were ordered not just to round up Jews, nomadic Gypsies, communists and other undesirables and imprison them, but were actually ordered to kill them, without regard to age or sex. Heinrich Himmler had only informed some of his staff of this top-secret project, and he and his aides had recruited people for special duties, using a process of weeding out those who were too humane, a process originally established by Theodor Eicke, the first S.S. Inspector of the Concentration Camp Service. Eicke was an Alsatian. Once the recruiters had rejected the sympathetic and moral volunteers, whom Himmler referred to as faint-hearts, they were left with 3,000 men (and some women). As expected many of the men came from the Concentration Camp Service, but as not enough S.S. personnel could be found the recruiters took in members of the ordinary police too. The men were placed into four groups. Einsatzgruppe A consisted of 517 personnel from the S.S. Security Police and Concentration Camp Service, 340 from the Waffen S.S., and 133 from the ordinary police forces. The female members were to be used as interpreters, clerks, and radio operators.

By the time of their entry into the Soviet Union none of the personnel were still under any illusions as to their real purpose. As can be imagined most of the men and women were moronic zombies, more amoral than immoral. However, some of the officers were intelligent. Of the eight men who would eventually command the four groups, four held doctorates.

Einsatzgruppe A entered Lithuania to be greeted with good news. A pogrom had preceded them. Identifying those Lithuanians who had taken part the einsatzgruppe recruited them as hiwis. When these local bully-boys and thugs expressed an interest in performing executions, they were allowed to do so. Some Lithuanian policemen also joined the einsatzgruppe, while on leave of absence from their regular duties.

The mission of the einsatzgruppe was death, and the officers began to organize special *aktion* in order to carry out this mission. The first aktion took place at Kovno, where the einsatzgruppe rounded up 416 Jews. These scared, innocent men were marched by a gang of Lithuanian hiwis to a spot outside the city and then were shot dead. Few Germans had been present at this first big aktion, and the anti-Semitic fervor of the hiwis impressed the einsatzgruppe men. The S.S. ordered all Jews in Lithuania to perform public service, often cleaning toilets and sweeping the streets. Any Jews who were too old or infirm to perform their act of atonement were handed to the einsatzgruppe for special treatment.

Throughout the rural areas of the east the four einsatzgruppe split up into einsatzkommandos and sometimes smaller sections in order to massacre village Jews, men, women, children, and babies. The einsatzgruppe found the Christian villagers to be ignorant and superstitious. Some kept garlic, special herbal compounds, and religious symbols near their doorways to keep out vampires and werewolves. The peasants had all been indoctrinated by their village priests, who were no less ignorant and superstitious. In some instances Christian villagers kidnapped Jewish neighbors and took them to the einsatzgruppen for extermination. Columns of arrested Jews who were marched out to the countryside were jeered and spat upon by their neighbors. There were some reports that villagers called a holiday and picnicked at the execution sites.

The einsatzgruppe were never short of hiwis, except in Estonia, but there were few Jews in Estonia anyway. Being professional murderers, the Germans were constantly astonished at the ferocity of the anti-Semitism they encountered, for the einsatzgruppe personnel were not all anti-Semitic. Most of the members would have murdered red-headed people if that had been the order.

By the end of August about 500 einsatzgruppe had shot 20,000 Jews at Vilnius. They could not have performed such a task had it not been for the several hundred Lithuanian hiwis. Surprisingly, 40,000 Jews still lived there, oblivious as to what had happened to their friends and relatives, and only now did the S.S. begin rounding them up to place them in a shrunken part of the Jewish quarter. This was christened the Vilna Ghetto and no one was allowed to leave without permission on pain of death. Meanwhile the einsatzgruppe personnel were mostly transferred to Kovno, where the surviving Jews were also being ghettoized. In Kovno 6,000 Jews had already been executed by the Hiwis and einsatzgruppe, and the remaining 30,000 were rounded up by Lithuanian police, German ordinary police, and German S.S. Security Police. Once the ghetto had been established with various thoroughfares being blocked off the Lithuanian police guarded the perimeter.

Inside each ghetto a Judenrat and a Jewish police force were created in order to run the day-to-day affairs. The members of these authorities were guaranteed better food rations and they and their families were immune to deportations for "resettlement." Always the nazis used euphemisms when dealing with people outside the S.S. Only days after the Vilna Ghetto was established, German, Lithuanian, and Jewish policemen began arresting all residents who did not possess German-issued work permits, and their dependents. This mass of 10,000 men, women, and children was marched away and handed to the einsatzgruppe.

In September, the issue of blank work permits to the residents of Kovno Ghetto was the cause of a riot. The people fought each other for possession of them, for to have one kept a man, his wife, and children safe. The ghetto Jews were not aware of the true destination of those who had already been deported, but they did not want to be separated from their families perhaps forever, nor did they wish to be worked to death in disease-ridden labor camps the way the people arrested by the N.K.V.D. had ended up. Whatever the true destination of the deportees, the Jews knew it would not be a pleasurable experience. The unarmed Jewish police could not control the mobs and eventually had to ask the Lithuanian police to step in. The Lithuanians were alarmed and a few panicked, firing submachine guns into the dense crowds. The riot was stopped as the people scattered indoors, but one of the many people who had been shot dead was a German police adviser.

The S.S. officers were angered by this death of a German, but despite the fault lying with the lack of discipline among the Lithuanian police the S.S. sought vengeance among the Jews. They ordered the Lithuanian police to arrest 1,000 elderly Jews and hand them to the einsatzgruppe for special treatment.

On 1 October 300 einsatzgruppe waited outside Vilna Ghetto as their Lithuanian hiwis and the Lithuanian and Jewish police arrested anyone found without a work permit. After sunset 3,000 Jews were marched to Ponary just outside the town, many of them holding lighted candles to help them find their footing. Once they arrived at the death pits they calmly stood on the edges of these mass graves and waited for the executioner's bullet.

Only now did the Vilna Jews realize the truth, and panic struck the community. Yet, the following day several hundred Jews allowed themselves to be peacefully arrested. It seemed that they were almost glad that the mystery was over. It was easier for them to accept death than it was to live in suspense. The Jews were now informed that a work permit protected a man, his wife, and two children under sixteen. If a man had more than two children under sixteen he had to make a decision as to which ones he would save. Naturally there was much bribery. A Jewish policeman might be induced to forget how to count with the offer of a warm coat or an item of cheap jewelry. A few Jews simply fled, for the perimeter was often poorly guarded.

On 4 October the S.S. learned of an outbreak of a contagious disease in a Kovno Ghetto hospital. They cured it by sending German and Lithuanian policemen to burn down the hospital, with the patients and medical staff still inside. On 24 October the Lithuanian Police and the einsatzgruppe hiwis scoured Vilna Ghetto for unproductive persons, finding 5,000 such people, many of whom had been hiding in cupboards, cellars, and secret compartments. They were marched to the death pits at Ponary.

Now the chief of the Jewish police, Jacob Gens, who was also a Jew, stepped in to personally choose who should live and who should die, by pointing out the weaklings as the residents of Kovno Ghetto were marched past him. His attitude was noticed by the S.S. Security Police and he was soon promoted to head the Kovno Judenrat. On 28 October Kovno Ghetto lost its unproductive elements when Lithuanian einsatzgruppe hiwis, and German, Lithuanian, and Jewish police searched the closely packed buildings. Approximately 10,000 souls were delivered to the einsatzgruppe. Between 3-5 November the Jewish police rounded up several hundred more Jews in Vilna who had been in hiding because they had not been able to acquire work permits.

In November a large part of Einsatzgruppe A was ordered to Riga, Latvia in order to begin aktion there. This gruppe of less than one thousand men was responsible for "purifying" all of Lithuania, Latvia, Estonia, and Northern Russia. In order to perform the duties prescribed by Himmler, the gruppe had to employ hundreds of hiwis.

As Einsatzgruppe B drove into Byelorussia it accepted several hundred hiwis almost at once. Many of the volunteers participated in the first big aktion for this gruppe at Bialystok in which 700 undesirables were shot. In late October at Borisov the einsatzgruppe personnel, some Byelorussian hiwis, and Byelorussian schumas (auxiliary policemen) held a pre-execution party becoming as drunk as humanly possible. Early the following morning the still-drunken killers roamed the streets of the town rousting out the Jews from their homes and marching them off to the countryside. In some instances the Jews ran for it and were gunned down on the spot. By late morning 8,000 Jews had been rounded up, but 2,000 had managed to escape from their guards who were by now suffering from hangovers. The rest of the Jews were massacred.

A few days later at Slutsk an equal number of German einsatzgruppe and Lithuanian hiwis ransacked the town in their search for Jews. Many of those found were shot dead in their tracks, and any Christians who tried to save their "one good Jew" were beaten senseless.

The highest number of volunteers came from Ukraine, and Einsatzgruppe C, which operated here, was never short of manpower. In Lwow the hiwis and mobs of Ukrainians and Poles launched an all-out attack on the Jewish quarter, murdering any Jew they caught in the street. Many a long-simmering grudge was settled as the mobs went after certain tradesmen. Jewish sources claim that 7,000 Jews of all ages were murdered in this pogrom. Certainly hundreds of Jews could be found hanging from lampposts the following day.

Further south Einsatzgruppe D, a smaller force of only 500 Germans, was under orders to purify the coastal areas of Ukraine and then the Crimean Peninsula as soon as it was captured, but the unit had to drive through Romanian-occupied territory to reach this area. When they did so the Germans were astounded at the fanatic anti-Semitism of some Romanians. Romanian soldiers and policemen attacked Jews in the liberated districts of Northern Bukovina and Bessarabia, beating, shooting, and stabbing them to death. The Ukrainian segments of these provinces also joined the pogrom. As a joke Jewish corpses were displayed in shop windows. In Jassy an army unit packed as many Jews as possible into a train of cattle cars. Then the train drivers were ordered to keep the train moving, criss-crossing the district. At the end of several days the train came to a halt and the doors were slid open to reveal 8,000 corpses. Those few who had miraculously survived were shot dead.

A party of Romanian policemen attached themselves to Einsatzgruppe D, which also took on some Ukrainian hiwis, and in the neighborhood of Storozhinets and Chernovtsy 12,000 Jews were executed in the first few days of liberation. The German executioners often stayed drunk on captured vodka as it helped ease their consciences, but the Romanians and Ukrainians only drank after the killings in a celebratory manner. Around Kishinev in the last two weeks in July Einsatzgruppe D, its hiwis, and the attached Romanians murdered 12,287 undesirables.

In Kiev as soon as it was liberated delayed action bombs began going off all over the city, killing hundreds of German soldiers and Ukrainian and Jewish civilians. Using this as an excuse, the commander of Einsatzgruppe C ordered retaliation against the Jews. Using 300 Germans and several hundred Ukrainian hiwis, the commander began rounding up the Jews for deportation. It was announced that any Jew who did not voluntarily come to the deportation centers would be shot. By 26 September 34,000 Jews had reported, and they were all marched to a wooded area known as Babi Yar. There took place the largest aktion. It took two days for the killers to finish off every Jew and even then a few adults and children survived for a time, dragging their bleeding bodies across the fields.

On 13 October the men of Einsatzgruppe C and one hundred Ukrainian hiwis dragged 11,000 Jews out of Dniepropetrovsk and murdered them. On 6 November men of this unit and several hundred Ukrainian hiwis massacred 15,000 undesirables outside Rowno. At Kharkov some einsatzgruppe placed 20,000 Jews in an abandoned tractor factory, and thereafter took out a few each day and shot them. They claimed they did not have enough personnel to kill all of the Jews at once. The real reason was that it gave the men an excuse to stay in one town for a while instead of roaming all over the countryside, where they risked running into partisans. The last thing these killers wanted was to confront an enemy who could shoot back.

When Einsatzgruppe D entered the Crimea it took on 500 Tatar hiwis in order to help butcher the Jews in this peninsula. Interestingly, a tribe of culturally Islamic people whose religion was Jewish was allowed to live in peace and to reopen their synagogues that the Soviets had closed. However, a tribe of cultural Jews whose religion was Islam were massacred. The einsatzgruppe evidently decided that their brief was to murder racial Jews not people who were solely religious Jews. They were allowed this laxity as the einsatzgruppe had never been given written orders for their mission. Officially the einsatzgruppe were an anti-terrorist force.

The Germans were in need of many real anti-terrorist forces quite soon, and not just to fight partisans. With the liberation of the Baltic States those Volksdeutsch who had been expelled by the Soviets could return. Administered by the VOMI department of the S.S., these people were soon allowed to take up where they left off. Other Germans were arriving too as colonists, administered by the Race and Resettlement Office of the S.S. To some extent they had been cajoled to settle in the east, but the benefits were good. Any of them who were in business could employ the natives cheaply, and any who were not were offered a variety of jobs, made available by simply firing the local natives. No taxes were payable for the first five years of colonization, and other special considerations were given. A few thousand Dutch families were recruited by the S.S. as colonists, too. Naturally this caused considerable ill feeling in the colonized districts among the indigenous population, and soon it became prudent for some colonists to carry sidearms. German security units that could have been used to good effect elsewhere were often tied up protecting colonists.

The reaction to the harsh policies of the nazi regime in the east forced some to form anti-nazi partisan bands, though they were not all pro-communist. The members of the Ukrainian National Revolutionary Army were beginning to complain about the atrocities they had witnessed, and in order to prevent a possible mutiny, the S.S. Security Police reacted in the only manner they understood, with brute force. They arrested the more vociferous rebels, but this only forced the whole unit to desert en masse. Under a Major Borovets these men formed a guerrilla band sworn to repel all Ukrainian enemies.

It was not the number of partisans that was hurting the Germans, but the number of potential targets that had to be guarded. The only answer was a full- and part-time militia. Each Baltic State had already recruited a militia, and the Byelorussians were allowed to recruit one, the Byelorussian Popular Self-defense Corps (B.N.S.). In the Ukraine a Ukrainian Popular Self-defense Corps (U.N.S.) was established. Within the area controlled by Army Group North a militia was established from Russian volunteers, called the Einwohnerkampfverbaende (Indigenous fighting bands). Army Group Center also created a Russian militia, called the Ordnungsdienst (Order Service), not to be confused with the ordinary Russian police who also had this name.

In addition Army Group North created some fourteen battalions of full-time militiamen, recruited from Russians, Finnish-speaking Karelians, Latvians, Estonians, and Lithuanians, called the Sicherungabteilungen (Security Departments).

To assist the local regular police, actual battalions of paramilitary auxiliary policemen were recruited as had been done in Poland already. Called schumas, which stood for Schutzmannschaften (Guard Man Squads), the men were trained to act as individual policemen or as whole companies of infantry as the occasion demanded. Usually the younger volunteers were placed in hunt formations and the older volunteers in sentry units. For their first few operations the battalions had German advisers from the S.S. and police, but usually the men operated under commanders of their own nationality.

After several months in combat the Roland and Nachtigall Legions were recalled and the men placed into the Ukrainian 201st Schuma Battalion. This proved to be a bad move, though, for now the men could see the atrocities of the nazis for themselves. By December the unit was becoming mutinous and the German police chose to disband it. The rabble-rousers among the men were arrested and sent to a concentration camp. Some of the men fled into the woods to form a guerrilla band, having come to the conclusion that Germany would never allow Ukraine to gain her freedom.

Besides these nationalist partisans and the communist partisans, there were a few small groups of Jewish partisans. Near Tomaszow Lubelski a Jewish band was in existence, but some local Poles found out about them and betrayed them to the security authorities. The information was acted upon immediately and the poorly armed band was wiped out.

To aid the German security divisions in their anti-partisan operations the Slovakian 1st and 2nd Divisions had been withdrawn from the front, but this still only put about 30,000 German and Slovakian infantrymen into the field on operations at any one time. As more and more civilian units and army rear-echelon units begged for protection, those Army and S.S. officers responsible for security were forced to turn more and more to hiwis and actual locally raised combat units.

In November 1941 a prisoner of war, Colonel Igor K. Sakharov, a Russian, was commissioned by the Abwehr to raise a force of anti-partisan soldiers. He gained 350 recruits from the prisoner of war camps almost at once. The commander in the field was to be Major Sergei Ivanov, and as he had gray hair the unit was nicknamed the Graukopf Battalion.

Also in November, Lieutenant-Colonel Helmut von Pannwitz was commissioned to raise several sotni (companies of a hundred men each) of horsed Cossacks from prisoners of war. He had been picked for the job as he had known the Cossacks as a youth and spoke passable Russian. Actually he was from the part of Germany that was occupied by the Poles in the inter-war period and he had lived there as a Polish civilian. He soon found there to be plenty of recruits for his sotni, and this is where he first came up with the idea of establishing a Cossack liberating army. Unfortunately he was incapacitated through illness in December. Meanwhile his Cossacks were soon busy patrolling the windswept snow-covered plains within fifty kilometers of the front line, searching for spies, partisan bands, and Red Army units that had infiltrated through the thinly defended front line.

Lieutenant-Colonel Henning von Tresckow, the chief of staff of Army Group Center, was commissioned to raise six battalions of Ukrainian and Byelorussian pioneers to perform light military construction and labor duties. He was impressed by the response, and he soon informed his friends Lieutenant-Colonel Reinhard Gehlen and Captain Wilfrid Strik-Strikfeldt. Gehlen would soon be promoted to head Foreign Armies East and Strik-Strikfeldt would work with him. These men would become very influential in the formation of units of eastern volunteers.

Between Orel and Kursk, and south of Bryansk, Colonel-General Rudolf Schmidt, commander of the German Second Panzer Army, went even further than other commanders and actually set up an autonomous zone called Lokot, with a Russian engineer, K.P. Voskoboinikov, as governor. With a population of 1.7 million the province was large enough to produce its own militia to keep out communist partisans, and as the German Army administrators had already introduced private ownership and capitalism, the Russian people of Lokot were kept happy. Unfortunately, Schmidt only controlled a small segment of the occupied east. Hitler could have greatly benefited from Colonel-General Schmidt's discovery.

In fact, by the end of 1941 Hitler had yet to sanction the employment of even one hiwi, let alone the recruitment of militia and anti-partisan units. Yet he was quite aware of the growing partisan problem. His advisers had been suggesting the creation of a major anti-partisan force of eastern troops, and Hitler finally had to give in, but he refused to use the Slavs, whom he hated. Instead he agreed to use people whom the Turkish government would smile upon. Turkey was neutral and could still swing either way in this world war, and Hitler knew it. To please the Turks and create the much-needed force, Hitler hit upon the idea of recruiting only Turkic-speaking Moslem troops. The Turkish language is part of the Turkic group, and the Turks have always felt an affinity towards speakers of the other Turkic languages, much more than, say, Frenchmen do for Spaniards, who both speak languages of the Romance group. Hitler also knew that Moslems shared his anti-Semitism to one degree or another. As the homelands of these people had not yet been liberated, the recruits would have to come from the prisoner of war camps. The army recruiters were surprised with the response, for not only did the volunteers see this as a chance to help liberate their homelands from the hated communists, but they saw it as a way of getting out of their terrible privation behind barbed-wire, where inadequate food, shelter, and medical supervision was slowly killing them. When the news was passed to the generals they expanded the order. Two legions were created, a Turkestani one from Yakuts, Dolgany, Tofalarys, Karagas, Tuvunians, Azerbaijans, Kumyks, Nogays, Karachais, Balkars, Turkmen, Khakass, Altays, Uzbeks, Khazhaks, Kirghiz, and Karakalpaks, and a Caucasian-Moslem one from Andis, Botlikhs, Godaberis, Chamalais, Bagulals, Tindis, Karatas, Akhvakhs, Tsaz, Kvarshi, Bezhtins, Ginukhs, Archis, Budukhs, Dargins, Kryz, Udis, Laks, Lezghins, Aguls, Rutuls, Tsakhurs, Tadzikhs, Chechens, Ingush, Kabardins, Circassians, and Khinalugs. Other lesser nations also supplied volunteers, and there was a considerable amount of crossover between these legions as the Germans never quite knew who or what they were dealing with. In fact none of the peoples in the latter group are Turkic-speaking.

The Germans expanded the order even further, making a very liberal interpretation of it by recruiting a legion of Armenians and one of Georgians. Both these nations are Christian and the Turks hated the Armenians, and would not take too kindly to the German recruitment of an Armenian legion that might have nationalist aspirations.

In addition to serving the Germans as militiaman, policeman, anti-partisan hunter, security guard, or hiwi, the people of the occupied-east could serve the Germans as a civilian industrial worker. By the end of 1941, 70,000 Soviet citizens had volunteered to work in Germany and another 100,000 had volunteered to work away from home but still within their nations. These men and women were treated reasonably well and the pay was good by Soviet standards.

Appreciated as this was it was not enough, for Germany desperately needed workers in industry and in agriculture. Too many of her men served in the armed forces, police, or one of the ancillary services. As yet Hitler had not compulsorily mobilized the women folk of Germany, nor did he want to for political reasons.

There was only one answer and that meant slave labor. Among the mass of people pushed and shoved aboard trains for Germany were half a million Ukrainian women destined to serve as housemaids for nazi party officials' wives. Eventually three million Ukrainians were deported for slave labor, half of them women. The workers' treatment depended on where they were sent. The destinations were Organization Todt, where some of the laborers would have to work close enough to the front line to come under shellfire, munitions plants guarded by the army, S.S. labor camps, German government labor camps, where the guards were government employees, and civilian labor camps operated on behalf of the large industrial companies in Germany, I.G. Farben, Siemens, Krupp and so on, where the guards were either company employees or Werkschutz, a government factory guard service. The German farms also received slave laborers. In many cases there were no guards, for no concentration camp inmates worked in the area, who were the real charges of the sentries. In these cases the treatment was fairly good, considering the workers were slaves. Not all of the slaves were manual laborers, either. Many became skilled machinists, and others worked as engineers and scientists.

The Ukrainians were treated better than any of the eastern slaves. They had the largest food ration, which was not too far below the German rate, and were allowed free time in the evenings and Sundays, but had to be off the streets by sunset. Fraternization with German civilians was frowned upon and both could be severely punished, but it did take place nonetheless. The Russians had more restrictions and a poor food ration. The Poles were practically starved.

Fritz Sauckel, the German forced labor recruiter, never had enough German staff, so he had to recruit 1,000 hiwis to help find and round up those citizens of the occupied east who had no gainful employment.

Meanwhile the Jews of Bessarabia and Northern Bukovina had been placed in several concentration camps in Transniestra. On 21 December at the Golta area under Colonel Modest Isopescu, the Romanians began to shoot their prisoners rather than feed them: 5,000 at Atmicetka, 18,000 at Dumanowka, and 48,000 at Bogdanowka. The remaining 114,000 Jews encamped along the Bug River were left to the elements.

Chapter 14

Yugoslavia: The Cauldron

Organized anti-fascist resistance was not long in appearing in the inhospitable mountains of Yugoslavia. In the late spring of 1941 a force called the Officers Movement, for lack of a more inspiring name, led by Colonel Draza Milhailovich fled to the mountains of southwest Serbia in order to prepare a guerrilla war against the Germans. For their part, the Germans, new to the countryside and lacking adequate intelligence, and most of all being distracted by their invasion of the Soviet Union, did not bother Milhailovich's men.

By the time the conflict between the homes of nazism and communism began, the Yugoslavian communists were already planning a campaign to fight the invaders and to gather non-communist recruits under their wing. Although the communists maintained that they would have made war upon the nazi/fascists even if Germany and the Soviet Union had remained allies, it was nonetheless noticeable that nothing really began until after Moscow was under attack and gave orders for the various communist parties to revolt, and that in Yugoslavia the fighting began due to a spontaneous non-communist uprising. There were in fact only a few hundred communist diehards in all of Yugoslavia, but they were all experienced at clandestine activity, some of them were veterans of World War One, a few, like Broz, were veterans of the Russian Civil War, and about 200 were veterans of the recent Spanish Civil War.

Josip Broz, known at this time only by the code-name Tito, ordered active resistance to begin on 4 July 1941, but he knew this would not happen for it would take time to raise and train and equip a guerrilla army. At first the activity consisted of ambushes of Serbian State and City Guards, with the object of trying to get the policemen to desert.

However, on 13 July the fiercely independent Montenegrin peasants shot up an Italian convoy near Kolasin and besieged the Italian garrisons of Bioca and Danilovgrad. Two days later, the Italian government ordered General Pirzio Birolli, the commander of the Ninth Army, to quash this revolt at once. Nonetheless by the 19th a Carabinieri outpost at Baranc had been overrun and the troops at Bioca deserted the town without much of a fight. Worse was to come; the 1,000 defenders of Danilovgrad surrendered after a week of battle.

Birolli's reinforcements were hurried to the threatened area, but a battalion column was ambushed while on its way to Podgoritza and lost one hundred dead. Still Birolli knew what he was doing, and his men soon occupied the mouths of the Zeta and Moraca rivers, having driven back the poorly armed peasants with a weight of infantry supported by artillery and aircraft. On the 30th the Italians began advancing into the mountains of Veljo Brdo and Trijebac, burning to the ground any village which offered the slightest resistance. Meanwhile mobs of Moslem peasants took advantage of the breakdown of law and order and looted nearby Christian villages, in some instances committing murder.

Now, loosely controlled by Milovan Djilas, one of Tito's deputies, the Montenegrin insurgents attacked the occupier in other areas of Montenegro. Nowhere were the Italians safe, and even minor missions had to be well-guarded. The Italian soldiers were suddenly afraid, for every harmless looking villager was a potential sniper, saboteur, or assassin. A Carabinieri outpost was overrun at Mojkovac. On 5 August, though, the rebels felt the full wrath of the Italians. The Venezia Division attacked Lipov and Kolasin, quickly taking the latter. Most of the peasant guerrillas fled in panic, but a rearguard of men from Durmitor fought bravely at Krnovo. With this action the Italians had the enemy on the run and dispersed. It looked like the end of organized rebellion. The Italians now began to rule Montenegro with the full brutality of a fascist regime.

Milhailovich was aware of the Montenegrin revolt and he was determined to follow it with a war of his own, but he suffered from political dissension within his ranks. Some of his men looked upon the guerrillas in Montenegro as the greater danger for they were being directed by communists. Others wished to side with the Serbian puppet government. The leader of the Cetniks, ex-citizens of the Austro-Hungarian Empire, who were Serbian-speaking and Serbian monarchists, was Kosta Pecanec, and he was urging his followers to aid the Serbian puppet government. These problems caused much soul-searching within the hearts and minds of the men of the Officers Movement. One of Milhailovich's sons would soon be serving with Tito.

Within Serbia hundreds of prominent citizens, including the Orthodox bishops of Nis, Zwornik, and Budimle, called upon the people to aid the Serbian government and the German "guest" forces to crush the communists. On 29 August the Serbian government received a new leader, Milan Nedic, an ex-general of the Yugoslavian Army and ex-Minister of War for Yugoslavia. He announced tough measures for dealing with all terrorists.

The Cetnik Movement split wide open. Those in agreement with Nedic joined his police and government or supported him in some way, and those opposed to the Serbian puppet government remained outlawed in the mountains. Soon the word Cetnik would describe the guerrillas, and not the supporters of Serbia.

On 21 September a gang of Titoists captured the town of Uzice in Serbia, quite close to Milhailovich's stronghold at Ravna Gora. Three days later a group of Milhailovich's men, henceforth called Cetniks, were argued and bullied out of Boza by a band of Titoists. Both Tito and Milhailovich knew it was time for negotiations between them, lest a war within a war begin between the Cetniks and the communists.

In answer to the terrorist problem Nedic formed the Serbian Volunteer Command (later Serbian Volunteer Corps). Led by Dmitrije Ljotic, it at first consisted of twelve companies of volunteers who were dedicated to salvaging what they could of Serbia, even if this meant fighting against Milhailovich and Tito. Some of the recruits were deserters from Milhailovich.

Meanwhile the Russian emigre population within the country, which could not rely on the occupiers for protection, feared that with communist partisans on the rampage it would only be a matter of time before communist assassins began to murder them and their families on the orders of Moscow. Therefore, they formed a Russian Defense Corps, with a nod from the local German commander, which consisted of 3,000 men, mostly serving part time, equipped with a rifle and a horse. Their purpose was purely self defense.

In southern Serbia and eastern Bosnia-Herzegovina the German 342nd Division went into the field on an anti-guerrilla sweep. About this time, October, there was an upsurge in activity in Montenegro, too. The Italians learned that Milovan Djilas had ordered a resumption of guerrilla action in order to convince the Italians that Montenegro would never submit. The Italian-controlled Montenegrin police and village militias seemed to be unable to report on guerrilla movements let alone stop them. When an Italian convoy of seventy men was taken prisoner near Jelin Dub on 18 October, after inflicting fifteen casualties on the communists, the Italians arrested ten members of the nearby village militia outpost and executed them for dereliction of duty. A few days later a large Italian column was ambushed for two days until it retreated, near Kuci.

As a new ploy the Italians offered an amnesty to all terrorists who surrendered their weapons. The Italians honored their offer, but there were few takers. The action against the village militia paid off. When the Moslem villages along the Ribarevina River were attacked by the communists, the militiamen put up a good defense.

But internal strife caused more problems for the guerrillas than a minor rebuff here and there. After thirty Germans were killed by Cetniks in Kraljevo, the German district commander ordered a massacre on 18 October. It is believed that at least 1,700 villagers were murdered. Only days later the Germans massacred 2,300 people in Kragujevac in retaliation for the killing of ten Germans by Cetnik guerrillas. Draza Milhailovich was made to feel like the murderer of his own people, when he heard the casualty reports. He vacillated when his hotheads urged more raids on enemy-occupied villages. On 28 October an argument between Cetniks who wanted to lie low for a while and communists who wanted to continue raiding ended in gunplay.

By the end of October in the city of Belgrade alone the German S.S. Security Police and the Serbian Police had executed 4,750 people for terrorist activities and as reprisals for terrorist acts.

On the first day of November, the Cetniks turned their guns on those whom they believed to be the greater danger to the Serbian people. They attacked the communist (Titoist) headquarters at Uzice.

The attack failed. Milhailovich claimed to control 5,000 men, and some women, but only a fraction of this force turned up for the battle. Obviously, as the Germans controlled the skies and the main roads, movement of large groups of guerrillas was slow and risky. Within a week Milhailovich's headquarters on Ravna Gora was surrounded by a communist guerrilla army. On 11 November Milhailovich made a compromise agreement with Pecanec. He would behave neutrally towards the Germans and Serbian government forces as long as he was threatened by the communists. During the siege the Cetniks captured thirty Titoists and shot them. They were all women.

The German command structure soon realized what was happening and decided to take advantage of this mini-civil war. The Germans had recently been reinforced with the 125th Regiment, 713th Security Division, 113th Division, and headquarters of the XVIIIth Mountain Corps, commanded by Lieutenant General Franz Boehme. Using all his field forces as well as the 342nd Division, Boehme launched an assault against the communists and Cetniks alike. When a column of Germans advanced on Uzice the communists besieging Ravna Gora abandoned their positions. This gave Milhailovich a chance to escape so that he could negotiate with the Germans. Mid-December saw the German capture of Uzice, but the rebels and most of the townsfolk had fled. The Germans were happy, though, for by the end of the year the communists had been driven into Montenegro, where they were no concern of the Germans, but would become an Italian problem. At this time there was no real liaison between the Germans and Italians, and therefore the Italians were not waiting for the communists. This lack of cooperation meant that Tito would live to fight another day.

On the last day of the year the Germans executed ninety communists who had been captured, in accordance with the rules of the Hague Convention. Some Serbian partisans had deserted their Cetnik or communist units and had gone home, but they found that there were plenty of informers who would quickly turn them over to the Serbian Police.

The war now emerged in Montenegro again. After an Italian patrol was captured near Nova Varos the nearby Italian garrison withdrew across the Lim River, to escape the invading communist army.

In the first two days of December 1941, the advanced units of Tito's army battered their heads against the Italian defenders of Plevlja, and the defenders claimed the victory, having inflicted casualties on the communists of 300 dead and 600 wounded. On 12 December the Italians counterattacked and almost caught Tito himself who had now come to see in person the state of the opposition at Drenovo. Meanwhile Tito had sent agents to Macedonia to try to gain control of all partisans there. The communists in Macedonia had risen against the Bulgarian occupation troops on 11 October.

By early 1942 Tito was already planning an invasion of Serbia, but how much this was really an invasion of German-controlled territory and how much it was really a retreat from Italian-controlled territory has never been fully established.

By the end of 1941 Yugoslavia was a theater of war and the lines had been drawn, but they had been drawn so faintly that there was much overlapping. In Slovenia law and order was defended by the Italians in the west and by Germans in the north and east. The district of Prekomurja was controlled by Hungarian troops. Many Slovenians had fled to independent Croatia and about 16,000 members of the Slovene intelligentsia had been deported to Croatia and Serbia from the German zones.

The Italians had allowed the Slovenians to set up a village militia for self-defense against communists and bandits, and belatedly they officially recognized it as the MVAC—Anti-communist Volunteer Militia. Then they began to advise and support it, recognizing a good thing when they saw it. The militia was divided into a part-time force, the Vaske Straze (Village Guards), and a full-time Legiya Smrti (Legion of Death). Many of the 6,500 members of the MVAC were ex-policemen. The communists called them "Whites."

Anti-fascist resistance in Slovenia was divided into two groups, the communists, who now and then took orders from Tito, and the Cetniks, who believed in Slovenian autonomy within a Serbian monarchy. However, the Cetniks were even less inclined to recognize a centralized leadership than the communists. The Cetniks were therefore a group of political clans of varying size, weaponry, and discipline. The major clans were the 3,500-man Roman Catholic Slovenian Legion, the 1,000-man Liberal and Socialist Falcon Legion, and the smaller National League. The most accurate description of these Cetniks is that each defended its own particular politico/religious ideology. The communists called all Cetniks in Slovenia "Blues."

Most of the time the Whites and the Blues fought the Reds, that is the communists, when they were not fighting each other, that is. The Italians only suffered when they got in the way.

Few Italian and German troops were required to keep order in Croatia, for the Croatian Army had increased in size to three corps, Ist at Zagreb, IInd at Brod, and IIIrd at Sarajevo. The army contained a total of five divisions, each of which consisted of three regiments, of three infantry battalions each, four engineer battalions, twelve artillery battalions, a regiment of three cavalry battalions (horsed), and an armored car unit. The total manpower of the army was

55,000. The prime purpose of the army was national self-defense against outside invaders.

It was the Ustaci which secured national interests within the borders of the new state. The Ustaci especially had its work cut out for it in the province of Bosnia-Herzegovina, as the population was only 25% Croatian and Roman Catholic, but 35% Moslem, and 40% Serbian Orthodox. Besides having fifteen part-time battalions and two rail security battalions, the Ustaci had two full-time completely dedicated units, the Black Legion and the Poglavnik Battalion. The specialty of the full-time Ustaci was to remove undesirables from the state. The Jews, Gypsies, and Croatian dissidents were arrested and placed in concentration camps. The Serbian Orthodox were encouraged to evacuate to Serbia taking only hand-carried belongings. In some isolated villages the Serbians were murdered. There is no accurate figure for Serbian expulsions, but it was certainly at least 200,000 people, and may have been much higher. The number of murders is also impossible to ascertain, but the communists claim a death toll of 200,000. It is more accurate to say, certainly, that about 200,000 Serbians were allowed to remain by converting to the Roman Catholic faith. It is also possible that upwards of 60,000 Gypsies were eventually murdered. The Moslems were left alone for the most part. Indeed the Moslems feared the Cetniks more than the Ustaci, for a few Moslem villages had been wiped out by Cetnik forays.

In addition to the normal Croatian police there were four State Police regiments, numbering 6,000 men, and a part-time Police Militia of 7,500 men.

As if this was not enough, the Italians formed their own Anti-communist Volunteer Militia in Croatia, which took orders only from the commander of the Italian "guest" forces.

The commander of the Croatian Army was Field Marshal Slavkovitez Kwaternik, a man who was often more responsive to the Germans and Italians than he was to Ante Pavelic's government. He supplied troops to both Germany and Italy for use on the Russian front.

However, the Germans did not get along well with the Ustaci. Not only did the men of Pavelic's pet force ignore the Germans in matters of discipline and security, but they disgusted the ordinary German soldiers with their atrocities. In the Foca area alone the Ustaci murdered 400 Serbians, but then again in this same luckless district 3,000 Moslems were massacred by Cetniks. It got so bad that the German command demanded that Jure Francetic, the commander of the 1st Brigade Black Legion, be dismissed due to his unbridled cruelty. Pavelic replied by promoting Francetic to commander of all Ustaci field formations.

Throughout Serbia a semblance of order had been created, the expulsion of the Titoists and the many minor terrorist incidents notwithstanding. One of the biggest Serbian operations took place in December, when the Belgrade city police rounded up all Jews. Any Jew who resisted or attempted to escape was shot dead on the spot, but most were peacefully handed over to the German

S.S. Security Police at the train station. These pathetic starving humans were then entrained for a new German concentration camp at Zemun, just outside the city. There in the next six months the Concentration Camp Service would work to death or murder in gas vans 15,000 Jewish men, women, and children.

As far as the Hungarians were concerned, one of the bad side effects of their liberation of their Magyar-speaking brothers just inside Yugoslavia was that they also acquired 25,000 people of the Jewish faith. The Arrow Cross members in the area did their best to alter this state of affairs by murdering and driving out the Jews, but although these fanatics were immune from punishment there was no government-sponsored campaign of anti-Semitism. By 8 January 1942, seventeen Hungarian soldiers had been killed by communist partisans while on occupation duty in Yugoslavia. In an act of retaliation General Ferenc Feketehalmi-Czeydner chose to exact revenge from the innocent in order to bring about a denouncement by the people of the terrorists. Between 17-23 January he unleashed his soldiers in the Ujvidek area. In one incident 550 Jews and 292 Serbians were forced onto a partially frozen river. Their weight cracked open the ice, and most drowned. Those who survived were shot down. The accepted death toll of the bloody week is 3,309. According to Jewish historians this was simply another act of anti-Semitism, but others suggest the operation, though horrific, did have a logical motive and was aimed at Jews, Serbians, and politically suspect Hungarians.

The Hungarian authorities had not sanctioned this operation, however, and once a public outcry came about the general and his aides were charged with murder. Then Admiral Horthy ordered the charges to be dismissed.

By the end of 1941 the Volksdeutsch of Banat had become victims of nazi aggression too, and a few of these German-speakers even ran off to join the Titoists. The S.S. Security Police did its job here just as heartlessly as if it was in the middle of Russia.

However, the Heimwehr continued to recruit honorable men as part-time militiamen, and the locally recruited S.S. men were placed into Einsatzstaffeln, which operated as full-time security units. Those men who wished to fight for the cause, but who could not pass the still strict S.S. recruiting standards, or who did not wish to be associated with that extreme right-wing organization, could volunteer for the German Army. Many of these volunteers were placed into a rail security battalion and three infantry battalions for duty in Yugoslavia.

In early 1942 the Bulgarians were drawn into the conflict further when the Germans requested military aid in Serbia. The Bulgarian government decided to fulfill the request by sending the First Army of the 7th, 9th, and 21st Divisions. They did this because the Bulgarians hoped that Hitler would intervene in their favor in their current argument with Italy over some Albanian-Macedonian territory, and also because they knew that as they had not allied with Germany in the war against the Soviet Union Hitler probably suspected their loyalty.

Tito launched his Serbian offensive in January, and coming so quickly after his defeat by the Germans, this move took the Serbians by surprise. The communists made good progress against the Serbian State Guard and Serbian Volunteer Command and they also entered Bosnia-Herzegovina. However, once the Germans woke up they began to repel the communist attacks and actually drive them back. The Croatian Army IIIrd Corps was also brought into action, and it too defeated the communists in Bosnia-Herzegovina.

Then the Germans launched a full-scale counterattack with Lieutenant-General Paul Bader's LXVth Corps on January 15, using the German 342nd and 718th Divisions and the Serbian Volunteer Command. In addition Italian and German aircraft hounded the communists. The combined Axis operation inflicted serious casualties on the enemy pushing him all the way back to Montenegro, from Zlatar Mountain to Prijepolje to Foca over the Lim River, and thence through Sandzak and into the mountains. At times Cetnik forces also harassed the communists in their snowy retreat. The Axis commanders thought that surely this was the end of organized communist resistance. The coup de grace came, it seemed to the Italians, when Moslem militiamen attacked the communists in the Lim valley and the Italians assaulted Prijepolje.

Yet unknown to the Axis commanders the main partisan force was already safe, and the defenders fighting valiantly at Prijepolje were only a rearguard. The rearguard abandoned their positions only at the last instant and crossed the frozen Lim River. The Germans had lost only 25 killed and 131 wounded in battle, but 300 men were laid low with frostbite, evidence of the terrible wintry conditions in which these men were fighting. The Germans counted 521 communists dead and 1,331 taken prisoner.

In February the Germans caught up with the communists and battled hard around Valjevo, suffering 500 casualties, but claiming to have killed 3,500 partisans. If this count is true, and it probably is, the number included innocent villagers who got in the way.

A Cetnik attack was barely held by the communists at Borac, but one outpost camp on Sinjajevina Mountain was captured by the Cetniks. Only the reaction of some part-time communist partisans staved off a major intrusion by the Cetniks into the loosely connected communist perimeter.

The Axis commanders were elated, because they believed that through international cooperation the communist menace had been eradicated. Only sporadic loner sabotage incidents would keep the security forces from getting bored.

In Banat the German authorities created the S.S. Prinz Eugen Mountain Division by launching another recruiting drive, drafting the S.S. Einsatzstaffeln en masse, and by bringing in a cadre of Germans, Austrians, and Volksdeutsch. While undergoing training the unit would perform minor sentry duties, but Himmler hoped to use the division in Russia.

Men and women who had been Yugoslavian citizens prior to April 1941 were by 1942 serving in militias, armed forces, and police units that owed their allegiance to nine different governments: German, Italian, Bulgarian, Hungarian, Croatian, Serbian, the Yugoslavian government in exile, Tito's communist council, and the Cetnik royalist council.

Cetniks operated in the Italian-controlled area of Slovenia and Montenegro, but as the Italians welcomed Serbian refugees from Ustaci atrocities, giving them food, shelter, and medical treatment, the Cetniks chose to leave the Italians alone, concentrating on the communist enemy.

In relatively minor actions throughout Yugoslavia between 16 February and 20 March 1942, Axis casualties were: German 37 killed, 65 wounded, and 45 missing; Croatian 75 killed, 305 wounded; Serbian 15 killed and 13 wounded; and Bulgarian 15 killed and 13 wounded. Italian losses are unknown. Hungarian losses were always low. The Serbian Werkschutz had proven itself not only as factory guards but as partisan hunters. These Serbians, Russian emigres, and Volksdeutsch would continue to serve in both capacities.

Unfortunately for the security of the occupied lands the communists had not been destroyed. In April the Cetnik base at Kolasin was attacked by a large force of communists. By now the Titoists had captured enough weapons that they were a formidable, if yet small, force. They possessed small arms of a great variety, vehicles, anti-aircraft guns, and mountain artillery. The Italians agreed that they should come to the assistance of the Cetniks and they consulted with the Germans about the operation. Surprisingly the Italians agreed that a German, Lieutenant-General Bader, should be in overall charge of the field forces.

The rescue mission began on 16 April with the German 718th Division, ten battalions of Croatian army troops and Ustaci, and General Roatta's Italian Second Army of three divisions. However, the Italians were slow in arriving at the battlefield.

The communists were driven back quite easily by this large force, but on 3 May the communists halted and began to regroup. On 16 May the communists attacked towards Kolasin again. They ran into the Italian Taurinense and Cacciatore della Alpi Divisions and were soundly defeated. In their usual manner the victorious Italians spent many days celebrating this success.

In Montenegro this spring the only major action was the defeat of a Moslem militia unit by the communists at Rakitnica, in June. Throughout May and June Hungarian, German, and Croatian units fought against pockets of communists who were loosely controlled by Tito.

Despite the successes there was cause for deep concern among the Axis commanders. Italy still had to keep sixteen divisions in her sphere of Yugoslavia and with four divisions in Albania and twelve in Greece this meant that fully half the Italian Army was tied down in inglorious occupation duty. The Germans had had to bring in reinforcements and this would soon give their Yugoslavian occupation commanders six divisions, including the home-grown

Prinz Eugen. In addition the local forces were being expanded. That these units were necessary was shown to be fact when in late June the communists broke out of Montenegro into Bosnia-Herzegovina.

There was a campaign going on in this area already. On 7 June the Germans had begun a sweep through eastern Bosnia with their 714th Division and the Croatian Army 1st Mountain Division. It was this act which had attracted Tito.

The communists attacked with four small brigades and by the 23rd they had made contact with the Axis forces. To date in the sweep the Germans had suffered 19 killed, 31 wounded, and 6 missing and the Croatians had lost 200 killed, 250 wounded, and 169 missing. In turn both had killed 1,748 guerrillas in battle and had taken prisoner 713, of which 275 were executed. Though the partisans had enough equipment to call themselves an army, they could not match the armored fighting vehicles, artillery, and aircraft of the Axis troops. Nor did the communists have all the peasant support that they required. The Croatian troops knew the terrain as well as the communists and often had friends and supporters in the mountain villages. This inequality accounts for the heavy losses of the communists and the light losses of the Axis. At this time there were also actions in western Bosnia.

The main opposition to the communist advance consisted of part-time Ustaci and Croatian police, and the Ustaci at the village of Kalinovik put up a very good defense. The communists flowed around any village that they could not conquer. The Axis troops considered themselves under attack at all times, but at one point in the campaign Tito ordered a retreat. It was impossible for the Axis defenders to know that they were under attack from partisans who were retreating rather than advancing.

The Cetniks entered the district and also nipped at the communist columns, and the Luftwaffe, Reggia Aeronautica, and fledgling Croatian Air Force patrolled the area constantly, picking off bunches of partisans like vultures pouncing on rabbits. Many villagers suffered when their homes, which were temporarily occupied by partisans, were bombed by Axis aircraft. Thus when the communists moved on they were often followed by hordes of peasant women and children who had nowhere else to go.

By 6 July the Croatian command was watching Tito's main column, identified by its radio traffic including communication with Moscow, approach the city of Sarajevo. Now the troops of the IIIrd Corps and the Ustaci sortied out from the city and pounced upon the communists sufficiently hard enough to inflict upon them one of their worst defeats. In the Bugojno valley the main column was surrounded by Croatian troops, Ustaci, Cetniks, and even local Croatian farmers armed with shotguns, knives, and pitchforks, while Italian aircraft continued to assault the communists. The Cetniks often attacked on horseback waving gigantic flags. The flags helped identify them to Axis aircraft. The fact that the Cetniks were anti-Axis and most bitterly anti-Croatian was overlooked in the euphoria of close combat with the communists.

The town of Prozor and its Ustaci defenders fell to the communists, but Tito now ordered a general retreat. On the night of the 15th the Titoist rearguard closed up to the Vrbas River. The following day his main column reached the village of Hurije, peopled by Serbians. The villagers welcomed the partisans not as communists but as Serbian freedom-fighters, despite the fact that the red star emblem was visible on most partisans' caps and that there were many Moslems and Croatians in the column. Tito himself was a Croatian. These villagers had yet to feel the brutality of the communist system. While halting at the village Tito heard that one of his columns had been repulsed at Bugojno village by a combined unit of Cetniks and Ustaci—an unholy alliance if there ever was one.

The Ustaci advanced on the next day, following the communists. If the Cetniks had reached Hurije first they would have admonished the populace for aiding the communists, and they might have executed the village headman. Their religious emblems and accompanying priests certainly would have impressed the peasants. However, it was an Ustaci unit that reached Hurije first, part of the notorious Black Legion. Hating all Serbians anyway, and seeing these villagers as supporters of the communists, the Ustaci massacred everyone they could lay their hands on. The crime of the villagers was to be devout Orthodox Christians and communist—at the same time!

On the edge of the Kozara Mountains the chasing Croatian 1st Mountain Division was severely hurt in a partisan riposte, to the point that the Croatian 3rd and 4th Mountain Brigades had to be brought up to the battlefield at once to reinforce the line. Late in the month the defenders of Bugojno village repelled another attack, but Zlosela fell to the communists on the 31st.

On 1 August reconnaissance aircraft and radio interception units brought in information to the Axis command that suggested all of the communists of Tito's main force were assembling on Malovan Mountain. This gave the commanders a major target and the orders went out to surround the enemy if possible.

The Croatian 1st Mountain Division would not be able to take part until it had regrouped. It had lost in this latest round of fighting 235 killed, 182 wounded, and 521 missing. Undoubtedly many of the missing had actually defected to Tito, but several had been killed in small patrol actions and their bodies had not yet been discovered. A few had been taken prisoner, for Tito did take prisoners at times to be used as slaves until they could be traded. Indeed on 4 August 700 Ustaci surrendered at Livno. The communists realized that these men had simply been cajoled to join as part-timers and did not agree with the Pavelic regime. Once their recruiters and rabble-rousers had been arrested, the rest of the men were simply disarmed.

The next Ustaci outpost to be assaulted was not so obliging. At Kupres the part-timers might have wished to surrender, but they were temporary hosts to an element of the Black Legion armed with light artillery. Under the stern eyes of the Black Legion commander all the Ustaci fought with courage for three days of major battle. The Ustaci casualties went unreported in this incident, but they claimed to have inflicted on the communists losses of 100 killed and 150 wounded.

Now Tito called off all assaults and ordered his partisans to concentrate on survival.

In the meantime between 10 June and 29 August in western Bosnia the Axis suffered losses of: German 71 killed, 187 wounded, and 8 missing; and Croatian 475 killed, 727 wounded, and 510 missing. They claimed to have killed 4,735 partisans and captured 12,207. The death toll may be true, but it includes communists killed by Cetniks, air attack, artillery barrages, and disease, as well as open battle. In addition a high proportion of the killed and prisoners were probably innocent of any partisan activity. This is especially noticeable when one realizes that the communists were suffering in other areas at the same time. In eastern Bosnia between 24 June and the end of August the Axis commanders counted partisan casualties as 4,963 killed in battle, 346 executed, and 6,641 taken prisoner. During June, July, and August the Axis counted enemy casualties as 1,031 killed, 273 wounded, and 2,168 captured, of which 212 were executed, in Croatia, for the Axis loss of: German 2 killed and 1 wounded; and Croatian 77 killed, 108 wounded, and 362 missing.

It is also noticeable that the Croatian Army and Ustaci had borne the brunt of the fighting, as is shown by their higher casualties, although poorer training did account for the higher loss among Croatian units, to some extent.

The execution of non-uniformed terrorists was sanctioned by the Hague Convention, but the communists were for the most part serving in an identifiable army. The executions listed above were performed by the Germans in retaliation for various acts of so-called terrorism, and by the Croatians for the same reasons. However, the Ustaci often massacred quite indiscriminantly, and added the resulting death toll to the enemy casualty list.

By September the Germans had their units spread over a large expanse: 718th Division in east Bosnia; 714th Division in west Bosnia; 704th Division in east Serbia; 717th Division in west Serbia; and the new S.S. Prinz Eugen Division in southwest Serbia. Bulgarian troops were aiding the Germans to control southeast Serbia. The Hungarians never aided the other Axis forces in Yugoslavia, but they eventually would have to increase their occupation garrison to a strength of five divisions in order to combat the partisans.

Chapter 15

The Middle East and the Failure of the Jihad

It is understandable that the Moslems felt resentment when the Europeans began to conquer their lands, especially as the Moslems had once controlled the eastern and southern Mediterranean coasts, the islands, and all of the Iberian Peninsula. Occupation of their lands by the Europeanized Turks was bad enough, but at least the Turks were Moslem. The Europeans were Christians and as such tended to be intolerant. Algeria fell to the French in the 1830s, Aden to the British in 1839, Tunisia to France in 1881 at the same time as the British overran Egypt. The interior Moslem nations of Africa fell to British and French influence in the latter part of the nineteenth century. Eritrea and Somalia fell to the Italians in the 1890s as did Libya in 1911. By this date the British and Russians had negotiated a protectorate over Iran. The French took Morocco in 1912, and by 1914 the British had spread their influence over Kuwait, Bahrein, Oman, and a few other sheikdoms on the Arabian coast. It was obvious to anyone that the British, French, and Italians coveted the remainder of the Middle East, which was under Turkish occupation.

The Turks then played into the imperialists' hands by going to war on the side of Germany in 1914. The British built up a large enough army to defend Egypt from a Turkish offensive and by 1916 were planning an invasion of Palestine. This year with British aid the Emir of Mecca, Hussein, launched a revolt against the Turks to liberate the remainder of the Middle East. Every Arab, and the British advisers, including the famous T.E. Lawrence, were at first convinced that the liberated lands would become one or several independent states.

However, the British had made other promises. The French wanted Syria, including Lebanon, and Palestine, so in May 1916 the Sykes-Picot Agreement was secretly signed, giving Syria to the French, certain Turkish concessions to the Russians, and the rest to the British. This agreement betrayed the Arab revolutionaries, but when Hussein learned of the agreement long before the end of the war he continued to lie to his followers, hoping to salvage something at the conference table.

In addition the British had made an agreement with the Jews of Europe, mentioned in the famous letter from Lord Balfour, the Foreign Secretary, to the Zionist Organization of Great Britain on 2 November 1917, giving them Palestine as a homeland. The purpose of the agreement, soon made public, was to attain Jewish cooperation in the war and to rid Europe of its Jews at the end of the war.

In September 1918 the Arab Army was victorious, entering the great city of Damascus a day ahead of the British forces. Within a month Turkey surrendered, and the Arabs now demanded their prize of liberty.

At once though they began to argue among themselves, tribe versus tribe, princely family versus princely family, and religious sect versus religious sect—Sunnites, Shiites, Druze, Jews, Maronites, Greek Orthodox, Syrian Orthodox, Eastern Catholic, Roman Catholic, and several Protestant faiths. In addition there were language arguments, Syriac versus Arabic, Kurdish, Turkish, Circassian, and others. Indeed before the land could be divided among the Arabs it was necessary to figure out exactly who was an Arab. The ultimate agreement was that anyone was an Arab who thought he was an Arab.

Hussein claimed to rule all of the Arabian Peninsula, except those lands already claimed by Britain. As the interior was worthless desert dotted with thieving nomadic tribes, the British did not argue this point. His son Faisal, who had led the Arab field force in the war, claimed Iraq, and as he was already in Baghdad with his army the British did not argue with him either. As for Abdullah, the other son, well he was in Damascus and was therefore a French problem. The British hoped that the Arabs would collapse into civil war so that the Allies would have a perfectly sound reason for taking over, but after two years the Arabs seemed to be doing reasonably well.

Then when the Treaty of Sevres formally accepted the Anglo-French claims, the situation changed drastically. The British troops who had not yet left the area ensconced themselves in Iraq, Palestine, and the land between. The French invaded Syria. The Arabs resisted the takeovers in Syria and Iraq, but superior firepower quickly forced the Arabs to accept the situation. To appease the Americans the British and French agreed to hold mandates over these lands, that is to educate them for self-government. Abdullah fled from Syria and the British allowed him to rule Trans-Jordan with some autonomy. Hussein was allowed to keep Arabia.

Within the Arabian Peninsula, though, there was turmoil, and in 1924 Hussein was overthrown by Ibn Saud. The Saudi clan had to fight for many years to pacify all of the large peninsula.

In 1921 the Iranians made a formal treaty with the Soviets, after defeating a Red Army, and this diplomatic move forced out the British as well as the Russians. Just days before the signing an Iranian Cossack, Reza Khan, seized power. In 1925 he took the title of Shah (Caesar). He ruled with a stern hand, a devious secret police, and aid from the Anglo-Persian Oil Company. Oil had been discovered in Iran as early as 1908.

By 1936 Syria was solidly controlled by the French, except for the Jebel Druz where Druz rebels still took potshots at passing patrols. Several revolts in the colony had been bloodily put down, but Lebanon had achieved a sort of autonomy, run by a Maronite Christian council. Iraq had achieved independence, but Faisal had only experienced this triumph for a few months, dying in 1932. A series of dictators ran the country after that. All of them had to toe the British line somewhat, as the British kept air bases in the country, interfered constantly, and of course controlled the country's oil outflow, through their concessions. Much of the Iraqi half of the profits went into the dictators' coffers. At least the Shah of Iran was spreading his wealth around a bit.

Trans-Jordan had a good deal of autonomy by this date, and even had its own army, the Arab Legion. In addition the British had a locally recruited unit, the Trans-Jordan Frontier Force. This should have meant that the Jordanians were pro-British, but there was much resentment for the way that the British had handled the raiding problem. For thousands of years the nomadic tribes had raided each other and they saw no reason to quit. However, when the Haweitat attempted to raid their enemies over the border in Arabia the British stopped them. Yet the British were never around to prevent the Haweitat from being raided. Arguments over customs and excise duties and border travel also caused ill-feeling. However, none of these or other problems were serious enough to fight over.

Palestine was different, for here the British had been allowing Jewish immigration. The Jews that came were not like the Jews of the Arab states who spoke Arabic and lived as Arabs, but were Europeans who spoke a variety of languages, centered around Hebrew, and who brought European ideas with them. They began to turn a peaceful lazy Arab community into a hive of commerce. At first the Arabs benefited, but eventually they saw this immigration as just another European invasion. The British had tried to placate the Arabs of Palestine, appointing an Arab Mufti (judge) for Jerusalem, Hajj Amin al Hussein, and sending pro-Arab governors, but the more fanatic Arab nationalists, men who had wrenched this land from the Turks, were not appeased. They attacked the Jewish settlements, and the Jews were forced to organize a defense force. The Jews did not like the British either, for they felt the British often turned a blind eye to Arab excesses.

In 1936 the Arabs felt that they could sit and watch their land being occupied no more. They reacted. At first it was only a general strike, but as the British security authorities began to put down the strike with violence the passive rebels became active rebels. Guerrilla warfare broke out in Palestine.

A year later the leaders of the Arab community, like the Mufti, were deported and exiled, but these were not the real leaders. The true leaders were those who were waging open war, like Fawzi al Kawukji, an ex-French Army officer. Many guerrillas were coming in from Syria, Iraq, Arabia, and Trans-Jordan to fight the British. There might have been problems in Egypt for the

British, too, but the British agreed to withdraw from Egypt and only to garrison the banks of the Suez Canal. Nonetheless a few Egyptians crept into Palestine to fight the British.

In the summer of 1939 the British finally made a deal with the Arab rebels. Palestine would be given its independence in ten years' time with an assured Arab majority. In the meantime Jewish immigration would be restricted to 15,000 per year.

The Arabs ceased fire, but the Jews who had been effective allies of the British now turned against the colonial master. The defense force plotted war against the British hoping to increase the rate of immigration. There was an added incentive for the Jews, now. They knew that the Jews of Eastern Europe were being persecuted, and for the British to curtail immigration at this date was practically a death warrant for thousands.

It would seem that Arab nationalism had been somewhat pacified by the end of 1939, but now coming upon the scene were secret agents from Germany and Italy. The Italian agents were not taken too seriously, for with their record of mismanagement and brutality in Libya for twenty-eight years, the Arabs believed that Italy could not be trusted. Germany was different. Germany had not tried to conquer Arab land, nor did it wish to. German missionaries had long been the friend of the Arab, and the nazi government was even more anti-Jewish than the Arabs.

Still when the Italians invaded Egypt the plotters saw their chance. Throughout every country of the Middle East, but most noticeably in Egypt, Palestine, Syria, and Iraq, the plotters readied their weapons, though there was no resistance when the British reoccupied Egypt as if it were still their colony.

The collapse of the Italians in the winter of 1940-41 caused the rebels to disavow the plotters at once. The fanatics hid their weapons and waited.

The British knew of the plots and counter-plots, but were intelligent enough not to overreact. However, the British war cabinet began to panic in April 1941. The Vichy French in Syria were a threat to the Middle East and the British had to maintain a constant vigil along the border. On one occasion French troops had entered Trans-Jordan. Arabs from British-controlled territories were receiving training and propaganda from German advisers in Syria. There were rumors galore, the most startling that Ibn Saud had made an alliance with Germany. In Libya the British were in retreat. On 1 April, a new dictatorship took over in Iraq. Led by Raschid Ali and four right-wing generals named the Golden Square, the new government was openly pro-German, and the rumors were that Iraq was about to join the Axis, which if nothing else would cut off the oil supplies currently entering British vehicles, planes, and ships, and redirect the oil to Vichy Syria and thence to Italy and Germany. In addition by mid-April the Allies were in full retreat in Greece and Yugoslavia. Lastly, more German aircraft were appearing in Italian bases throughout the Mediterranean. The entire Middle East was threatened.

Actually Hitler's dreams of an Axis Middle East were just that, dreams. It was coincidence that made several incidents appear to be part of a coordinated action. Hitler did not believe his tiny force in Libya could liberate Egypt, nor did he think Vichy France would attack British territory from Syria. Indeed he was ever anxious that the French in Syria would join the Allies. His victories in Yugoslavia and Greece were sudden opportunities, and his swift victories there surprised him as much as it did the Allies.

When he moved an airborne division to Greece he did so with the idea of either occupying Malta or any other Allied-held island. There was no basis in the rumor that the paratroopers were preparing to land in Iraq, but some Iraqis and many Britons believed that to be true.

The British overreacted. The weakest link in the enemy plan appeared to be Iraq, for although that country possessed a police force of 10,130 and an army of 368,000 including reservists and had recently been armed with up to date weapons by the British, the British believed through their intelligence operatives that the Iraqis would not fight for Raschid Ali. Another British advantage was that the British had an air base not far from Baghdad.

One of the provisions of the establishment of Iraqi independence was that the British were allowed to transport troops across Iraq at will. Using this ploy the British landed British and Indian troops at the port of Basra and the nearby airbase at Shaiba.

On 27 April Raschid Ali denounced this publicly as an invasion, for the British had not moved from these two bases. Of course he was perfectly correct, but at this stage of the war the free world was inclined to believe the British protestations.

The British civilians who worked in Iraq did not trust their own government any more than the Iraqis did and they prepared to evacuate the nation, setting up defenses in the meantime. On 30 April two Iraqi brigades positioned themselves around Habbaniyah airbase, a move designed to worry the small garrison of R.A.F. personnel and the 1,200 Assyrian and Kurdish Levies who worked for the British. They settled down to peer with binoculars at the airfield, military buildings, English-style township for dependents, and the nearby lake. At the same time Raschid Ali cut off the oil pipeline and diverted the oil through a disused system to Syria.

On 1 May the Iraqis watched the British aircraft take off and land unhindered, probably unaware that hotheads had already shot at British oilfield workers. The following morning at 5 a.m. the tired Iraqi soldiers watched as several planes calmly took off, circled and flew over them. They were still admiring the view when the first bombs fell among them. The explosions shattered their bodies and their formations. The war had reached Iraq.

Wellington medium bombers later arrived from Shaiba and bombed several Iraqi targets. The Iraqis had only light anti-aircraft guns, but they did put up their handful of fighter aircraft to challenge the British. Two British planes fell to ground fire and five were shot down by Iraqi fighters, but the day definitely belonged to the British who had the advantage of surprise—attacking without a declaration of war.

The Iraqi anti-aircraft gunners were jittery, as can be understood for this was their first war. At Baghdad airport they blasted away at an incoming aircraft and cheered when it went down in flames. Unfortunately it was a German aircraft carrying the German Military Mission to Iraq. Other German aircraft managed to fly in to Mosul without incident, having refueled at Vichy bases in Syria. From this Iraqi airfield the Germans began bombing and strafing British troops.

On the first day of war the British had to quell a riot in Basra and defend against snipers there and at Shaiba, but other than that they saw no major Iraqi reaction. The Iraqis were indeed stunned. The average Iraqi soldier did not understand international politics and could not understand why the British had turned on the people of Iraq so ruthlessly. Still Iraqi propaganda urged the troops to hold on until relieved by the German paratroopers.

On the night of 5 May the Iraqis at Habbaniyah were attacked by Britons, Kurds, and Assyrians. Following orders the Iraqis fell back to Fallujah. At dawn, though, an Iraqi rearguard held up the enemy advance until the British brought up armored cars.

On 10 May the Arab Legion of Emir Abdullah, currently taking British orders, sniped at the Iraqi fort at Rutba. The garrison called for reinforcements at once, and within hours some troops did arrive. Also coming to the rescue was a band under Fawzi al Kawukji. However, after British armored cars had shot up the walls, Fawzi thought better of his rash move and fled with his men. The next morning, following a British air raid, the garrison fled too.

For the next week the air raids continued—Iraqi troops being shot up by British planes, and German and a few of the surviving Iraqi warplanes shooting at the British and their allies. Here and there the Iraqis had to fight off raids by teams of the Arab Legion. The temperature was often as high as 120°F and there were sandstorms. The Iraqi Arabs did not like to fight in the desert anymore than the British, and the constant air attacks unnerved them. More unnerving, though, was the waiting for the German reinforcements.

By mid-May the Iraqis had a brigade at Ramadi, two brigades at Fallujah, and a division at Baghdad. As yet no mobilization of reserves had taken place, and most of the air force had been destroyed. Several German aircraft had been destroyed by British air raids on Mosul, and even in Syria the German planes were not safe from the R.A.F.

On the morning of 19 May the defenders of Fallujah were assaulted by a force of British, Indian, Assyrian, and Kurdish infantry, supported by air, artillery, and armored cars. The brigades were ordered to fall back at once, but about 300 Iraqis were either late in getting out and were taken prisoner or they deliberately surrendered.

Raschid Ali and his generals tried their best to instill some spirit into their men, and by the 22nd they were ready. A brigade charged into Fallujah. The sudden bellicosity surprised the Allies, and the Iraqis entered street after street to find it deserted. But then the Assyrians and Kurds ran out of the buildings where they had been hiding and the Iraqis found themselves in full-scale battle, in some places hand to hand. The Iraqis soon ran for it. The following day the Iraqis charged again, but this time the British were prepared, though the Iraqis did manage to capture the southern part of the town for a few hours.

Now the Iraqis concentrated on the defenses of Baghdad.

On the morning of the 28th the Allies were approaching Baghdad from north and south, their columns having come from Habbiniyah and Trans-Jordan. The Iraqis had been reinforced with a total of three German squadrons and one Italian squadron, but not by any ground forces. Indeed as the German airborne division had landed on the island of Crete the Iraqis knew that no more reinforcements were coming. There was more bad news. An entire Indian division was coming upriver from Basra.

The orders from the Golden Square were to resist, however, and resist the Iraqis did, using artillery and aircraft to assault the Allies who were massing for a charge. When the Allies did attack they found the city gates defended by ditches, barbed wire, machine gun nests, and artillery. The Iraqis had their backs to the wall and they were fighting well. On the night of the 30th, though, Raschid Ali fled to Iran. Those leaders that were left notified the British embassy, which had not been bothered by the "war," that they wished to surrender. The following morning the Allies entered the city.

Only an occasional air raid by German and Italian aircraft broke the silence of the next few days. The Iraqis had suffered about one hundred killed and five hundred wounded, but the total Allied loss was only twenty killed and forty wounded.

Fawzi al Kawukji had not surrendered in 1939 in Palestine and he had no intention of surrendering now. He withdrew nearer to Syria. As mentioned above, however, the British continued their air raids on Syria and then followed this by a full-scale invasion on 8 June. The British announced that they would give Syria and Lebanon their independence, so that any local men who continued to fight in French uniform were now fighting against their own futures. Few Syrian Arabs believed the British propaganda. Fawzi did not believe it either and he planned to fight the British when they reached his hide-out. However, action came for him at once. A group of his men just inside Iraq encountered a British mechanized column. As the Arabs caught the British in an ambush they were victorious, the British being forced to run for it. This incident had perhaps made Fawzi somewhat overconfident.

For the next two weeks he and his men sniped at passing British vehicles between T3 and Palmyra in Syria, and then his men captured an entire truck convoy. As the French fell back under constant British pressure Fawzi was left to bear the full brunt of the Allied forces in this area. After Fawzi had been wounded he had had to put his deputy Aref Abd er Razeq in command. Razeq was a good leader and in any case if he got into trouble he had seven advisers with him, German members of the French Foreign Legion. The Germans advised that Fawzi fly to Athens to seek medical aid from German doctors and he agreed to do this. He did not trust the French doctors as he was a deserter from the French Army.

Now the Germans took over Fawzi's forces. A diplomat, Rudolf Rahn, formally accepted the force as the Arab Legion of the German Army and began to recruit Syrian Arabs and Iraqi refugees in the Aleppo area. On 9 July the small army attacked Raqqa, a garrison now in the Allied rear. The Indian defenders fought very well and by nightfall the Germans advised that their Arab Legion withdraw. The Germans wanted the unit more for its propaganda value than its fighting quality and they did not want it wiped out so soon.

The following day the Vichy command in Syria surrendered. Now there was a mad scramble as the few Germans in the country and the more fanatical members of their Arab Legion fled north to Turkey before the British closed off their retreat. About 300 men of the German Arab Legion managed to escape into this neutral country.

After a diplomatic intervention the Germans gained Turkish permission to transport the Arab Legion to German-occupied Greece, where the men were reunited with Fawzi. They were quickly joined by about 130 other Arab nationalists from various countries.

The British did not feel secure in Iraq, yet, for neutral Iran lay to the east. Iran had really not shown any serious anti-Allied bias, but the British had all but conquered the Middle East and only Iran stood in the way. Afghanistan toed the British line and to the east of that country lay British-controlled India.

The British knew that the Soviets also coveted Iran, and someone suggested that the British dust off the old 1907 Anglo-Russian agreement. That this would be unprovoked aggression did not seem to matter to these "defenders of democracy." Naturally the Soviets jumped at the chance. Apart from their natural love of conquest the Soviets were facing a German invasion by this time and they desperately needed Iranian oil.

The agreement was that the Soviets should be given occupation over the northern third of the country, and the British jurisdiction over the southern third, with the middle maintained as a protectorate. If the Iranians resisted the invasion, so be it.

On the morning of 25 August 1941 the Iranian Armed Forces command was informed that Soviet troops had crossed the northern border and that an invasion fleet, probably British, was approaching the coast. Within an hour British aircraft were flying over the country dropping leaflets to inform the Iranians that they should not concern themselves that they were being invaded and conquered.

However, the Iranians were concerned and they showed it by opening fire on the aircraft with anti-aircraft guns and fighter planes and shelling the British fleet with gunboats. The British navy had tackled bigger fish than this, so it was no effort for them to cripple four gunboats and blow two sloops right out of the water. Admiral Bayendor was killed defending his country against the aggressor.

British paratroopers had landed to guard the British oilfield workers in the country, and by dusk two Indian divisions were ashore. In the north the Soviet advance was slow, but ceaseless. The coastal oilfields were already in British hands.

The Iranians chose to stop the British at Paytak Pass, but throughout the 26th the Iranians were seriously unnerved by heavy British bombing. Their air force seemed to have disappeared and the troops felt very lonely. On the next day when the British and Indians charged them they did not put up too much of a fight. Only an hour later the British were pouring through the pass.

The next morning a new premier, Ali Furanghi, announced a surrender. The Iranians counted about fifty killed and two hundred wounded in action against the British-controlled invaders, and inflicted casualties of twenty-two killed and forty-two wounded. The casualties in the Soviet invasion are unknown.

The Anglo-Soviet agreement was implemented and in 1942 American troops arrived in the British sector. The Iranian government was forced to do Allied bidding and when a certain General Zahidi became outspoken, the British sent an S.A.S. team under Captain Fitzroy MacLean to kidnap him. With a forceful hand and good intelligence work the British kept control of Iran and Iraq. The desert tribes and bandits saw the occupation troops as a source of profit, though, and there was constant raiding throughout the next few years. In the Iranian province of Azerbaijan the Soviets brought in Azerbaijani communists who rabble-roused for an independent, but communist and pro-Soviet, Azerbaijan. Few people were fooled by this as they knew the Soviet record of brutality in Soviet Azerbaijan. The Soviets also infiltrated communists into the Iranian government. Any outspoken Iranian critics of Soviet behavior were ruthlessly dealt with in the Soviet style.

Hajj Amin el Hussein, the ex-Mufti of Jerusalem, had been living in exile in Iran and he had fled to the Japanese embassy for sanctuary. Later with the aid of anti-British Iranians he escaped, eventually making his way to Greece. He negotiated with the Italians and then with the Germans, and found the Germans to be more powerful and more aware of Arab problems. He chose to side with them and publicly announced this. He was soon made an S.S. gruppenfuehrer and used to sway the Moslems to the nazi cause. He was especially useful for morale purposes in the case of the German Arab Legion and the ex-Indian Army Moslems who were now serving in the German-sponsored Indian Legion.

Chapter 16

The Americans and the Un-Americans

Within the United States there were three factions which wanted to prevent their country from aiding Britain in her European War: the pacifists, the isolationists, and the fascists. The pacifists abhorred American involvement in any war. The isolationists only wanted to stay out of other people's wars, believing that a war would only be justified if American interests were under direct attack. These men and women had witnessed a million Americans go off to fight in a European war in 1917 and only 80% of them had come back in one piece. What is more these isolationists believed that the British, French, and Italians had not fully appreciated the American sacrifice and that the political situation in Europe had actually become worse due to the conflict. In other words, American blood had been shed in vain.

In the early years of World War Two the No Foreign Wars Committee and the America First Movement both gained great popularity. The most outspoken speaker of the latter was Charles Lindbergh, an American of Swedish extraction who had proven his courage as a pioneer aviator. Many Americans felt that if he was against the war then he must have sound reasons.

The American fascists were against an alliance with Britain, because that country was the only Western European bulwark standing against the spread of their own ideology. Fascism, in many guises, had been long in America, but for the American fascists it was the Negro rather than the Jew who appeared as the "enemy in our midst." Serious race riots between Whites and Blacks competing for housing and jobs had broken out in East St. Louis in 1917, Washington, D.C., Chicago, New York City, and Omaha in 1919, and Tulsa in 1921. Several southern towns had also seen mob violence. In total the death toll was in the hundreds and the injured numbered thousands. At times the regular army had been forced to take over security. In the 1920s the Ku Klux Klan, a half-century old semi-secret organization, increased its membership, because its stance of being pro-American-White-Protestant and anti-everything else had become popular again. On occasion its murderous violence sickened even rabid racial bigots.

Anti-Semitism had become strong when at the turn of the century tens of thousands of European Jews had entered the country and at once had begun either creating or taking over small businesses. Anti-Jewish groups often doubling as anti-immigrant groups sprang up, and on one occasion all of New York City was forced to a standstill while police searched for time bombs supposedly planted by anarchistic immigrants. None were found. In 1920 Henry Ford, the motor industry inventor and businessman, put out a book, *The International Jew*, blaming the Jews for having started the Great War for profit.

In 1934 the popular radio speaker Father Charles E. Coughlin, a Canadian priest of Irish extraction, who broadcast to America from a Detroit radio station, altered the philosophy behind his messages to one of extreme right-wing reactionary socialism, anti-Semitic and anti-British. He became more popular than ever. At one time he had ten million radio fans. He was less successful in politics. In 1936 for the Presidential election he allied with Dr. Francis E. Townshend, a California socialist, and Huey Long, the very dictatorial governor of Louisiana, to create the National Union for Social Justice political party. They did not stand a chance against the Republican Party or against Roosevelt's Democrats, but their 882,000 votes showed that somebody had taken them seriously.

By the late 1930s a host of fascist groups were gaining strength: the Silver Shirts of William Dudley Pelley; the American White Guard of Henry D. Allen; the American Defenders; Defenders of the Christian Faith of Reverend Gerald B. Winrod; the Knights of the White Camellia of George Deatherage; the Black Legion; the Christian Front; the Sentinels of the Republic; the American Vigilant Intelligence Federation; the Friends of Progress of Robert Noble and Ellis O. Jones. Some of these groups took the field as strike-breakers, challenging union members who held such "communist" ideas as work safety and overtime pay for extra hours.

Some of these organizations had contacts with the German and Italian governments, but the greatest overtly pro-German group was undoubtedly the German-American Bund. Practically a third of all White Americans were of some German ancestry, but the Bund concentrated its efforts on actual immigrants who were German-speaking and their sons and daughters. In 1930 there were 1,608,000 German-born and 370,914 Austrian-born residents in the United States. Led by Wilhelm Kunze the Bund members openly paraded in uniforms with swastika flags. The party leaders preached the nazi ideology, but remained pro-American too, White-Christian-American that is. One of the largest rallies took place at Camp Siegfried, Long Island, in 1939 where 3,000 adults met, guarded by uniformed party militiamen. The same year in New York City Fritz Kuhn of the Bund drew a crowd of 22,000 at Madison Square Garden. Simultaneous rallies and meetings of the Bund had to be held in many cities due to the immense size of the United States, so no actual national rally ever took place.

When Germany prepared for war in the summer of 1939, thousands of

German immigrants to the United States returned to serve their fatherland. They were accompanied by many sons of immigrants, who themselves had grown up as Americans. A few nazis who had no German connections also went to Germany. Americans of Italian birth or parentage also sailed to Italy to serve Mussolini. The government of Roosevelt made much of the 7,000 or so Americans who entered Canadian or British service, but kept quiet about the volunteers for Germany and Italy. The fascists blamed Roosevelt for much of their troubles, even trying to elicit support by spreading the rumor that Roosevelt was of Jewish extraction. There was no denying that the President had many close Jewish friends.

In the summer of 1941 President Roosevelt took the United States into an undeclared war against Germany. Several Bund leaders now fled the country, suspecting that all-out war was near. Kunze was arrested in Mexico and repatriated to the United States. For his general anti-government feeling he was sentenced to fifteen years' imprisonment.

After the Japanese attack on the United States bases in the Pacific on 7 December 1941, all Americans, Bundists, fascists, pacifists, and isolationists included, found themselves at war. Lindbergh served with distinction against the Japanese.

Few of the Americans who entered Axis service in Europe gained prominence. Those who did were broadcasters like: Fred Kaltenbach, a one-time favorite journalist of William Randolph Hearst, who served German radio; Ezra Pound, the poet, who broadcast on Italian radio; and Mildred Gillars, who became Axis Sally.

In 1943 some of the Bundists, currently serving in the German Armed Forces, toured the prison camps full of Americans captured at the Kasserine Pass debacle. They managed to create an auxiliary unit of the S.S. called the American Free Corps, but with never more than a hundred members it remained purely a propaganda tool. By far the majority of the Americans and ex-U.S.A. residents preferred to serve on an individual basis, and most of them remained anonymous. Only a handful became famous, such as Joachim Ribbentrop, who became Foreign Minister, Ernst "Putzi" Hanfstaengel, a confidant of Hitler and Foreign Press Chief, Baldur von Schirach, Chief of the Hitler Youth, and Gustav Krupp von Bohlen und Halbach, the boss of the great Krupp arms company.*

Of course the majority of the Volksdeutsch in the United States had nothing to do with fascism. The German-born General Walter Krueger served admirably in the Pacific, and the racial-German Dwight D. Eisenhower commanded the Allied Expeditionary Forces in Western Europe.

Naturally the large American corporations had interests in countries that

*A second cousin, Charles Bohlen, was Roosevelt's adviser on Soviet affairs.

eventually became part of the Axis or were conquered by Axis troops, and this in itself was no cause for concern as long as during the conflict the American owners and directors did not aid and advise those factories and laboratories to assist the enemy. Indeed it would have been correct for the Americans to have sabotaged in every way the ability of their foreign concerns to support the enemy. Unfortunately, it seems that some major corporations continued to operate their "enemy" factories, mines, banks, laboratories, and installations by using either neutral citizens as couriers or by using company interests in neutral nations, usually in South America.

According to investigations by Charles Higham, some of these companies were the Chase National Bank (later Chase Manhattan), Davis Oil Company, Ford Motor Company, General Aniline and Film, General Motors, International Telephone and Telegraph, Morgan Bank, National City Bank of New York, Sterling Products Inc. (Winthrop Chemical and Bayer [aspirin] Company), R.C.A., and Standard Oil.

Higham also implicates directly such families as the Morgans, Du Ponts (despite their Jewish connections), Rockefellers, and Fords. One of his accusations is that oil belonging to Standard Oil of New Jersey was transferred from American oil tankers, which had risked being sunk by German U-boats, to Panamanian-registered ships, which in turn transferred the oil to German ships, so that the U-boats could be refueled at sea. He also charges that Davis Oil Company knowingly put its oil into the U-boats. There is even a charge, bordering on the outlandish, though not necessarily false, that William Rhodes Davis did not die of a heart attack, but was murdered by British MI6 agents. It is interesting that Davis had helped form the America First Movement and the No Foreign Wars Committee. This author's investigations have followed Higham's and have gained evidence that suggests the Davis Oil Company, a transporter not a producer, continued its illegal actions long after Davis' death. It is fact that the well-known businessman Leonard Smit of New York City was jailed for smuggling diamonds illegally to Germany in December 1943, and that many journalists were angry that the prosecutors had only scratched the surface of his illicit business dealings.

Due to the exceedingly complicated nature of business dealings with the Axis during the war, the whole truth of it will probably never be known. Several companies managed to get Roosevelt's permission to trade with the enemy, under the idea that failure to do so would do more harm to the United States than the enemy. In addition all major American companies traded with neutral nations that also traded with the Axis. The Americans were quite aware that much of the goods and fuel shipped to Spain was destined for Germany with hardly a stopover on Spanish soil.

There is, however, no evidence as yet to support the belief that American strategic bombing was influenced by major corporations which did not want their foreign concerns damaged.

Chapter 17

The Crooked Cross and the Hammer and Sickle

Once the fluid Eastern Front had frozen into solid ice at the end of 1941, the Axis partners had time to take stock of the situation. The Finns had settled for their original goals, though even they had occupied some territory that was Soviet before 1939. Here they found willing recruits among the Karelian population. The Romanians had superseded their original demands and now had troops in Eastern Ukraine. The Germans had planned to occupy all of the European portion of the Soviet Union, but had not fully obtained that goal. What was more important to the general course of the war was that the Red Army had not only survived the greatest offensive in history, but had produced reinforcements out of nowhere and had regained some ground. Moscow, Rostov, and Leningrad were still holding out against the invader.

Those Germans who were not blinded by nazi propaganda and who were strategically knowledgeable were aware that once having lost in 1941 Germany could no longer achieve total victory. They knew that Germany might still attain favorable terms in a compromise peace, though, and they too continued to fight. On the Eastern Front the Axis partners were deadlocked. On the Western Front, which as yet had no land battlefield, the United States was now a fully-pledged ally of Britain. In North Africa Rommel and his Italian friends were in full retreat. In East Africa the last Italian garrisons had capitulated. In occupied Yugoslavia it looked like a running guerrilla sore would soon break out into open warfare. These were grave setbacks indeed. One of the gravest tragedies was the horrific losses on the Eastern Front. Finland, which had not yet recovered from her losses in the Winter War, had now suffered more casualties. Romania had been stunned by the losses taken at Odessa. The Germans suffered the most, counting by the end of the year 830,403 men lost through deaths, wounds, losses as prisoners, injuries, illness, and frostbite. Army Groups North and Center would soon be reorganizing sixty-nine of their seventy-five infantry divisions with seven instead of nine infantry battalions, with many infantry companies established at a strength of eighty men rather than one hundred and eighty. By the end of 1941 it was not uncommon to find German battalions commanded by captains, as the senior officers had become casualties. Nor did the terrible wintry conditions and minor offensives of early 1942 bring any respite. In the first fifty-nine days of the year the Germans lost another 175,233 on the Eastern Front.

There were several remedies for the lack of manpower in the German Armed Forces, all of which had to be put into force during 1942: the conscription age was lowered to eighteen; the volunteer age was lowered to seventeen; the small number of reservists who had been let loose after the fall of France would have to be recalled, up to the age of forty-five; the conscription of newly-acquired German citizens would have to be implemented, though at different age levels than in "old" Germany; rear-echelon units would have to be combed for non-essential personnel; personnel over thirty-five years of age, and thus not normally eligible for combat status, might have to serve in the front line; and training units would have to double as sentry units, thus damaging irrevocably the training schedule. Hitler also had to urge his Axis partners to supply more troops to the Eastern Front and to other German-occupied areas. All of these were official remedies, that is approved by Hitler. On an unofficial level the German units in the east would have to take on more and more volunteers from the indigenous population and from prisoners of war. Civilian industry did its part by releasing 370,000 men who had hitherto been considered essential personnel. Their loss to German industry had to be made up from slave labor.

The use of ex-Soviet citizens as volunteers had of course already begun. Officially Estonians had been used in Erna, Ukrainian nationalists had been recruited, in December the four supposedly Moslem Turkic-speaking legions had been established, and the Cossacks were being recruited on a small-scale. Hitler had been convinced by his nazi racial theorists that all Cossacks were descendants of the Ostro Goths, an ancient Germanic tribe.

At divisional and regimental levels many German officers had authorized the use of defectors and volunteers for minor chores. After a few weeks these men and women were found reliable enough that they were allowed to work without German supervision. Later some of the men were armed for self-defense, and a few units used them as small scouting sections. To identify them from the enemy each was issued an armband, the most common one being *Im Dienst der Deutschen Wehrmacht* (In the Service of the German Armed Forces), to be worn over their civilian or Red Army coat.

As time went on these hiwis were acknowledged as partners, the size, strength, and morale of any hiwi unit depending on the intelligence of the German officer who employed them. By early 1942 almost all German units were using hiwis, not just army outfits, but the different S.S. organizations, the Reichs Labor Service, the National Socialist Transportation Corps, Luftwaffe, Navy, Organization Todt, TeNo and others. The Romanians and Italians also used a few hiwis, but they did not pay as well or treat their charges as well as the Germans. Even front-line German units were soon using hiwis. From one battalion to the next their use differed, reflecting the attitude of the battalion commanders. Some officers looked upon them as comrades in arms, some saw them with skeptical eyes, still others used them as little better than slaves, and of course some officers refused to use them at all, as the Fuehrer had not authorized it.

There were desertions and revolts by hiwis, especially in units commanded by arrogant nazis, but more than ninety percent proved their loyalty and keenness to defeat the communists, whether in the act of washing soldiers' socks or hunting down partisan snipers.

There is much to indicate that Hitler did not even learn of the existence of the hiwis until spring 1942. The truth was kept from him as much as possible, for he did most thoroughly disapprove of treating "subhuman" Slavs as equals. Therefore there is no accurate count of the number of hiwis in service by this date, but this author believes it must have been at least one hundred thousand. If one assumes that for every hiwi working in a rear-echelon unit one German soldier could be released for front-line duty then the value of these people can be fully appreciated.

In addition to the hiwis were those Soviet citizens who wanted to serve in their own major front-line units with national identification under German orders. Units such as these were far harder to hide from Hitler. One could hardly report, for example, that a particular village had been captured by a unit that was not allowed to exist, nor could one requisition supplies for the continued maintenance of that unit. At least in the case of hiwis one could report that a particular village had been captured by, say the 100th Jaeger Division, without bothering to mention that of the company involved a few of its men were Georgians, or Ukrainians, or Russians.

The use of the Estonians and Ukrainians notwithstanding Hitler had consistently refused permission for all-Slav military units to be formed, and that was that—at the Fuehrer's headquarters one did not question the Fuehrer's orders. But a thousand miles to the east military necessity made a mockery of those orders. On 22 August 1941, almost the entire 436th Infantry Regiment of the Red Army deserted en masse at Mogilev, its commander, a Don Cossack, Major Ivan Nikitich Kononov, asking that his Cossacks be allowed to fight against the communists. After witnessing that they performed their test duties adequately and willingly, the local German commander illegally acknowledged the force as the 102nd Cossack Regiment attached to the German Army. Soon the Cossacks were serving in small sections, performing scouting and guiding. Such was one foreign volunteer unit created. There were many similar cases.

In time all German-organized combat units made up of Soviet citizens serving in their own nationally identifiable groups were nicknamed Osttruppen (Eastern troops) to distinguish them from the hiwis.

Northern Sector

The Latvian and Estonian Civil Guards were ordered to deliver their fitter men to the German Army for front-line duty and at first several officers refused to acquiesce to this misuse of their policemen, but once these trouble-makers were arrested by the German S.S. Security Police and sent to the concentration camps the men were duly transferred to the front line as ordered. They were formed into an Estonian and a Latvian Legion, hurriedly trained, and assigned to a position north of Lake Ilmen on the flank of the 250th Spanish Blue Division.

The Spaniards had already seen some hot combat in the cold snow and on 27 December 1941 Commandante Roman's 2/269th was forced to retreat from Udarnik, losing some men as prisoners. Eventually the Spaniards counter-attacked and restored the line, and Commandante Rebull's 1/269th also advanced. The Spaniards came across their compatriots who had been captured, finding them ritually pinned to the ground with bayonets. Not surprisingly the Spaniards fought on with a frenzy when they reached the enemy defenses near a church. A fierce battle ensued, forcing the Soviets to flee across the frozen river Volkhov. Here for a few minutes they were devoid of protective cover and the Spaniards took the opportunity to slaughter great bunches of them.

A suicidal mission was offered to the Spaniards in January. The remnants of the German 290th Division had been trapped at Vsvad, and a small party was ordered to get through to them. Leaving on the 9th Captain Ordas took with him an anti-tank gun company and a provisional company of 200 ski-troops. The heavy equipment and supplies were carried in horse-drawn sleighs driven by seventy hiwis. It took two days for the little column to cross frozen Lake Ilmen in a blizzard with temperatures at -68°F. By the time the troops reached the shore one hundred and two were maimed with frostbite. The unit had not yet reached the front line, but had only reached forward positions manned by the German 81st Division. On the 17th Lieutenant Otero de Arce led a patrol of thirty-six Spaniards and forty Latvians of the Latvian Legion, which was under the orders of the 81st Division, to capture a village. They quickly lost the village to a Soviet counterattack, though. Other patrols were sent out, but about one hundred and thirty men were currently disabled with frostbite, and one patrol of twenty-three Spaniards and nineteen Latvians was ambushed, only five Spaniards and two Latvians surviving. By the 20th Ordas was wondering what he could do for the trapped division for he had only twenty infantrymen fit enough to fight! Yet when he heard that all available troops were to attack so that the division could break out Ordas and his survivors joined the Latvian Legion in their attack on the 24th. The operation was successful, but only twelve Spaniards were still standing at the end of it.

Ordas was decorated with a Spanish medal and his men received a collective Spanish award, and the Germans handed out thirty-two iron crosses to the Spaniards. The Germans were surprised by the bravery of the Latvians, and they awarded several specially struck medals to them, as they were ineligible for German awards.

In the meantime the Soviets had launched an offensive, forcing some German units to withdraw and thus creating the Volkhov Pocket just north of Novgorod. The Germans, however, were unable to counterattack until the snow had melted and the spring sunshine had baked the ground hard. Only spoiling attacks were to take place, moves which it was hoped would prevent the Soviets from advancing any further. In this tenuous northern sector the Netherlands Legion entered its 2,500 men into line at Gusi Gora north of Lake Ilmen in January, while the 900 men of the Flemish Legion were transferred to the Volkhov Pocket just in time to repel a Soviet attack at Kopsy. During this fighting, on 22 January, Raymond Tollenaere was killed. The Flemings fought well, but it was obvious they still suffered from morale problems, due to the fact that their commander Michael Lippert was far too arrogant. In February the Norwegian Legion (also designated the 266th Battalion) of 1,200 men settled into the Leningrad sector.

February saw the renewal of Soviet action. At Demiansk the entire German 290th, 30th, and S.S. Totenkopf Divisions were cut off, but they managed to chop their way through the Reds and reach the main German line on the 25th. Near Gusi Gora the Netherlands Legion came under major assault, the Dutchmen only managing to hold on by the skin of their teeth. The Dutch doctors and nurses of the Netherlands Field Hospital who arrived in early March came just in time to aid the German medical staffs who were busy with the mounting Dutch wounded. By the time the Soviets called off their bloodthirsty assault, the Netherlands Legion had suffered eighty percent casualties.

The Flemish were mentioned in dispatches for their bravery exhibited on 10 February, and as a reward were ordered to go over to the attack. For six solid days they flung their flesh against a wall of Soviet firepower, to no avail. Then the attack was called off. It was just as well, for only seventy Flemings were still standing.

In April the legions began to receive back their wounded who had been more or less healed, and the Flemish and Netherlands Legions received reinforcements. The Dutch welcomed 2,600 members of the Weer Afdeling, who grumbled that they had never volunteered to actually risk their lives for the cause. The Flemish were built up to a strength of 1,116, but as yet all of the officers were German. By May the Norwegian Legion was in poor shape for not only had it suffered casualties, but the S.S. had released some men for their lack of nazi ardor. Yet the unit remained in line.

By May, though, the ground had been baked hard enough to be traversed by wheeled- and tracked-vehicles and the snow had disappeared. It was time for the Axis to launch its spring offensive. Major attacks took place in the northern sector with the objectives of capturing Leningrad, linking up with the Finns, and diverting enemy forces from the southern sector. As part of the general German plan the Western European legions were in the thick of the fighting.

When the Flemings had lost their commander, Michael Lippert, in April, who had not been grieved, they were visited by Hans Albert von Lettow Vorbeck, ostensibly as he was to soon command them. The men were wary of this nephew of a famous German general of World War One, but he was soon found to be likable. However, he was then transferred elsewhere. The new Fleming commander was Josef Fitzhum.

The Danish Frikorps had been assigned to beef up the crippled Totenkopf Division and as part of that force participated in a major attack at Demiansk on 20 May. By 2 June the Danes had suffered terribly and their Volksdeutsch commander, Lieutenant-Colonel Christian Frederik von Schalburg, had been killed. Knud Martinsen took the Danes back into the attack on the 4th, but failed to break through. The Danes now received von Lettow Vorbeck as their new leader. On the 10th the Frikorps repelled a Soviet counterattack, but lost their new leader in the terrible fighting. To date the Danes had suffered forty percent casualties in three weeks.

In the heat of late spring the whole Axis front in the northern sector charged over the tops of their trenches towards the enemy, with the German generals hoping that the Volkhov Pocket could be straightened out. East of the Keresti River the Spaniards were attacking, with one element of their division fighting at Bolshoye Shomolshe. Between the two Spanish forces the Flemish were attacking just west of Ossiya. The Netherlands Legion charged forward so fiercely that they broke through and captured the commander of the Soviet Eleventh Army.

On 22 June the Spanish 3/262nd was ordered to halt, for though it had only lost nine dead and sixty-seven wounded in its latest attack it had advanced further than any other unit east of the Keresti River and was in danger of being cut off. Yet at Bolshoye Shomolshe the reconnaissance unit of the Blue Division was still being held up, two of its squadrons having suffered fifty percent casualties. The next day a major Spanish effort was made supported by German artillery, Stuka divebombers, and a few German armored vehicles. By dusk the enemy was on the run, and the reconnaissance unit, the 3/262nd, and the Flemish Legion had broken through and taken hundreds of prisoners. The Volkhov Pocket now began shrinking as the Spaniards and Flemings continued to make good progress and on the northern edge the Norwegian Legion advanced.

On the 25th Maloye Shamoshe fell to the Spaniards and the Axis troops were now able to simply mop up the pocket. All told 32,000 prisoners were captured in the pocket. The Spaniards took 5,097 of these for the loss of only

274 casualties. One of the men captured by Dutch troops was Lieutenant-General Andrei Vlasov, a Soviet hero.

In July the Netherlands Legion was taken out of the line for a good rest, having only 1,755 men left. The Flemish Legion was transferred to the Leningrad front under a new commander, Conrad Schellong. On 17 July and again on the 23rd the Danes were subjected to painful charges by fanatic Reds, but they held their position. Two days later the Frikorps, which had suffered seventy-eight percent casualties, was withdrawn from combat. The men were soon informed that they were going home to Denmark for a well-earned rest.

Southern Sector

Hitler had chosen an economic objective for his 1942 offensive, the oil- and mineral-rich Caucasus. Not only were the natural resources valuable to the Soviet Union, but across this expanse lay trade routes to the Middle East including Soviet-occupied Iran and the oilfields there. The Axis commanders had learned that the destruction of the Red Army was an unobtainable goal as long as the Soviets were willing and able to trade space in the tradition of Russian generals going back centuries. However, unlike the Russian armies of the past the modern Red Army required fuel to move, and the Axis generals believed that if they could cut off the Red Army from its source of fuel then it would be immobile and therefore vulnerable to a final Axis offensive.

In order to succeed Hitler would require every available man at the front, with the bulk of them in the south. He controlled directly or indirectly 232 divisions of which 170 contained German personnel. However, the maintenance of this number of German divisions relied on the extensive use of hiwis and on the creation of new divisions from recruits rather than putting those recruits into the old formations that had been depleted through casualties. Most of the German divisions would be going into battle with no more than two-thirds of their established strength. In April 1942 Adolf Hitler formally authorized the use of hiwis.

The southern sector received sixty German divisions, of which ten were armored, and forty-three divisions from Axis partners, of which one was armored. While the Fourth Panzer Army aimed at Voronezh, the Sixth Army was aiming to follow the Don River along its south bank, stop where the Don turned southwards, and then leap to Stalingrad on the Volga River. Both formations would come under Army Group B. Army Group A was to take Rostov with the First Panzer Army and then break out to the Caucasus, while the Seventeenth Army protected the rear communications and the coastal flank. The German Eleventh Army was to rid the Crimea of the enemy once and for all.

This plan would leave the Sixth Army exposed at Stalingrad, so to protect its flanks and rear Hitler could only use the Axis partners. The southern flank of the Sixth Army would be held by the Romanian Fourth Army and the northern flank would be protected by the Romanian Third Army. Holding the south bank of the Don in the rear of Sixth Army would be the Italian Eighth and Hungarian Second Armies. It was obvious to anyone who could see the whole picture that the rear and flanks of the Sixth Army were the weak links as the Axis partners had obsolete equipment and no real purpose being so deep into Russia.

The Crimea offensive came before the major moves in the southern sector, for the Axis commanders did not want a Soviet force on their southern coastal flank. That the enemy was still on this "island" was not evidence of demerit to the German and Romanian troops fighting in this campaign nor to their commander, General von Manstein.

When only Sevastopol was still holding out in December it seemed that the Crimea campaign was over, but then despite the hideously cold weather the Soviets made a series of amphibious assaults on the Kerch Peninsula. One of them met the Romanian 8th Mountain Brigade at Feodosia on December 29, and the brigade commander was forced to put his engineers into line and leave his artillery exposed until his infantry could form for a successful counterattack. But when Soviet tanks suddenly appeared the Romanian infantry fell back to east of Stary Krim. The Romanians had been taken totally by surprise for there appeared to be no Soviet ships to the south large enough to land tanks ashore and the eastern shore was frozen. The sea was indeed frozen, and the Soviets had simply driven their hundreds of tanks across the frozen sea. This gives one an idea of exactly how cold the temperature was. This meant a renewal of the Crimean campaign and the German command was to feel that the fighting here deserved special recognition, so eventually a special badge was awarded for veterans of the Crimea battles.

On the northern slopes of the Yaila Mountains the Romanians stood alongside a German division and battled against charging Soviet infantry. On the fifteenth day of the new year von Manstein counterattacked with three-and-a-half German divisions and a Romanian mountain brigade, and within three days the enemy had been pushed back to the tip of the Kerch Peninsula, having lost 6,700 killed, and 10,000 men, 177 guns, and 85 tanks captured.

For a time the line was still. To hold the northern flank von Manstein brought up the Romanian 18th Division, which had been resting. On 27 February the Soviets chose this ill-equipped force as their target and attacked it with every available man, gun, tank, and plane. Not surprisingly the forward observation posts were overrun at once, but the line itself held and the German reserve counterattacked at once and restored the situation by the end of the day. On 13 March the Germans were struck by a major Soviet assault for a week, but the Germans held their holes in the ground and then went over to the assault with an armored and two infantry divisions. They did not get far. Six days later, the Soviets struck again and failed. Another Soviet attack between 9 to 11 April also failed.

As can be seen, if the Axis did not remove the enemy from the Crimea once and for all they would eventually lose it. A Soviet force in the Crimea could threaten the south Ukraine, and planes of the Red Air Force stationed there could threaten the sea lanes of the Black Sea and bomb Romanian oilfields.

The Romanian 19th Division had recently been rested and the Romanian 4th Mountain Brigade was still in good shape having been on sentry duty on the southern central coast of the Crimea. Both were brought up to the front in April. Von Manstein was under orders to capture the naval base of Sevastopol which was still in Soviet hands, but at Kerch the enemy had seventeen infantry divisions, two cavalry divisions, three infantry brigades, and four armored brigades, and they were being watched by only five German infantry and one German armored divisions. Obviously either the Sevastopol enemy or the Kerch enemy had to be dealt with, but the Axis could not fight both. Fortunately help was at hand, and it was non-German aid that solved this German problem. The help came in the form of the Romanian VIIth Corps. Containing the 10th Division and the 8th Cavalry Brigade, it was soon reinforced with the 19th Division and given the job of holding the northern end of the Kerch line. Now von Manstein could use his German units to assault. His plan was for the German, that is southern, half of the line to go over to the offensive, which would, he hoped, at least spoil the enemy's intentions of attacking and possibly drive them across the straits forever. Attached to the German Brigade Group Groddek was a Romanian motorized unit.

On 8 May the German and Romanian motorized and armored units drove forward. At once victory was in sight. On the 11th German tanks broke into the enemy rear, and now the Romanian VIIth Corps also attacked. With their rear cut off by an unfrozen sea the Soviets began to panic. German and Romanian motorized troops reached Kerch on the 16th after fighting their way through sixty miles of enemy rearguards, and the Romanian 8th Cavalry Brigade cut a swath with its vehicles and saber-wielding horse cavalrymen all the way to the warm sea south of Kerch. The Soviet pocket was then sliced into mouthsized bites by the Romanian and German infantry. It was a great time for Romanian-German cooperation. By 20 May the two Axis forces had captured 258 tanks, 1,133 guns, and 170,000 men. The eastern half of the Crimea was now turned over to the Romanian VIIth Corps (10th and 19th Divisions, 8th Cavalry Brigade, and 4th Mountain Brigade, which had been renamed the 4th Mountain Division, but had not received any reinforcements to match its new status). The Romanians spent several weeks mopping up the area, for the Soviet stragglers hid in caves and in the Yaila Mountains, and only gave the Romanians a target when they ventured forth in search of food.

In the meantime von Manstein turned his attention to Sevastopol. The

Romanian Mountain Corps with its 1st Mountain Division (ex-brigade) and 18th Division was ordered to advance over the toughest terrain on the Sevastopol front, to wit a patch of almost unpenetrable undergrowth before Gaiteny and two hills called the Sugarloaf and Fedyukinny Heights. Naturally the Romanians put the mountain troops in front of the hills. To cover their advance the Romanians emplaced thirty-four medium and light artillery batteries, knowing that they would be needed. The enemy possessed a wealth of artillery including some 305mm coastal guns.

The Romanian and German artillery pounded the enemy defenses for five days before the offensive, while the Romanian and German air forces sent as many sorties against the enemy as possible. Even the Axis anti-aircraft guns were turned upon the fortress, when not in use against the scant Red Air Force presence. As a surprise the Germans sent a regiment of remote-controlled tanks each packed with explosives into the enemy lines. The coastal waters were patrolled by German, Italian, and Croatian small craft with the objective of preventing the enemy from resupplying by sea.

On 7 June the infantry and assault engineers of the Romanian and German divisions leaped forward. It was already 100°F and the activity of running, jumping, and dodging enemy bullets and shrapnel soon caused each man to sweat until he was soaked to the skin. The sweat ran into the eyes, stinging them, and making it hard to scan the undergrowth to locate the enemy machine gunners. The areas between patches of foliage were lined with masses of barbed wire and every flat space was covered by enemy fire. The infantry took many minutes just to gain a yard or two. The Axis base line was shelled by artillery and mortars incessantly, causing casualties among stretcher bearers, medical orderlies, returning wounded, messengers, telephone linesmen, and the rear headquarters of the battalions and regiments. Yet oblivious to casualties the Romanians worked calmly, making up for lost men with guts and sheer determination. At the front itself the Romanian infantry charged from one pillbox to another, making room for the assault engineers who followed immediately behind with flame throwers and explosive charges. When one pillbox was blown apart and burned there was no time for cheering. The Romanians prayed silently to Jesus for having survived one more hour and then ran to the next clearing and the next pillbox. The Romanian mountain troops had it better in that they had trained just for such terrain and they worried far more about the enemy than the natural defenses. These men, whom some Germans thought to be cowardly, battled against superhuman odds. After eleven days and ten nights of hell the Sugarloaf was captured. The infantry of the Romanian 18th Division had learned the hard way that the toughest terrain was the safest. Now they cut their way through the undergrowth inch by sweating inch. To enter into a clearing of even four feet width invited Soviet bullets. In this manner many Soviet snipers and machine gunners were bypassed. This did not mean that the Romanians ceased to suffer casualties, for they were still susceptible to artillery and mortar fire and some of the bushes were sown with booby-traps and land mines. This was indeed a soldiers' battle, and Major-General Lascar could only busy himself with making sure that the front-line troops were supplied with enough ammunition and food. He did venture into the fight at times, though, lending his advice as a sort of roving platoon commander. Von Manstein received reports of his bravery and leadership from the German liaison officers with the 18th Division. After twenty days of butchery the Fedyukinny Heights were taken by the Germans from the flank. For the first time the men of the Romanian 1st Mountain Division were able to walk several hundred yards erect. So far their advance rate had been 330 yards per day.

On the twenty-second day of battle a gigantic explosion was heard all over the battlefield. Soviet political commissars had blown up a cave complex near Inkerman that contained supplies and ammunition rather than let them fall into Axis hands. The fact that the caves were being used as a refuge and contained tens of thousands of Soviet civilians and wounded and medical staff did not seem to affect their decision. If there had been any doubt among the Romanians as to what kind of enemy they were fighting, no doubt existed now.

On the 29th the Romanian 18th Division was told to hold the enemy's attention while a German unit made an amphibious assault in the enemy rear. The envelopment worked and suddenly thousands of Soviets began throwing up their hands. Behind the German amphibious force the Romanian 4th Mountain Division landed men and these were soon put to mopping up the shore, and later conquering bypassed pillboxes in the Balaclava area. In three days the Romanian mountain troops took 10,000 prisoners.

By this time the city of Sevastopol had been captured and the surviving enemy were huddled on the Khersones Peninsula under Romanian and German air and artillery bombardment. But the defenses collapsed under a German infantry assault on 4 July—30,000 Soviet soldiers threw up their hands, though some of the female soldiers fought to the death.

The senior Soviet staff had already fled by sea, but one boat with a general aboard was captured by Italian vessels.

The Crimean campaign was over, but the Axis troops here were still subject to Soviet air strikes. Only one day after the anti-aircraft guns were removed from Yalta naval base the Red Air Force struck, destroying shore installations, sinking two Italian MAS boats and damaging three.

It was already time for the finishing moves of the great southern sector offensive into the Caucasus. Fortunately for the Axis the enemy had played right into their hands. On 12 May the Soviets had made a spoiling attack by two armies towards Kharkov, but the German Sixth Army had held. Near Kiev a party of teenagers of the Reichs Labor Service (R.A.D.) had been forced to lay down their shovels and pick up rifles when the Soviets broke through and attacked the airfield they had been refurbishing. With the older cadre directing the defense the young workers repelled the enemy until German troops could counterattack. In this battle the Ukrainian Sumy Militia also performed favorably, and the Sixth Army was able to counterattack while the First Panzer Army hit the enemy in flank. The Soviets were cut off and crushed, and 241,000 Reds went into Axis captivity. This left a gap in the Soviet defense line exactly where part of the Axis offensive was to take place.

One of the units chosen to help hold the Don River in the Axis rear was the Wallonian Legion. This body of 2,000 men had served on anti-partisan operations with the German 100th Jaeger, 68th, and 97th Jaeger Divisions. Leon Degrelle had insisted on entering the legion as a private as he had no military experience. Within a few months, though, he had risen to the rank of lieutenant, nine promotions, and had received the Iron Cross second and first classes. He had been severely wounded and there is evidence that not all the promotions were political. In order to replace losses the Wallonian volunteer age was stretched from 18 to 35 years to 16 to 45 years, and this brought in 400 recruits in March and another 380 by May, including John Hagemans, the Rex Youth Leader, and Joseph Pevenasse, another Rex official. The commander, Colonel Pauly, had been replaced by Lucien Lippert. All of the unit's personnel were Wallonians, but there were some German advisers and technical sergeants.

On 10 June the First Panzer Army attacked the Izyum line and quickly crossed the Donets. It reached Kupiansk on the 22nd. On the 28th the major offensive began. South to north the Axis attacked the enemy in Eastern Ukraine, the Seventeenth Army going for Rostov, the First Panzer Army for Chertkovo and Millerovo, the Sixth Army towards Novaya Kalitva on the Don River, the Fourth Panzer Army towards Voronezh on the Don, and the Second Army to a point north of Voronezh.

It took several days of rough fighting, but the Germans reached the Don, but they did not attempt to cross. Rather they let the Fourth Panzer Army advance eastwards with the Soviet-held Don on its left flank. This move startled Stalin and his generals. Once the panzers had driven on, the Sixth Army followed to protect the immediate rear of the Fourth Panzer Army from an attack from the other side of the Don or from one of the many bridgeheads that the Soviets still held.

Further south the First Panzer Army, which contained as well as German divisions the Slovakian Mobile Division and the multi-national Wiking S.S. Division, had taken its objective and had swung southwards to take Rostov from the east. When that city fell the German Seventeenth and First Panzer Armies poured into the Caucasus. On 9 August German tanks entered the oil center of Maikop, having cut off a Soviet force in the Kuban. On the shore of the Kuban German troops had landed from the Crimea. Ironically in this heart of the Soviet oil region the German vehicles then ran out of fuel and had to stand to for several days waiting for the fuel truck convoys. In the first week of September the Germans then fought their way over the Terek River near Mozdok and entered the nation of Ossetia. Further German and Slovakian attacks failed to liberate the homelands of the Chechens and Ingush around Grozny. To the east the Germans did better, entering northern Daghestan and sighting the Caspian Sea. Among the liberated people were some Terek Cossacks who had been in rebellion since 1931!

General von Kleist had been arguing for mountain troops for the Caucasus and he eventually received a Romanian mountain division. These soldiers did Romania proud in the next few weeks. Another reinforcement was the Wallonian Legion, which the Germans described as fresh, ignoring its battles against the partisans. This was an insult, really, for too many of the names that had been on the rolls in May were by now on the casualty lists. The unit now had a standing strength of 1,000, and it was ordered to brave shot and shell in a major assault. These Belgians obeyed, but within days the legion was almost wiped out, suffering no less than 854 casualties. Degrelle was wounded twice again, but he remained with the unit. Not surprisingly he was promoted again—there was no one else. It must be noted, though, that his rank was a legion position only and he did not have the authority to give orders to German armed forces personnel. In late September the legion received 140 new volunteers and in November came another 226, plus many wounded men had been returned to duty. Most of the latest batch of volunteers had been taken prisoner by the Germans in 1940 and had volunteered when Rexist recruiters had toured their camps.

The Wiking Division continued to attack, leading with the Nordland Regiment. The Finns lost heavily taking Hill 711. In November the entire Axis line in the Caucasus, most of it on the Terek, was assaulted by Soviet forces that had sneaked across the Caspian Sea. Unfortunately, the Romanians bore the brunt of the onslaught and the failure of this one small division brought all thought of another Axis advance to an end.

By the end of November the line was static, and assisting the Germans in the Caucasus were the Romanian 6th Cavalry, 9th Cavalry, 1st Mountain, 2nd Mountain, 3rd Mountain, 4th Mountain, 10th, and 19th Divisions.

Miles to the north the Fourth Panzer Army had continued to follow the Don eastwards and then stayed with it as the mighty river curved southwards. However, the Sixth Army, no longer following the panzers, soon broke out across the Don and charged for the city of Stalingrad on the Volga River. By August 23rd the Sixth Army had reached the Volga on both sides of the city and was battling for the suburbs. The Romanian Fourth Army followed the Sixth Army and eventually settled on the southern flank of the Sixth Army, between it and the Fourth Panzer Army. Behind it came the Romanian Third Army which took up positions on the north flank of the Sixth Army. On the left flank of the Romanian Third Army was the Italian Eighth Army, facing northwards, and to its left flank was the Hungarian Second Army on the south bank of the Don facing northwards.

The Hungarians had rejoined the crusade in the spring at the request of Hitler and had sent their Second Army commanded by General Jany, consisting of the 102nd and 108th Divisions and the IIIrd Corps of the 6th, 7th, and 9th Divisions. The Second Army was reinforced in August with two more corps headquarters, the IVth, controlling the 10th, 12th, and 13th Divisions, and the VIIth, controlling the 19th, 20th, and 23rd Divisions. The Hungarian 1st Armored Division did not reach the front until October, but was placed in reserve in any case. On the face of it this was a powerful army, but the so-called armored division only had eighty-five Czech-built 38-Ts and twenty-two obsolete German-built Mark Is, with a few even worse Hungarian-built light armored vehicles, plus the army's rear-echelon personnel were not just Hungarians, but Serbians, Volksdeutsch, Slovakians, and Ukrainians, who did not like the idea of fighting for Hungary, though they did at least agree on the choice of enemy, and the labor troops who performed all mindless manual labor consisted of 55,000 Jews, who were unarmed, ill-clothed, and often unfed. As for the Hungarian fighting troops, many had come to the Eastern Front after only eight weeks' training.

The Hungarians had been engaged in light action near Kursk in June, but other than that had seen little fighting this year. According to Allied propaganda the Hungarian 6th, 7th, and 9th Divisions had suffered badly in July, and the 7th and 14th Divisions had been hurt in August. As can be seen the Soviets were not even sure which divisions they had been up against let alone how many casualties they had inflicted, but the Hungarian government did admit that by early September their war casualties were 14,531 dead.

The Hungarians made an attack at Voronezh on 14 September, but this rash act brought them nothing but another 2,000 dead. They then settled down to face the Soviet bridgeheads on the Don.

Also at the request of Hitler the Italians had expanded their expeditionary corps with the addition of the IInd Corps, of the Sforesca, Ravenna, and Cosseria Divisions, and the Alpine Corps, of the Julia, Tridentina, and Cuneense Divisions and 23rd March and 3rd January Blackshirt Groups. The original expeditionary corps was renamed the XXXVth Corps and would contain the veterans of the Pasubio, Torino, and 3rd Rapid Divisions. Replacements for the veteran units were told gruesome stories of how cold it became in winter on the Russian steppe and how terrifying the communist enemy could be. Two battalions of the Croatian Legion were attached to the 3rd Rapid Division. This gave Mussolini a total of 227,000 men serving on the Eastern Front formed into the Eighth Army of General Italo Gariboldi and the Vicenza Division which was guarding the Italian lines of communication from partisan attack.

The Italians began to move on 11 July, attacking and overcoming rearguards and bypassed units for a month. The horse cavalry of the 3rd Rapid Division performed excellent scouting missions and even fought a major action at Krasny Luch, but as dismounted troopers. The Italians then settled into their positions along the Don. By mid-August the line was not yet fully defended, and the Soviets saw their chance. For three days the Italian infantry withstood the assaults. On the 24th the 3rd Rapid Division was brought up to counterattack between Yagodny and Chebotarevsky. During this maneuver Colonel Bettoni saw that his Savoia Cavalry Regiment was in danger of being outflanked, so he ordered the 2nd Squadron of horse cavalry to charge the enemy. When Captain de Leone received the order he obeyed with eagerness. It is not every day a cavalryman receives an order to charge with the sword. While the enemy's head was kept down by artillery fire the Italians began their last cavalry charge in history.

The captain's horse soon fell, riddled with machine gun bullets, but his men carried on, galloping at a frenzy straight towards the enemy. The artillery fire ceased and now the horses smashed into the mass of Soviet infantry, the horsemen slashing the upraised faces of the terrified Red infantrymen with their sharp sabres as they rode right through the Soviet lines. On the enemy flank the 1st Squadron attacked dismounted with rifles. Bettoni had ordered the 2nd Squadron to be followed by the 3rd Squadron, a normal cavalry tactic, and it worked yet again. The Soviets had turned around and were firing at the backs of the 2nd Squadron as the surviving horsemen roamed the enemy rear, so they did not see the new wave of sabre-wielding cavalry. The horses slammed into the Soviets, knocking some of them over, and the sabres scarred deep into the heads and shoulders of the infantry. This was too much for the usually cool Reds and they fled for the river from whence they had come. The Italian artillery was redirected to follow the fleeing enemy.

It is estimated that of those Reds who survived to reach the other side of the river about 300 were wounded. It is known for sure that 600 were captured, often several by one horseman and his sword. One hundred and fifty dead Soviets were counted, and among the booty were hundreds of small arms and four field guns. Italian casualties were only 39 men killed and 74 wounded and 170 horses killed or crippled. Except for the families of the Italian dead, it was a glorious day for Italian arms, for they had met the enemy at uneven odds and had won a small but noticeable victory. The Soviets made no more attempts to advance in this sector.

By November 1942 the Romanians had 267,000 military personnel serving on the Eastern Front and guarding lines of communications. As the Romanian Third and Fourth Armies slotted into place to protect the flank of the Germans at Stalingrad the Soviets took note of this, and based on the knowledge that the Romanians were poorly equipped compared to the Germans the Soviet generals decided to cut off the Sixth Army in Stalingrad by smashing through the Romanians. The front was relatively quiet at this time, except within the great city itself where the Soviets and Germans battled tooth and nail for every building.

The most startling observance is that south of the Fourth Panzer Army lay a gap of 200 miles. This gap was patrolled by Luftwaffe planes and mobile detachments of the German 16th Motorized Division, but this was totally inadequate and is a perfect item of evidence of how short of manpower Hitler really was in relation to his ambitions. A gap in a front line the distance between London and Manchester in England or New York City and Washington, D.C. in the United States is farcical. It was most fortunate for the Axis that this gap did not lie in Russia, but in Kalmyk. The kalmyks are a Buddhist Mongoloid people and they resented the religious and economic oppression of the communists. It was indeed liberation day when the first German troops entered the area. As the entire region was open to Soviet attack the murder squads of the Einsatzgruppe came nowhere near this area, and the administration was left to front-line German officers who in effect gave the Kalmyks their freedom. In return several young male Kalmyks offered their services as scouts and guides. Indeed so many volunteers stepped forward that it was decided by the Germans to create the 103rd Kalmyk Defense Troop of horse cavalry. These osttruppen were so valuable that the 16th Motorized Division expanded the unit, eventually to two brigades of two battalions each. The Kalmyks proved so trustworthy that only three Germans were assigned to them, and then only for liaison work. With this added unit the job of the German motorized troops became less difficult, but remained tasking nonetheless. Of great help had been the man who appeared out of nowhere to administer the Kalmyk troops. Rudolf Vrba was one of those sinister figures who slide in and out of history like a James Bond. He was accepted as he was one of the few Germans who could actually communicate with the Kalmyks, and he insisted upon being addressed as Doctor Doll. The man's true nationality, however, is in constant doubt.

The enemy opposition in Kalmyk consisted of horse cavalry raiders and bands of partisans who were using this gap as an infiltration area. The partisans were for the most part ethnic Russians, and though they played down their communism when it suited them they found no solace from the Kalmyk villagers. Of course this information was passed back to Stalin who made a mental note that in future the Kalmyk nation must be considered an enemy of the Soviet people.

Hitler had not authorized the creation of a Kalmyk unit, but the German troops knew that he had authorized the use of hiwis and that was good enough for them. Besides Hitler never came to see for himself what his German brothers were up against. The general impression throughout the German Armed Forces was that the worst that could happen to a German officer who recruited foreigners would be that the unit was simply disbanded and the officer given a verbal reprimand. There was a good chance that the fait accompli would be accepted by higher command. Whether Hitler liked the idea or not, or even realized it, his continued offensive relied in part on tens of thousands of hiwis and osttruppen, made up from people whom he considered to be subhuman and not worthy of bearing arms. Those "subhumans" who showed courage under fire could not even be decorated with German awards unless Hitler had authorized their unit. Instead they had to make do with their own internal unit awards.

Chapter 18

United in Fear and Ignorance: Anti-Bandit Units in the East

By autumn of 1941 Heinrich Himmler had become dissatisfied with the einsatzgruppe executions. He was amazed to learn that villagers were allowed to witness the massacres, especially in Ukraine, for this threw out all pretense at secrecy. If the Jews of occupied Europe learned that they were all to be murdered they would hardly remain docile. Worse, the German people were hearing rumors of the massacres from returning wounded and soldiers on leave, and, though currently disbelieving the rumors as propaganda begun by the enemy, the people might eventually decide that there is no smoke without fire. If so, the German people might actually revolt against the nazi regime. Life was never boring for the Gestapo and Sicherheitsdienst personnel of the S.S. Security Police stationed at home in Germany.

The murder process was haphazard. Whenever hiwis were used they sometimes did not bother to fill in the mass graves. Even senior einsatzgruppe officers were often drunk on duty, as they found it morally easier to kill while blurry-eyed and senseless. As a result many shootings were inaccurate and survivors were managing to crawl out of their graves on the night following the aktion. As well, there seemed to be no method. Whole villages of Jews had been mysteriously bypassed. Where aktions were performed by only hiwis the discipline was often nonexistent.

Reinhard Heydrich has been credited with coming up with the solution. He declared that corpse factories would have to be erected, places where undesirables walked in but never walked out, and where a small dedicated staff could keep discipline and secrecy and follow a schedule. Heydrich knew that the Soviets had established extermination camps in the mid-1930s, but he felt German ingenuity could improve upon the Slavic model.

The first place chosen for the experiment was Chelmno Concentration Camp. It was provided with shooting pits and a gas chamber which was fed by an engine's carbon monoxide. By the time the first Jews were sent here in December 1941 thousands of Jews had already been executed in Poland, some quite publicly, for petty infringements, such as a shouted insult or a sarcastic look on their face. Yet the Judenraete (Jewish Councils) of the ghettoes refused to believe the stories of the einsatzgruppe in the east, but instead preached that this extended pogrom would end like all the others in past history, with most of the Jews surviving, a little leaner perhaps, but alive nonetheless. The intellectuals in the Jewish communities reminded their people that even in London and Paris two hundred years before, the nobility had banqueted while outside the mansion walls the ordinary folk had starved to death. In other words, injustice was nothing new and it did not have national origins.

At the beginning of 1942, Chelmno was opened for business after a few successful dress rehearsals. The S.S. personnel who handled the actual exterminations were selected from inner perimeter camp guards in the same manner as the einsatzgruppe had been chosen. Chaim Rumkowsky, the leader of the Lodz ghetto, was ordered to hand over 20,000 of his people to the S.S. Security Police for "relocation." By his own admission he managed to convince the S.D. officers to halve the number. He may not have known the true destination of these unfortunates, but he certainly knew that a mass movement by foot, truck, or freight train in a cold Polish December would freeze to death the elderly and the sick and give pneumonia and influenza to the rest, which as they were all emaciated by this date would be fatal to a high percentage of them.

Rumkowsky ordered his Jewish Police to assemble 2,000 recent arrivals and all the non-Polish Jews, that is the Germans and Austrians, and all the criminals in the ghetto jail. Most of the latter had been imprisoned for stealing food for their families. By the end of January 1942, Rumkowsky had filled the quota. The men, women, and children were handed over to S.S. sentries who placed them onto freight trains with sealed boxcars. Upon arrival at Chelmno the survivors of the freezing cramped journey were ordered out onto the small platform, where they were separated into workers and nonproductive elements. Several of the Axis personnel were S.S. hiwis of various national origins. The outer perimeter guards, who oftentimes never met the prisoners, were made up of hiwis, S.S. reservists, wounded Waffen S.S. men who were unfit for combat duty, and occasionally someone who should have been fighting at the front but who had convinced the powers that be to keep him out of danger.

In the interior of the camp the manual labor was performed by Sonderkommandos, prisoner workers who were paid by being exempt from execution, until the starvation diet made them unproductive. The Sonderkommandos became adept at removing the clothing from the living victims and jewelry, watches, hair, gold teeth, and tattoos from the dead victims, before the bodies were cremated. The S.S. Concentration Camp Service ran on a limited budget and needed all the profit it could get. Once the monster of Chelmno was fed, Rumkowsky was informed that he had to supply more Jews. The monster would never be sated. Rumkowsky complied and began to supply Chelmno on an almost daily basis.

Other extermination camps were now being created in occupied Poland, the most efficient being the extermination center at Birkenau, which was part of the Auschwitz complex of labor and concentration camps. Soon the S.S., hiwis, and Sonderkommandos had their mission down to a fine art. The gas chambers were christened delousing shower rooms, and in some camps the new arrivals were welcomed by a roving orchestra of prisoner musicians. Many of the newcomers were induced to write postcards to their relatives of the "having a wonderful time, wish you were here" variety. Minutes later they were massacred to the tunes of Strauss.

In March 1942 Lwow ghetto was ordered to supply all nonproductive Jews, that is those breadwinners who were not currently employed by a German concern, and their families. Though the Judenrat complied with the order, the Jewish Police proved inefficient in the roundup, probably from a lack of ardor. After a few days the local district S.S. became impatient and they sent in German S.S. Security Police and Ukrainian hiwis to do the job. They soon arrested 15,000 people. Not only did this mean that Lwow was short 15,000 human beings, but the world was short 15,000 human beings, for their destination was newly opened Belzec extermination camp.

By April 1942 Rumkowsky had supplied the nazis with 44,000 people, but the ghetto survivors were restless now for they suspected the worst. On 4 May, when he was ordered to supply yet more bodies, he offered up only some recently arrived non-Polish Jews. Still, his Jewish Police managed to come up with 10,600 of them.

The einsatzgruppe had largely become redundant by spring 1942. The S.S. men and women of A and B were assigned to other duties, many of them to the extermination camps, but if any of the ordinary policemen wished to serve in an S.S. unit he at first had to formally enlist into the S.S. The hiwis could serve in the camps or go to other types of camps and prisons as sentries, and many did so for the duty was easy—if one did not have a conscience—and treatment by the S.S. of its auxiliaries was very good. Several camps became almost the exclusive preserve of hiwis and the large German-run special camps even used hiwis. Belzec had many Estonian and Ukrainian hiwis, and Sobibor and Treblinka used Ukrainian hiwis. If any of the einsatzgruppe hiwis chose to go home he could do so, but he usually joined one of the part-time militias so that he could keep a weapon for self-defense.

Einsatzgruppe A reported that in its first five months of aktions its 900 or so German personnel and several hundred Russian, Latvian, Lithuanian, Estonian, and other hiwis had executed, by 25 November 1941, 1,064 male and female criminals, 56 captured terrorists, 653 mentally ill, 44 Polish dissidents, 28 Red Army prisoners of war, five Gypsies, one Armenian (presumably a dissident), and 136,421 men, women, and children whose crime was being

Jewish. Within another sixty-seven days the unit had added 92,631 more Jews.

Einsatzgruppe B and a few hundred Byelorussian and Lithuanian hiwis had shot 45,467 people by 14 November. In the last few days of July 1942 the remnants of Einsatzgruppe B murdered 10,000 Jews near Minsk. Half of the victims were German Jews who had been herded here over the months.

Einsatzgruppe C and several hundred Ukrainian hiwis had shot 95,000 enemies of the New Order by 1 December 1941. By late March 1942 the tractor factory of Kharkov had been emptied of its 20,000 Jewish inhabitants. Most of them had died from hunger and cold rather than by shooting.

Einsatzgruppe D consisting of only 500 Germans, some Ukrainian hiwis, and 500 Tatar hiwis shot 92,000 people by 8 April 1942.

Actually not all the victims were shot for some einsatzkommandos experimented with gas vans, which had their exhaust systems fed into the rear. The victims were loaded into the backs of the vans, locked inside, and then taken for a ride. After fifteen minutes or so of driving the bouncing and screaming from the back stopped.

From the summer of 1942 onwards Einsatzgruppe C and D remained in being, taking a few veterans from A and B, and performing Hitler's cleansing mission in Eastern Ukraine and the Northern Caucasus. In these areas they would run up their tallies to a total of 363,211 victims.

In May 1942 Moses Merin, the leader of Sosnowiecz ghetto, was ordered to hand over a quota of Jews. By mild coercion and promises he assembled one thousand volunteers for resettlement. The nazis expressed dissatisfaction at this low number, though, so the Jewish Police began arresting people in the following categories: criminals, petty offenders, mentally ill, cripples, and non-Polish Jews.

In July 1942 Czerniakow, the leader of the Warsaw ghetto, was secretly informed by the Jewish Gestapo that deportation was to begin soon. However, in case he had any ideas of failing to comply with the order the S.D. arrested his wife before demanding the quota on 21 July. Then without his permission Lithuanian and Latvian schumas and German and Polish ordinary policemen sealed the ghetto walls tightly, while fifty Germans of the S.D. and Gestapo and 200 Latvian and 200 Ukrainian schumas entered the narrow streets and began to search for people who did not possess work permits. The Jewish Police also assisted the roundup. They had a new commander, Jacob Lejkin, who had replaced Josef Szerynski, who had been imprisoned after being caught with his hand in the cash register. He had siphoned off valuable loot which should have gone into the S.S. coffers.

On the 23rd Czerniakow committed suicide rather than be a party to such an inhumane act. His protest was hardly noticed by the nazis. The nazis hit upon a new idea. They offered a free hot meal to anyone who volunteered to be resettled, and even this paltry bribe brought a high response. Naturally any sign of a physical scuffle on the part of a recalcitrant Jew resulted in him or her being shot dead on the spot. By 31 July the senior S.S. officers were dissatisfied with their catch. Therefore they brought in more reinforcements—more Ukrainian, Lithuanian, and Latvian schumas and German gendarmerie. Many of these policemen had to come hundreds of miles for this aktion.

Josef Szerynski was paroled by the S.S. to aid the nazis in the roundup, but on 20 August he opened his front door to be greeted by a young man who promptly shot him in the face with a pistol and then fled. In itself the wounding of Szerynski was not important to the nazis, but the manner of the act was. The German S.S. Security Police realized that a conspiracy must exist, for a ghetto Jew did not acquire a pistol and ammunition on his own—it took contacts with the Polish black market or terrorists.

Confirmation came the very next day, when a party of Ukrainian schumas were shot at. They had scattered for cover and had then fired indiscriminately at doors and windows.

On 27 August the deportations from Warsaw suddenly ceased. Two-thirds of the population had been "resettled," and 2,648 unarmed civilians had been shot dead in the winding streets. Some of the victims had been shot for sport by bored schumas.

In September Lodz ghetto, which had been spared for a few months, was once again called upon to fill the deportation trains. The latest quota was particularly heartrending: all sick, all people over sixty-five years of age, and all children under ten. The Judenrat refused to administer the order and ordered the Jewish Police not to assist. The nazis therefore recruited a mob of Jewish policemen, firemen, and Judenrat food distributors to carry out their orders, in return for exemptions for their own children. After a few days the touring S.D. officers espied too many children still at large so they sent in their own men to simply kidnap the children off the streets.

The Warsaw respite proved illusory. After only two weeks the deportations began again on 5 September, and within a week another 10,000 people had been deported. By now the schumas were roaming the streets shooting people just for the fun of it. By 21 September the nazis had emptied the Warsaw ghetto of 253,741 men, women, and children, all of whom had been sent to extermination camps. This left, according to S.S. statistics, about 50,000 people.

On the 21st the S.S. Security Police reneged on their contract with the Warsaw Jewish Police and began arresting them and their families. Yet 380 hand-picked policemen were allowed to remain, proving that the nazis still required the assistance of at least some Jewish policemen. The ghetto inmates were now assured that there would be no more roundups. The only ones left were Judenrat employees and munitions workers, and their families.

On the night of 23 September the village of Tuczyn near Rovno, which contained 2,000 Jews, was surrounded by a force of German S.S. Security

Police and Ukrainian hiwis. The buildings were then set alight and as the Jews came running out they were machine gunned to death. The perimeter was poorly guarded, though, and several hundred Jews managed to reach the safety of the woods.

By the end of 1942 the city of Warsaw, excluding the ghetto, had increased its population to 921,000 Poles, as the number of refugees from Wartheland had more than offset the number of Poles murdered or imprisoned by the authorities. The Reichsdeutsch minority increased to 16,078 as more and more good jobs were taken from Poles and offered to the German labor market, and as those German workers brought their families. The Volksdeutsch population also increased to 14,682, reflecting the attraction of the city and its large garrison as a safe haven for those Volksdeutsch who had been living in rural communities where anti-German terrorism was on the increase. The increased Volksdeutsch figure also showed that some Poles had tired of living on semi-starvation rations for years and had suddenly remembered they were of German descent and had declared themselves to be Class IV Volksdeutsch.

This year the authorities had finally come up with a racial standard for Wartheland. About one million two hundred thousand Poles had already been kicked out of Wartheland and put on the open road, while German colonists had been coming in. The Germans were Volksdeutsch who had been driven from their homes by the Soviets and who had chosen not to go back to their now liberated homes, plus released reservists aged forty-six and over, wounded veterans, and those unfit for military duty who were encouraged to settle on the new frontier. By the summer of 1942 only 57% of Warthelanders including Silesians were still declaring themselves to be Polish citizens. The new orders from Berlin changed this. According to German law any foreigner who was German-speaking was declared to be a German citizen, Class III Volksdeutsch. Individual will was not taken into consideration. This order did not apply to Jews or to Gypsies. Husbands of Gypsies could therefore find themselves conscripted into the German Armed Forces even though the S.S. was trying to kill their wives. All non-Jews and non-Gypsies of Eastern Europe were allowed to declare themselves to be German citizens even though they did not speak a word of German, but they were considered to be Class IV Volksdeutsch, that is on parole. In addition all Polish-speaking residents of Wartheland who had lived there before 1919, or who were children of those who had lived there, were declared to be Volksdeutsch Class IV. This did increase the rationing and employment status of millions of Poles at one stroke, but it also made the men between 18 and 45 susceptible to military conscription if they were not employed on essential duties, although it must be remembered that many of the men of this age group were currently prisoners of war having been captured in 1939. Still, a voluntary declaration of German citizenship could get one out of the prison hell camps. This law did not apply to the 100,000 Kashubians who wished to remain non-German, and they and the 300,000 Poles who had moved to Wartheland since 1919 were expelled. They trudged along the dusty roads to the General Government, but once there if they could not find work at once they were susceptible to the slave labor recruiters.

About 200,000 Wartheland Poles refused the offer of German citizenship and voluntarily moved to the General Government. A few German-speakers went with them, and indeed the Polish resistance movements contained some German-speakers.

All citizens of Luxembourg were declared to be German, regardless of whether they spoke German, French, or Letzteburgesch. In fact, use of the latter languages was outlawed in August 1942. Professor Damian Kratzenburg's Volksdeutsch Bewegung (Ethnic German Movement) looked upon these new orders as a mixed blessing. These fascists wished for the state to come under German authority, but they did not like the German government's acceptance of the Francophiles. The language law provoked a general strike, but the S.S. Security Police put it down quickly. Within the tiny state 1,200 Jews were arrested and the rest were expelled to France. Two thousand Luxembourgers had already joined the German S.S. and Armed Forces by this data, but the new law soon put 13,000 Lxembourger conscripts into the German Armed Forces. By the end of 1942 tens of thousands of men from Alsace and Lorraine, taken from France, and Eupen-Malmedy, taken from Belgium, also found themselves conscripted. In 1943 another 44,000 men were conscripted from these areas including Luxembourg.

In 1943 another 78,000 Volksdeutsch were conscripted in Wartheland, all of them, in theory, real Germans. It is difficult to assess the number of Polish-speakers conscripted by the Germans in the war, but counting those who were German citizens prior to 1 September 1939 it must certainly total about 200,000. There is evidence to show that recruiters who had not managed to find their quota in Wartheland sometimes slipped over the border into the General Government and press-ganged young Poles. By German law, of course, these soldiers were not Poles at all but Class IV Volksdeutsch. The conscription of Czech-speakers in the Protectorate of Bohemia and Moravia did not take place as haphazardly as it did in occupied-Poland, but those who had declared themselves to be Volksdeutsch, or who had been declared by their parents, were taken into the armed forces in masses beginning in 1942.

The Partisan Problem

From the August 1939 border of Germany and Poland stretching all the way to the Red Army lines in Russia the hills, mountains, forests, swamps, and isolated villages were infested by bands of partisans. In ex-Soviet territory the Soviets operated Red Army and N.K.V.D. partisans, and in Ukraine various bands of nationalist partisans fought the Soviets and the nazis alike. In Poland there were no less than nineteen groups of which two were communist.

Some of these bands were military-like in discipline, others were well-meaning but ill-disciplined, and still others were just gangs of criminals.

To protect as many potential targets as possible, the German authorities expanded the militias. In Estonia the Civil Guard was administered in thirteen regional defense units and a rail security force, and its name was later changed to the Self-Defense Corps. The Latvian and Lithuanian Civil Guards also took the same name.

The Byelorussian Self-Defense Corps was expanded to include 55,000 members, a formidable force on paper, but the members were spread all over the nation and rarely assembled above battalion level. The similar Ukrainian Self-Defense Corps soon reached a strength of 180,000. There were some smaller militias, too. The Lokot Militia was expanded by Voskoboinikov when he learned the partisans were trying to gain control of the autonomous state. In the Haivoran area sixteen companies of Ukrainian militiamen were formed to guard installations. The Sumy Militia of northeast Ukraine had fought well against partisans and against a Red Army breakthrough.

The police commanders also recruited more personnel. The Estonian schuma was reorganized into twenty-five battalions: 29th to 45th, 50th, and 286th to 293rd. The Latvians created forty battalions: 16th to 28th, 266th to 282nd, 311th to 313th, and 316th to 322nd. The Lithuanians expanded to twenty-three battalions: 1st to 15th, the Lietuva Battalion, and the 251st to 257th. At first these policemen were not adequately uniformed, making do with bits of their own national army and police uniforms and bits of German uniforms, but by the spring of 1942 they began to receive their own uniforms decorated with German police insignia, for it must be remembered that the schumas were auxiliaries in the German Police not in any local national police force. However, most members of the schumas wore a national identification patch. As German policemen they could be sent anywhere the chief of the German Police, Heinrich Himmler, wished. A battalion of Lithuanian schuma was sent to Italy and another to Yugoslavia. The Byelorussian schuma was formed into eleven battalions: 45th to 49th, 60th, 64th to 67th, and 69th. The Ukrainian schuma had no less than seventy-one battalions: 51st, 53rd to 57th, 61st to 63rd, 101st to 111th, 113th to 126th, 129th to 131st, 134th to 140th, 143rd to 169th.

In addition in Byelorussia, Ukraine, and occupied-Russia the German Police established the Hilfeswachtmannschaften (auxiliary sentry squads), abbreviated to Hiwas. These were sentry companies of about two hundred men each and they had the status of German auxiliary police. By summer 1942, there were about one hundred of these companies controlled by German Police and S.S. officers. At first each hiwa was only issued with ninety rounds of ammunition in case any of them defected to the partisans. Ninety rounds would not last long.

Within the liberated Crimea the S.D. formed six battalions of German auxiliary police made of Tatars. As the troops were treated quite well by the S.D., the unit proved itself to be a reliable force.

The districts behind the lines continued to be administered by the German Army which had created its own indigenous militias in Russia and which constantly clamored for more German Army anti-partisan units. In answer Army Group North was reinforced with a German police regiment and an army bicycle battalion of over-age reservists, and Army Group Center got an army security regiment. These few troops were totally inadequate.

Colonel von Treskow's six pioneer battalions had been armed to protect themselves and little by little these Ukrainians and Byelorussians found themselves spending more time hunting partisans than performing construction work.

As the army received less than was hoped for, Colonel von Pannwitz was ordered to take his Cossack sotnis and form a larger body out of them. By spring 1942 he had established the von Jungschulz and Platow Regiments, each of three battalions. From his advisory headquarters at Kherson in south-central Ukraine the German-Polish colonel would soon be sending his Cossacks to ride against partisans wherever they showed themselves. In the autumn he traveled to the Kuban and the Don and Terek valleys to discuss the recruitment of Cossacks from those areas. He found an interested party in the person of Nikolaj Kulakoff, the Ataman of the Terek Cossacks. Von Pannwitz was offering more than his orders had authorized him to. He was determined to create a Cossack Liberation Army.

Many temporary units were created, too, some of which may never be officially remembered. For example, in the Crimea when stragglers were found hiding in the Yaila Mountains several companies of Ukrainian hiwis were assembled to aid the Romanians in rooting them out.

The Caucasian Moslem Legion was now in action, but its men fought in separate battalions, except for the 450th Regiment raised by Colonel Meyer-Mader for it proved that it could handle large-scale action.

Yet, more and more German soldiers were thrown into the partisan war, some even while on leave or recuperating from wounds. Replacements and returning wounded were placed in march battalions for days on end so that they could protect themselves from partisan snipers. After it had suffered 50% casualties in battle at the front the 638th Regiment (French Volunteer Legion) was withdrawn for a good rest in March 1942 and sent to Poland, but the men spent most of their time guarding installations from Polish terrorist saboteurs. The aging Colonel Labonne was recalled home and the unit was split into two separate battalions, the 1st under Major LaCroix and the 3rd under Major Demessine.

The result of Hitler's authorization of hiwis in spring 1942 was not just that many German officers saw this as a carte blanche for raising osttruppen, but also the condition of the hiwis was greatly improved. Uniforms of varying descriptions were supplied to the male hiwis, and some female hiwis in certain cases, and new disciplinary regulations standardized their pay and treatment. The hiwis were given their own rank and decoration structure, and often the only distinguishing mark from a hiwi that an ostruppe wore was that he was allowed to wear the German Armed Forces eagle on his breast. Several divisions now began using companies of hiwis in the front line.

The number and description of German anti-partisan units is indeed somewhat baffling, and post-war apologists for the murder squads of the einsatzgruppe often try to lose these units among the general term of anti-partisan security units. However, this is not borne out by facts. Indeed, to describe these murderers as ordinary soldier-policemen is to insult those brave men of bona-fide fighting outfits. There are several recorded instances in which einsatzgruppe men were asked to supply aid in an emergency anti-partisan operation by officers of the Army, S.S., and Police, but the killers always refused, claiming that they had orders from the highest level to refrain from anything that would jeopardize their mission, and it must be said that they did have such orders and that getting oneself killed could constitute jeopardizing one's mission. If any einsatzgruppe men did become involved in combat it was because they had come under attack not because they had willingly offered aid to a beleaguered and hard-pressed garrison. There is, however, a possibility that some of the einsatzgruppe hiwis were loaned to combat formations, as hiwi records are practically nonexistent. An einsatzgruppe killer was no more a real soldier than the Tower of London executioner was a chivalrous knight in armor.

Anti-Partisan Operations

In addition to German units and German-sponsored units the Axis consisted of partners, but when these partners were asked to provide anti-partisan forces they responded poorly in the opinion of the Germans. The Romanians did put two divisions on security duty, but only in Romanian-occupied Ukraine where there had been very little resistance activity. The Hungarians supplied five divisions to the Germans, but they were in a bad state. The Germans put the best, or rather least worst, on rail security duty and the other four on minor sentry duties.

It was thus the German-controlled units that bore the brunt of the anti-partisan war.

The first major operation in the east, that is what had been Poland and Soviet territory, took place between 19 to 31 March 1942. Operation Muenchen aimed at destroying an impudent partisan group that had captured the countryside around Yelna and Dorogobuzh. Once V-men had scouted the area the Germans attacked with one security and two panzer divisions and their hiwis, but only the hunt regiment of the security division fought a serious action. The partisans were equipped with horse cavalry, artillery, and tanks, but were driven back towards Dorogobuzh after German aircraft had caught some of them in the open.

This was the first real setback for the Soviet partisans, but the military defeat did not bother them as much as the lack of recruits. Their recruiting drives were meeting opposition at the hands of the indigenous militia and police even in small villages, so the Soviet leadership stepped in with new orders. From spring 1942 onwards the partisans were empowered to conscript all Soviet citizens, males and childless females aged 17 to 50 years. Refusal was punishable by death. The recruits were sent into their first battle unarmed as they were on parole. Desertion was punishable by the death of the individual and his, or her, entire family. Pregnancy caused by conception after the conscription date was also punishable by death. On occasion the partisans would call in a Red Air Force strike on a village that had resisted their recruiters.

In such a manner the partisans increased in strength, but not surprisingly many Soviet citizens willingly gave information to the authorities about terrorist activity. The partisans were not loved anywhere, not even in actual Russian territory. Whenever possible the Red Air Force dropped supplies, equipment, and replacements to the partisans and therefore more and more the partisans took on the appearance of a major military force fighting a guerrilla campaign and less and less that of a popular uprising of peasants which Soviet propaganda described.

The sophistication of German-controlled army, militia, S.S., police, and hiwi anti-partisan units had to increase accordingly.

The partisans continued their activities in Lokot and succeeded in assassinating Voskoboinikov, but fortunately for the Axis the militia commander emerged as a leader. Bronislaw Miechislaw Kaminsky, a half-Russian whose other half was Polish and Jewish, took over the political controls and increased the size and power of his militia. Within weeks he had five regiments (battalions really), an artillery battalion, and a tank company equipped with Red Army equipment which had been begged, borrowed, and stolen from the Germans. Kaminsky was politically astute and he christened his militia the Russian National Liberation Army (R.O.N.A.) and did not suffer any visible signs of German displeasure by using this presumptuous title. He preached that his troops were the forerunners of a new anti-communist Russian state.

Unfortunately, besides being a military and political leader of ability he was also one of the cruelest psychopathic killers known to modern history. There are stories, unverifiable, that he murdered some of his own men in frenzied rages with his bare hands. However, he did succeed in a series of battles in driving out the partisans, and by the summer of 1942 he was strong enough to loan to the Germans a unit for rail security duties at Briansk outside the borders of Lokot.

Elsewhere partisan raids had picked up. In a district administered by Army Group North, General von Wirth was assassinated. In western Russia the German garrison of Prigorye near Smolensk was wiped out. In the Crimea a thousand Germans were killed or wounded in ambushes. In the Briansk area three Hungarian battalions failed to trap a partisan group and suffered 400 casualties.

Beginning on 24 May the authorities assaulted the partisans of western Russia with an army of three panzer and six infantry divisions accompanied by hiwis, a police regiment, and the Russian Graukopf Battalion. Air support was on call. By the end of Operation Hannover the Axis troops had lost 550 killed and 1,650 wounded, but they had killed in action or executed 10,500 partisans.

In March 1942 the S.D. began forming a special unit of Russians called Druzhina under the command of Colonel V.V. Gil. Gil, a Kuban Cossack, whose real name was Rodinov, had once been the chief of staff of the Red Army 229th Division. Department I was trained for overt operations and Department II was trained for covert work. By June the unit was ready, but its first mission was called off at the last moment. As it was spare, the German Army commandeered the unit for front-line duty at Nevel northeast of Polotsk.

In June V-men entered the Briansk forest to begin Operation Vogelsang. They were quickly followed by a panzer and two infantry regiments with their hiwis. In one week they lost 58 killed, 130 wounded, and one missing, but they killed 1,193 partisans, arrested 498 suspected partisans, and forcibly evacuated 12,531 villagers from areas where the partisans had been living.

Though it had taken casualties, the Graukopf Battalion grew to a disciplined force of 3,000 men. The Germans gave the unit a new commander, Vladimir Boiarsky, late of the Red Army 41st Guards Division, and a new name, the Versuchs Brigade, but the men called themselves the Russian National People's Army (R.N.N.A.). The very name alone caused many Russians to volunteer for the force. Legally the existence of this unit as a fighting force was on shaky ground and the possession of such a nationally conscious title would have given Hitler heart palpitations if he had heard it, but the recruits did not know this, nor did the unit's officers who were now wearing Tsarist uniforms inform them.

At Novocherkassk Sergei Pavlov formed a unit of Don Cossacks who were given German auxiliary police status. By August the men were patrolling on horseback the valley of the Don just south of the river which was currently the front line.

The Waffen S.S. had been using a horse cavalry brigade at the front for a year and then with an eye to anti-partisan warfare they increased the brigade to divisional-size as the S.S. Florian Geyer Cavalry Division. Not enough young volunteers were coming into the Waffen S.S. from Germany, so to fill the ranks of this division S.S. recruiters went among the Volksdeutsch community near Melitopol in the Ukraine. This community had suffered badly in June 1941 when the N.K.V.D. had arrested the able-bodied menfolk and deported them for slave labor. Some of the men had hidden and survived, and there were plenty of eager youngsters willing to avenge their loved ones.

The French Volunteer Legion fought one of its toughest battles in June 1942 while on an anti-partisan sweep. The 3rd Battalion was ordered into action near Volost by its commander, Major Demessine, and its intelligence officer, Lieutenant Jacques Doriot, but the enemy was waiting and prepared. The French suffered high losses, and were astonished to find that the action was little different than front-line combat. The 1st Battalion, now under Major Bridoux, son of the French Minister of War, was attached to the 186th Security Division for an assault on partisans near Smolensk. Here too the French were alarmed at the strength and weaponry that some partisan groups could muster.

The entrance of the German forces into the Caucasus changed the nature of the volunteer situation again. The Caucasian Moslem Legion was now able to recruit directly from its homeland, while some of those already serving were allowed to visit home. The Chechens and Karachais were discovered to be already in conflict with the Soviets and their guerrilla groups were accepted as militias. Other ethnic groups were encouraged to form self-defense militias.

About this time, late summer of 1942, Hitler was informed of the existence of the Georgian and Armenian Legions and the Azerbaijani element in the Caucasian Moslem Legion, which had been serving loyally as sentries and on minor partisan hunts. He surprised everyone by agreeing that these nations should have some autonomy. Unfortunately for these people the nation of Azerbaijan and most of Georgia were never reached by Axis forces. The new status did cause more Georgians and Armenians to volunteer from the camps and hiwi detachments, and the Azerbaijanis were soon socially promoted by being given their own independent legion.

In the southern half of the German-occupied Caucasus the army controlled things, and not only did they not oppress anyone, but they opened all religious buildings and allowed nationalist culture to flourish. The Tats, a Jewish people who speak an Iranic language, were left to live in peace. Only in the north Caucasus were the S.S. Security Police and einsatzgruppe operating.

In August 1942 Hitler lifted most of the restrictions on the raising of osttruppen. This reappraisal came as a direct result of the increase in partisan raids. The order came at the time of the liberation of the Kuban and the Terek valley and much of the Don valley and more and more Cossacks were recruited from their farms. General Wagner established the Kuban as an autonomous zone and placed Timofey Domanov at its head, and a militia was established.

Hitler also demanded that all employees of German civilian organizations of the government and party be armed for self-defense. In August a Dutch unit of the Transportation Corps (N.S.K.K.) was ambushed by a large but badly disciplined and led partisan force. The Dutchmen turned the tables on the enemy and captured a thousand prisoners, and earned twenty-five iron crosses.

In the late summer the German 287th Regiment arrived at Stalino to undergo advanced training. Its 3rd Battalion was called the German Training Detachment (D.A.L.) and was made up of Arabs serving in the German Army, most of them veterans of the Arab Legion raised in Syria.

In September the Lokot Militia (R.O.N.A.) began a series of pre-emptive strikes, hitting the partisans just outside the borders of Lokot. At the same time near here in the Briansk region Operation Dreieck began on the 16th. For two weeks the Germans and the R.O.N.A. hunted down the enemy, killing 2,244. Kaminsky gave the Germans the first evidence of his brutality in this operation. One enemy group escaped the net and broke out westwards. About 1,600 German troops chased the enemy, but by early October they had only caught up with forty-five stragglers, all but two of whom were killed.

So far the anti-partisan operations in the east had been directed at local level by officers of several branches of the security forces without much coordination. Heinrich Himmler decided that a coordinator was needed and he rushed to put one of his own men in the position before an army general got it. He persuaded Hitler to appoint S.S. Obergruppenfuehrer Erich von dem Bach Zelewski as Reich Plenipotentiary for the Combating of Partisans. This S.S. general had recently suffered a nervous breakdown after having witnessed too many executions of Jews. Now Himmler believed the man to be cured of his faint-heartedness, and as he liked him he entrusted him with this important position. The fact that Zelewski was part Polish with two Jewish brothers-in-law was disregarded.

The first operation to be coordinated by Zelewski was in November, a sweep of the Polotsk lowlands in Byelorussia. This move by the 12th Panzer Division to ensnare the headquarters of a partisan band was unsuccessful. The senior S.S. officers were soon complaining that the army officers were not ruthless enough in their searches and interrogations, and they claimed that if let loose on the populace they could attain better results.

There was also a danger of Soviet troops slipping across or around the front line. On 4 February 1943 a Soviet brigade made an amphibious invasion of Ozereyka Bay in the Crimea, which was defended by German artillery and elements of the Romanian 38th Regiment. As the German gunners fired frantically, Captain Radiu led his company of Romanian engineers in a counterattack, and later Captain Dabija Nikolai arrived with a company of Romanian infantry. These few troops held the enemy and shelled his ships until German tanks and infantry could drive the enemy into the sea. The victors counted 620 Soviet corpses and thirty-one destroyed tanks. Radiu was killed.

Chapter 19

The Protected Ones: The Czechs

When the Russo-German War broke out in 1941, it came as a cataclysm that made up the minds of many Slovakians that at last liberation from the fascists was possible. As about 10% of the people were communists a resistance movement was quickly organized, which manifested itself in various forms from simple passive non-cooperation in the cities to open guerrilla warfare in the high mountains. More German guest forces were brought in to combat this partisan presence and three Slovakian army divisions had to remain constantly available for anti-partisan duty. The tiny air force of two fighter squadrons and a reconnaissance group served under Luftwaffe orders. The German S.S. Security Police and their men and women recruited from the local Volksdeutsch kept constant vigil over the lives of the natives. In Ukraine two Slovakian infantry divisions were serving on lines of communications protection duties, and the Slovakian Mobile Division was doing good service at the front. Altogether the three divisions in the east contained 42,000 troops.

Communist saboteurs also began interfering with the normal run of operations in the Protectorate of Bohemia and Moravia, especially in the armaments industry, trying to prevent the manufacture, assembly, and transportation of weapons and ammunition from the well-known armaments plants in the nation. Communist rabble-rousers were trying to turn an unruly population into a rebellious one. The new ideological war had caused the man in the street to choose sides, and the political and cultural oppression of the Czechs and the racial oppression of the Jews was affecting consciences. Perhaps of more immediate import, though, was the crippling black market and war profiteering.

By September 1941, Hitler had come to the conclusion that von Neurath could not control the Czechs, and on the 23rd he placed that diplomat on permanent sick leave. The Protectorate's State Secretary, S.S. Obergruppenfuehrer Karl Hermann Frank, a Sudeten, had hoped that as he had "suffered" under Czech oppression for years he would now be given the opportunity to dish it out for a change, but this was not to be. Advised by Himmler, Hitler decided that the best man for the job was S.S. Obergruppenfuehrer Reinhard Heydrich, the man who had just set into motion the genocide of the Jewish race.

Heydrich took over on 27 September and true to his reputation he began ordering death sentences and arrests. The S.S. Security Police had been under his command since before the war and armed with lists of names of those who had been investigated he now knew exactly whom to arrest. He reaped the benefit of his own spies. Of course this information had been deliberately withheld from von Neurath just for such an occasion.

The day after he arrived six executions were ordered, twenty on the following day, and fifty-eight on the 30th. The number decreased after this date, but executions took place daily and the names of the victims were published.

However, the people soon realized that only about half of the victims were terrorists. The rest were known criminals, black market operators, and war profiteers. Some were Germans, and one of those placed on death row was none other than Premier General Elias. As most of the people looked on the terrorists as brainless hotheads anyway, the general mood was of justice having been done.

In the first two months of Heydrich's rule about 5,000 persons were arrested on charges of treason by the Czech Police and the German Police and S.S. Security Police. This crippled the major resistance organizations, and made Heydrich a prime target.

The major result was far worse for the resistance, and that was that the S.S. regime was seen by many to be beneficial to the populace. Heydrich increased the food ration for all Czechs, which brought a decline in the phony registrations of hungry Czechs as Class IV Volksdeutsch. Factory canteens were installed on a national scale, something that the pre-war Czech government had never bothered to do. The Czech Police received better treatment too, and pensions were established for men wounded on anti-terrorist duty and for loved ones of policemen killed in action. Within weeks the Protectorate was far more secure and productive than von Neurath could ever have hoped for. Heydrich did not even use a bodyguard when he drove to and from work, between his headquarters in Prague and his home where he lived with his wife and children in a suburb of the beautiful city. He bragged "My Czechs will never harm me."

The people were still not free, though, and no better sign of this came than on 18 December 1941 when forced labor was introduced. All males aged 16 to 65 and females aged 17 to 45 who were not employed on useful duties were to be conscripted to work in Germany. This law eventually affected about a quarter of a million Czechs, who were sent to Germany, and an equal number who were transported to a German concern in the Protectorate. All those who had declared themselves to be Volksdeutsch were exempt, but these men were eligible for military conscription. These phony Volksdeutsch were nicknamed by the Czechs "Margarine Germans" for they had become Germans simply to acquire better food and treatment.

Another of Heydrich's benefits was the continuance of a provisional Czech government. The new premier was Dr. Jaroslaw Krejci, with Minister of Propaganda Emmanuel Moravec, Minister of Interior Richard Bienert, and Minister of the Treasury Josef Kalfus. Some minor officials were German and Volksdeutsch. The government, in theory, still commanded the Czech Army which was standing at 7,000 men.

One of the more comical acts of the S.S. was the racial census, overseen by the Race and Resettlement Office (R.U.S.H.A.). Himmler had ordered this to try to put some sort of order in the Volksdeutsch system. However, the results proved most confusing: 45% of all non-Jewish and non-Gypsy civilian residents of the Protectorate were deemed to be of Germanic or Nordic blood and 15% were deemed to be of Alpine Celtic blood. These were acceptable to the German government. The remainder were judged to be of Slavic stock.

The confusion came about, though, when the Sudetenland received a census. There, where everybody was a Class III Volksdeutsch German citizen, the result was that only 25% were judged by R.U.S.H.A. to be of Germanic or Nordic stock and about 70% of Alpine Celtic stock. There were even many Slavics. As the nazis held the Nordics to be of the highest order, the Germanics second, and the Alpine Celtics third, then in terms of their own race policy they should have liberated Bohemia and Moravia and conquered the Sudetenland rather than the other way around. This proved that the nazis' racial policies were nonsense.

Of course, intelligent people had known this all along. In the 1930s the racial standard for entrance into the S.S. had been very high. Neither Hitler nor Himmler could have passed the racial entrance exam. Hitler was more Alpine Celtic than Germanic and also had some Slavic (Czech) blood.

The Czech government-in-exile in London had expressed great concern when the world learned that Heydrich was taking over the reins in Prague for it feared mass executions and arrests. The exiled politicians had therefore parachuted some of their soldier saboteurs into the Protectorate to make contact with the resistance. These men were ordered to study a method of assassinating Heydrich.

However, by 1 April 1942 the government-in-exile had an even greater need to get rid of the man. This day Heydrich issued decrees of pension systems, unemployment benefits, and other social aids. This was given as a reward for increased production in the factories and decreased incidents of sabotage and also as an incentive towards peaceful cooperation. The British government already considered all Czechs to be enemy unless proven otherwise and Heydrich's methods were not going to change the minds of the British. The Protectorate was becoming a member of the Axis family. Of the sixteen Czech agents flown in from Britain, by May 1942 only two had survived the watchful eyes of the Czech Police and the German S.S. Security Police.

The exiled politicians in London had to remove Heydrich for he threatened their survival. The Czech Provisional Government called the exiled politicians traitors and puppets of the English. If Heydrich succeeded in pacifying the Czechs without further bloodshed then the exiled politicians might as well give up all hope of seeing their nation again. The Czech resistance movement also had a score to settle with Heydrich. To try to win world support if not Czech support the exiled politicians popularized Heydrich to the world as "the Butcher of Prague." Of course as far as the Jews were concerned he deserved this title.

On 27 May 1942, while Heydrich's chauffeur-driven car was quietly gliding through a suburb of Prague, two soldiers of the British-sponsored Free Czech Army jumped in front of the car at a hairpin bend and one threw a grenade into the open-topped vehicle. As they ran off the grenade blew up in the rear, but the poorly made device only wounded Heydrich. He drew his pistol and fired at the escaping terrorists. The chauffeur also drew his pistol and followed them, firing as he ran. One of the would-be assassins ran straight into two Czech city policemen, gunned one down, and made his getaway. Meanwhile a passing baker's van had stopped and the driver had put Heydrich in the back and driven him to a hospital.

The authorities went berserk. Hitler went into a rage and ordered Frank to find the terrorists at once. The entire city was sealed by Czech police, Czech gendarmerie, German police, and German S.S. security police with the aid of three battalions of German army troops and some Waffen S.S. who were stationed in the city. A body of S.A. made up of Germans and local Volksdeutsch and a unit of the N.S.K.K. were also drafted to the job. Once done, the Czech and German police began to search every last building.

This operation netted a profit for the discovery of illegal items and the capture of wanted persons provided the jails with plenty of occupants, but no evidence was found to link any of these people with the assassination attempt. While the streets were being secured, inside the hospital the Czech doctors and nurses were fighting to save Heydrich's life. German medical specialists were flown in from Berlin.

Benes, the leader of the Czech government-in-exile, proclaimed to the world that the people of his native land had spontaneously risen against the oppressor, but he did not mention that in fact the attack had been planned by his military staff for months. At first Hitler believed the Allied propaganda, but wiser heads prevailed and convinced him that the act was the work of a handful of London agents. Many senior Germans were afraid that Hitler would wreak vengeance on the Czech people, and their fears were not just based on moral grounds, but if the Germans overreacted then it might throw the Czech people back onto the Allied side. If so, then the Allied agents would have succeeded, for many Germans were convinced that that had been the real goal, to force the nation onto the Allied side, even at the cost of much innocent blood.

Already in the week following the attack thousands of Czechs had been arrested and 157 had been shot as convicted terrorists. President Hacha publicly acclaimed the executions and pronounced Benes to be the number one enemy of the Czech people. His mouthpiece, Dr. Moravec, made it clear in several radio broadcasts that the people as a whole had not been involved in the attack.

All of this argument and diplomacy became redundant on 4 June when Heydrich died of his wounds. President Hacha put the nation into a state of mourning, and when Heydrich's body was laid in state tens of thousands of people passed by the coffin to pay tribute, not all of them German by any means. The body was then taken to Berlin for a state funeral, which the members of the Czech Provisional Government attended.

Unknown to the German people the S.S. Security Police had already begun to crackdown hard on the Czechs. In Kladno district Czech and German police surrounded the village of Lidice allowing no one to leave. Later all the women and children were evacuated by S.S. Security Police, and then an S.S. murder squad of twenty-three men entered the village. None of the Czech police knew the true purpose of the action, but they soon realized it when they heard the rattle of machine gun fire. According to S.S. figures 170 males were executed, and eleven late arrivals were then dispatched with a few bullets. In addition, fifteen hostages from the surrounding area were shot. The women were transported to a concentration camp, and ninety children also went to a camp. However, eight children of obvious Germanic appearance were sent to Germany to be adopted by innocent German families. The village itself was burned to the ground, and later youths of the Reichs Labor Service blew up the rubble with explosives.

On the 16th a member of the Free Czech Army assassin gang defected to the police, and with his help some members of the resistance were captured. Within two days one of the resistance prisoners betrayed the actual assassins. They had been hiding in a church in Prague.

At once a Waffen S.S. unit of 759 soldiers was dispatched to the scene, and all seven terrorists were either killed or they committed suicide to avoid capture. However, the fight lasted several hours and the German casualties were ridiculously high.

Until this incident the terrorists were considered to be heartless murderers by the Czech people, but once they realized that these young men were willing to sacrifice their lives for Czech freedom and had performed in battle so well, they became heroes. The church in Prague became Czechoslovakia's Alamo.

In retaliation for hiding a terrorist the entire village of Lezaky was wiped out on the 24th by an S.S. murder squad, only the children being saved. In the three months following the assassination the authorities executed 1,357 Czech men and women and imprisoned 3,188. One of those executed was General Elias.

The Czech agents had won. Henceforth the people of the Protectorate began accepting less and less the reality of Axis occupation and pining more and more for the dream of Allied liberation.

Within Slovakia the Slovakian police, Hlinka Guard, locally raised S.S., and German S.S. security police began to round up the Jews in April 1942, an operation overseen by Dieter Wisliceny. He ignored the outcry of the intellectuals. By October, though, the Roman Catholic government stepped in to halt the deportations as the intellectual outcry was having political effects. Many wealthy Jews had remained safe by bribery, but 58,000 others had not been so fortunate. They had been sent to extermination camps.

Chapter 20

Axis France

In German-occupied France, while the placards, posters, leaflets, newspapers, cinema newsreels, and radio stations were trying to recruit volunteers to fight the Soviets, the authorities were busy rooting out the enemy in their midst—the Jews. Rumors abounded in the second week in July 1941 that there was to be another mass roundup of immigrant Jews in Paris. Late on the 15th orders came in for the following morning for all off-duty city police, police reservists, police from neighboring districts, and cadets from the Police Academy to report for a special operation. This gave the Paris Police Prefect 9,000 men. As well, the Parti Populaire Francais loaned four hundred of its militiamen for the roundup.

On the morning the police and militiamen were issued with lists of people to be arrested. These were immigrant Jews, some of them naturalized French citizens, males aged 16 to 60 and females aged 16 to 65. Exemptions were made for Jews married to non-Jews, wives of prisoners of war, pregnant women, and women with children under two years of age. Just over 7,000 people were arrested and taken to the sports stadium.

For eight days the arrestees were kept under guard, and the French authorities did not even supply food, water, or toilet facilities. The shock of what a French authority could do caused great despair and there were some suicides. The frightened teenagers trying to look brave, the mothers pining for their children, and the older men and women who feared the worst would have suffered death and disease if it were not for the climate which was warm and for members of the Red Cross and a Quaker organization who brought food and water.

On the ninth day the Jews were placed on trains and taken to Beaunes la Rolande and Pithviers concentration camps. There they were guarded by French police. They were joined at a later date by 5,800 more immigrant Jews from Paris. Smaller roundups took place in other parts of France. Of all the policemen involved only one resigned rather than be a party to such an atrocity.

Terrorist activity had stepped up considerably after the invasion of the Soviet Union as many communists had been straining at the leash for a year and were now let loose by their commissars. The German Military Government of occupied France decided to make an example at once to prevent the outrages from worsening. In retaliation for the death of a German soldier, it was announced that one hundred political prisoners were to be shot. Pierre Pucheau, who was the Vichy Minister of the Interior, and in theory in charge of occupied France as well as Vichy France, argued with the German Army and succeeded in lowering the figure to fifty and getting only communists put on the death list. These fifty prisoners were guarded by French police until the execution day, 23 October, and then they were handed over to the German S.S. Security Police. Twenty-seven were shot at a sand quarry near Chateaubriant and twenty-one at Nantes prison. However, the very next day the Germans shot one hundred hostages in Bordeaux.

This did not stop the terrorist acts, and indeed by the end of November they were averaging three a day in the occupied zone. On 21 November in Paris a bomb was thrown at a bookstore frequented by Germans. Patrolling city policemen witnessed the attack and a gunfight broke out between them and the terrorists, but the culprits escaped. On 12 December the French police arrested one thousand Jews of the professional classes, doctors, lawyers, architects, and so on in the occupied zone, declaring these to be hostages in case of further terrorism.

At the end of 1941 the French people were reminded that the greater war was still going on for the British stepped up their air raids. Factories and rail yards were the main target and as a result the French people suffered casualties. As the French were in effect at war with the British many people thought these raids were deliberately aimed at innocents. This was natural fodder for the fascist propaganda animal. Not only were the British stealing France's colonies, not only were they aiding the communists, but they were killing French civilians, destroying their homes, and removing their livelihood. On 3 March 1942 British bombers struck at the Renault plant in Paris, killing 623 civilians and injuring 1,500.

Despite such provocation the Germans felt that the Vichy regime was not reacting sufficiently, and they convinced Petain to dismiss Darlan. The new vice-premier was none other than Pierre Laval, though Petain seems to have hoped that the new Minister of War, General Eugene Bridoux, could temper Laval. Darlan remained as Commander of the Armed Forces.

On 5 May 1942, due purely to Himmler's greed, the S.S. demanded and received from Hitler command of the French police in the occupied zone, and gave the job to Higher S.S. and Police Leader Karl Oberg. This brought forth only a mild protest from Laval, possibly as he owed the Germans a favor. Ironically it was the German Military Government which complained the loudest. The generals ruled Northern France and the Atlantic coast with a stern but reasonably fair hand, and they feared that the S.S. would bring only cruelty, stupidity, and overreaction to the administration.

Actually Laval had other things to worry about, for this same day the British attacked again. The French-controlled island of Madagascar contained several ports, the largest being Diego Suarez on the northern tip. The British Admiralty had been alarmed by a recent Japanese raid into the Indian Ocean and they feared that the Vichy government might open the port to Japanese warships. This was not altogether a groundless fear for the Japanese were currently using bases in French Indo-China.

On the morning of the 5th British carrier-borne planes struck the defenses of the port without warning and sank a sloop, a submarine, and an armed merchant cruiser. Later two French submarines returning from patrol were also sunk. A few French vessels managed to escape. Then British troops landed and battled with the garrison of a battalion of Senegalese, three battalions of Malgache (local natives) and French artillery under the command of Colonel Clairebout. After two days of action the garrison pulled back into the interior of the thousand-mile-long island, having suffered 200 killed and 500 wounded. The island garrison contained a total of 20,000 troops, but in keeping with French policy the men were ordered not to attack the British invaders.

The authorities in occupied France had their hands full in June. Sabotage was on the increase and as some of this was coastal a French Naval Police was created to search for saboteurs along the coasts and in the shipping yards. The police in the rest of France were busy too this month, for the German government demanded that all immigrant Jews in the unoccupied zone be handed over to them. The Vichy government did not refuse and their police began to arrest these helpless people all over the country. However, most of them were held in French camps and only a trickle was allowed to flow to the Germans. Life in the French camps was no picnic, though. It is estimated that of the 7,500 German Jews deported to France and subsequently imprisoned there in the fall of 1940, only 5,500 were still alive by the summer of 1942.

There were good signs, though. By June 1942 France had full employment again and the economy was showing evidence of getting better. This did mean that few people were volunteering for work in Germany, so the German labor office hit upon a new idea. For every three volunteer workers who went to Germany one prisoner of war would be released. It is understandable that the loved ones who had not seen their menfolk for two years were in agreement with this offer, but few others were willing to take advantage of it. Eventually 240,000 volunteers went to Germany under this so-called "releve" system, but obviously this was not nearly enough. There were still one million eight hundred thousand French prisoners of war. Laval, therefore, introduced conscription. Instead of the twenty-year-olds serving in the Workshops of French Youth, henceforth they would be sent to Germany as "volunteers." Runaways were to be arrested by the police and imprisoned.

Karl Oberg went one step further. He declared that a runaway from forced labor in the occupied zone would be shot, and if he could not be found all his male family members including cousins over the age of eighteen would be shot in his place!

The Vichy government also changed its military policy. In July, the Laval regime accepted the French Anti-Bolshevik Legion as part of the French Armed Forces and changed its name to the Legion Tricoleur. This legalization did bring an increase in recruitment, for now men could enlist to fight the communists without being considered a nazi. As well, the German N.S.K.K. opened its ranks to Frenchmen and quite soon 2,000 men were taken in and formed into two regiments. Though civilians the men were uniformed in a medium olive green tunic, brown shirt and black trousers, and were eligible for medals while on paramilitary duty. Their purpose was to drive, maintain, and direct vehicles for whatever organization required the transport. Whenever a man was permanently assigned to another unit as a driver, mechanic, or traffic director he received the uniform of that unit, but kept his N.S.K.K. insignia. In partisan areas he would be armed. The Allies considered them to be soldiers.

In August 1942, unknown to most Frenchmen, the French guards of the concentration camps began to hand over the Jews to the S.S. for "resettlement in the east."

The German government demanded still more workers and now Fritz Sauckel came upon the French scene, bringing a few German labor experts to round up slave labor in the occupied zone. He also recruited Frenchmen as employees, who were paid on a commission basis. To steal his thunder, not to mention his slaves, the Vichy government came up with a new law, S.T.O. (Obligatory Work Service). This stated that all men aged 20 to 50 years not employed on essential duties were to be conscripted for forced labor in Germany. They were to be under guard and have none of the privileges of the volunteers, such as pay and vacation time, and for an infringement of the rules they could end up in a concentration camp. Also, all men aged 18 and 19 and 51 to 66 plus all unmarried females aged 20 to 35 were conscripted for useful work near their place of residence. This seemed on paper like slavery, but it was not much different from that imposed on their own people by some of the Allied governments. The Vichy S.T.O. organization prevaricated for much of the time and did not start sending large numbers of workers to Germany until February 1943, and then only men aged 20 to 22, who would have been sent under the new amendment to the Workshops of French Youth law anyway. However, the police were brought in if anyone tried to escape the S.T.O.

One of the new police organizations that sometimes found itself looking for forced labor evaders was the Groupes Mobiles des Reserves set up by Rene Bousquet, the Secretary General of Police. Its purpose was to replace the Ministry of Defense's Gardes Mobiles that had been disbanded by the Germans. The plan was to set up fifty-seven 200-man companies of full- and part-time police.

The most important month for France since June 1940 was November 1942, and by coincidence the main event took place about the twenty-fourth anniversary of the French victory in World War One. The Anglo-French War had continued in September when British forces advanced south from Diego Suarez to occupy all of Madagascar. By November only a few French colonial troops remained in a pocket on the south coast.

At the same time a massive armada of British and American ships was sighted in the east Atlantic heading for Gibraltar. The Axis knew that it could be a reinforcement for Montgomery's forces in Libya, but the French commanders were aware that it could also be an invasion task force aiming for French North Africa or worse for France itself. All Vichy units were alerted.

It is ironic that after eleven months of trying to decide whether or not they should concentrate on Germany or Japan and if on Germany should they liberate France from the Germans, the Americans decided to attack the French. The Americans naively assumed that the French would not resist if they realized the task force was American, so to this end American emblems were painted on the sides of the vessels and on the aircraft, American troops would land waving gigantic American flags, and each man would wear a Stars and Stripes patch. British units accompanied the Americans, and their ships and planes would also use American insignia. It would be the first time in history that the British would go into action with someone else's flag, as if they were ashamed of their own. Though American bombers had been hitting French ports since August, the American generals believed that the memory of Lafayette and the Rock of the Marne were too powerful to allow the fascists to sway the French people into a Franco-American War. They also had a French general of their own, Henri Giraud, who had escaped from the Germans, and who was to broadcast over the radio on the day of invasion. The Americans believed that British-sponsored Charles de Gaulle was not acceptable to the vast majority of Frenchmen. In this latter belief the Americans were correct, but in all else they were grossly wrong. Giraud was no good to them for most Frenchmen had never heard of him, and the illiterate Algerian and Moroccan defenders of North Africa had never heard of Lafayette, either.

On 5 November two items of bad news reached Vichy. In Madagascar the last troops had surrendered to the British and the British and American task force had just passed through the straits of Gibraltar.

On the night of the 7th Major-General E. Bethouart, who had been in contact with the Allies, was secretly notified that the Allies were going to invade North Africa at 2 a.m. At once he sent off a party of trusted men to arrest the members of the German Armistice Commission, another group to await the Americans at Rabat beach, and a battalion of confused soldiers personally led by himself to seal off and occupy Army Headquarters at Rabat. As soon as he had accomplished these missions he sent dispatches to General A.

Nogues, the Resident-General of Morocco, and to Admiral F. Michelier notifying them of the invasion and that the new political leader of France was General Henri Giraud. Nogues vacillated, but Michelier reacted at once. He believed the talk of an invasion to be a ruse and he ordered the French troops to arrest Bethouart on a charge of treason.

However, the first of 18,500 American troops was already ashore in Morocco before the French realized what was happening. The invasion beaches were near Mehdia, Fedala, and Safi. It was still dark when coastal patrols began opening fire on the Americans. Just before 7 a.m. off Casablanca French shore guns and the battleship *Jean Bart* began shelling two U.S. cruisers and the battleship *Massachusetts.* No casualties were inflicted on the Americans and the return fire was so accurate that the French ceased fire for a while. However, seven French destroyers managed to slip out of the harbor and head for Fedala.

As the French destroyer captains were preparing to devastate the troop transports off the beachhead they suddenly spied an escort force of an American cruiser, a light cruiser, and two destroyers, and not willing to challenge the big guns, they withdrew. Now eight French submarines entered the action, and they kept the Americans busy, though shells did sink one of the French destroyers. Later the destroyers attacked again accompanied by a light cruiser, but this resulted only in the loss of another French destroyer. The action was finally ended when American carrier planes struck every one of the French warships, sinking two destroyers.

From daylight onwards American soldiers had been landing on either side of Oran in Algeria, and the French defenders had been forced to fall back by them and the excellent Anglo-American naval gunnery and air strikes. Within the harbor, however, the French were victorious. Two small British transports shot straight into the port carrying 400 American troops. The French met them with a hail of fire from all sides and within hours the crews and passengers had suffered fifty percent killed. The survivors then surrendered. At La Senia airfield the French defenders also managed to halt the Americans, even though the invaders had now landed tanks, and when the Americans reached the suburbs of Oran they were stopped by good defenses.

At Algiers the invaders met a mixed response, for many of the senior French officers had pro-Allied sympathies. At the main barracks and headquarters only token resistance was offered, but some strongpoints did resist fiercely. The shore battery at Cap Matifou only surrendered after two naval bombardments and an air raid had devastated the gun positions. The harbor itself also proved to be well defended. Two British destroyers entered, but one was driven off by heavy gunfire. The other reached a pier and unloaded American rangers and British commandos under a hail of bullets. About 8 a.m. the destroyer was forced to retreat by shellfire, and this left the ground troops with only their hand-held weapons for protection. They fought on until noon and then surrendered as they had run out of ammunition.

By this time General C.E. Mast had proven he had Allied leanings and Admiral Darlan himself ordered him to be removed from command and arrested for treason. Darlan was in Algiers and had been held under house arrest since the morning by pro-Allied French officers. He was rescued by a detachment of French police and then he announced that the garrison was to repel the invaders.

However, once he was informed of the military situation he knew that this was an impossible order. Before sunset he ordered the Algiers garrison to cease fire. The following morning Darlan and his staff opened negotiations with the Allies in a quiet Algiers far from the sound of gunfire in Oran and Morocco. American Major General Mark C. Clark, British Lieutenant-General Kenneth Anderson, and pro-Allied French generals Mast and Giraud argued with the Vichy commanders for possession of North Africa.

Near Oran the French counterattacked, and they did not make much of an impression on the Americans, but unknown to them the American commander here, Lieutenant General Lloyd Fredendall, had panicked. One more push might have brought about a favorable situation at this port. In Morocco too the defenders showed more spirit, now that the initial shock of the invasion had worn off and now that the French officers knew who was on which side.

The talks came to a head on the morning of the 10th when Clark threatened to throw Darlan in jail and call off the negotiations. Darlan wished to keep power in his own hands regardless of the political situation, so he yielded at 11:20 a.m. ordering a complete ceasefire throughout North Africa. By the end of the day all the French troops had been notified and the battle was over. The short Franco-American War and the longer Anglo-French War were over.

The Allies, who still maintained they had arrived as liberators, had sunk four destroyers and eight submarines, damaged a battleship and six destroyers, and inflicted casualties of 490 killed and 969 wounded. Allied losses were 2,300 killed and wounded.

On the 10th Laval was in conference with Hitler and Mussolini at Munich when the embarrassing news reached them. Hitler became extremely angry and demanded that Tunisia, which was still under French control, be opened to German and Italian troops at once. They would fight to defend that colony even if the French would not. Laval tried to debate the point, but Hitler had never gone in for such niceties as diplomacy and he stopped the conversation cold when he declared that German and Italian forces would enter not only Tunisia but Vichy France at midnight.

Hitler kept his word. The following day German paratroopers landed at Bizerte and Tunis and later transport aircraft brought in more men and equipment, and Italian forces entered Tunisia from Libya. The French did not offer resistance.

Within unoccupied France the people awoke to the sound of military convoys. They peered out of their bedroom windows and saw the Germans.

Though Germany had defeated them two years earlier, these people for the most part had not yet seen the Germans. Now every inch of French soil was under occupation. The German S.S. Security Police had been operating clandestinely in Vichy France for months, but now they openly followed the army convoys in uniform or in their black overcoats, which were as good as a uniform. By the end of the day they had commandeered the best hotels and chateaux and were strutting about in arrogance. The German troops liaisoned with the French Army to find billets. The swastika flag now flew alongside the Tricolor in every hamlet, village, town, and city of France, except for the extreme southeast portion which came under Italian occupation. Corsica also went to the Italians.

Petain and Laval protested, but felt there was little they could do. Bridoux ordered that there was to be no resistance. The Vichy government knew that the S.S. would soon round up those many immigrant Jews that the French Police had failed to hand over to them, so the Laval regime begged to be allowed to do it themselves. This was agreed. Laval wanted as much control over police operations in France as possible. Already the outspoken antinazis were being rounded up by the S.S. Security Police, including General Jean de Lattre de Tassigny who had publicly demanded that the French Army resist the Germans.

However, within days there was no Vichy French Army as the Germans and French made new treaties demobilizing the entire force except for the 1st Infantry Regiment, which was allowed to exist as a show force, the Legion Tricoleur, which was currently battling for its life on the Eastern Front, and the garrison of French Indo-China. The French Air Force was dismissed and its equipment confiscated, but at the moment the French Navy was left alone, although German troops had gone as far as the gates to Toulon Naval Base.

On 27 November, after the Germans had blocked Toulon harbor as much as possible with sea mines, they charged into the naval base. Immediately the French captains either ordered their vessels to make a run for it or to scuttle. Those that tried to make for the open sea either struck mines or were hit by German divebombers. Only a few small vessels reached neutral Spain or Allied ports. Hitler's gamble failed, though, and he lost his only chance of gaining a fleet in the Mediterranean.

Many of the French people who had cooperated with the Germans over the last two-and-a-half years now turned against them, and reluctantly opted for the Allied cause. However, those who had openly sided with the Germans for the survival of their country now saw that they were on one side of a civil war. They knew that they had better win, for if they did not there would be no mercy from the resistants, especially the communists. For better or worse their futures were tied up with the fortunes of Germany.

Chapter 21

The Godforsaken Crusade: The Russian Front 1942–1943

By the beginning of November 1942, the Axis southern sector of the Eastern Front was guarded by the following units: in northwest Georgia the German Seventeenth Army, and to the north of Georgia and Azerbaijan the German First Panzer Army, both of which contained German and Romanian divisions; to the north of here the German 16th Motorized Division and the Kalmyk Legion patrolling a vast area; then holding a solid front the Romanian Fourth Army backed by the German Fourth Panzer Army just south of Stalingrad; holding out in the city of Stalin among piles of rubble the Sixth Army battling against suicidal defenders; northwest of the city the Romanian Third Army; to the Romanians' left rear the Italian Eighth Army facing the Don River to the north; and on the left of the Italians the Hungarian Second Army along the Don just north of Novaya Kalitva. This gave the Axis: five panzer, four mountain, and thirty-one infantry divisions of the German Army; one armored, six cavalry, four mountain, fourteen infantry divisions of the Romanian Army; one armored and eight infantry divisions of the Hungarian Army; and one cavalry, two motorized, three mountain, and three infantry divisions of the Italian Army. In the immediate rear there were one Italian, two Hungarian, and several German divisions protecting the lines of communications.

The Romanian divisions were poorly equipped, and though the Germans had been willing to help all they could spare were half a dozen 75mm anti-tank guns to each division and eleven Mark IIIs and eleven Mark IVs to the Romanian 1st Armored Division.

On the morning of 19 November the infantry of the Romanian Third Army were preparing to continue a light attack in the hope of closing up to the Don everywhere along the long front, when a massive Soviet offensive rammed into them. The Ist Corps in the Kletskaya area was struck by the whole Soviet Sixty-fifth Army. The infantry did not stand a chance against the heavy artillery bombardment, countless blasts from rocket launchers, waves of Red infantry, and spearheads of tanks. A quick reinforcement by the 7th Cavalry Division made no difference. The ill-prepared 7th and 11th Divisions were smashed by the Soviet Third Guards Army, and Major-General Lascar's Vth Corps was cut off almost at once by the Soviet Fifth Tank and Twenty-first Armies. Within hours the rear-echelon units were fleeing in the snow as the Soviet tanks broke through the main line. The Romanian 1st Armored Division was ordered up from the reserve, but it ran straight into the armored spearhead of the Fifth Tank Army. The result was a massacre.

The German Sixth Army on the right flank could do nothing as they had their hands full themselves. The Red Army tanks charged through wherever they saw an opening. By nightfall of the short wintry day the Romanian Third Army had been chopped into pockets. However, the darkness did not bring a halt to the fighting, the running, the dying, and the freezing.

The following dawn showed the Soviet Twenty-first Army to be behind, south of, the Romanian Vth Corps, but Lascar did not panic. He organized a counterattack to his rear and by dusk much of the corps had broken through the enclosing ring. The Romanian IInd Corps on his flank was now also on the run southwards, the men struggling through the deep snow with Soviet tanks nipping at their heels.

The same day at first light, the Romanian Fourth Army south of Stalingrad was assaulted by the Soviet Fifty-first, Fifty-seventh, and Sixty-fourth Armies. The Romanian VIth Corps of the 1st, 2nd, and 18th Divisions, which bore the brunt of the attack, simply ceased to exist as a fighting force. The 20th Division of Major-General Dragalina on the army's northern flank was not heavily assaulted and it succeeded in dodging the main force of the enemy by side-slipping northwards into Stalingrad. The Romanian 1st Cavalry Division moved out of the path of the enemy tanks and hid in the rear of the German Sixth Army, but the 8th Cavalry Division was soon surrounded.

On the third day of battle Major-General Lascar learned by radio that Adolf Hitler had awarded him the oak leaves to the Knight's Cross, Germany's highest medal, for his courage and leadership. He was the first non-German to be so honored. Lascar had too much on his mind to ponder this laurel for he and his men were being chased by tanks, assaulted on the flanks by infantry and horse cavalry, and murdered by long-range rocket and artillery barrages, while struggling through deep snow. The rivers and water courses were frozen solid and did not hinder the enemy. In fact the heavy Soviet tanks used them as highways. Lascar was freezing, exhausted, and frightened, but he continuously handed out orders, setting up rearguards and flank blocking positions. Already the casualties were high. The 13th Division reported 3,763 casualties and the 14th Division reported 2,261 casualties after only two days of combat. Since the reports had come in more men had been lost. Men were literally dropping in their tracks from cold and fatigue. Their comrades were too exhausted, too cold, too scared to stop and render assistance, and kept on trudging through the snow. Thousands were abandoned to their fate. Only the Third

Army's Ist Corps was better off, having been able to move westwards nearer to the Italian Eighth Army, which still held a quiescent front on the Don. The IInd and Vth Corps were moving southwards towards the only defense line that the Romanians could think of, the Chir River, but in some places it lay seventy miles to the rear of the original Romanian front line on the Don. It was a long shot, but the Romanians were told to aim for that forlorn hope, that chance in a million, for that ultimate salvation, which might, just might, mean continued life and freedom for some of them.

On the 23rd Major-General Sion reached the German 22nd Division with only 3,604 survivors of his division, but he still had to fight on to help the Germans hold back the enemy. Within days he and many of his Romanians would be dead.

The collapse of the Romanians on both flanks meant that the Sixth Army was cut off. As early as on the 21st German troops had sighted Soviet tanks to their rear and by the end of the day no truck convoys could get through. The worst news that General Paulus received was that this day some of his men had died of starvation. The poor condition of the Russian roads in winter and partisan and Red Air Force attacks had slowly strangled his supply lines until only a bare minimum of ammunition and food was getting through. Now, however, that the lines had been cut completely he would have to rely on Reichmarschal Hermann Goering's boasts of air supply. Within the lines of the Sixth Army the quartermasters were ordered to stockpile any food that was available and to start cooking their transport, the horses.

On the 24th the Romanians of Third Army were at the end of their tether. They had been running and fighting for six days. The 6th Division was completely out of ammunition and Major-General Stanescu ordered a surrender. Before the day was out Major-Generals Lascar and Mazarini were also discussing terms with the Soviets. The Soviets had so far counted 30,000 Romanian prisoners.

Colonel-General Friedrich Paulus knew that the situation was grim. He was aware that the Romanians were brave, but he had been placed in an impossible situation by Hitler. He had now not only his own men to feed but two Romanian divisions as well, and he was surrounded. He had no illusions that the Romanians could restore the situation. He knew them well.* He therefore asked for permission to break out towards the Don. Hitler refused, for he wanted to hold on to the city for prestige reasons, the worst reason for a military maneuver. Paulus was flabbergasted, but he obeyed. Having never been a line commander until he was suddenly jumped to an army command in the spring, he assumed that Hitler knew what he was doing.

Stalingrad now had a perimeter of 150 miles held by nineteen German divisions, the Romanian 20th and 1st Cavalry Divisions, and the Croatian

---

*He had a Romanian wife.

369th Regiment.* Counting rear-echelon personnel, including a Luftwaffe flak division, there were 270,000 Axis personnel, and this was an incomplete count.

On the Don to the right of the Italians the Romanian Ist Corps had managed to hold a rigid defense line using the 7th, 9th, and 11th Divisions, but along the Chir River General Dumitrescu and his surviving Romanian officers were trying desperately to gather enough stragglers to form a barrier against the Soviets who must surely continue their assault. The IInd Corps had two complete battalions of infantry and many ad hoc companies and platoons made up of rear-echelon personnel. The Vth Corps was in even worse shape. The men of the Third Army knew that they could not hope to hold their holes in the snow for they were short 40,000 combat troops, 34,000 horses, and the equipment of five divisions.

South of the Don-Chir confluence the Romanian Fourth Army was settling along the Don into a new front line. It was in better condition that the other Romanian army, but not sufficiently to repel another attack.

The Germans had no reserves to speak of, so they formed several temporary units. One of them was led by Colonel von Pannwitz, who was ordered to take time out from his regular duties. He was given a thousand German infantry and six tanks. With this paltry force he nonetheless ambushed and crippled a Soviet cavalry brigade just east of the Don. Then he attached stragglers to his force, some German rear-echelon troops, a Romanian artillery battery, and three battalions of Russian horse cavalry, who had been training nearby and performing patrol duty. With his larger command he held part of the front and repelled several enemy probing attacks. At Kotelnikovo he defeated a Soviet cavalry division and at Nebykov he destroyed a Soviet infantry division. Understandably, von Pannwitz was awarded the oak leaves to the Knight's Cross and Marshal Antonescu awarded him the Order of Michael the Brave 3rd Class.

The only effective reserve for the entire front was the German XLVIIIth Panzer Corps, but this unit with its highfalutin title only contained the 13th Panzer Division and the crippled Romanian 1st Armored Division, and on the 27th it was completely surrounded northwest of Kalatch. At this moment the Romanian Fourth Army was facing two Soviet armored corps and nine infantry divisions, and the Romanian Third Army was up against an armored corps, two cavalry corps, and thirteen infantry divisions. The defenders of Stalingrad were currently under pressure from six armored brigades and twenty infantry divisions, but by the end of the year the attacking Soviet forces around the city would increase threefold.

In the Kotelnikovski area the German Fourth Panzer Army was currently under attack, but it was also trying to form a relief column. Its southern flank

*Not to be confused with the 369th Division in Croatia.

was wide open and covered only by a few German and Kalmyk reconnaissance troops.

On the 27th Major-General Gheorghe Stavrescu's 14th Division, which had been surrounded for more than a week, finally capitulated. One thousand Romanian survivors were still holding out at Morozowskaya under a Major Rascanescu of the 15th Division.

The situation on the Eastern Front was more serious than at any time to date. It was only natural that the Germans blamed their Romanian allies, and that the Romanians blamed their government for having placed them so far into Russia, when their original goal had only been to liberate Bessarabia and Northern Bukovina. The more thoughtful could see that it had been Hitler's and Antonescu's greed that had caused the Axis to bite off much, much more than it could chew. Fortunately for these Axis troops, the German XLVIIIth Panzer Corps succeeded in fighting its way to safety across the Chir just west of Petrovka and the Italian Eighth Army, which held the Don east of Veschenskaya, had not been assaulted.

The next round of battle began on 7 December when a Soviet armored corps forced its way over the Chir about twenty miles northwest of the Don-Chir confluence. It took a counterattack by a panzer and an infantry division of the German Army and an infantry division of the Luftwaffe to crush the enemy advance. Further attempts by the Soviets to pierce the defenses lasted from the 11th to the 19th.

The strength of any prolonged offensive spearhead is in its flanks and as the Germans had left their flanks to partners, the decision of victory or defeat lay with non-Germans. The Soviet choice of hitting the Romanians was shown to be a good one, for not only did it cut off an entire German army in Stalingrad but it almost knocked Romania out of the war. The Germans had to launch a relief expedition at once, but once again the flanks were left to the Axis partners. Only after three weeks of fighting was the Fourth Panzer Army in a position to begin the counterattack, but to do so it had to rely on Romanians to guard its immediate flanks and Italians and Kalmyks to protect its greater flanks, and the Kalmyks could barely hold their own against the many cavalry raids in their sector. If the Soviets were going to attack again the obvious area would have been the open flank to the south, but the Soviets had learned a thing or two since the debacle of the year before. The Soviets chose to repeat a similar attack to that launched on 19 November. The Soviets had an ace up their sleeve, too. What Axis commander would have thought that the Soviets still had enough reserves left to launch another major offensive in a totally different area?

The Italians were in even worse shape than the Romanians had been. They held their line primarily with infantry and light artillery, having only fifty-five tanks, none of them a match for the Soviet T-34. The 270,000 men only possessed 380 anti-tank guns, and the infantry were spread thinly, about 300 per thousand years. The heavy snowfall was not a problem for the three alpine divisions who were trained for such conditions. For the other Italian soldiers the snow was like glue. The land was flat, but that did not help, for it only allowed the wind from Siberia to gain speed before it sliced into the hands and faces of the Italians like razor blades. Exposed skin became frostbitten within minutes, and the joints of the bones seemed to freeze solid. Anyone who had been foolish enough to retain gun oil on his weapon now had a useless block of ice in his hands. In some cases fires had to be started under the trucks so that the engine could be warmed enough to start!

Supplies reached the front-line troops only after weeks of travel, and only sporadically. The worst thing was that the Italians knew they were here only for Mussolini and his dreams of glory. The idea of the noble and holy crusade against atheistic communism had been sufficient to bring a flush to the cheek as the women of Italy cheered the fresh drafts when they left home in the spring and summer, but the memory of the cheers had been drowned by the sound of the cold Russian wind. When the Italians learned of the Romanian collapse they began to feel that they were the only Axis troops left in Russia and that they might soon have to face the entire Red Army. They prayed to Jesus and Mary that this would not happen. Their prayers were not heard.

On 11 December a Soviet infantry division assaulted the Montebello Legion, and two guards divisions hit the 63rd Tagliamento Legion, both blackshirt formations, and an armored corps and an infantry division attacked the Ravenna Division. The Italian forward observers just disappeared and the front-line infantry had to run for it or be crushed. The German 298th Division on the flank, here as a corsetting unit, sidestepped, hoping to hold up the enemy and give the Italians a chance to regroup.

The Italians did manage to erect a new barrier and bring the enemy attack to a stop by redirecting artillery, throwing in reserves, and standing solidly against the hordes of enemy infantry. The Italian generals began to breathe easier. It had been a heartstopping moment.

On the 18th Soviet peripheral attacks struck the Germans and the Romanian 7th and 11th Divisions, while the First Guards and Sixth Armies mashed the Italian IInd Corps of the Sforesca, Ravenna, and Cosseria Divisions, and the XXXVth Corps of the 3rd Rapid, Pasubio, and Torino Divisions into the snow. The Alpine Corps of the Julia, Tridentina, and Cuneense Divisions fared much better, for at least these men could move in the snow. Partially surrounded almost at once, the mountain troops had to turn about and slice their way through the enemy in order to retreat south. There was no hope of rebuilding the line this time.

The horse cavalry of the 3rd Rapid Division were annihilated, but the mechanized part of the division survived by retreating. The Croatian Legion was destroyed.

Within hours of the Soviet attack every Italian soldier from general to private in all units from artillery to cooks and laborers had come to the full realization that it was every man for himself. The worst dream possible had become reality. Stumbling along with heavy feet and numb hands, with rifles frozen and useless, the troops stopped only long enough to catch a painful sharp breath and then rushed on once more. They congregated into columns, more or less corresponding to unit designations, and were spurred on by the sound of gunfire to their rear. Every few minutes artillery salvoes blasted huge holes in the mass of humanity, but ignoring the screaming wounded the majority of the men moved on with rags wrapped around their frozen feet and some with blankets around their shoulders. As many were weaponless they resembled beggars rather than soldiers of a fascist army. These were no crusaders now. The trains full of flowers and daubed with chalked slogans were just a cruel memory.

Suddenly Soviet tanks, infantry, and horse cavalry would appear on the flank and sometimes in front of the column. The column would simply curve to one side and take up a new direction of movement like a green worm slithering across the snow-covered steppe. The men did not know where they were going and did not care much. It was enough to just place one foot in front of the other without worrying about navigation. Here and there a priest could be seen giving last rites to a dying man, as much to give comfort to himself as to the dying man.

At Meshkov one column found its way barred by the enemy, and the senior officers forgot their pains and tried to organize the mob into a fighting formation. Eventually enough willing Bersaglieri were found to launch an attack. The men were formed up and sent against the occupied buildings in waves across the snow, but in their hundreds they were scythed down by machine guns, their scarlet blood desecrating the pure white snow with ugly blotches. Once it was realized that the way ahead was firmly blocked, the column slithered to the side and moved off in another direction. Every few minutes stragglers were picked off by roving bands of Cossack horsemen.

On the 20th a column entered the valley of Abrusovka, which was protected on both sides by Soviet artillery. Yet with Red Army tanks only yards to the rear the men could do little else but charge, run, and then stumble forward into the valley of death. The enemy artillery worked overtime blasting the Italians to pieces with direct fire. Suddenly a few Germans appeared in trucks. As they drove past the Italians the latter screamed, yelled, and waved their arms for the trucks to stop. Some Italians jumped onto the sides or flung themselves at the fenders. A few ran in front of the vehicles. But the panicky Germans pushed, shoved, kicked, and shot the Italians off the trucks and in some cases ran over the men in front. As the trucks drove on leaving them behind the Italians stared with disbelief and hatred. At the tail of the column, which was just entering the valley, the enemy tanks caught up, mashing under their treads anyone who did not have his hands up. Groups which tried to flee to the flanks were gunned down.

Yet here and there small mobs of Italians miraculously glided through the explosions, seemingly immune to the slicing shrapnel, and these few escaped the valley.

The collapse of the Italians sealed the fate of the defenders of Stalingrad. Marshal Antonescu bypassed the German chain of command and ordered the Romanian Fourth Army that if attacked again in strength it should withdraw. He did not know yet the full extent of the disaster, but he knew he was in danger of losing his entire expeditionary force.

On 10 December the German Fourth Panzer Army had sent its main battle force towards Stalingrad, but once again the Germans had to rely on aid from partners. As the Germans attacked towards the east, they knew that the enemy was already to their rear (west). On their northern flank they placed the Romanian VIth Corps and on their southeast flank the Romanian VIIth Corps and gave orders to hold the base line and not to attack, but the VIth Corps did actually advance a few miles. The Germans were finding the opposition to be tough. However, when von Manstein was forced to send one panzer division to aid the Italians this left his spearhead with only two panzer divisions, which had a much reduced strength of only thrity-five tanks and a few thousand infantry between them. Unbelievably, though, the Germans were only thirty miles from Stalingrad by the 19th.

Far to the south the 16th Motorized Division and the Kalmyks had been reinforced at last, with the "European" Wiking S.S. Division, which by now also had a few tanks.

Late on the 19th, though, the enemy counterattacked against the German relief force and the Romanian VIth Corps. The Axis held off the sudden move, but they were aware that this spelled the death certificate for Stalingrad.

On the Don front the Romanian Ist Corps, beefed up with IInd Corps elements, had repelled light probing attacks for a few days, but when the Italians retreated the Romanians felt very isolated. On the 20th the Romanian 7th Division began withdrawing south without orders, and within hours the headquarters of the two corps were doing likewise. By the following morning the whole Romanian Third Army was in full flight. Once the men were out of the trenches and onto the open steppe they became perfect targets for Soviet tanks and aircraft. The men were vaguely aware of their destination, Milyatinskaya, but were not sure where it was exactly. It lay another seventy miles ahead of them. The Romanians found little consolation when they saw that German units were retreating equally as fast.

From the 27th to the 30th two Soviet armies pushed the Fourth Panzer Army and the Romanian VIth and VIIth Corps all the way back to Kotelnikovo. The men were brave, but they were hopelessly outnumbered. They cried as they knew that with every yard of retreat it was another nail in the coffin of the German and Romanian defenders of Stalingrad. The German commanders now requested that the remaining Romanian formations be sent home, except for the Popescu Group of the 5th and 8th Cavalry Divisions, which was part of Romanian Fourth Army.

The Axis situation looked completely disastrous by the new year. German formations were holding a line from the Don, southwards along the Kalitiva River, thence eastwards to the Tzimbiya River, and then back westwards along the Sal River. Hundreds of miles to the south across a great gap lay the German First Panzer and Seventeenth Armies, which were now under orders to break off action in the south Caucasus and retreat out of the Caucasus as quickly as possible through Rostov. This would be a tense operation, for the front on the Kalitiva River was only a hundred miles from Rostov.

The Italians were raking up a corps-sized unit built around the Vicenza Division, and the Romanians were putting together a scratch force from all units. In Stalingrad the Axis troops were still holding out, but they were running out of horses, dogs, cats, and rats to eat.

Then came an even greater debacle. The German Fourth Panzer Army collapsed, and the Soviets drove all the way to the Manich River before they were held by ad hoc forces. Now the enemy was only twenty miles from Rostov, and the two German armies to the south still had a distance to go before they would reach that city.

The Axis collapse of the Romanian, Italian, and German units was not the fault of any group of individuals in southern Russia, but the miraculous way they constantly created new defense lines was the result of the sheer hard work and courage of several Romanian, Italian, and German officers, most notably General von Manstein.

By 12 January the front ran from Manutchskaya, which was twenty miles east of Rostov, almost due north to the Donets, where that river curves westwards. This section was held by: the German XLVIIIth Panzer Corps; German Army Detachment Hollidt, containing some German formations and the Romanian 7th, 9th, 11th, and 14th Infantry Divisions, 7th Cavalry Division, and 1st Armored Division; and the Fourth Panzer Army, which as well as German units had the Romanian 5th and 8th Cavalry Divisions, and the 1st, 2nd, 4th, and 18th Infantry Divisions. Westwards along the Donets to Voroshilovgrad was the German Fretter Pico Group, which had German and Romanian scratch units. From Voroshilovgrad to the Don lay the remnants of the Italian Eighth Army and then the still unharmed Hungarian Second Army. The most vulnerable part of the line was the Don front held by the weak Hungarians, for though they were still in original shape they had a greatly extended defense line. The Germans had loaned them as much equipment as could be spared, the most effective being twenty-two Mark IV tanks and some 38t tanks.

On the 12th the Soviets launched a test attack on the Hungarian 7th Division, and within twenty-four hours it collapsed under the weight of the assault. On the 14th the Reds chose the Hungarian 12th Light Division, and after twenty-four hours it was in a deplorable state. Within another few hours it began to come apart. On the 15th, while this division began to disappear the Soviets struck the other Hungarian units, forcing the 19th and 23rd Divisions to retreat at once lest they be outflanked.

A day later the Italian Eighth Army ordered a complete retreat, the Vicenza Division and the Alpine Corps fleeing as best they could. Now General Gusztav Jany felt he had no choice but to order his Second Army to retreat also. The last unit to abandon the front was the Hungarian 9th Light Division, and the Hungarian 13th Light Division retreated in good enough order that it was able to cover the retreat of the flanking German 168th Division, but nonetheless this was a rout and after a few days the scene was a repeat of the previous Romanian and Italian retreats. The men of the Alpine Corps were unbelievably performing the same terrifying duty as in December, fighting through enemy units and partisan groups while under air attack, being chased by enemy tanks, and struggling through the deep snow. Tens of thousands of Hungarians, Italians, and Germans died from bullets and shrapnel, starvation, disease, and exhaustion. Whole groups of men often panicked and ran the wrong way, straight into the teeth of the Soviet tanks. Stragglers were sometimes tortured to death in hideous manners.

Von Manstein had the ability to pull out a reserve force like a magician pulling a rabbit out of a hat, and once again his skill was desperately needed. He held the Donets River west of Voroshilovgrad as far as Izyum, but west of that town there was nothing to stop the enemy. When Soviet forces probed this gap von Manstein grabbed the Wiking S.S. Division and threw it in at Groshino to stop the enemy tanks on 10 February. The struggle lasted several days, and then von Manstein plucked out more reserves and struck the enemy column in flank, cutting him off from the supply crossing places on the Donets River. By the end of February the Soviet tank thrust was destroyed, having lost 23,000 dead, 615 tanks, 425 guns, and 9,000 men taken prisoner.

At last the Axis could breathe freely, for the great Soviet offensive was over, but the Germans needed Axis partners more than ever now, for the Germans had also suffered badly in the winter, most seriously at Stalingrad.

After tens of thousands of men had been evacuated by airlift, mostly the wounded, and others had died, Paulus could still report on 22 December that he had a ration strength of 253,600 Germans, who were members of the army, luftwaffe, Organisation Todt, and N.S.K.K. Actually some of the latter unit were Dutchmen. He also had about 2,000 Croatians, 13,000 Romanians, and 19,300 hiwis. This gives a rough indication of the ratio of hiwis to German troops. Some formations were quite willing to use hiwis. At the end of 1942 the 134th Division declared that half its personnel were hiwis!

It is interesting that of the Germans trapped in Stalingrad by this date only 25,000 were infantrymen. It is obvious, therefore, that the perimeter was being manned for the most part by cooks, clerks, maintenance men, construction engineers, labor troops, and other rear-echelon soldiers, and that probably some of the N.S.K.K. and Organisation Todt men were serving in a front-line capacity, too. Certainly everyone was subjected to air raids, artillery barrages, and most horrific of all the endless hunger and cold.

Each day at least some part of the perimeter was under attack. The Romanians held the southern sector and were never forced to face a major assault, but this did not lessen their suffering very much. In fact it may have been worse in one respect. The Romanians became convinced that the Germans were shortchanging them when it came to supplies, food, and ammunition. If the Germans felt deserted by their Fuehrer, then the Romanians and Croatians here felt that doubly so.

By 25 January the Luftwaffe had flown out 42,000 wounded and diseased, certain technical specialists, and the staffs of three divisions, but the last flight had been made, for now the perimeter began to crumble and the airfields were too close to the firing line for planes to land. There were still 18,000 wounded and diseased waiting to evacuate, but by now no method of transporting them. The German and Romanian air forces were still doing their best to drop supplies by parachute, but they had to brave heavy flak and fighter concentrations. It was impossible for them to come even near the tonnage promised by the boastful Goering.

At the end Paulus was promoted to field marshal by Hitler in the hopes of strengthening his resolve, for no German field marshal had ever personally surrendered. It was not the resolve of Paulus and his men that required strengthening, but their stomachs and their weapons that required filling. The promotion only served as a going away present. On 2 February the last large pocket surrendered. Stalingrad had fallen.

Coupled with the collapse of the partners this made the winter of 1942-43 the worst military disaster under German command in history, if one excludes the surrender at the end of World War One. The Hungarians, who had only been in heavy action for a few days, had lost 35,000 killed, 35,000 wounded, and 26,000 missing. The Hungarian armored division reached safety with only six tanks. The Hungarian generals had often complained that passing German troops had sometimes harassed their unarmed Jewish labor troops, but once the retreat had begun the Hungarian generals forgot all about those Jews. They were not even counted among the casualties. So to the number of missing above must be added the 50,000 Jewish labor troops who fell into very unsympathetic hands when they were overrun by the Soviets. The Hungarian government now insisted that their troops be used only in anti-partisan duties and under no circumstances should they be expected to hold a front line again. To make sure that this happened Horthy ordered all units home, but for the 102nd and 108th Divisions which were guarding lines of communication. Most of these Hungarians were stationed in Galicia and were later joined by seven more Hungarian divisions, but the Hungarians had made truces with all non-communist partisan groups. Their duty could not be considered serious combat.

The Romanians withdrew their survivors from the front in February and found that they had lost 173,000 killed, wounded, and missing. Not all the missing were prisoners, for many lay covered by snow and would only be discovered in the spring by the Soviets, and many had drowned in semi-frozen rivers that had cracked open when hundreds of men had frantically run across them. The only organized Romanian force was the group that had been serving in the Caucasus and had by now retreated to the Kuban with their backs to the sea. This eight-division force would remain on this static front. The Romanian Air Force also remained at the front, scattered all over, using seventeen fighter, twenty bomber, eighteen reconnaissance, and one naval squadrons with a total of 350 aircraft. The aircraft were of various types. There were even some British-made Hurricanes. The Romanian Navy had been built up to a fleet of seven destroyers and many smallcraft, but it hugged the coasts, ever fearful of Soviet submarines and air power.

Of the Croatian expeditionary force, only the bomber group of the air force remained at the front. The 369th Regiment had been devoured at Stalingrad, and the Croatian Legion had disappeared in the turmoil of the Italian collapse. Altogether 5,000 Croatians were missing. A small Croatian naval force of 900 men manning twelve minesweepers and coastal artillery was operating on the Black Sea coast under German naval orders.

The Italians had registered 66,000 missing, of which a high number were lying dead in the snow. This brought Italian casualties on the Eastern Front to date to 85,000 dead and missing and 30,000 wounded. As noted above the Alpine Corps survived the best. The Julia Division, which had come to Russia with 16,000 men and 4,000 mules, had fought very well and had never been overrun, and had gone home with 3,200 men and forty mules! The Tridentina had a surviving strength of 6,500 men, the Cuneense only 1,600, and the Vicenza, which had been in the rear most of the time, counted only 1,300 survivors! In addition of the several thousand troops directly controlled by Alpine Corps headquarters, 880 survived.

The debacle only made Mussolini more defiant. He insisted that the surviving Italian troops not be placed on secondary duties, but rather be kept in the front line. The Germans, desperate as they were, replied by sending the Italians home.

The German losses were 400,000 killed, wounded, and missing. In total about 825,000 Axis troops were lost to the war effort, although perhaps 100,000 could eventually return to duty after time in hospital. The Axis computed that the Soviets had lost 750,000 troops.

In the southern sector the Germans were outnumbered eight to one, and elsewhere on the Eastern Front five to one. Half a million Germans were taken away from their essential industrial jobs and drafted into the armed forces after this devastating campaign, but as the German units were already short that number before the Soviet attacks this move damaged industry far more than it helped the army.

By 19 January the Red Army claimed to have taken 27,600 Hungarian, 22,000 Italian, and 2,500 German prisoners, but any Soviet announcement can be dismissed as nonsense. Propaganda was one of their major weapons and it was used to the point that they did not know the truth anymore. The true figure may have been far higher or far lower. However, it is known that of all the Axis troops declared missing only 20% could be found alive in Soviet camps by the spring. It is also known that many of the prisoners were deliberately starved to death, to the point that cannibalism was not unknown, and in some places the prisoners survived by eating the feces of their guards, to the merriment of the sentries. The Soviet intention was that no one should survive, but then, when British and American officers began asking questions, the Soviets changed their minds and decided to help some of their prisoners through the crisis. Of those who had surrendered this winter only 6,000 ever saw home again, and only a few hundred were non-Germans.

In the Caucasus the Axis troops had held on until Hitler ordered them to withdraw. He had waited until the last possible moment. The First Panzer Army slipped through Rostov, and the Seventeenth Army with all the Romanian units had moved to the Kuban. Hitler ordered that peninsula to be defended as a jump-off place until the next Axis offensive. The order to retreat meant that the Germans and Romanians had to abandon heavy equipment, stockpiles of supplies, and above all a friendly population, to retreat hundreds of miles, while enemy tanks and horse cavalry nipped at their heels. The Red Air Force was gaining strength every day, no matter how many planes they lost to the Axis air forces and flak units.

Tens of thousands of Georgians, Kalmyks, and Moslem Caucasians now retreated alongside the Germans. Women and children fled too, for even though they might not have agreed with their male relatives' choice of friends they knew that the returning Soviets would not look kindly on any relative of a "turncoat." If the osttruppen found it hard to assert their national aspirations under Hitler's rule, they knew it was absolutely impossible to do so under Stalin, despite the fact that Stalin was a Georgian who despised the Russians. The osttruppen retreated to the Kuban and through Rostov to the Ukraine taking their families and often times elderly parents with them. Once in safety the men could be placed in regular military formations. For these people the German Army was the only place of refuge.

The troops of the Slovakian Mobile Division were rebellious in their retreat. No one could disguise the fact that all was not well, and fear, rumor, and mistrust ravaged the unit. The more farsighted and the more pessimistic in the force saw the Soviets someday marching through the streets of Bratislava while the N.K.V.D. arrested anyone who could add two and two. Then the division was almost cut off while on the road to Krasnodar. The Soviets broke through into the central Kuban, putting themselves between the Slovakians and the sea. Several members of the force took this opportunity to desert and ask the Soviets to be allowed to fight against the fascists, but the division remained cohesive. The majority of the men were flown out by Luftwaffe transports, unfortunately abandoning their equipment. The planes landed in the Crimea and the Slovakians were immediately put to defending a stretch of the coast in case of a Soviet amphibious assault.

Northern Sector

History has somewhat ignored the northern sector of the Eastern Front during the great battles in this winter, but the combat was deadly here even though little ground changed hands.

The Finnish front had become a permanent border, practically. In April 1942 the Finns had lost a thousand casualties but had held a Soviet assault along the Svir River. Elsewhere only company-sized attacks broke the monotony of trench warfare. In May, though, the enemy had launched a serious attack on General Dietl's German and Austrian mountain troops west of Murmansk and gained up to sixteen miles in places. A lesser attack failed against the Finnish IIIrd Corps east of Salla. In August a Norwegian ski battalion of the Waffen S.S. arrived to aid the 6th S.S. Nord Division in its cold stationary struggle.

To the south of the Finnish front Leningrad still held out, miraculously, defying all reason. In addition to German troops, who pounded the city's defenses incessantly, the Norwegian Legion manned a section of the front, which had become a permanent line. In July the Flanders Legion joined them in order to keep up the Axis assaults. About this time the commander, Conrad Schellong, was replaced by Julius Gevaerts.

The front was also static further southeast. Having destroyed the Volkhov Pocket the German generals were now content to keep things immobile for a while, preferring not to rock the boat while the bulk of their reserves were in the southern sector of the Eastern Front. At times the Netherlands Legion entered the line to fill in gaps, but after its high losses in the spring it was in no position to fight a major battle. This period meant a relatively quiet time for the Spaniards, too. In August Major-General Esteban Infantes arrived as second in command of the division to be trained to take over some day. Other Spanish replacements were brought up to allow the veterans of one year's service in the unit to go home if they wished. It was believed in Madrid that one year on the Eastern Front was enough for anybody.

On 23 August the Blue Division was pulled out of the line, but the rampant rumors about a long well-deserved rest were quashed when the trains disgorged the men near Vyriza, who were then assigned to the German XXIVth Corps. The corps headquarters placed the division into line at Pushkin-Slutz-Krasny Bor, close to Leningrad. This was a long front of eighteen miles and the Spaniards were facing the Red Army 3rd Division. The outgoing Germans of the 121st Division told the Spaniards that this was a quiet sector that only brought death and disfigurement to twenty men per day on average.

Meanwhile the Flanders Legion was also moved, so that it could take part in several fights at Kolpino from August to October. It was in October that the men of the Norwegian Legion heard the news they had been begging for—they were being pulled out for a long rest.

The military situation changed in November when the winter brought snow and frozen lakes and rivers. The Russians had always bragged that their best general was "General Winter" and once again they planned to use their terrible wintry conditions as an ally. The frozen surface of Lake Ladoga once again became a highway for supply trucks to and from Leningrad. All along the Volkhov and Leningrad sectors the action stepped up in December as the Soviets probed for weaknesses. The Germans called up their formations in reserve, which included the rested Norwegian Legion, which was put into line at Krasnoye Selo just south of Leningrad, the Danish Frikorps, which had been relaxing at home in Denmark, and which now went to Kondratovo, and the Netherlands Legion, which went to beef up a German unit.

Beginning on Christmas Eve the Dutch, Danes, and their flanking German units were subjected to heavy assaults day after day, but the defenses withstood the avalanche. Only around Leningrad was it still quiet. This soon changed, though, on 12 January as the Leningrad garrison charged out of its trench system. By the 15th the Norwegians and Germans here were in dire straits. Suddenly the Soviet attacks petered out, and the Danes were allowed to pull out and move a few miles to Moschino, while the Netherlands Legion was able to pull out altogether and entrain for Thuringia in Germany for a rest and a hero's welcome. A couple of weeks later the Norwegians were pulled out for a rest.

The Spaniards were still up front. Major-General Munoz had finished his combat tour and had gone home, stopping off at Berlin on the way where Hitler presented him with the oak leaves to the Knight's Cross. At the front Major-General Infantes was now in command. On 16 January 1943 Infantes was ordered to hand a battalion over to a neighboring German unit temporarily, and he chose the 2/269th of Captain Patino. This battalion was offered a point in the line that had not been fully constructed yet, but for five days it was relatively quiet. In the half light of a late frozen morning the Reds came at the Spaniards. There seemed to be millions of them, and Captain Massip's company was quickly surrounded. The Spaniards did not think of retreating, though, and Massip directed the defenses brilliantly. By 2 p.m. it was dusk already and now Massip, who had coordinated his move with Patino over the radio, and the rest of the battalion launched a counterattack. The fighting continued for the next twenty hours, the entire night, where figures could be partially distinguished against the white backdrop of snow.

The Reds withdrew at dawn, 10 a.m. Four hours later the battalion was relieved by a German unit. Now Patino could take roll call. Out of the 800 men he had had the previous morning, only seventy were still on their feet, and some of them were lightly wounded. Massip would be awarded Spain's highest award for this encounter.

Incredibly just two days later the Germans ordered the remnants of Patino's battalion to reenter the line to help stabilize it after another enemy offensive. So far only a few partly patched up wounded had reached Patino's seventy heroes, but he obeyed the order. On the 25th and 26th the Spaniards battled for every ounce of snow, and the Russians now withdrew for good. They had had quite enough of such suicidal resistance. Patino and many others lay wounded, and the survivors were sent back to the division. Infantes had expected a battalion to return, but all he got was twenty-eight exhausted and sick veterans. Each wore a German decoration earned in the battle.

Infantes soon had his hands full. On 10 February the depleted Blue Division was attacked by a major do or die enemy force of two armored regiments, four infantry divisions and three infantry brigades. The Soviet generals were hoping to punch a hole in the enemy line and free Leningrad once and for all.

Actually in the front foxholes at the time of the attack were the 262nd Regiment, the divisional reserve battalion, a reconnaissance group, a ski company, and some engineers. The preliminary artillery barrage alone was enough to devastate an army, and following this effort, which had been feebly countered by the Spaniards' own artillery regiment, the Red Army advanced with their tanks driving forward as peacefully as on a Sunday drive through a Moscow suburb.

Here and there small outposts of Spaniards clung to snow, soil, and sanity, peppering the Soviet infantry with machine gun and rifle fire as they walked bunched up behind the tanks. Captain Ruiz de Huidrobo held his position until he was gunned down, an act earning him Spain's highest award. Only the ski company and elements of the 1st Battalion of the 262nd Regiment managed to outrun the advancing enemy. These breathless survivors soon ran into rear-echelon personnel at Krasny Bor. Then the fighting began again as the Red Army seemed unstoppable. Corporal Ponte blew up a Soviet tank with a magnetic mine, but he was killed in the process—earning another of Spain's highest award. Within hours the enemy had reached Infantes' headquarters, and all the Spaniards were struggling for their lives with the iron monsters.

Almost at the last possible instant the German 112th Division counterattacked, and this move attended by Stuka divebombers which aimed their cannon and bombs straight at the tanks broke the motion of the Soviet offensive. Then on the flanks the Latvian and Flanders Legions counterattacked. Soon everywhere the enemy had been brought to a halt and was digging in.

Infantes knew that he could not hold what he had, even so, and he ordered all troops to reform on the east bank of the Ishora River in order to prevent a complete encirclement. He quickly rushed the 1/263rd and 2/269th to hold the line. This was proved to be a good idea, for no sooner had these two battalions arrived than they were attacked by Soviets who had broken through. They held their trenches, regardless, and on the morning of the 11th the stragglers began reaching this defense line. As they stumbled in dazed and exhausted they were hurriedly placed into scratch units and thrown into the line. The senior officers collected Spaniards, Germans, Latvians, and Flemings, and the men were soon standing shoulder to shoulder facing the communist onslaught. It was a case of every man doing his duty to the last bullet, last knife, last bare hands.

The struggle went on and on, and the men lost all sense of time, especially as much of the fighting took place in darkness. When the enemy finally withdrew the defenders realized that they had been fighting on this line for six days.

With their infantry destroyed the Soviets could only retreat to the Neva River, leaving only a few rearguards behind, but even these few men were not needed for the Axis survivors of the Battle of Krasny Bor were in no condition to counterattack. The German 112th Division was crippled, the Latvian Legion severely depleted, and the Spaniards had suffered 3,645 killed, wounded, and missing, with the infantry companies losing 75% of their strength. As for the Flemings, only sixty of them were still standing in line.

On 25 February the Danes and the Germans launched an offensive of their own at Moschino, and the heroism of the Danes was reported to the highest authority. The Reds only stabilized the front in March. The Danes were then withdrawn from the line on 20 March.

In March the Spaniards only lost thirty men a day on average and so considered this to be a quiet period, and more one-year veterans were allowed to go home. On 19 March the division was assaulted, but the enemy made no gains this time. In mid-May the division was given a shorter front to defend, only fifteen miles between Pushkin and Slutz and thus the daily casualty rate shrank to between ten and fifteen. The enemy did not try anything serious against the Spaniards, even though the Blue Division was outnumbered five to one.

In March the Flanders Legion, which now stood at company strength, was attacked along the Neva River, and not only held, but counterattacked, and gained a better position from which the Flemings, aided by a few German tanks, defended the line against swarms of Reds for eight days. When the legion was relieved it had only forty-five men still in the front line.

Chapter 22

Osttruppen: Indigenous Security Forces in the East

By the end of 1942 the entire picture of the anti-partisan war in German-occupied territory of the Soviet Union and Poland had begun to change. Instead of it being a soldier's battle with orders countermanding other orders and units changing chains of command seemingly at whim, a more orderly administration was created. This was in part due to von dem Bach Zelewski who was coordinating all anti-partisan action and also to General Walter Warlimont who was the liaison officer between the Army and the S.S. for such operations.* It was not solely due to the Germans, though. The osttruppen began to get political, and they knew that good performance and discipline would help them when it came to dealing with the logical Germans to decide their political future.

In October General Pyotr Krasnov, a 75-year-old ex-general of the Russian White Army and ex-headman of the Don Cossacks, formed the Cossack National Council in Prague. For reasons that are obvious his council made Adolf Hitler the titular head of the movement, but other than this it was a purely nationalist Cossack movement. Quite soon several men announced that they were adhering to this cause. These included men who were currently osttruppen, others who were prisoners of war of the Germans, and others who were emigres. Two of the latter were Generals V. Naumenko and Andre Shkuro. Krasnov had once commanded troops in battle against Stalin himself at Tsaritsyn (Stalingrad), and since the Russian Civil War he had made a living in the west as a novelist. Shkuro had been forced to swallow his pride, for he had been a leader of the Kuban Cossacks, and had made a living in a circus. The commanders of the various independent companies, sotnis, and battalions of Cossacks currently serving the Germans were soon urging that their men adhere to this political cause. Von Pannwitz was glad that the two regiments he had raised

---

*Warlimont's wife was a member of the American Anheuser-Busch brewery family.

had formally acknowledged the council, for he had always been eager to liberate the Cossack homelands from the communists.

Von Pannwitz had already been given permission by the German Army to increase the size of his force to a full division and he had begun to recruit all the Cossack osttruppen and hiwis he could find, plus he had recruited directly from the homelands that had recently been liberated, the Don Basin, the Terek Valley, the Kuban and the Trans-Baikal area. The German objective was to get all Cossacks into one unit, but it was soon learned that there were more than enough Cossacks for one division.

What was really needed was someone to standardize all the osttruppen, not just the Cossacks. In this aspect the army won and were allowed to place one of their own men into the position, to the chagrin of the S.S. Lieutenant-General Heinz Hellmich was made Inspector General of Osttruppen on 15 December 1942.

One of the things he did first was to discover why these men had become osttruppen in the first place. He learned that the primary reason was survival—individual survival and national survival. The eastern peoples knew that soldiers are paid, fed, clothed, housed, when not on operations, medically cared for, given leave and passes, and in general they survive, barring unfortunate periods in battle. On the other hand prisoners of war and slave laborers held by the Germans had a high mortality rate. As for national survival, the overriding cause was a hatred of communism. These men were happy to be partaking in a war to destroy that devil, even if it meant siding with another kind of devil. Indeed, some men enlisted to escape the communist commissars who had been incarcerated in the prisoner of war camps with them. Hitler had ordered that all commissars were to be shot, but few of his so-called supermen had carried out the order, for they were too moral to kill surrendering soldiers.

A few men had enlisted from the camps in order to escape at the earliest opportunity, but in fairness it must be stated that desertion among the osttruppen was only 10%, which was not high when one considers that all were subjected to communist propaganda through the radio stations, air-dropped leaflets, and secret agents, many of them were often on their home ground and therefore had the ability to hide, some had witnessed German-sponsored atrocities, and that from the summer of 1943 onwards it was obvious that Germany was losing the war.

Hellmich also had to judge which units were worth keeping. In fact just counting the osttruppen proved to be a problem, for the members of the General Staff refused to admit to Hitler how heavy their dependence on osttruppen and hiwis really was.

The following is this author's estimate of the osttruppen at the beginning of 1943:

First came the legions. The Azerbaijan Legion, which had recently been given its own national status, had about 36,500 personnel formed into independent companies and battalions spread all over the east performing anti-partisan sweeps. A body of Azerbaijani politicians was recognized as a potential provisional government for the state of Azerbaijan.

The Georgian Legion currently claimed 19,000 troops split asunder in the same manner as in all the legions. Georgian political leaders had spent years in Paris claiming to represent the people of Soviet-occupied Georgia, and now with someone at last smiling on them they hoped to be able to go home someday to a free land. However, the small part of Georgia that had been reached by the German forces was not deemed ready for an autonomous government as yet by Hitler's political advisers.

The Armenian Legion of 7,000 men was also split up into companies and battalions and had no political leadership worth mentioning. The Turkish government would hardly agree to a gift of Armenian autonomy by Hitler, and he knew it. While he was still trying to woo the Turks into the Axis, Hitler could not afford to be benevolent towards these traditional enemies of the Turks. In any case while Armenia remained under enemy occupation a decision was not urgent. Another factor was that in November 1942 several Armenian units had mutinied. The revolts were quickly put down and the communist infiltrators who had caused them were taken care of by the S.S. Security Police.

However, the Turks were pleased by the existence of some of the other legions. The Turkestani Legion consisted of 20,550 troops who spoke Turkic languages. The men were divided into companies and battalions on tribal and language lines, and like all legions it was split up for political as well as practical reasons. Hitler did not want to be faced with actual armies clamoring for independence, but his armed forces could handle the independent battalions if they became rebellious. The president of the Turkestan Liberation Movement, Veli Gajun Chan, had been diplomatically lobbying for more recognition by Hitler, but he became angry when he received complaints from his people about the behavior of the einsatzgruppen. Evidently some Turkic-speaking people had been mistaken for Jews and had been murdered. They had probably protested their "innocence," but as they did not speak German or Russian they had probably not been able to convince their executioners. There is also the possibility that some of the hiwis knew that they were killing these innocents but had deliberately told their German bosses that the victims were Jews. In any case it was difficult for Chan to make his complaints understood for according to the official German government pronouncement the einsatzgruppen did not exist, but were figments of Stalin's imagination. The Turcomans came into a better situation when they were assigned to an actual division. The German 162nd Division had lost much of its infantry in battle and the Turcomans seemed ready-made as replacements. Therefore six battalions of this small division were rebuilt to contain 950 Turcomans and twenty-seven German advisers each. The rest of the division, three other infantry battalions, artillery, engineers, heavy weapons, and rear-echelon personnel were made up of Germans. However, there were problems. The Turcoman captains and majors were being advised by German sergeants and this caused a class conflict, and due to an inexcusable foul-up some of the Germans who arrived as advisers had recently been prisoner of war camp guards. Naturally it was difficult for these men to adjust. They had been propagandized into hating their prisoners from the Red Army, but now they were to suddenly start treating them as equals. One other problem was that not all that many Germans could be found who spoke Turcoman, or any Turkic language, and few of the Turcomans showed the aptitude or the inclination to speak German. One other problem was that as the unit was training in Ukraine the divisional staff became afraid that while on an evening's pass the Turcomans might be approached by communist agents-provocateur. Therefore the division was transferred to Germany to be out of harm's way. One minor problem was that recruits continued to pour in, but none were Turcoman, and few were Turkic-speaking. They had been assigned to this unit by well-meaning but ill-informed German officers.

The Caucasian Moslem Legion claimed 15,000 members, divided into companies and battalions and also into a militia in their homeland. The Germans did not recognize any political leadership for this legion.

The Kalmyk troops were serving more or less as a militia, but also due to the military situation as a front-line force. In late January, though, all the men became regulars as they retreated with the Germans. Consequently, there were by now about 5,000 Kalmyk soldiers.

The Estonian Legion that had been formed almost at a moment's notice was still being used as a front-line unit, and the Latvian Legion was in a similar position, though it was far larger than its Estonian counterpart due to a major recruiting drive in 1942. There was also a Lithuanian Legion, but it had only been used in anti-partisan actions. The German Army did not intend to use its five battalions as front-line troops. The S.S., which normally had its fingers in everyone's pie, did not bother with the Lithuanians, because Himmler was repulsed by their strong Roman Catholicism. He considered them to be little better than Poles.

The Versuchs Brigade (RNNA) numbered 10,000 Russian personnel by this date divided into an engineer, an artillery, and four infantry battalions, but in mid-December Field Marshal von Kluge had made the mistake of ordering the brigade to be split into companies, temporarily, for some anti-partisan sweeps and patrols. This deed taught some of the more far-seeing men that the Germans did not intend to use the unit as a liberating army. This disillusionment, plus the tedium of long boring patrols across windswept snowy plains in Western Russia caused about 300 to desert.

There was as yet no accurate count of Cossacks, for von Pannwitz had assembled, or had ordered to assemble, 15,000 Cossacks for his division, but there were still several independent units floating around. Most of these troops had pledged allegiance to the Cossack National Council.

The various osttruppen legions thus numbered approximately 150,000 troops. The political councils and committees did not just claim to own legions, though, for there were some considerable militias in the east, as well.

The Caucasian Moslem militias had become regulars in early 1943 as the Germans retreated from their homelands, but most of the other militias were still extant. As the German Seventeenth Army had been ordered to hold the Kuban to the last man, the Kuban Cossack militia was still alive and kicking, and performing valuable security duties here.

The Estonian Self-Defense Corps now numbered about 8,000 full- and part-timers, and the Lithuanian Self-Defense Corps had about 32,000 troops. The Latvians had been recruiting heavily throughout 1942 and by early 1943 had about 94,000 full- and part-time soldiers.

The Ukrainian Self-Defense Corps had no less than 180,000 militiamen, and the Byelorussian Self-Defense Corps had 55,000, but some of the Byelorussians had been formed into a full-time unit of six battalions under the name Byelorussian Security Corps and under the guidance of Obersturmbannfuehrer Siegling.

The Lokot militia (R.O.N.A.) was doing well and was respected as an antipartisan unit, despite the excesses of its commander, Kaminsky. It now had 20,000 full- and part-time troops.

The Sumy militia had been destroyed in battle in the autumn and winter of 1942, battling partisans and Red Army units that had broken through. Its 10,000 men had been whittled down to a force of 600 survivors. The Haivoran militia and the Sicherungsabteilungen had both been disbanded, their personnel presumably going into other units.

With the addition of smaller militias the total number of militiamen was probably around 400,000.

In addition to these soldiers there were the policemen. Each occupied district had its own police force, for the sake of convenience called Ordnungsdienst by the Germans. These men and a few women were only concerned with antipartisan operations whenever attacked by urban guerrillas. For major police operations against terrorists the Germans preferred to use their own field units of the German Police, which in early 1943 took the title S.S. Police Battalions and Regiments, not because their personnel were S.S., for they were not, but because they received their orders from the S.S. The locally raised field units of the German Police were called schumas and hiwas, for short, and must not be confused with the Ordnungsdienst. In addition, German police units took on hiwis now and then.

The Estonians had about 13,000 schumas, and the Latvians had about 20,000, but recently the Latvian 16th, 19th, 21st, and 24th Schuma Battalions had been commandeered by the German S.S. and placed into the Latvian Legion for front-line duty. The Lithuanians had about 12,000 schumas. The Byelorussians had eleven schuma battalions and the Ukrainians had seventy-one. The hiwa companies contained a total of about 20,000 Russians, Ukrainians, and Byelorussians. Some of the schuma battalions were quite sophisticated, containing horse cavalry and light artillery. A few of the Ukrainian schuma policemen were Cossacks.

The Cossacks did have their own unit with auxiliary police status, namely the regiment commanded by Colonel Sergei Pavlov, which was currently guarding General von Manstein's headquarters at Novocherkassk.

The S.S. had two auxiliary police units, Druzhina, which had 2,000 men, who had sometimes served at the front line, and a force of six battalions of Crimean Tatars called the Crimean Self-Defense Corps. These 10,000 Tatars patrolled their liberated homeland and often times were used on anti-partisan sweeps in southern Ukraine.

This total of about 150,000 auxiliary policemen means that the total of osttruppen available to the German Army, S.S., and Police was at least 700,000.

It was a formidable task for Hellmich to ascertain who he was the inspector general for and how he could standardize their formations, but he was not in charge of the hiwis. Indeed who was?

The German generals were loath to admit the true extent of German dependence on the hiwis due to Hitler's insistence upon considering the Germans to be the master race and therefore not reliant on subhumans. Yet many German units would have disappeared if it were not for their hiwis.* Whenever the subject of hiwis arose at supreme headquarters the generals usually managed to fob Hitler off with some fictitious figure and description, but in March 1943 when General Hellmich was pressed for a count he answered that he believed that in addition to the osttruppen there were about 310,000 hiwis. However, in June 1943 when General Zeitzler attempted to minimize the participation of the easterners in the war on the Axis side he declared to Hitler that there were only 220,000 hiwis.

If one takes a compromise figure between these two officers', of say a quarter of a million hiwis, then this figure would probably not be too high, and indeed may be far too low. Hellmich was in charge of all osttruppen and Zeitzler was the chief of staff of the German Army. If anyone knew the true extent of hiwi participation then it would be these men.

There is no account of the number of Volksdeutsch from Latvia, Estonia, Lithuania, Ukraine, and Russia who served in the German Armed Forces and Police as Class II, III, and IV citizens, but it must certainly have been at least 40,000.

Suffice it to say then that in early 1943 there were one million men, who were indigenous to land claimed by the Soviet Union prior to June 1941, who

---

*Interestingly, during the Vietnam War many U.S. units used hiwi-type troops.

were currently serving as uniformed members of German-controlled field formations, and that this does not count the ordinary policemen on the beat in the occupied cities and towns. If these easterners had not been serving then their place would have had to have been taken by Germans. However, the Germans had no surplus manpower. They were constantly short half a million men as it was. If they had suddenly been forced to come up with another million troops, then Hitler would have had to evacuate at least some of the nations he had invaded and probably would have been forced to make peace with one or more of the Allies. Not surprisingly when Hitler once mentioned in passing that the eastern units should all be disbanded his generals told him at once without hesitation that if this happened the front would collapse and the war would be lost.

As a comparison, may the reader realize that in 1940 when the British went to war against Germany in the Franco-Belgian campaign they fielded only half a million men. In World War One the United States only fielded one million men.

Anti-Partisan Warfare

The war by the Axis units against the terrorists, resistance, partisans, guerrillas, bandits, franc-tireurs, irregulars, or enemies of the state, or whatever one calls them was becoming more and more brutal with each passing day. The German S.S. officers claimed that the soldiers of the German Army were not ruthless and thorough enough. The army officers complained that the S.S. men and police were far too indiscriminate and callous, and in some instances downright cruel. In response to the S.S. complaints Hitler proclaimed on 16 December 1942 that henceforth no one would be court-martialed for a crime against the public if committed while he was on an anti-partisan operation. This order astounded the army officers, and they complained that this was a license to kill, rape, and loot. In reaction to their complaints Hitler proclaimed two weeks later that henceforth partisans were to be taken prisoner if possible. This did not revoke his earlier pronouncement, but it did at least calm down the generals. At the headquarters the response was one thing, but in the field it was something different altogether. It effectively meant that the commander on the scene was the law, and if he was a sadist then all hell would break loose.

In Poland in order to aid the Polish and German Police, including the one Polish schuma regiment, a Polish militia was formed from Class IV citizens. These militiamen were primarily to be used as sentries and as guides. Polish forest rangers were also armed to be used as guides whenever the authorities went after a terrorist band.

Army Group Center was currently battling the partisans in its rear areas with three army security divisions, a bicycle regiment, a cavalry regiment, a tank battalion, the Russian Versuchs Brigade (R.N.N.A.), the 102nd Cossack Cavalry Regiment, and minor miscellaneous companies, but this force was not enough. The other army groups had even less security troops. To help, Hitler hit upon an idea that was not as good as it looked. Nine divisions were moved into Poland and the eastern territories from Germany to aid in garrisoning important towns and guarding installations and to be on call for emergency action, but five of these so-called divisions were actually replacement depots, in which newly-trained recruits, men returning from leave, and recuperated wounded were placed while they waited for transportation to their units, often as members of march battalions. With the members changing every few days there could be no finesse in their assaulting technique. They were simply mobs of soldiers. The other four divisions were even worse for they were training units, which should have been spending their time preparing the seventeen- and eighteen-year-olds for battle rather than farming them out for petty security duties. This is another example of how short of manpower the Germans really were.

There were some officers who had ideas as to how to increase the number of Axis troops. One was Colonel Reinhard Gehlen, chief of the army intelligence section known as Foreign Armies East. He had made contact with several Germans who had knowledge of the Russian people and had set aside a few buildings to house a party of advisers who had recently been serving in the Red Army. Captain Wilfried Strik-Strikfeldt, a Russian Volksdeutsch, ex-officer of the Tsarist Army, and ex-official of the Red Cross, who had spent the inter-war years in Latvia, screened these Russians for security reasons and found them willing to cooperate to put out propaganda leaflets, but the Army High Command (OKH) had refused this gesture.

After Stalingrad, however, the generals proved more receptive, and negotiations began, at first at low level. Situated at Dabendorf, just outside Berlin, the advisers were technically members of the propaganda section of Foreign Armies East, but they saw themselves as pioneers of a Russian government that would restore freedom to their people. In January 1943 they gained a powerful ally, Alfred Rosenberg, the Reichsminister of the occupied east.

In February the group finally gained recognition. Hitler agreed that any eastern soldier who wished to could acknowledge the group as the command staff of a Russian Liberation Army (R.O.A.). The leader of the group became the commanding general, General Andrei Vlasov. Though a Soviet general Vlasov had actually been an adviser to Chiang Kai-Shek in his troubles with the Chinese communists, in the days when Stalin played both sides. In 1941 he was jumped from divisional command to lead the Thirty-seventh, Twentieth, and Second Shock Armies in succession. He had been responsible for the defense of Moscow when that city became a battle zone. He had then gone on to attack in the northern sector to create the Volkhov Pocket. However, by May the Second Shock Army had been destroyed for among other things the Soviet supply system had broken down and many of the troops had starved to death. On 6 July Vlasov had been found wandering in the woods alone by a Dutch patrol.

Though soldiers who recognized their allegiance to this force could wear the colors of Saint Andrew on their sleeve topped by the letters R.O.A., they did not receive any orders from Vlasov for he was more a political adviser than a general. Indeed he did not have the authority to look after their welfare. That was Hellmich's job. Vlasov was therefore never sure of which units he actually controlled. Some Russian units refused to acknowledge him, like Gil's Druzhina, but other non-Russian units did. Vlasov was an imperialist and wanted the various national committees to acknowledge Tsarist imperial rule over them, but those that did so behaved this way only because they saw safety in numbers. They knew that they would have to struggle for further German recognition, and the stronger they were militarily the easier their political struggle would be.

At least the propaganda about the R.O.A. worked. More prisoners of war stepped forward to form all-Russian battalions and even some Red Army troops defected to join the R.O.A.

Other senior members of Vlasov's committee were Georgyi Zhilenkov, who had once been a secretary of a Moscow suburb Communist Party branch and later an army brigade commissar, and Colonel Vladimir Boiarsky, late of the Red Army.

With the creation of this "army" and its committee and the amount of propaganda that the Germans issued about it, it gave heart to the other imprisoned nations. Several national committees sprang up, each hoping for recognition from Hitler. The Ukrainians were particularly angry that their massive aid to the Germans had as yet gone unrecognized. They had attempted to establish a national committee as early as eight days after the German invasion of the Soviet Union, but their provisional president Yaroslav Stetzko had been thrown into a nazi concentration camp.

The Germans announced that they had room for more Cossacks now. The German Army had decided that horse cavalry were obsolete by 1940, but the vast expanse of the Soviet Union and the lack of armored vehicles had changed their minds. The idea of chasing partisan horse cavalry with German horse cavalry recommended itself, and in 1942 each army group was assigned a cavalry regiment. However, not enough trained horsemen could be found in the German Army so the Cossacks were to be used to fill the gap. In January 1943 Captain Boeselager, who had been ordered to create one of these regiments, attracted 350 Cossacks to Smolensk, the training depot. Later he recruited another 300 Cossacks for this unit.

The first major anti-partisan operation of 1943 was Operation Hornung, in which Germans, hiwis, and Byelorussian militiamen guarded the exits of the Pripyet marsh, while a German assault force entered that large wilderness.

The marsh was in fact too large to guard completely and the partisans easily escaped. By the nineteenth day, 26 February, the Axis had suffered two Germans killed and twelve wounded and twenty-seven non-Germans killed and twenty-six wounded, but the S.S. officers who were in overall charge of the operation had ignored Hitler's orders and had shot 7,378 captured partisans and suspected partisans, the majority being simply villagers who lived in the vicinity of partisan activity. In addition 2,219 partisans were actually killed in battle, and the Axis troops confiscated enemy supplies, namely 559 horses, 9,578 cattle, 844 pigs, 5,700 sheep, and 223 tons of grain. To deny the partisans any shelter ten villages were burned to the ground. As a sideline, 3,300 Jews were discovered in hiding and shot. The S.S. officers bragged to von dem Bach Zelewski that they had destroyed a major partisan army, but when quizzed further admitted with embarrassment that they had only captured the following weapons: fourteen pistols and one hundred and seventy-two rifles.

These S.S. officers had acted the way most ignorant people act when faced with insurmountable frustration. They had lashed out blindly, indifferently.

The militiamen who had been serving in their homelands of the Caucasus were now coming into Ukraine and looking for duties, which would in turn provide them with food and money. Younger brothers, uncles, and even fathers of osttruppen were now signing on the dotted line. Their women and children often accompanied them, living off the scraps of an army the way camp followers had been doing for centuries. Many an osttruppe would have his family's welfare on his mind, while he battled for his life. No one who had had even the faintest contact with the Axis armies wanted to remain behind and trust to communist good will.

Sergei Pavlov found a camp for his men's dependents and then set up his new headquarters at Krivoi Rog. The Germans in this vicinity eagerly accepted his Cossacks as an anti-partisan force.

The Kalmyk Legion found a home along the Dniester River, where it was employed to prevent partisans from crossing.

One of the best documented terrorist operations or anti-bandit operations as the authorities called them came from a quarter that the Axis had not bargained for—the Jews. At first it was identified with the budding Polish underground movement. The Polish resistance movements were slowly being diluted into one or two major units, politically, while growing stronger militarily, despite the fact that the Germans thought they had killed off the intelligentsia capable of organizing such a thing. By the end of 1942 the German authorities had executed or killed in action 17,000 terrorists and members of the intelligentsia and had imprisoned tens of thousands, in Poland, not counting Jews. Yet the resistance increased.

By May 1942 the numbers of sabotage incidents in the General Government were being listed in the hundreds each month. On 19 May a bomb exploded near the Warsaw Gestapo headquarters, and six days later the Kripo headquarters in Warsaw was blown up. In retaliation for these acts, on 27 May 201 men and 22 women were picked up off the streets at random by S.S. security police and taken to Magdelinka village where they were shot. On 23 July fifteen army trucks in a Warsaw garage were destroyed. On 30 September an entire factory was burned to the ground. On 8 October all rail lines leading out of Warsaw were simultaneously cut by explosions. These were just the headlines in the news of resistance acts. There were countless acts in which trucks were damaged, motorcyclists hurt by a wire strung across a road, telephone poles cut down, windows broken by thrown stones, and such. The authorities could not feel safe anywhere, except inside the Jewish ghettoes. Inside these prison-neighborhoods the nazis were so complacent because they believed "their Jews" would never turn against them. The Polish underground members were usually so anti-Semitic that they always voted against getting involved with the ghetto resistance movements. A few pistols and bullets were sold to the Jews, but by and large the Poles thought it a waste to put these weapons inside the ghetto where they would probably never be used.

Not all the Jews had been ghettoized. In the summer of 1942 the Polish Police, Polish forest rangers, and German Police began making continuous forays into the Parczew forest to hunt for the thousands of Jews who had escaped the net and were hiding here. This duty was usually not dangerous for the Jews did not possess weapons, and those that did have them did not know how to use them. Most Jews had found excuses to avoid military conscription in pre-war Poland and therefore knew nothing of military training. The policemen knew there was always a danger of running into escaped prisoners of war or actual terrorists, so they had to keep their wits about them. In fact there were two small Jewish partisan bands operating here.

The S.S. had looked upon the attempted assassination of Szerinski as an aberration, and the shots fired at the schumas as a last gesture by the same person. However, they became alarmed on 29 October 1942 when Jacob Lejkin and his aide were gunned down in a ghetto street. Most S.S. did not mind the Jews killing each other, but the S.S. Security Police thought differently, realizing the implications of these incidents. They informed their Jewish employees that this revolt must be nipped in the bud at once.

While the Jewish Police and Jewish Gestapo hunted every nook and cranny for the killers, the Judenrat announced that these terrorists were troublemakers who would cause a severe backlash by the Germans. However, the Jewish resistance now knew the truth about the nazi extermination policy and felt there was nothing to lose. On 28 November Yisrael First, the liaison man between the Judenrat and the German Police, was shot dead in the street.

The acts of resistance by the Warsaw Jews gave heart to other Jews in Poland, and soon Jewish resistance was growing all over the General Government. On 22 December Jews blew up a cafe in Cracow killing twenty Germans. In retaliation forty hostages were shot.

In January 1943 ostensibly in retaliation for terrorism in the General Government, 35,000 Poles were deported for slave labor. In truth they would probably have been arrested anyway for the German industrial complex needed workers, but the authorities always tried to get as much mileage as they could out of every act. By this method they hoped that the loved ones of the deportees would blame the terrorists rather than the authorities. In 1942 in the General Government the terrorists had killed 86 German, 84 Polish, and 17 Ukrainian policemen and 108 Polish government employees.

It was in January that the S.S. chose to rid themselves of the problems of the Warsaw Jewish resistance by eliminating all the Jews of Warsaw. Higher S.S. and Police Leader Sammern was notified that all the Warsaw Jews were to be sent to the camps no later than 15 February. At once this dutiful officer began organizing the police operation.

On 18 January he entered the ghetto with a few Germans of the S.S. Security Police, 200 German gendarmerie, and 800 Latvian and Lithuanian schumas. He held in reserve a unit of German policemen from the Lublin Regiment. Only about 600 Jews had been rounded up when the police began to receive fire from pistols and homemade hand grenades. As they were not used to being shot at by Jews, the policemen fled. The senior officers of the S.S. Security Police had panicked more than anyone.

The aktion continued for another three days, and the police sprayed windows and doorways with bullets in return for just one shot. Another 6,000 pathetic starving humans were kidnapped and deported to the extermination camp at Auschwitz. In an anger caused by ignorance the S.S. ordered everyone to be kidnapped, men on their way to work, kids on their way to school, food lines of housewives, and whole buildings emptied. Hundreds were shot in the streets, and hundreds more were hit by stray bullets fired indiscriminately. Some bullets ricocheted out of the ghetto.

On the 22nd the nazis did not return. The idea that Jews could fight back astonished the nazis, and it would take a while for them to get over the shock.

Elsewhere in Poland the authorities were faced with an increasing rebellion. Every day some member of the authorities was under fire in the General Government, and even in Wartheland there were incidents. Every few days a sentry was found with his throat cut.

In March the Jews of Cracow were deported, pacifically, without giving the nazis much trouble. This now meant that in Poland only Lodz and Warsaw ghettoes still had substantial numbers of Jews. The Warsaw Jews had survived yet again, and the resistance remained active and acquired more weapons, having shown the Polish underground that weapons sent to the ghetto would be used. In February five members of the Jewish Gestapo were assassinated. Their employers, the S.S. Security Police, did not overly concern themselves, for the Gestapo personnel were on the deportation lists, too.

On 13 March a mob of Jewish workers refused to go to work and began fistfighting their Ukrainian werkschutz (factory guards). Armed Jewish resistants heard the commotion, flocked to it, and joined the fight, killing one guard and wounding another. The other guards ran for it. Later in the morning German S.S. Security Police entered the ghetto and arrested a suspect, but as they neared the outer gate with him they were ambushed by armed Jews. The suspect was rescued and two Germans were shot dead.

The Higher S.S. and Police Leader now ordered a repeat of the aktion of January. Hundreds of Germans and schumas entered the ghetto streets to deliberately shoot anyone they could see. All told about a hundred people were killed and several hundred wounded.

Himmler now gave his permission to liquidate the Warsaw ghetto once and for all regardless of what it took. Those nazis of various nationalities who had been killing Jews for years had always claimed to be soldiers in a war. Now Himmler gave them a chance to prove it. Sammern was given a deputy to control the aktion, Brigadefuehrer Jurgen Stroop, who had moved from the concentration camps to combat duty with the Totenkopf Division. He was now given a combat command of his own. He was to root out the Jewish bandits, and then deport all the remaining Jews to the camps.

On the morning of 19 April 1943, Stroop sent in his assault team. It consisted of 234 German policemen and gendarmerie, 375 Ukrainian werkschutz, borrowed from Trawnicki labor camp, and 830 Waffen S.S. The latter were all eighteen-year-old recruits, who had been in the armed forces less than a month, and their older training cadre. They were told that the enemy were not just Jews, but communist terrorists. The perimeter of the ghetto was sealed tight by Polish police.

It has since been estimated that the Jews had about a thousand armed resistants, the term "armed" being a very loose one indeed. At first the Axis troops used members of the Jewish Police as shields, but soon found that the guerrillas hated the Jewish Police almost as much as the Germans and were shooting back without remorse. By the end of the day only a few hundred Jews had been arrested and the authorities had taken casualties. A light tank and two armored cars of the gendarmerie had been damaged by Molotov cocktails, a German had been killed, and fourteen S.S. men, two gendarmerie, two Polish policemen, and six Ukrainians had been wounded.

Stroop gained better control over the situation the following day and his men managed to arrest several thousand residents. He became angry when he learned that some of the German employers of Jews in the ghetto had been hiding as many as 5,000 Jews in their factories. Stroop could not understand how some Germans could put their Christian morals ahead of an order from Heinrich Himmler himself. When it was realized that many Jews were hiding in the sewers, Stroop ordered chlorine gas to be pumped into them through the manholes to drive them out. The day's aktion cost him two dead and ten wounded.

Stroop had noticed that after some badly aimed Molotov cocktails had set several buildings on fire plenty of hiding Jews had suddenly emerged rather than be burned alive. This gave him an idea. From now on he would return the shots not just with rifle and machine gun fire but with blasts from flame throwers and artillery. He borrowed the necessary weapons from the Waffen S.S. training barracks and from an anti-aircraft unit. The Warsaw ghetto now began to disappear in smoke and flames.

The armed Jews barricaded themselves in rooms and cellars with broken furniture and unhinged doors. Stroop referred to these in his daily reports to the Higher S.S. and Police Leader as bunkers. He was under pressure to finish the aktion as soon as possible from the commanders of the police units, Trawnicki labor camp, and the Waffen S.S. training barracks, who all wanted their personnel returned so that they could get on with fighting the real war. Stroop was also under pressure from Himmler, who knew that the longer the situation continued the more publicity it drew. Few Germans were still believing that the operation was an anti-partisan fight, for it was obvious to anyone near Warsaw that the enemy of the S.S. was every Jew armed and unarmed. The S.S. Security Police was also worried that the Polish underground movements might take advantage of the situation and increase their activity.

Because of all these pressures Stroop continually referred to the aktion as a battle against well-armed terrorists who were dug in prepared defensive bunkers. He could not hide the fact that his casualties belied the claim that his men were pinned down, for compared to the number of Jews he was arresting they were ludicrously small. They were: on the 21st of April, four wounded; 22nd, three dead and one wounded; 23rd, three wounded; 24th, three wounded; 25th, four wounded; 26th, one wounded; 27th, four wounded; 28th, three wounded; 29th, none; 30th, one wounded; 1st day of May, two dead and two wounded; 2nd, one wounded; 3rd, three wounded; 4th, none; 5th, one wounded; 6th, two dead and two wounded; 7th, one wounded; 8th, two dead and three wounded; 9th, none; 10th, four wounded; 11th, one dead and two wounded; 12th, one wounded; 13th, two dead and four wounded; 14th, five wounded; 15th, one wounded.

Only now after almost one month could Stroop declare to his superiors that the ghetto was Jew free, and even then he had to admit that he was putting in the 3rd Battalion of the 23rd Police Regiment to mop up a few holdouts in the burned-out rubble. These German police reported shooting incidents for another three weeks.

What of the casualties inflicted upon the enemy? Stroop boasted that his men had arrested 55,000 men, women, and children. He praised the bravery of his men, German police and S.S., Polish police, and Ukrainian werkschutz, and recommended several for decorations.

During the long struggle there had been skirmishes between the authorities and terrorists outside the ghetto, but these were coincidental and often precipitated by the authorities making a sweep of a particular group of buildings or acting on a "tip." One of the resistance movements, the communist People's Guard, claimed to have shot up some Axis personnel who were guarding the ghetto perimeter, and it is true that some of the communist leaders were racial Jews, so this claim is liable to be correct. The other Polish resistance groups did not aid the Jews except to smuggle in some food and a few weapons, usually for profit. The greatest aid to the Jews came when the Red Air Force launched a long-range raid on Warsaw. Some of the bombs struck the ghetto and, though they killed a few Jews, the bombs allowed many Jews to escape to the outside world during the commotion. However, the world outside the ghetto was hostile, too, and many a Jew was turned in to the authorities by a good Pole doing his duty.

Of far more importance to the Poles at this time was the discovery by German troops of mass graves around the Katyn forest. Inside lay the rotting remains of approximately 14,000 Polish Army officers of all ranks who had been taken prisoner in the short 1939 campaign by the Red Army. Stalin, fearful that the Polish officers would revolt in favor of Germany, had ordered them to be killed. Fortunately he had changed his mind and thus not all the Polish officers in his captivity had been executed. Naturally the Germans made as much propaganda out of this find as possible and, so no one could say it was a nazi plot, neutral citizens and British and American prisoners of war were taken to the death site to identify the dead from their papers and uniforms. There was soon no doubt that the Germans had been telling the truth. This created great anger among the Poles directed against the Soviets, not that any Poles had much love for the Soviets anyway, but this did not mean that the Poles suddenly started liking the Germans. Indeed the news of the find confirmed the belief of many Poles that they had no friends anywhere.

The news from Katyn caused Himmler to realize that if the Soviets gained any more ground in battle they might begin to discover the mass graves of the Jews. In a belated action he gave orders to Paul Blobel to take charge of a labor gang of Jews to traverse the east looking for these mass graves. Once discovered the Jewish slaves were to dig up the corpses and burn them. Once the mission was accomplished these Jews would then be executed by an S.S. murder squad and their bodies burned. Blobel knew one place to start. He had been in charge of the Babi Yar massacre.

The Warsaw ghetto uprising was the greatest of all slave revolts against the nazi authorities, but it was not the only one. Indeed once the Jews heard that there were resistants in the Warsaw ghetto it gave encouragement to their own ideas about revolt. However, the futility of using bare hands against machine guns has always been obvious. The following are some of the incidents in 1943 in the nazi-occupied east:

In January a newly arrived shipment of Jews at Treblinka extermination camp and the camp's sonderkommando revolted against the S.S. guards. The result was that one thousand Jews were shot to death, but the firing was so indiscriminate from the panicky guards that several were struck by their own bullets.

In Bialystok a gang of Jewish rebels killed eight S.S. men before they were caught. Sentenced to Treblinka, the rebels refused to obey orders when they arrived and were shot down on the spot by Ukrainian guards.

Also at Treblinka a young Jewish woman stripped at the order of a guard, but then realizing she was going to be executed she grabbed the rifle of the Ukrainian guard and shot him dead. She then killed another Ukrainian and wounded a third before she was overpowered. The guards then proceeded to torture her to death.

In June the sonderkommando of Belzec extermination camp was suddenly transferred to Sobibor extermination camp. Fearing the worst the men ran off and had to be hunted down one by one and shot.

Between 16 to 23 August Bialystok ghetto was in revolt, though the rebels possessed few weapons. Vilna ghetto also experienced a revolt about this time. By this date the only other ghettoes still in existence were Lodz, Kovno, Siauliai, Riga, Minsk, and Lida. Lublin ghetto had been finished off when a group of S.S. killers from Auschwitz and Maidanek camps led by Scharfuehrer Otto Mohl had run rampage through the streets killing off the last of the Jews.

Generally speaking there was no danger for the guards, male and female, German, Ukrainian, Lithuanian, Estonian, or others, for the instances of revolt were so few as to be negligible, and as has been seen they were futile. However, the guards were often afraid, for they were always outnumbered, sometimes as much as one hundred to one, and as the prisoners had nothing to lose by rebellion they were potentially a great danger. Over the years, though, the guards became complacent. Often one guard with a holstered pistol would take charge of a work detail of scores of prisoners.

In the summer of 1943 the situation changed. In August there were serious revolts in the following labor camps: Krychow, Konin, Gleboku, Lackie Wielkie, and Jaktorow. The commanders of the other camps learned of these happenings, but each one believed his prisoners were different, and blamed the revolts on poor discipline. Franz Stangl, an Austrian, had done well creating Sobibor extermination camp, and in 1942 had been placed in charge of the larger Treblinka. There had been isolated incidents here, but he never expected an actual revolt. On 2 August this happened, though, and for a few minutes his guards were stunned. Exactly a month later another revolt took place and also failed, but each time the workers at the labor and extermination complex learned something. Then on 13 September came the great revolt. The guards were attacked and twenty Germans were killed, and part of the camp was burned, and then the prisoners ran for the gate, ignoring the tower machine guns. It is believed that about 200 inmates survived to reach the woods. The Germans and their Ukrainian helpers were shocked and panicky.

On 10 September a work gang revolted at Miedzyrzec labor camp and killed two German guards before five of them were shot dead and the revolt quelled. The greatest escape took place at Vilna ghetto in September, when the inhabitants were threatened with death if they disobeyed an order. Hundreds of Jews of all ages rammed their way through a barrier of Lithuanian Police, and most of them survived to reach the countryside.

Stangl had thought that he had left Sobibor labor and extermination camp in a peaceful status and that the Jews would give no trouble to his successor, another Austrian, Franz Reichleitner. And this was true for a year. However, in August the sonderkommando had refused orders and had to be shot down on the spot. The Ukrainian guards suffered no casualties, but the very act of mutiny unnerved them. Then on 2 September an outside working party of thirteen prisoners killed their Ukrainian guard and ran off. The guards were extremely angry that one of them had died, disregarding the fact that this was an extermination camp, and one can imagine the brutality with which they reacted.

Some of the inmates were Red Army prisoners of war and they did not intend to be worked to death. They organized a revolt and on 14 October they judged the time to act to be now. This time they and the other male and female prisoners of Sobibor, mostly Jews, attacked the guards with woodchopping axes. As most of the guards wore holstered pistols they did not stand a chance. Then all 600 prisoners charged the gate and broke down the wire with the weight of their bodies, though the tower machine guns sprayed them with bullets. Those who survived these guns and the guns of mobile squads of guards also had to run across a minefield. Rashke estimates that 140 prisoners were killed or wounded in this way and the wounded soon killed. The camp had lost eleven S.S. men killed and at least two Ukrainian hiwis killed. Other Ukrainians may have died, and several of the guards were wounded by prisoners armed with captured weapons.

The surviving camp commandant radioed for help and the KdS at Chelm sent him seven S.S. men to take charge of the panicky Ukrainian guards. These then spent the next twenty-four hours hunting down those inmates who had not been able to escape, finding and killing 160 altogether.

It is noticeable that this camp had contained only thirty S.S. men, not all of them on duty at any one time, and 200 Ukrainian hiwis. To date this small dedicated group had massacred a quarter of a million people. The KdS had in turn notified all the security forces in the area that an estimated 300 inmates had escaped. Of course the ordinary German soldiers and policemen were told that the escaped men and women were prisoners of war, communist terrorists, and habitual criminals. The surviving escapees were hunted down by the German soldiers in the vicinity, a special detachment of German Feldgendarmerie (Military Police), and the Polish Police. As well, there were groups of Polish partisans in this area, and they also hunted down the prisoners, eager to kill a few Jews and communists. The N.S.Z. (National Armed Forces movement) was the most Jew hating of the Polish groups, but all of them contained some anti-Semites. At the end of the first week of liberty about one hundred prisoners had been killed, many of them turned in by Polish farmers.

However, these revolts were successful in one sense. The guards would never be as complacent again, and in fact Treblinka and Sobibor were closed down.

In Bialystok ghetto the Judenrat was ordered to hand over 9,000 people for an unknown destination. The officials complied, but the Jewish Police refused to execute the order. The frustrated authorities therefore had to do the job themselves, with German S.S. security police, hiwis, and the city police. During the roundup a Gestapo man was shot dead. In a frenzy of anger the nazis opened fire on the crowd and killed 120 and wounded many others before they calmed down. Following this incident the Judenrat put up a reward for information leading to the arrest of the terrorist. Rather than cause further bloodshed the man gave himself up. However, Bialystok ghetto did not last long.

To the east of Poland the authorities decided that the answer to the increasing number of guerrilla acts was an increase in the number of search and destroy operations. From 22 February to 8 March 1943 took place Operation Kugelblitz in the Velizh-Vitebsk area of northeast Byelorussia, launched by Third Panzer Army. As this was an army mission the troops did not leave a trail of senseless destruction behind. Many Cossack and Tatar hiwis were used here.

In 1943 as the Soviet war machine began to advance, many people who had performed light duty or offered minor aid to the Axis knew that if the communists returned they and their families would die. More recruits were therefore available for the Axis authorities to help prevent such a thing from happening. The Germans had already launched a massive recruiting drive in Latvia, and now they announced that the Estonian Legion of 969 combat personnel was to be expanded and in return for Estonian loyalty the state would receive some sort of self-rule. In Lithuania 3,000 men were recruited for construction engineer battalions to be assigned to the Lithuanian Legion. In Operation Winterzauber Latvian and Ukrainian schumas swept Latvia looking for partisans.

Another autonomous area was created in March, in the Globoku district. In an unusual move Druzhina was appeased and the unit became the militia for this area. The officers were allowed to recruit the locals and suddenly it looked like the Germans were going to take seriously the claims of the Druzhina soldiers to be members of a Russian liberation army.

Another major operation took place between 21 March and 2 May, Donnerkeil, and again it was a reasonably humane affair as it was directed by the German Army, despite using rebellious Cossacks.

Throughout the early part of 1943 von Pannwitz had been building his Cossack division. He gained Kononov's 102nd Cossack Regiment and many more volunteers on an individual basis. Those Cossacks who had fled from their homelands had brought their women and children with them and they created a small temporary town outside Mlawa (Lielau) in East Prussia. Here the division was assembled and trained with the troops divided as follows: the 1st Brigade consisted of the 2nd Siberian Ussuri, 4th Kuban, and 1st Don Regiments, the latter being the ex-102nd Regiment; and the 2nd Brigade consisted of the 3rd Kuban, 5th Don, and 6th Terek Regiments. This gave von Pannwitz 12,000 Cossack horsemen. In addition the non-Cossacks who had been sent to the division, who were mostly Caucasians, were placed into a Caucasian horse-drawn artillery regiment. About 60% of the troops were ex-prisoners of war. Many of the German advisers and technicians were actually Austrians and Volksdeutsch. Colonel Alexander von Bosse, the commander of the 1st Brigade, was a Latvian Volksdeutsch.

The Kalmyk Legion was also assigned to this base as some German officers wanted to amalgamate the two, believing any Soviet citizen who could sit on a horse was a Cossack. The Germans soon found this belief to be quite erroneous and the Buddhist Kalmyks were never mixed with the Russian Orthodox Cossacks. Both forces were used for minor sentry duty while undergoing training and refitting.

The Ukrainians were also at last gaining recognition. The German government finally gave permission for a combat-worthy division of Ukrainians to be formed. This was no sudden move for it followed two years of petitions and negotiations, however it was surprising to the Ukrainians that Heinrich Himmler agreed to give the soldiers S.S. status, not as hiwis, but as members. His one proviso was that the men be Galician Ukrainians, for that district had once been part of the Austrian Empire. Hence the division was to be called the 1st Galizien Division (Halychina in Ukrainian). In reality Ukrainians from all over that nation served in the force. Himmler also wanted to limit the force to a division of 15,000 men, but when the recruiters went out they found 80,000 volunteers, men who were currently working in necessary professions or already serving the authorities in some capacity, many as militiamen. The S.S. recruiters therefore managed to pick the cream of the crop and urge the others to remain in their positions. With so many men to choose from the age requirement was made 18 to 30 years, except for officers. The first men were accepted on 8 April and by 14 July the ranks had been filled, and the organizer, Obergruppenfuehrer Otto Waechter, considered the recruitment job to be done. Now came the basic training.

The Ukrainians demanded and received their own N.C.O. and Officers Training Schools, which meant that the men would not have to fight under too many German officers and sergeants, though the senior staff were German S.S. officers, and as the Waffen S.S. could not supply all the required personnel there were even some German Army officers and sergeants. Most of the officers would be Ukrainians, many of them middle-aged veterans of the Ukrainian War of Independence. Two well-respected officers were Alfred Bysanz and Dmytro Palijiv, both of whom had worked for a decade for Ukrainian independence. As members of the S.S. the men were well paid, well treated, and recognized as equals (in theory), and their families received monetary compensation while the breadwinners were away. One further request that the Ukrainians made, which was agreed to by the S.S., was that the division only be used against communists. These Ukrainians had no quarrel with the British or the Americans, and indeed some of the older officers had fought alongside the British twenty-five years earlier.

Following basic training the men received advanced training as radio operators, weapons specialists, engineers, drivers, mechanics, cooks, clerks, artillery gunners, and so on. Himmler was determined that the unit would not be committed to battle until it was fully trained. The division impressed Himmler and he soon renamed it the 14th S.S. Division.

These soldiers were serving so that Ukraine might gain at least autonomy within the sphere of the Germans, if not full independence, for they desperately needed to control their own affairs and have cultural and religious freedom, a combination of which they had never fully experienced. These men were prepared to fight and die not to rid the Anglo-Americans of their personal liberty, as the Allied propaganda stated, but rather to attain the same rights that Americans and Britons took for granted. To this end they always looked upon themselves as soldiers of a free Ukraine, and never as S.S. men, regardless of what insignia they wore.

They believed this even more when it was announced that the Germans had finally recognized the Ukrainian Liberation Army. That there was no such army, and that even if there was the group of Ukrainian politicians who were negotiating with the Germans would never be allowed to control it, was totally irrelevant, for the news was a light at the end of the tunnel. However, all Ukrainian osttruppen and hiwis were allowed to pledge allegiance to this body, and as a result more companies and battalions were recruited. Many prisoners of war who had held out for two years in an emaciated condition now considered this particular army worth joining. That the Allies would consider the whole lot of them to be German soldiers was not understood at the time, and as long as there was no guarantee that the Allies would win the war this belief held by a few foreigners was unimportant. What counted was that this was the only feasible method by which their political goals might be attained. By August the political leadership of the Ukrainian Liberation Army claimed that 75,000 troops had pledged allegiance.

Himmler had really jumped the gun and had stolen a march on the German Army, for the army was supposed to have raised the Ukrainian division. However, he had not yet been able to gain control of the Russian Liberation Army

(R.O.A.), and this frustrated him. Jealous of the army's control of this new force he ordered his S.S. Security Police, now led by the devious Sud-Tyroler Ernst Kaltenbrunner, to arrest twenty-eight Russian members of the army's leadership on trumped-up charges. The German Army was not powerful enough to prevent this and all twenty-eight were executed. However, Vlasov's cabinet was not touched. The S.A. also lusted after the R.O.A. and sent Sergei Froehlich, a Russian Volksdeutsch, as a liaison officer.

Not all Ukrainians were elated at the progress of the few politicians, for some were communists, like General Nikita Khrushchev, who, though he always spoke proudly of his Ukrainian nationality, had in fact turned his back on his people a decade before during the great Stalin-organized famine. Other Ukrainians hated the communists, but hated the nazis, too, and this gave rise to the nationalist partisans.

In the spring of 1943 the authorities began to come under attack from a new group of partisans, the Ukrainian Insurgency Army (U.P.A.), concentrating most of their activity in Galicia. Here the communists had been unable to gain much support, and the authorities had had so far a more or less peaceful time, being only on the lookout for raids by a few Polish N.S.Z. Whenever the N.S.Z. or the U.P.A. accidentally ran into a communist partisan force, be it Polish, Ukrainian, or Russian, the result was a fight to the death.

In April 1943 German police outposts at Horokhiv, Tsuman, and Olyka were destroyed by U.P.A. raids, and at Yarmolynci an entire Ukrainian schuma battalion killed its German advisers and defected to the U.P.A.

This made the U.P.A. quite impudent, and the result was that on the 21st the garrison town of Ivanova Dolnya was attacked by a fearsome force of U.P.A. and several hundred Germans and Polish policemen were killed and wounded.

On 8 May the German police and Polish police garrison of Kremianets launched a search and destroy mission through the nearby Ukrainian villages, during the course of which some suspects were executed. On the return journey the column of a few hundred Germans and 180 Poles was ambushed by a large band of guerrillas, and suffered ninety casualties. The enemy was discovered to be the U.P.A., and the next day a German police battalion attacked a guerrilla concentration at Yapolot near Kostopol, but despite having some light artillery the Germans were repulsed by the U.P.A.

Meanwhile a nearby force of U.P.A. had been battling against a band of N.S.Z. since the 7th. When the Germans learned of this they took advantage of the situation and attacked the U.P.A. on the 10th. Due to heavy firepower, though, the spearhead was soon brought to a halt. One result of this attack was that the U.P.A. moved away from the N.S.Z. and the latter group was allowed to escape. Though both partisan groups hated the communists and the nazis they also hated each other.

On the 12th a German S.S. unit assaulted a U.P.A. faction at Kolky, but suffered fifty killed and wounded for their efforts, and the guerrillas escaped. Two days later a German battalion attacked a U.P.A. group near Labosha, but in maneuvering the main column was ambushed and lost thirty-five dead. The battalion was then pinned down and reinforcements had to be brought up before the battalion could disentangle itself. This same month the city of Zhitomir was raided by the U.P.A.

On 23 June a train carrying a unit of the German S.S. Security Police was blown up by U.P.A. saboteurs. When the dust settled the U.P.A. opened fire with machine guns. Altogether 150 Germans were killed.

On 20 August the garrison of Kamin Koshyrsky, consisting of 147 German police, 200 German soldiers, some luftwaffe rear-echelon personnel, some S.S. security police, and a body of Polish militiamen, came under fire from mortars and a 75mm cannon. As the shocked Germans and Poles ran for their defensive pits and shelters, an advance section of the U.P.A. charged through the town firing at everyone who moved. The result was a bloody slaughter. Later a party of guerrillas grabbed as many supplies and as much equipment as they could carry off. Suddenly the raid was over. The authorities counted one hundred Germans and ten Poles dead, many wounded, and fourteen Germans and a Pole missing believed taken prisoner.

In a major anti-partisan battle at Radovychi on 7 September, 300 Germans were killed.

About this time the U.P.A. was totally reorganized by its commander, Taras Bulba Chuprynka (real name Roman Shukhevych), who hoped to unite all nationalist Ukrainian partisans and especially absorb the Ukrainian Nationalist Self-Defense Force (U.N.S.) made up of Galicians. One of his major coups in the military sphere was when Commander Vovchak's group ambushed a German police column near Klevan-Kortylisy and killed S.A. General Viktor Lutze.

In November when the rains gave way to snow, the authorities launched a search and destroy mission in the Carpathian Mountains. In these high narrow passes guerrillas had taken to ambushing Axis convoys and messengers. The sweep was made by German policemen, and they soon suffered high casualties. On 27 November two German divisions were sent against a partisan group that had been identified, but only one battalion of U.N.S. was found. Even then the Germans suffered sixty killed in action and the U.N.S. succeeded in escaping. A nearby unit of U.P.A. also escaped.

The U.P.A. claimed that in October and November of 1943 they inflicted losses on the Axis of 1,500 killed and wounded for the loss of 414 of their own men, and they also inflicted losses on communist partisans and the Polish N.S.Z. This is possibly a fairly accurate count, for though the authorities would claim a higher guerrilla loss, how could they tell whether a man killed in a village was really a partisan or not and if so what group he belonged to?

A major confrontation took place on 4 December near Sambir when two

German police regiments were driven back from a U.P.A. hideout with a loss of 316 dead. One week later a U.P.A. group was surrounded at Kropyvnyk by two German police regiments, but it succeeded in fighting its way out.

Galicia, southeastern General Government, and western Ukraine were the battleground of the Ukrainian nationalists and they made life extremely difficult for the authorities in 1943. The Axis were also in a bad way because the only regular combat troops in this sector were passing through on their way to the front and rarely did the police have any help from the army. The army and the S.S. were far too busy fighting even greater anti-partisan actions in Russia, Byelorussia, and the vast Ukraine.

It was hoped that a series of operations in May and June would crush the bulk of the Russian guerrilla opposition once and for all. In May Operation Maigewitter was fairly successful and also humane as it was an army affair. Colonel von Renteln's new Cossack Regiment performed well alongside the 8th Panzer Division. Nevertheless, Operation Robber Baron was aptly named. As it took place near Lokot, Kaminsky loaned some of his R.O.N.A. to the Germans and their hiwis, and the Germans saw that he had passed his cruelty on to his men. The area proved clear for the most part as it was swept by five infantry and one panzer divisions, but where there was opposition the fighting was tough. A total of 1,584 partisans were killed on the battlefield and 1,568 suspects were arrested. North of Briansk there was another mission, Operation Freischutz, in which over a period of ten days two infantry divisions and two additional infantry regiments killed or captured 2,000 partisans. Yet another simultaneous operation, Nachbarhilfe, was killing or capturing 864 guerrillas.

Once the operations were over Kaminsky refused to withdraw his unit, but instead annexed the territory to his Lokot state. For the time being the German Ostministerium chose to ignore this act.

Operation Cottbus began on 3 June between Lepel and Borisov northeast of Minsk with Obergruppenfuehrer von Gottberg controlling 16,662 Axis troops, including Druzhina and the Dirlewanger Brigade. Oskar Dirlewanger was one of those characters that only Himmler could have found a use for. He had been thrown out of the S.S. after he had been convicted of child molestation and had spent time in a mental home. Brought out of banishment by Himmler, he had been charged with raising a brigade of professional poachers who were currently doing prison time for this offense. The idea in itself was good for these illegal hunters would have made good scouts for an anti-partisan unit. However, an entire brigade of them was no better than any other trained unit. The result was, though, that Dirlewanger recruited every kind of criminal but poachers: convicts, habitual criminals from the concentration camps, and S.S. men like himself who had fallen afoul of the S.S. regulations. All of these were promised an amnesty if they fought well. While training in Poland the unit had been used to guard work details of Jews, and they were given a chance to vent their frustrations on the helpless.

When Cottbus began Dirlewanger allowed his men to do just about anything they wanted, bearing in mind Hitler's pronouncement that no one would be punished for deeds committed on an anti-partisan mission. At the end of the three weeks von Gottberg praised his Russians and Germans. They had a body count of 9,500 dead enemy. The combat had been serious but at no time had the Axis troops been in a hurt. They had lost only 59 killed and had captured only 492 small arms. Obviously most of the dead were innocent villagers. In west Russia the authorities had also launched another serious mission in June. Controlled by the S.S., ten battalions of German police and Polish police, two Hungarian security regiments, three battalions of Cossacks, and various S.S. personnel killed or captured about 15,000 partisans and suspected partisans.

Due to the excesses of the troops whenever under S.S. orders, the German Armed Forces High Command (O.K.W.) gave orders that in the future all partisans who surrendered were to be taken prisoner. This really only reinforced the Fuehrer's order of the previous December, but it was meant as a protest. Unfortunately whenever Axis units were in action outside the army-administered districts they did not come under the command of O.K.W., but under von dem Bach Zelewski or one of the Higher S.S. and Police Leaders, all of them S.S. officers. Heinrich Himmler would continue to act as a mutinous warlord and support his men in arguments with the army.

In June the French Volunteer Legion was organized into three battalions again, and though not under a regimental headquarters they were all assigned to the German 186th Security Division as the unit's strike force.

On 23 June Hitler became alarmed about the high number of osttruppen and hiwis, and in one of his more intransigent moods he ordered that no more units of easterners were to be formed. This order was blatantly ignored, even by himself.

Chapter 23

The Nationalist/Fascist Alliance in the Balkans

Yugoslavia

Within the pacified areas of occupied Yugoslavia there was little for security units to do except remain alert. The Russian Defense Corps was allowed to expand in peace and was officially recognized by the German government as an auxiliary police force. This force began to get more recruits, as the younger members of the emigre community became of age, Russians who had never seen Russia, and also as the recruiting offices recently opened in ex-Soviet territory began to reap their human harvest. In addition to Russians a few Ukrainians and Cossacks were recruited. The German commander, Lieutenant-General Steyffon, was succeeded by a Russian, Colonel Anatole Rogozhin. Before the end of 1942 the force was encompassed within the German Army without losing its auxiliary police status and fielded three horse cavalry regiments and ancillary units including a reserve manpower pool, totaling 15,000 personnel. The unit's prime mission now was to protect the Belgrade-Nish rail line.

The Hungarians were rarely subjected to partisan raids and they hardly ever left their occupation zones to aid the other members of the Axis. However, a Hungarian river boat flotilla did assist German troops to destroy a partisan unit on the Sava River.

In fact only in Slovenia and Montenegro did the situation refuse to conform to Axis plan. In Slovenia the Italians only remained in the towns if possible, and when forced to move between them to resupply they had to protect their convoys well. The valleys were usually safe for the Cetniks controlled these with the aid of a truce of sorts with the Italians, but the mountain roads were the playground of the communists. The communists became so much of a problem in western Slovenia that the Italians were forced to launch a major offensive against them in July 1942 northeast of Ljubliana. The spearhead of the force was made up of seven infantry divisions and a blackshirt legion, and the flanks and more inaccessible areas were patrolled by the Whites and the

Blues. General Mario Robotti also had considerable air support to call upon, which was very useful in discovering partisan hideouts. When contact was made the roughest fighting took place in the sectors swept by the Whites, and the Granatieri, Cacciatore della Alpi, and Lombardia Divisions. The enemy was hurt but not destroyed.

To the east in German-occupied Slovenia the authorities found that they were up against some members of the Slovenian-speaking community of Carinthia. When the Germans had entered Austria in 1938 the S.S. Security Police had arrested the leading intellectuals of this small community, and cultural laws were soon passed outlawing the Slovenian language even in the privacy of one's home. As a result many fled into Yugoslavian Slovenia, but in April 1941 Hitler's armies had caught up with them, so many Carinthians had gone underground for fear of being arrested. When Tito sent his agents into the mountainous nation in early 1942, they found several thousand willing recruits.

The Titoists claimed that in the next few months they inflicted casualties on the Axis of 3,800 dead and 2,000 wounded, and this figure can be accepted as pure fiction. However, the authorities were under fire in one way or another every few days, and retaliations were made. In some villages terrorists were publicly beheaded by the Germans. In April 1942 the Germans began to expel the intelligentsia from the nation, but this time it did not mean removal to other parts of Yugoslavia as it had done for the Serbian and Croatian residents of German-occupied Slovenia, but rather removal to the territory conquered from the Soviets. The deportations were heartless, but not many people were affected at first.

In Bosnia-Herzegovina the Cetniks were left alone by the Germans, and were able to rescue their brothers from Ustaci atrocities, while at the same time the Cetniks fought the Ustaci and other Croatian units on occasion. Some Cetnik groups also spent their time committing atrocities against the Moslem population. One of the worst acts of this kind took place at Sandjak in which about 9,200 people died.

Throughout this area and all of Croatia the Ustaci massacres became more and more brutal. Whenever ammunition ran short the Ustaci hanged, stabbed, and beat their victims to death. No Serbian or Jew or Gypsy was safe. In some instances victims were buried alive. All of the town Jews had already been incarcerated in concentration camps by the Croatian Police, and in August 1942, when the S.S. Security Police asked for them, the Croatians found only 9,000 diseased and emaciated Jews to be left. These few remnants of the Jewish population were transported to the extermination camps in Poland.

In Banat more young men were enticed and cajoled into joining the German Armed Forces or one of the paramilitary units. Banat volunteers for the police were formed into three regiments and ten independent battalions and informed that they could be sent anywhere the chief of police, Heinrich Himmler, desired, if necessary even to the Russian Front.

Those Yugoslavs who were unfortunate enough to live in the proximity of Bulgarian garrisons were in constant danger of being looted, raped, and murdered, for discipline in the Bulgarian Army was lax and cruelty was a way of life for many of the Bulgarian peasants. Most of the Bulgarian occupation troops were middle-aged and missed their families and farms. The pride of the Bulgarian manhood was still facing the Turkish border in case of attack by Bulgaria's traditional enemy. In March 1943 in retaliation for a partisan attack on Skoplje, which killed thirty-two Bulgarians and wounded twenty-six, the Bulgarians arrested 1,003 innocents and later shot 288 and imprisoned the remainder. Even the Bulgarian government was militant and Hitler had to intervene in order to calm them down when they and the Italians began sabre-rattling over a border dispute in southern Yugoslavia. Each claimed Macedonia.

By November 1942 Tito's partisan army was stronger than ever, for although the casualties lost had decreased his number of veterans he was gaining recruits all the time, many of them witnesses to nazi/fascist atrocities and excesses. Women joined him to proudly bear the duties of nurses, cooks, laundresses, radio operators, messengers, interpreters, and spies, and many fought as infantry. This month Tito's main force captured Bihac and proclaimed the force to be the Yugoslavian National Liberation Army. He retained military command but in theory passed political control to an all-party council. At this moment in time he did not want potential recruits to think of his force as just a communist army. He also hoped to woo the British into supplying him, and to this end he constantly denounced by a mobile broadcasting radio station the Cetniks who were receiving British air-dropped supplies and who had British advisers, for according to Tito the Cetniks were now effectively on the Axis side.

As for the Cetniks it must be realized that Milhailovich never had complete control over his men, as they were scattered all over Serbia, Bosnia-Herzegovina, and Slovenia, and secondly he knew that his full-time force of perhaps 30,000 ill-armed troops, many of them horse cavalry, could not hope to defeat the Croatians, Italians, Germans, Hungarians, and Bulgarians, but by using these nation's armed forces he might be able to defeat the communists. He knew that not all of Tito's men were communists, but he also knew that as long as they obeyed a communist commander they might as well be.

Indeed Winston Churchill, who had reports from his advisers with the Cetniks at his fingertips, was not totally opposed to the idea. He always had one eye on the post-war world. The advisers told Milhailovich that if the British landed on the coast of Yugoslavia they would need assistance from the Cetniks, that is from a well-armed, trained, and disciplined unit, but that a mob of starving wretches on the run from Stuka dive-bombers would be useless to the British. In fact they would be a liability. They advised Milhailovich that his mission was to build up his strength and not get involved in major actions with the occupation authorities.

Those authorities were more than ever determined to crush the Titoists and consequently new formations and combinations of formations were put together. The Croatian Army gathered a field force of an infantry regiment, four mountain brigades, and artillery and armored cars. The Croatian Police offered a mobile brigade of gendarmerie, and the Ustaci put forth a defense brigade. Within Croatia the German Police created their own gendarmerie made up of thirty battalions of Croatians, which used German advisers and technicians and had the status of auxiliaries of the German Police. In addition, the German Army created the Devil's Division. Actually the 369th Division of the Croatian Army, it used German advisers and technicians and was divided into three regiments, the 373rd Tiger, the 392nd Blue, and the "new" 369th.

In January 1943 the Axis launched Operation Weiss, a combined offensive aimed at wiping out the main force of the Titoist communist partisans, which was still defiantly holding on to Bihac. The Titoists here were behaving as if there was no war, holding judicial courts, teaching children in schools, and operating a socialist economy. This would be the fourth Axis attempt to crush Tito in eighteen months. In the second week of January the Axis troops began to move into jump-off positions. From the north came the Croatian strike force and the Devil's Division, and from the northeast came the German 717th Division, a regiment of the 187th Division, and the 7th S.S. Prinz Eugen Division made up of Volksdeutsch, mostly from Banat. From the west coast the Italian Vth Corps was on the march. To Tito's rear, the valley of the Neretva River, lay a Cetnik army of 12,000.

On the morning of 16 January 1943, the battle opened for real with German and Italian aircraft blasting apart the little province that the Titoists had created. Communist anti-aircraft guns fought back, but they were inaccurate due to a lack of trained crews. On the borders of the partisan zone Axis heavy artillery plastered the light defenses of the guerrillas. Titoist artillery replied, but only sporadically. This day the Germans and the Ustaci went over to the attack, and though they were stopped, the enemy was forced to radio for support. The German commanders thought they had the enemy where they wanted him, but the next day the front-line positions were emptied of defenders. Aerial reconnaissance soon informed the Axis generals that the communists were all on the move towards the Neretva. Axis air and artillery barrages continued to harass the retreating enemy while the Germans and Croatians advanced, overcoming suicidal rearguards.

The Italians had a garrison at Prozor in the path of the communists and were rushing troops to aid the Cetniks on the Neretva. "The Communists must not be allowed to cross that river," was the order. However, what the Italian generals described as "rushing" the Germans described as "crawling," and the Germans urged the Italians to hurry. The answer was that "Prozor will hold the enemy anyway."

By the 20th the German troops and the Ustaci were being held by a large rearguard at Kordun, though the Germans brought up more artillery and a detachment of tanks. The Titoists matched them with artillery and opened fire with concealed anti-tank guns. During the struggle Colonel Jure Francetic of the Ustaci was killed in action.

Still by early February even the slow Italians were now reaching the Neretva in places and the Axis were sure that they had the enemy trapped. The aircraft continued to attack the enemy columns, though in the highest mountain passes visibility was poor and the cloud low. The Axis troops had begun following the communists again and soon entered the snowy mountains too. Rainstorms drenched the troops and then severe frosts froze them. The communists could be tracked by the impedimenta of their retreat, broken wagons, dead horses, and dead people. Typhus was downing as many partisans as bullets, and a large number of the partisan dependents were abandoned to die in the snow from various causes. The Axis did not have an accurate count of the number of enemy, but usually overestimated it. At this time Tito had 20,000 fighting personnel, of which 4,500 were wounded and sick who had to be hand-carried. Most of the partisan vehicles had been left behind in the valleys, and the few horses in the column were being used to drag artillery and flak guns.

The Axis artillery was mostly horse-drawn, too, and in these mountains the gunners had to help their animals pull the heavy equipment. Going down icy glaciers was even worse, and required many men pulling on ropes to guide the cannons safely to rest.

On 16 February the partisans launched their major effort, trying to overcome the defenders of Prozor, the 3rd Battalion of the 259th Regiment of the Murge Division, but the Italians bravely battled for twenty-four hours, though outnumbered. However, the partisans then brought up artillery, which the infantry battalion could not match. Now the 600 Italians began to suffer heavily, and when they ran low on ammunition the commander negotiated a surrender. A few Italians fled from the scene, not wishing to trust the communists. This was shown to be good policy, for the Titoists quickly massacred the Italians. The Titoists had become extremely angry at being held up for a day, but at last their way was clear to the river.

The best the Italian generals could do was apologize to the Germans and strike at the Prozor bottleneck with every available warplane. Of course the other Axis units had not done too much better. To date in this offensive the German units, including the Devil's 369th Division of Croatians, had suffered 335 killed, 101 missing, and several hundred wounded, and the Croatian-controlled units had lost 700 casualties. The Axis field units claimed to have killed 8,500 guerrillas and taken prisoner 2,010, but in fact the dead included all bodies found, victims of air and artillery barrages, disease, and the extreme cold, regardless of age, and the prisoners were civilian dependents who had been following the partisans, but had been unable to keep up.

On 19 February the German 717th Division caught up with the main force and battled hard against a substantial rearguard at Ivan Sedloe, but it was not until the 21st that the Germans broke through and destroyed the fanatic defenders. During this fight the Italians, who had brought up their VIth Corps as well, were also held up by a column of guerrillas at Konjic, and it was only when the Germans advanced again that the Italians saw their enemy flee for fear of being cut off.

The Axis began to follow again, but they were often new to the terrain and moved slowly, ever wary of an ambush by a solitary sniper or a battalion rearguard. Partisan artillery shot back at them now and again. Once in a while the Axis troops could hear their artillery and air support strike the enemy and the sound gave them heart. The infantry of the 717th Division were middle-aged reservists and not mountaineers and this mountain warfare was often too much for them. The field commanders received a stream of complaints from their generals, demanding to know why the movement of troops and equipment was taking so long, and under their breath the officers wished that the generals would come and see for themselves the type of terrain and wintry conditions in which they had to fight.

On the 22nd an Italian battalion defending Jablanica was completely swamped by thousands of bearded barbaric-looking partisans. This gave Tito a second place to cross the river, but in an incomprehensible order he commanded that the bridge be blown. This meant that his only crossing point was near Prozor. Later it came to light that Tito thought the Cetniks were going to use the Jablanica bridge from which to strike him in flank, but this may have been decided with hindsight to cover up a stupid mistake.

The Axis were jubilant, for not only was the Tito main force still straddling the Prozor crossing area, but the column that had reached Jablanica now had to double back slightly. A few men and women could cross the swollen river with ropes, but the heavier equipment and the stretcher cases would have to be left behind unless they could reach Prozor.

Guided by a Cetnik unit the 717th Division reached Vilica Guvno on 2 March to discover a well-prepared rearguard. The Cetnik and German charge against dug-in machine guns and mortars brought heavy casualties and no gains, and the divisional commander had to call for reinforcements. Within a couple of days he received the Devil's Division and the Ustaci brigade.

By the night of 6 March some enterprising guerrillas had constructed a one-man plank bridge over the river at Jablanica and the column here chose to cross by this method. Most of the wounded had been sent to the main column.

By the morning of the 7th a substantial number of partisans were on the opposite bank of the river at the two crossing points, but they had abandoned their heavy equipment, including artillery and heavy mortars. In addition the land was flatter here, and visibility was better, which meant that Axis warplanes could catch them easily and other planes spot for Axis artillery.

It was now that the Cetniks decided to throw in their main force, for they had been waiting on this side of the river, and they now saw the enemy to be on his last legs. With great courage, but a lack of tactical sense the Cetniks charged the Titoists by the thousands, on foot and on horseback. The leading Cetniks waved gigantic flags, not just as rallying points and as morale boosters, but to let the Axis aircraft pilots know who they were, for today the Cetniks were on the Axis side. But the partisans brought in more and more men as they crossed the river and the Cetniks were simply slaughtered as they charged into the massed machine guns. By the end of the day the Cetniks crawled away to lick their wounds. The partisans had won the field and they were safe from Axis ground units. By the 9th all the partisans were on the far bank and were digging in along the cliff crests to stop the Axis regulars from following.

Southeast of Sarajevo a large partisan column retreated towards the Drina River, and the Italians and Cetniks combined to halt it, but at the end of March the partisans punched a hole right through the Axis line. The Italian field commander ordered a retreat at the beginning of April, and the partisans were allowed to capture Foca.

The partisans were now deep into Montenegro, and this meant that the Italians were bearing the brunt of their activity again. Only a few days after arriving, the Titoists captured the Italian garrison at Podgoritza. This alarmed the Italian command that the Titoists might be thinking of entering Albania. When the Cetnik garrison of Niksic made threatening moves, the partisans lashed back and the Cetniks ran away.

The Axis generals were angry that the fourth attempt had been unsuccessful, and consoled themselves with the thought that at least the partisan army had been driven away from the bauxite mines that were vital to the Axis war effort.

While the regular Axis units took roll call and refitted their exhausted battalions, Milhailovich's troops languished in despair. Their casualties had been extremely high, and coupled with the number of troops who just went home for a while, this brought his main force down to about 9,000. Although Milhailovich conferred with German and Italian officers in order to coordinate operations, he still had his British advisers and was in radio contact with British headquarters in Cairo. The pro-Allied Yugoslavian government in exile recognized the Cetniks as the Yugoslavian Army of the Homeland and made Milhailovich the minister of war of the royalist government. They and Milhailovich knew that most of his troops would return and had only gone home to take care of the social and economic problems that women and children get when their menfolk are away for long periods of time.

The Axis commanders were not planning to languish, though, for they could not afford the time. The Italians for one were in constant action due to Tito's forays in Montenegro. They suffered badly at Javorak. The main reason was the wider war. The Anglo-Americans were winding up their African campaign, and the powers in Rome and Berlin believed that an Allied amphibious invasion of southern Europe was a serious possibility. They knew that it would come while the weather was good, but other than that had little idea of when or where. Yugoslavia was a potential target, especially as it was in turmoil, and therefore the order went out to smash the Titoists as soon as possible. In any case wherever the landing took place it would not do to have Axis reserves tied down in a guerrilla war in the mountains of Montenegro.

The Axis commanders also knew that the Cetniks would ally with the Anglo-Americans if they arrived on the Yugoslavian coast. Therefore the Croatian Army and the German 104th (ex-704th) Jaeger Division and newly arrived 1st Mountain Division advanced along the Italian-controlled coast against the Cetniks. In most instances the Cetniks were peacefully disarmed, only a few of these irregulars fighting to the death or fleeing. Within days Major Pavel Djurisic and his 4,000 men along the coast were prisoners of the Germans. Draza Milhailovich was almost caught, but he and his British advisers managed to escape into Serbia. The Italians had refused to take part in this operation, but at least they did not refuse their Axis partners entry into what was technically their terrain.

The Axis units moved into jump-off positions in the first two weeks of May, and the need for their urgent aid was shown again on 14 May when the Italian 383rd Regiment was sorely defeated at Bioce.

The following day the Axis began their fifth offensive against the Titoists. The opening round went to the Axis as they struck with air raids and long-range artillery barrages. At least the weather was good and the Axis infantry knew they would not be freezing again. When the partisan perimeter was attacked by the Axis the infantry joined in mortal combat. On the north flank of the partisans the Devil's 369th Division advanced from the Drina River. From the east the 1st Mountain Division attacked towards Kolos with the Bulgarian 61st Regiment on its right. Also on the east the Italian Taurinense Division was attacking Pijevlija. From the southwest the Italian Venezia and Ferrara Divisions and the German 7th S.S. Prinz Eugen Division advanced towards the Piva River. From the northwest the German 118th (ex-718th) Jaeger Division with elements of the German Brandenburg Division was moving up. In command of the entire operation was the German General Luetters. In reserve he had the Bulgarian 62nd Regiment, the German 104th Division, and 11,000 troops of the Ustaci and Croatian Army.

The partisans were trapped in the Lim and Tara valleys and on Mount Durmitor and had no heavy equipment and many wounded and sick. Tito also had a tiny team of British liaison officers for the first time. The peasant soldiers laughed at such a response after two years of requesting aid, but Tito treated them well, realizing their potential. Tito constantly demanded that they radio for British air support, even one squadron, but their pleas met with deaf ears at British headquarters. The only protection from Axis aircraft was the mountain mist that hid the narrow passes and crevices and the heavy rains that also hindered the Axis advance.

The Germans and Bulgarians were held up at once by a heavily manned perimeter defense, though they did not have to face the sort of enemy firepower they had witnessed in the fourth offensive. Air support was on call and coupled with the Axis artillery this told the Axis troops that it was only a matter of time before the guerrillas collapsed.

In fact the partisans began to move out immediately, leaving only strong rearguards. Aerial reconnaissance informed the Axis command that Tito had split his forces into two columns, one which was aiming for the Sutjeska River and the other, which contained the wounded, which was aiming for the Tara River. Luetters notified the Italian outposts on the Tara to be on their guard.

The Italians fought well and repelled the enemy everywhere along the Tara, and within a few days the partisans had to retreat. It was soon realized that this column was now trying to join the other one, but as it carried the wounded and sick it moved very slowly. Luetters knew that if Tito waited for it he might seal his own fate. To this end the Germans attacked repeatedly against the rearguard of this main column, hoping to keep the two forces from uniting, while some German troops tried to infiltrate around the flanks.

By now Tito thought that he was well and truly trapped, so he ordered what was left of his mountain artillery and mortars to be buried and the horses and mules that had been carrying this and other equipment on their backs to be slaughtered for food. One German party broke through for a time and Tito was wounded and cut off with a small unit for a day or so.

To take some of the pressure off his main army Tito ordered all his other units throughout Yugoslavia to go onto the offensive, and within days every Axis security unit was either on the alert or in action. This told Luetters that he was definitely putting Tito in a strain. On 5 June the main partisan column crossed the Sutjeska, and the troops of the 1st Mountain and 7th S.S. Prinz Eugen Divisions, which were the only Axis mountain units in the battle, were ordered to smash through the enemy rearguards at once. The partisans were heading for the Zelengora River and might possibly elude the elaborate trap after all. The Germans soon reached the Sutjeska with elements of the 7th S.S. and the 118th Jaeger Divisions, but found only a large rearguard of about 1,200 guerrillas. The German infantry tried to sneak through in places to cut off the rearguard from its escape and within hours some Germans had done so, having reached the bridge. The Germans then assaulted the enemy, but during the night the guerrillas broke out of the encircling ring and crossed the river at another place. Even the Banat Volksdeutsch of the S.S. had to begrudgingly respect the fighting ability of the communists, men who had been their fellow citizens only twenty-six months earlier. By 12 June every partisan was over the river.

The Germans followed at once, battling against more rearguards until the 18th. That day no significant enemy concentration was found. The enemy had eluded the trap.

The Titoists were relatively safely established in the Vlasic Mountains and at Visetc on the coast. During the mopping up, that is the next phase of action in which the Axis troops searched for enemy stragglers and hiding wounded, the Italian Ferrara Division earned a fearful reputation for massacring villagers. The Bulgarian 61st Regiment also murdered a few innocents when it could not identify true partisans. The German 1st Mountain and 7th S.S. Divisions rested, for they had borne the brunt of the battle and had suffered heavily. The Germans now brought in more units to help secure their occupied territory, ever mindful of the potential Anglo-American invasion. Among these units were the S.S. Danmarck Regiment and the S.S. Nederland Brigade.

Greece

The Greeks are a violently independent people, and as soon as the government surrendered to the Axis small groups of soldiers and civilians fled into the mountains rather than surrender. Their first problems were not how to fight, though, but how to survive and how to identify which villages were friendly. The summer was no problem, but these partisans knew that winter would test their fortitude to the limit. As opportunities presented themselves they skirmished with the occupation troops and as time went on these bands began to group together for mutual self-protection. It was late in the year before any of these groups began to think of political motives, and this only happened when the intellectuals began to arrive from the towns, hoping to create order out of the confusion, and most of all hoping to back their own particular ideology with an army.

The first political group to become established was the National Liberation Front (E.A.M.), which was a coalition of left-wing parties, the important ones being the Socialists (E.L.D.), the Agrarian Socialists (A.K.E.), and the communists (K.K.E.). The fighting section of the E.A.M. was the National Popular Liberation Army (E.L.A.S.). This group gathered considerable support throughout the mountains of the Peloponnisos, Roumelia, and Macedonia.

Meanwhile in the Epirus Mountains Colonel Napoleon Zervas had established the National Democratic Greek League (E.D.E.S.), which accepted men and women of all political persuasion except communists. The third major group was a band named after its leader, Psarros.

There were two other groups, but these were made up of Macedonians, and both were opposed to Greek rule as well as rule by the invaders. The Defenders of Northern Greece (Y.V.E.) and the Kaltchev force. The latter was a partisan group, but its members felt that the presence of communists in the mountains was a greater danger to the Macedonian people than the presence of Bulgarian troops in the towns. Some Macedonians who accepted the Bulgarians as the protectors of Macedonian culture, a tenet of official Bulgarian propaganda, joined this group.

By early 1942 disillusionment had swept the partisans, for they were still living little better than bandits and had made no serious efforts against the occupation authorities. The communists had all joined E.L.A.S. and were slowly but surely gaining control of that army. Rival groups did not like to see such a large communist army in Greece, but instead of uniting against it quarreled among themselves. Two new political groups sprang up, the National Union of Greece (E.E.E.) and the National Guerrilla Anti-Communist Action Alliance (E.A.S.A.D.), both of them vehemently anti-communist. However, the arguments between these factions did not result in gunfights, and only manifested itself in a lack of inter-group cooperation. When Major Kostapoulis and his followers became disenchanted with E.L.A.S., he simply left to form his own group.

The British and later the Americans and Soviets sent advisers to the partisans, but never could figure out who was the more effective. Liaison officers with the E.L.A.S. claimed that E.D.E.S. was useless, and liaison officers with E.D.E.S. radioed headquarters that the communists were little better than a mob of ignorant peasants. By February the Allies were recognizing only three groups, E.L.A.S., E.D.E.S., and the National and Socialist Liberation, E.K.K.A. of Colonel Psarros. The other groups received no aid from the Allies and only had what they had captured in battle.

For the first year there was no battle. The Axis authorities knew of the guerrillas in the mountains, but left them alone to squabble. An Axis offensive would only have unified them. The Axis could afford to do this for there was little action anywhere. The first serious incident came when an E.D.E.S. group ambushed an Italian convoy on the Arta-Yannina road in June 1942 and killed all sixty soldiers.

The lack of effective partisan resistance meant that the authorities were not too oppressive, and the Greeks managed to survive fairly well during the occupation. The treatment of the people depended not only in which zone they lived, the Bulgarian, Italian, or German, but often on the disposition of the district commandant. The Jews of Greece suffered worst. Seventy percent of the nation's Jews, 55,000, were residents of the city of Salonika in the German zone. These Ladin-speaking people were noticeably non-Greek and had always wished to be left alone. Few Jews had assimilated. The German authorities had issued anti-Semitic laws at once, but it was not until July 1942 that the S.S. Security Police began to crack down. This month all Jewish males were conscripted for forced labor, and the working conditions were made as harsh as possible. The officers then proceeded to make a good profit by ransoming the Jews for considerable sums of money. By the end of the year all the Jews had bought their freedom, except for twelve percent who had died due to the bad treatment.

The Italians had not just occupied most of Greece, but had actually annexed part of it, but they searched for allies in their political moves. They found some support in the Arumanian community. The Arumanian-speaking people of the Pindus Mountains call themselves Vlachs, and the Italians looked upon them as some sort of long-lost Italians. Their chief, Diamandis, was put in charge of the Vlach Legion, which was used to guard the roads in their land against partisan movement. In return the Vlachs were left alone to rule themselves, and Diamandis was encouraged to think of himself as a future king of the Arumanians. Not all Vlachs supported this idea. The deputy leader of E.A.M., Tzimas, was a Vlach.

The Italians had no such luck with the Macedonians. The Y.V.E., which was renamed the Panhellenic Liberation Organization (P.A.O.), began to ambush Italian vehicles regularly, but refrained from entering the German-occupied zone. These Macedonians felt that one enemy at a time was enough. For this reason the communists accused the P.A.O. of making a truce with the Germans, but then again the communists accused everyone of being Axis-dominated.

By the summer of 1942 the Axis occupied Greece with the Bulgarian IInd Corps in Thrace, the German 22nd Parachute Division on the island of Crete, the 11th Luftwaffe Field (infantry) Division in Attica, and some independent German army and police battalions in Athens and Salonika. The rest of the country was occupied by the Italian Eleventh Army.

The reasonably peaceful situation changed in the spring of 1943, when Allied advisers began asking the partisans to launch an offensive. The motive was to hold the enemy's attention and make him think that the Anglo-Americans were going to invade Greece. In return the Allies would drop by parachute much-needed supplies. The greatest problem for the advisers was not to get the guerrillas to fight, but to get them to coordinate their actions. Thus the only major action in May was a joint E.D.E.S./E.L.A.S. ambush of an Italian column which killed eighty Italians including a general at Domenico.

Indeed the guerrillas were arguing among themselves even more, and at Agrinio a party of E.D.E.S. arrested some E.L.A.S. members. Political commissars hurried from one mountain top to another to smooth over the differences, while the British and American advisers were often kept in the dark as to what was really going on. The Kostapoulis organization was forced at gunpoint to rejoin E.L.A.S.

The Germans came to the conclusion that the Italians had allowed the situation to go on for far too long, and they brought in their own troops to enter the supposedly Italian-controlled zone and extinguish the partisans once and for all. They were worried that if the Anglo-Americans did land here they would link up with the partisans who had been allowed to grow for more than two years without one major offensive against them.

The German 1st Mountain Division, which had been battling the Titoists, was ordered to drive through Albania into northern Greece. The E.A.M. learned of this and placed an E.L.A.S./E.D.E.S. force on the border in the

Albanian village of Leskovic in early June. These Germans had learned anti-partisan warfare the hard way, and they were not about to be caught unawares. Instead of the Greek partisans ambushing them, the German unit's reconnaissance troops infiltrated through the woods and struck the village in flank while artillery opened a barrage on the enemy. The Greeks were stunned by this onslaught and they fled quickly. The Germans also reinforced the Peloponnisos with their LXVIIIth Corps, consisting of the 117th Division, which had experience of warfare against the Titoists, and the 1st Panzer Division, which was resting from front-line duty. Several independent battalions of the German Army also arrived to garrison out of the way places. The local Greeks learned that many of these reinforcements were Austrians and newly conscripted Poles.

The Germans also demanded that the Greek government help. The new prime minister of this semi-autonomous government that in theory ruled all Greece, except that annexed by Bulgaria and Italy—Thrace and a strip along the Albanian border—was Joannes Rallis, a man who insisted that he ruled not only with Axis permission but with Allied permission—which ignored the pro-Allied royalist government in exile currently based in British-controlled Cairo. To aid the Axis in their anti-partisan moves, he recruited from the right-wing faction enough auxiliary police to create the Laocoon Battalion. Some of these men came from the Greek Police and Gendarmerie, and others had been members or supporters of extreme right-wing parties before the war. An additional aid was that some villages were judged to be right-wing and nationalist enough to have their own militia, so that they could repel partisan food gathering patrols. Rallis also tried to make contact with some of the smaller guerrilla groups to convince them to support the government. The Axis commanders approved of this, but being military men they tended to put their faith in a good old-fashioned full-scale offensive. They did like what they saw of the Laocoon Battalion in its first sweep in the Peloponnisos, and they allowed Rallis to recruit another 14,000 Greeks into his Security Battalions.

The Axis offensive moves began with an attack near Porta in Roumelia by the Italian Pinerolo Division and Aosta (horse) Cavalry Regiment, but the attackers were soon pinned down by a large group of E.L.A.S. and after three days of battle the Italians withdrew, having suffered 500 casualties.

One of the greatest sabotage actions took place about this time. E.L.A.S. men blew up the Kournoso rail tunnel seconds after an Italian troop train had entered it. The resultant death toll was about 500. In retaliation for this and other acts the Italian garrison of Larissa executed 118 political prisoners. The E.L.A.S. then announced that in future they would not take Italian prisoners. At Bougazi an Italian battalion was forced to retreat by a partisan raid.

Though political commissars tried to calm their men, a group of E.L.A.S. battled with a group of E.K.K.A. near Kalambaka. Casualties were light, but this spelled the end of cooperation between these two groups. By early July the political heads of the various main groups had managed to coordinate a general partisan offensive in answer to requests by Allied advisers. At Rovilista an Italian column was repulsed by an E.L.A.S./E.D.E.S. ambush, suffering about 120 killed, wounded, and missing. At Monotiano the eighty-five-man garrison was overrun.

On 10 July 1943 the Anglo-Americans invaded southern Europe at Sicily. The German and Italian commands knew that the Allies did not have sufficient naval power to land elsewhere as well and therefore the garrisons of Yugoslavia, Albania, and Greece breathed a sigh of relief.

For the partisans this meant they too could stand down, but the good weather and their recent successes spurred them on to bigger and better things. The Italian garrison of Almyros was attacked, but the defenders fought with courage and repelled the guerrillas. In retaliation the Italians murdered 38 villagers. In Thrace a Bulgarian column was all but wiped out by an E.L.A.S. ambush.

The Allied advisers tried to be everywhere offering advice and encouragement, but they often got caught by surprise. A British officer with an E.L.A.S. patrol barely survived a skirmish with a P.A.O. patrol.

The Polish soldiers of the German Army, who were legally Volksdeutsch Class IV, proved quite unreliable and so many surrendered to the partisans at the earliest opportunity that the guerrillas requested an officer of the pro-Allied Polish Army be assigned to them to screen and administer them.

Albania

It has been related how Mussolini's blunder into Greece in November 1940 soon brought defeat and the Greek Army pouring into southern Albania. The two Albanian battalions in the Italian Army flat-footedly refused to fight the Greeks and some even ran off to defect to the Greeks. The ringleaders of the mutiny were imprisoned. The rest of the Albanian soldiers were placed on sentry duty. Not until the offensive of April 1941 was all of Albania reunited under the Italian flag. By all of Albania it is meant not just the state in existence prior to 1939, but those villages of Albanians in Yugoslavia and Greece. These were unified into one nation, Albania, but it was an Italian-controlled Albania.

To give the Albanians some recognition King Vittorio Emmanuele created an Albanian Royal Guard, which helped guard him in Rome. It was made up of young Albanians who could see no further than a pretty uniform. Within Albania the fascists were given more recognition and they in turn preached to their compatriots that cooperation was the only road to national survival. Four legions of Albanian blackshirts were formed for ceremonial and light security duty, and on occasion they assisted the Italian secret police in hunting terrorists. The mutiny of the Albanian soldiers was overlooked and more recruits taken in to form an artillery and six infantry battalions and some anti-aircraft batteries. Two of the infantry battalions were made up of blackshirts. When these units were inspected the Italian generals liked what they saw and restructured the infantry into three regiments of two battalions each. This put a total of 7,000 Albanian-speakers into the Italian Army in addition to the blackshirt legions. Some of these men were ex-Yugoslav and ex-Greek citizens, but all considered themselves to be Albanians. They did not see any contradiction in being Albanians and Italian citizens at the same time, just as Scots are proud of who they are, but also consider themselves to be British citizens answerable to an English government. This idea of Albanian national consciousness within an Italian framework was made more predominant when the Italians dismissed the Albanian premier, Shefket Verlaci, in December 1941 and replaced him with Mustafa Merlika Kruja, who immediately announced a greater fusion of the two nations.

The year 1941 was a period of major change in the life of the Albanian people, for though the Italian military had suffered setbacks the fascist spirit spread through the land, and the ordinary people, uneducated peasants for the most part, accepted the political status quo and decided to make the best of it. Looking around them they could not see anyone with a better idea. The ideas of Western democracy were as alien to them as the doctrine of Islam was to the Anglo-American people. Only the Albanian communists saw things differently, and only then because their "god" had been attacked by the fascists in the Soviet Union in June 1941. Their leadership was strong and wily, but their following negligible.

On 16 September an all-party conference was held illegally in the small town of Peza in order to create a National Liberation Movement, but the right-wing parties identified the manipulations and behind the scenes intrigues of the communists at work and refused to join. Instead they set up their own National Front, known as the Balli Kombetar, with Midhat Frasheri as leader, with the avowed policy of kicking out the Italians, destroying communism, and gathering together all Albanian-speakers into a Greater Albania. This was not the only coalition of anti-fascist parties. A force called Legality was established by Abas Kupi in the Kruje area, which aimed at similar goals to the Balli Kombetar, but also maintained its loyalty to King Zog. Another major force was the Roman Catholic band set up by John Markagjon, which took its support from the small membership of that religion in the country, though most Roman Catholics naturally supported the Italians, taking their advice from the Pope. Within days of the conference armed clashes were taking place between the National Liberation Movement and the other groups.

By the beginning of 1943 General Enver Hoxha, the communist leader of the National Liberation Movement, had a guerrilla army of about 10,000 fighters in a stronghold in the mountains of the southern part of the nation. The other groups collectively had about the same number of troops and held positions in the north of the country.

On the second day of the year two battalions of Italians made a sweep southeast of Vlova, but were defeated by a large band of communists at Gjormi. The Italian command was surprised and naturally the communists were encouraged. The Italian and Albanian leaders of the nation had been slow to recognize the danger of allowing their political enemies to militarize. True the enemy had divided on ideological grounds, but almost all left-wingers in the country were supporting Hoxha and this the fascists had not counted on. From now on the members of the security forces never knew from where the next guerrilla attack would come. Sentries had to be doubled and trucks convoyed in case of ambush. One sniper's bullet could keep a barracks in turmoil for the rest of the day and night.

The next major attack took place at Voskopoja, in which the Italians were wiped out. In February the Italian government came to the conclusion that the military command was not doing enough and they imposed General Pariani on the country to wipe out the partisans. He paid his respects to the Viceroy, Francesco Jacomoni, and to the Albanian government, and then set to work.

One of the methods was to increase the Albanian participation in the cleaning up of their own country, and soon a fourth regiment of Albanians was being trained by the Italian Army. This 4th Regiment was recruited from the Kosovo district, which had been part of Yugoslavia, and it was grouped together with the 1st Regiment into the new 1st Brigade.

Things had also been moving on the political front. The Italians had not been happy with Kruja, and on 19 February 1943 they replaced him with Ekrem Libohova, but he resigned in despair only twenty-eight days later. The new premier was Maliq Bushati, but this did not work either, and on 12 May a refreshened Libohova took office again. This time Libohova took the bold step of announcing a good deal of autonomy for Albania including the transference of the Albanian units of the Italian Army into a new Albanian Army. It goes without saying that he had cleared this with the Italian government beforehand.

By this date, though, communist guerrilla activity was stepping up to become very serious. In a battle around Permet the Italians suffered about 500 casualties. In July there were major clashes between the communists and the Italians near Mallakastra and Tepelina, in which the Italians barely held their own, and in August the National Liberation Movement stated their statistics of enemy (Italian and Albanian security forces) losses as 1,000 in July and 1,500 in August. As the fascists never gave out their exact losses to the public, one wonders how the communists came to this figure, and as it is offered in round figures it must be highly suspect. The point is that in Albania in the spring and summer of 1943 the Italians were fighting a major guerrilla war, but that they were fighting in theory for a political ideology and not just for their own aggrandizement. They were also assisted by countless Albanians, members of the Italian Army, members of the Italian Blackshirt Legions, and the local

Albanian Police, plus they were aided by the general population. By the summer of 1943 as many Albanians were serving in the security forces as in all the partisan armies combined, and thousands more were working as civilians in the small factories and on the farms, which directly and indirectly supported the regime.